THE

EMERGENCE

OF THE

GREAT

POWERS *1685-1715*

---

hARpER TORChbOOKS

*A reference-list of Harper Torchbooks, classified
by subjects, is printed at the end of this volume.*

THE RISE OF MODERN EUROPE

Edited by WILLIAM L. LANGER
Harvard University

* *In preparation*

THE
EMERGENCE
OF THE
GREAT
POWERS *1685-1715*

BY JOHN B. WOLF

UNIVERSITY OF MINNESOTA

HARPER TORCHBOOKS THE UNIVERSITY LIBRARY

HARPER & ROW, PUBLISHERS, NEW YORK

To

AUGUST C. KREY

and

LAWRENCE D. STEEFEL

THE EMERGENCE OF THE GREAT POWERS, 1685-1715

Copyright, 1951 by Harper & Row, Publishers, Incorporated
Printed in the United States of America

This book was originally published in 1951 by Harper & Brothers in The Rise of Modern Europe series, edited by William L. Langer.

First HARPER TORCHBOOK edition published 1962 by Harper & Row, Publishers, Incorporated, New York and Evanston.

TABLE OF CONTENTS

MAP

ILLUSTRATIONS

The illustrations, grouped in a separate section, will be found following page 112.

INTRODUCTION

OUR age of specialization produces an almost incredible amount of monographic research in all fields of human knowledge. So great is the mass of this material that even the professional scholar cannot keep abreast of the contributions in anything but a restricted part of his general subject. In all branches of learning the need for intelligent synthesis is now more urgent than ever before, and this need is felt by the layman even more acutely than by the scholar. He cannot hope to read the products of microscopic research or to keep up with the changing interpretations of experts, unless new knowledge and new viewpoints are made accessible to him by those who make it their business to be informed and who are competent to speak with authority.

These volumes, published under the general title of *The Rise of Modern Europe,* are designed primarily to give the general reader and student a reliable survey of European history written by experts in various branches of that vast subject. In consonance with the current broad conception of the scope of history, they attempt to go beyond a merely political-military narrative, and to lay stress upon social, economic, religious, scientific and artistic developments. The minutely detailed, chronological approach is to some extent sacrificed in the effort to emphasize the dominant factors and to set forth their interrelationships. At the same time the division of European history into national histories has been abandoned and wherever possible attention has been focused upon larger forces common to the whole of European civilization. These are the broad lines on which this history as a whole has been laid out. The individual volumes are integral parts of the larger scheme, but they are intended also to stand as independent units, each the work of a scholar well qualified to treat the period covered by his book. Each volume contains about fifty illustrations selected from the mass of contemporary pictorial material. All non-contemporary illustrations have been excluded on principle. The bibliographical note appended to each volume is designed to facilitate further study of special aspects touched upon in the text. In general every effort has been made to give the reader a clear idea of the main movements in European history, to embody the monographic contributions of research workers, and to present the material in a forceful and vivid manner.

A century or more ago, the first great historians of the modern school, notably Ranke and his contemporaries, were fascinated by the problems connected with the growth of the modern state and the emergence of the new states system. Many of their works are still interesting and instructive, for they set standards of historical work which are still recognized. In some respects they seem to have exhausted the field, for relatively little new work was done on the seventeenth century during the last generation, at least by way of synthesis. To most laymen the period of Louis XIV was one of hopelessly complicated dynastic struggles and never-ending wars. And so it was in a sense. But looked at afresh there is still much to be learned from the politics and conflicts of that age, while the epoch-making scientific discoveries of the contemporary world have given the period of Newton, Leibniz and their colleagues a new and surpassing interest. Professor Wolf has re-examined his subject with a modern eye, by no means glossing over the stormy military events of the period, but laying great stress on the administrative structure of the new states of Europe and particularly on the cultural and intellectual revolution which in those years forced upon Europeans a complete reorientation of thought. He has taken full advantage of the numerous though scattered monographic studies and has provided the general reader with an authoritative and well-balanced review of a crucial chapter in European history.

WILLIAM L. LANGER

PREFACE

THE reconstruction of the history of a single generation always presents difficulties, for it is practically impossible to bring both the forces of inertia and those of change into focus at the same time. The former, deeply embedded in institutions and in the hearts of men, are obviously important determinants of the historical process, but the process itself is unstable. It is normal for living things to strive to maintain a form that cannot endure in the flux of life, and man, as a biological phenomenon, cannot escape this trait either physically or historically. At some periods the forces of resistance appear to be greater than those of movement, but in an era of great wars, revolutions, and new discoveries, the forces for change are clearly ascendant. It should cause no surprise, therefore, that in this volume movement is brought sharply into focus, while the conservative factors are kept in the background.

Like every history this one rests upon assumptions. The first is that the great wars of the period were immediate determinants of the historical process and, therefore, should be the main political theme. The wars did not necessarily accomplish the aims of those who fought them, but they did forge the institutions and give the forms to European society that were to be characteristic of the next two centuries. I am not unaware of the many other determining influences, nor are they neglected in this volume, but I have been unable to escape the conclusion that the wars regulated the timing and set the direction of the historical process. Political Europe of 1715 was not, of course, the work of one generation; the generation of 1685–1715, however, was the one, goaded by war and revolution, that molded its structure. A second assumption of the book is that man's interest in and the extension of his understanding of the cosmos, of the earth, and of mankind itself were the primary determinants of that intellectual movement generally called the Enlightenment. Many dark and ancient preconceptions still colored man's explanation of the universe and his conception of his destiny, but the "crisis in the conscience of Europe," to borrow Hazard's expression, developed significantly from the labors of seventeenth-century scientists, explorers, and philosophers who challenged time-honored beliefs with facts. These two assumptions account for the organization of the book.

But yet a third assumption is implicit in the presentation of the material. Western civilization has progressively altered the forms that characterized its medieval origins; in this particular period the process was tremendously accelerated, so that within a relatively short span of years the forms of the eighteenth and nineteenth centuries became sufficiently fixed to make their outlines identifiable. Ever since the fourteenth century the classic pattern of medieval Europe had been fading; in this period, however, the secularization of politics, the extension of the centralized, bureaucratic state, the rise of the great military powers, and the emergence of the balance of power on a continental scale all marked radical breaks with the medieval political synthesis. At the same time the Cartesian *esprit géométrique,* generalized in the intellectual life of the elite, implied a striking rupture with the past. Much of the medieval world was gone before 1685, much of it still remained in 1715, but in the intervening thirty years new forms emerged to give direction to European life.

Like most writers I am indebted to many people. The financial aid which Dean Theodore C. Blegen and the Graduate School of the University of Minnesota provided gave me both research assistance and an opportunity for travel. Professor William L. Langer, as editor of this series, generously gave me of his time and his wisdom; his editorial labors have greatly benefited both the style and the substance of this volume. Professors Walter L. Dorn, Herbert Heaton, and Lawrence D. Steefel read all or most of the manuscript in an early draft. Professors Frederick B. Artz and John Bowditch read all or most of it in relatively finished form. Professors David H. Wilson, George W. Anderson, Henry Guerlac, and Mr. Roger Derby read chapters that dealt with their fields of specialization. I have profited greatly from the constructive criticism of all these men. There are also many others to whom I am indebted in the departments of history, art, music, romance languages, philosophy, political science and economics at the University of Minnesota, colleagues who patiently listened to my problems and gave me criticisms and suggestions in areas where their knowledge exceeded my own. I wish, too, to thank Professor J. U. Nef for an extended exchange of letters that were both stimulating and useful. Miss Joanne Amspoker assisted in preparing the bibliography; Miss Virginia Hulce helped to make the manuscript ready for the printer. Naturally none of these people are responsible for errors of fact or interpretation that may appear in the book.

I wish also to thank the librarians of the Widener Library, the New York Public Library, the Library of Congress, and particularly the Library of the University of Minnesota. I have acknowledged the sources of the pictures in the captions. Mr. Robert Kress helped me prepare the photographs.

Lastly I wish to thank Professor A. C. Krey for the encouragement he unfailingly gave me, and my good wife, Theta H. Wolf, for her forbearance when my behavior became eccentric, for her willingness to listen when I had to talk, and for her assistance at various stages of the manuscript's development.

JOHN B. WOLF

Bone Lake, Wisconsin
July 5, 1950

EUROPE
CIRCA 1700

To Danubian Monarchy, 1699-1720
To Savoy, 1699-1714
To Prussia, 1702-1720
To Russia, 1699-1721

Scale of Miles
0   200   400

KM. OF NORWAY

SWEDISH

SCOTLAND

UNITED KINGDOM

IRELAND

ENGLAND

NORTH SEA

KM. OF DENMARK

OB

ATLANTIC

OCEAN

(To Hanover, 1714)

HANOVER

BRANDENBURG

UNITED NETHERLANDS

SP. NETHERLANDS (To Austria, 1714)

A. OF COLOGNE

SAXONY

THE EMPIRE

ALSACE (1681-1697)

EL. OF BAVARIA

Rhine R.

Da

KINGDOM OF FRANCE

FRANCHE COMTÉ 1678-1714

SWITZERLAND

SAVOY

MILAN

MANTUA

DANUBIA

Vigo

KM. OF PORTUGAL

KINGDOM OF SPAIN

PAR MODENA

REP. OF GENOA

TUSCANY

PAPAL STATES

VENETIAN REPUBLIC

Rome

CORSICA (Genoa)

RA

(To Austria, 17

Cadiz

MINORCA (To England, 1713)
Port Mahon

KM. OF SARDINIA
(To Austria, 1714
To Savoy, 1720)

KINGDOM OF THE TWO SICILIES

Gibraltar (To England, 1713)

MEDITERRANEAN

SICILY (To Sav To Austr

MOROCCO

ALGERIA

TUNIS

MALTA

Chapter One

THE INSTRUMENTS OF HIGH POLITICS

I. DYNASTIC POLICY AND REALPOLITIK

IN MEDIEVAL Europe the dualism between crown and country, prince and people prevented the full mobilization of military or political power. The feudal hierarchy stood between the king and the people and according to both political theory and legal practice lands, provinces, and kingdoms were items of inheritance rather than integral political entities. This condition encouraged dreams of universal monarchy like that of Charles V, yet also fixed rigid limits on power by assuring the local autonomy of territories only superficially united by the person of the prince. Politicians and statesmen from the days of Louis XI to those of Richelieu recognized the evil inherent in this personal conception of sovereignty, but the roots of the system were too deep to be cut in a single generation.

By the seventeenth century, however, this traditional dualism was beginning to fade. Two hundred years of warfare, commerce, and political reorganization had been furthering the identification of prince and kingdom, but it was not until the era of world wars, beginning with the Turkish siege of Vienna (1683) that the process of history became accelerated enough to define clearly the political forms prevalent in the eighteenth and nineteenth centuries. When the smoke cleared from the battlefields of those great wars (1683–1721), a new political organization stood out in clear relief. Fantasies about a universal empire had all but vanished and what had emerged was a Europe governed by a balance of power between great military states. Kings by divine right, who ruled within the limits set by medieval constitutions, had been replaced by princes who were the chiefs, or at any rate the titular chiefs, of great military and civil bureaucracies. Princes had become identified with their states, and the time was not far off when the people too would become an integral part of the sovereign power.[1]

The resolution of the time-honored dualism helps to explain the anomalous pattern of politics at the end of the seventeenth century. The great

[1] Cf. Chapters Four, Five, and Six.

military powers did not emerge full blown in their new role. They too were the creation of princes, of men who believed they were fulfilling the dynastic ambitions of their forebears at the very time when the imperious demands of a new age were forcing them into the role of state builders.

The myth of divine right, dominant in the seventeenth century, encouraged the dynastic illusion. Churchmen, statesmen, philosophers, and parliaments proclaimed untiringly that God had placed princes over men and had appointed them His agents.[2] Even in England, where one king had been beheaded and another driven from his throne, many of Queen Anne's supporters and, indeed, that good lady herself, believed that God rather than parliament was the source of royal authority. The Whigs might pretend that it was otherwise, but theirs was revolutionary talk in a Europe governed by duly anointed kings. Locke and his friends saw that the ancient dualism had become anachronistic, but most of Europe refused to recognize the changes taking place in the political arena.

As long as divine right was regarded as the ultimate source of royal authority, dynastic politics played a role out of all proportion to their actual significance as a factor in international affairs. At first glance the idea of divine right might seem to suggest a force supporting the *status quo;* would not an aggressive war to deprive a prince of territory given to him by God be a violation of the divine intentions? Even a "modern" political theorist like Pufendorf could argue that there was an "obligation to restitution [of a conquest] . . . until the expelled prince and his heirs are all deceased or until such an unfortunate prince hath quite abdicated or relinquished his claims. . . ." [3] But dynastic politics were served by various interpretations of God's intentions with respect to a society of princes who were interrelated by marriage. Sandras de Courtilz's analysis of the hazards and advantages of royal marriages may seem unduly cynical, but only to those unfamiliar with the procedures. Royal marriages and the conventions governing the rights of succession, as that publicist pointed out, were the raw stuff of diplomacy for those who practiced dynastic politics.[4] The system did, in fact, justify cynicism, for it rested on the proposition that while God may have designated princes to rule, men made conventions and treaties to regulate the procedure by which God appointed rulers, and then proceeded to interpret those treaties to suit

[2] J. Hitier, *La doctrine de l'absolutisme* (Paris, 1903), 11–59.

[3] Samuel Pufendorf, *Of the Law of Nature and Nations* (English edition of 1700), 576.

[4] Sandras de Courtilz, *Nouveaux intérêts des princes de l'Europe, où l'on traite des maximes qu'ils doivent observer pour se maintenir dans leurs états et pour empêcher qu'il ne se forme une monarchie universelle* (Cologne, 1685), 304–319.

themselves. The most important political problem of Europe at the end of the seventeenth century, the question of the Spanish succession, arose directly out of the conflict between the Bourbon and Hapsburg heirs to that throne. God's expressed will was not in itself sufficient to settle the dispute. Though dynastic claims provided legal rights, the question was discussed and finally solved not in those terms, but in terms of *Realpolitik* and military power.[5]

In the Europe of the late seventeenth century the idea that the state encompassed and transcended crown and land, prince and people, was becoming established, reflecting a great revolution in political conceptions.[6] Hailed by Grotius and the coterie of publicists who were developing the concept of international law, this new ideal was written into the public law of Europe by the great treaties from Westphalia (1648) to Nystad (1721). Thenceforth, not princes ruling by divine right, but civil and military bureaucracies provided order and form to society. Driven by the demands of war, kings and statesmen were forced to concentrate their attention upon the political and economic realities and to shape their policies to suit the interests of their states. Machiavelli had insisted upon state interest as the proper basis for politics; in the seventeenth century his ideas, buttressed with doctrines of natural law and natural rights, increasingly became the motive power of political action.

The pace of the revolution that transformed the king into the chief of a bureaucratic machine was accelerated by the very forces that created it. In earlier centuries lay scribes had joined the king's government and, as secretaries, had discharged many administrative and judicial functions. But in the course of the seventeenth century these men of the pen had won a sensational victory over the men of the sword even in the domain of political action. At the opening of the century the councils of princes had still been composed of great noblemen and of clergymen who were the sons of noblemen, in short of men whose feudal conceptions were ill suited to the political requirements of the emerging states system. But within the century these aristocrats had been displaced by the rising class of career bureaucrats, whose relatively humble origins made them conscious of the state rather than of estates. These officials, many of them learned jurists with university educations or sons of royal officials with bourgeois backgrounds, together with a sprinkling of great lords who

---

[5] Even in the twentieth century a Bourbon prince has expounded and defended the idea that the Bourbons had been designated by God for the Spanish throne. See Sixte de Bourbon, *Le traité d'Utrecht et lois fondamentales du royaume* (Paris, 1914).

[6] G. N. Clark, *The Seventeenth Century* (Oxford, 1929), 124 ff.

were willing to stake their fortunes on the state, formed the nucleus of the civil and military bureaucracies. Their careers and fortunes depended upon their service to the state and the favor of the prince; their duties almost forced them to see the problems of politics in operational terms. Commerce, finance, fortifications, the delineation of frontiers, the collection of taxes, the administration of revenues, and the organization of armies and navies were their daily tasks. Such problems were becoming the primary concern of governments and therefore became inevitably issues of high politics. Louis XIV may well have dreamed of the Bourbon dynasty's ruling Germany, France, and Spain, but the Rhine frontier, the Dutch commercial monopolies, the growth of English commerce, the strategic importance of fortifications, and the problems of maintaining a navy at sea were the concerns of his principal advisers. In time the exigencies of war and politics forced even Louis to accept the role of chief official, administrator of a civil and military bureaucracy.

The same process was at work elsewhere. As Europe came to be ruled by great military states, those states had to act increasingly in terms of state interest. The great political problems that grew out of the decay of the Holy Roman and Spanish empires seemed to reflect dynastic politics, but in the actual course of events political realities, based upon military, commercial, and financial considerations, became the predominant counters. The rise of great standing armies and their maintenance in the field made strenuous demands upon the treasury and the credit of the kings. In order to assure a continuous flow of revenue from taxation, required to meet the mounting costs, governments had to formulate and implement policies that would increase the riches of their potential taxpayers, and officials primarily interested in maintaining the power of their state inevitably urged policies that coincided with state interest. Thus European governments were assuming a characteristically modern shape and thereby rendering dynastic politics altogether anachronistic.

II. DIPLOMACY AND DIPLOMATIC ORGANIZATION

As the center of gravity in political action shifted from dynastic policy to *Realpolitik,* the procedures of diplomatic intercourse underwent corresponding changes. For almost two centuries Europe had groped toward an organization of diplomacy appropriate to the needs of the emerging states system. By the end of the sixteenth century many of the more important princes had abandoned the old system of occasional missions and had established regular embassies at foreign courts. In the course of the next century even the lesser princes had found it necessary to maintain permanent agents in the great capitals to represent their interests and to keep themselves informed about major political developments. The needs of the time had created the institutions necessary for the conduct of politics on an international level.

The process had been slow and at times painful. When Richelieu became a secretary of state under the regency of Maria de' Medici, he was charged with foreign as well as domestic correspondence. He found, however, that his office possessed no copies of recent instructions to the French ambassadors abroad; to secure this essential information he had to beg the envoys to send him copies of their letters and instructions. A decade or so later, when he became the trusted minister of Louis XIII, Richelieu continued to supervise both foreign and domestic correspondence; no special bureau for foreign affairs was created until after his death. In 1661, when Louis XIV became his own first minister, the "foreign office" consisted only of a secretary and five other individuals who acted as clerks, code experts, mail censors, etc.; it still retained the peripatetic characteristics of the earlier era when the king's chancellery accompanied him on all his travels. But by the end of Louis's reign the French foreign office had become a permanent, organized bureau, with extensive archives and a whole hierarchy of officials and clerks. Decisions of policy were still made by the king and his councils, but the bureau carried out negotiations and supplied much of the information upon which policy was based.[7]

The French foreign office became a well-developed institution earlier than those of other states. In England, for example, foreign correspondence was still divided between the Secretaries for the North and the South, whose duties included domestic as well as foreign affairs. The Vienna Hofkanzlei, likewise, handled all correspondence, foreign and domestic, pertaining to the emperor's role as ruler over the complex of states and provinces that was becoming the Danubian Monarchy. However, when Peter the Great organized a bureau for foreign affairs he had no difficulty in finding models. The increasing specialization of function was becoming common everywhere; the ever-growing complexity of international relations obliged governments to set up special offices to conduct routine foreign affairs and to receive and record information.

At first no single official was given pre-eminence in the treatment of

[7] C. G. Picavet, La diplomatie française au temps de Louis XIV (1661–1715) (Paris, 1930), 27 ff. This is a remarkably thorough and fine study of the mechanics of French diplomacy.

diplomatic affairs. The practice throughout the seventeenth century was for an ambassador to negotiate with any officer who might have the ear of the prince or the responsibility for his government. Even the direct command of Louis XIV failed to stop this practice until the last years of his reign. It was easier to enforce the channeling of all correspondence between an ambassador and his own government through the bureau for foreign affairs, but even this was not the universal practice in France at the opening of the eighteenth century. Nonetheless, by 1700 the idea that a single official should represent his king in the conduct of foreign affairs had become fixed, thereby establishing the position of the emerging secretaries for foreign affairs as responsible servants of their governments rather than as mere letter writers.

In the century from 1585 to 1685 the role of the ambassador reached its full development. A number of books, all more or less modeled upon Gentile's *De Legationibus* (1585) and Antonio de Vera y Cuniga's *El Ambaxador* (1620), explained the duties, privileges, and immunities of ambassadors and set patterns for their behavior. The congresses of Westphalia (1648) and Nijmegen (1678) further hardened the form of diplomatic usage and in each of the principal capitals local etiquette and procedure regulated the position of the diplomatic corps. This was a century when problems of precedent and protocol were sometimes settled by duel, sometimes by edict, but once they were solved they became the very fabric of the diplomat's life.

The diplomat served as the eyes, ears, and mouth of his government. The Venetians, whose diplomatic organization was a model for all Europe, had long since demonstrated the advantages to be derived from diplomacy. In an age with relatively simple and hopelessly inadequate means of communicating intelligence, the ambassador was the reporter of a wide range of information from court gossip to economic and political developments. There were histories, geographies, and guidebooks purporting to provide information about Europe, but they were neither up to date nor sufficiently exact for the purpose of policy decisions. It is not entirely clear how much Louis XIV, Leopold I, or Innocent XI actually knew about Europe, but their diplomatic agents were undoubtedly their principal and most trusted sources of information. Of course, the diplomat, duly accredited to a brother monarch, was not the only source of intelligence. Europe swarmed with secret agents; some of them, like Villars when he followed Charles of Lorraine's armies in Hungary, were men of high place and favor; others were specially commissioned officials whose training enabled them to understand and conduct negotiations on technical, commercial, or military problems; still others were relatively humble men, adventurers, merchants, publicists, who accepted a fee in exchange for espionage or news letters.[8]

The personnel of the diplomatic corps underwent an interesting change in the seventeenth century. Earlier in the century it was customary in Catholic countries to use churchmen for many missions. They understood Latin, they were accustomed to handling affairs, they could be rewarded for their services by remunerative benefices. Important noblemen or great soldiers were also commonly chosen as ambassadors since their personal prestige reinforced that of their prince. But by the end of the century clergymen were less numerous, and even though there were still a few great nobles in the diplomatic ranks, the newcomers, men of the lesser nobility or the newly ennobled official class, constituted the majority of the diplomatic corps. Like the army, diplomacy had become a career and the men who followed it were officials of the new type whose fame and fortune depended upon service to the state. These new officials, in turn, emphasized the importance of state interest in diplomacy.

The education of the diplomat was not standardized. In the mid-seventeenth century Latin, Spanish, and Italian were all languages of diplomacy; by 1715 French had become essential, Latin was still important, but Italian and Spanish had declined to purely local use. The career diplomat acquired his linguistic facility both in school and in the course of his training. Many successful ambassadors had some legal education and most of them had also some experience in finance or administration. Others had been educated to be courtiers and heads of noble families, and not a few became diplomats after a career in the army. Ordinarily, however, professional diplomats had undergone apprenticeship. Young men, usually relatives of officials or of favored courtiers, were sent with embassies as clerks or assistants; thus they acquired a knowledge of Europe, and an understanding of the king's affairs.

Neither ambassador nor secretaries for foreign affairs as yet exerted much influence in the formulation of policy. The ambassador, though not a robot at the end of a telegraph line, acted under precise instructions, any deviation from which might be repudiated. The secretary of state, in turn, was primarily an executive officer, implementing the decisions of the prince. If he happened to be a strong character, skilled and experienced,

---

[8] Cf. O. Krauske, "Die Entwicklung der standigen Diplomatie," *Schmollers Forschungen*, III (Leipzig, 1885).

he could no doubt exercise a considerable personal influence, as did men like Colbert de Croissy and Torcy in France. But in general the important decisions were made by the prince. Some rulers, like Leopold I and Louis XIV, discussed important issues with their councils, while others, like William III and Peter the Great, acted quite independently. It must be remembered, however, that with the growing complexity of affairs, more and more reliance had to be placed on subordinates for the execution of policy. Everywhere the institutions for the conduct of foreign affairs were becoming established and their responsibilities defined.

III. ARMIES AND NAVIES

The necessary concomitant to the rise of great military powers was the development of standing armies and fleets. Between the era when the Roman legions disappeared from western Europe and the end of the seventeenth century neither the political nor the economic structure of Europe could support extensive military establishments. Hans Delbrück is probably right when he insists that a well-developed money economy was a prerequisite to the reappearance of the legions,[9] but centralized political power was also necessary before the feudal levies and the disorderly bands of condottiere soldiers could be replaced by regular armies of disciplined, uniformed men. The state's authority as well as its treasury had to be developed before the governments could exert effective control over the military.

The new armies that emerged in the last third of the seventeenth century did not at first represent a radical break with the past. The king initially took over the condottiere bands and used them as a standing army. It was not until the opening of the eighteenth century that the effects of new discipline, new *esprit de corps,* and new uniformity gave the armies of Europe a modern character. Nonetheless, the shift of power from the hands of a free captain to those of the king's officials immediately brought far-reaching consequences.[10] The standing armies were at once the expression of the authority of the central government and the instruments for increasing its power. The civil disorders, characteristic of the dualism that had disturbed all Europe from the sixteenth to the last quarter of the seventeenth century, came to an end with the rise of strong military forces. No longer could a Count Mansfeld defy the emperor, a Condé rebel against his king, or a religious party hope to establish a re-

---

[9] H. Delbrück, *Geschichte der Kriegskunst* (Berlin, 1920), IV, 259.
[10] Cf. General Weygand, *Histoire de l'armée française* (Paris, 1938), 145 ff.

public within the kingdom. At the same time the necessity to feed, clothe, equip, and pay an army obliged the king to create bureaucratic machinery to collect taxes and administer revenues. This in turn facilitated the development of the bureaucratic police state characteristic of the eighteenth century. When great political upheavals led to war on a scale never heretofore seen on the continent, these armies became the instruments of the power that shaped the Europe of the next two centuries.

The structure of the standing army revealed its condottiere origins. The ranks were filled, theoretically at least, by volunteers who made soldiering a profession. Actually many of these volunteers came from the lower classes, among whom poverty drove able-bodied men into the army. Volunteers alone, however were usually not numerous enough to fill the ranks, and since the recruiting officers faced both unemployment and punishment if they failed to secure enough men, more drastic measures were adopted to obtain recruits. Men who were not interested in the soldiers' pay or freedom from taxation, became "loyal soldiers" through guile or force. The prisons yielded some; the press gangs that operated on the highway and in taverns brought in others. In both France and Prussia, where the armies were relatively large in relation to the population, the militia became a source of men for the regular army. Louvois even considered a plan that much resembled compulsory military service.[11]

More important to the inner organization of the armies was the fact that by 1700 the hierarchical organization was becoming fixed. General Weygand's statement that the "hierarchy founded on seniority regulated the rights to command and advancement," [12] refers to the ideal rather than the fact; actually advancement depended upon many things, seniority among them, but the important thing was that a chain of command had become established. At the apex was the marshal, who took his orders directly either from the war minister (France), or the war council (Austria), or the king (Sweden); under him were fixed gradations of rank down to the common soldier. This orderly picture contrasted sharply with the armies of a half century before, in which the captain or colonel was almost a free agent. Commissions were not always given for

[11] G. Girard, *Le service militaire en France à la fin du règne de Louis XIV* (Paris, 1921), 22–161; C. Jany, *Geschichte der königlichen-preussischen Armee,* I (Berlin, 1928), 546 ff. Spanheim remarks that the French king could find soldiers because, by ruining commerce, the government left men with the army as the only place "to find wherewith to live." E. Spanheim, *Relation de la cour de France en 1690* (Paris, 1900, ed. by E. Bourgeois), 495–96.

[12] Weygand, *op. cit.,* 145.

merit or seniority. A great nobleman who could raise a regiment easily became a colonel. A wealthy man could purchase a commission suitable to his station in life. Favor, position, and political influence secured commissions for others. Max of Bavaria, August of Saxony, and Louis of Baden received their commands in the imperial army because they were sovereign princes; Eugene of Savoy, Villars and Catinat obtained theirs through proven worth plus political influence. The practice of placing a cash value on commissions in general debarred men without financial backing from high command, but in actuality the rigidity of the system was attenuated by the fact that the king often rewarded meritorious services by grants of either money or commissions.[13]

Although sons of the bourgeoisie could and did enter the officer corps, most of the officers were still drawn from the nobility, and, whatever their origin, the officers simulated the code of behavior inherited from the traditional ideal of the feudal knight. *La conduite de mars* (1685), a military etiquette book, was widely translated and printed in many editions; it obviously was a standard text for officers. The book rehearsed the whole mythology of chivalry as the basic pattern for the "compleat officer"; the anarchistic freedom of the feudal knight might be disciplined, but his ideals and code of honor still colored the art of war.[14]

The new armies were riddled with graft and corruption just as their predecessors had been. The king paid for soldiers who appeared only at reviews; the supply lines were pilfered, and expense accounts were padded. The rise of army commissars and inspectors, the lists of penalties, and the numerous instances of corrupt practices indicate that all armies suffered alike. In France, for example, enrolling men just for reviews was punishable by branding and mutilation for the men, and by fine, imprisonment, or discharge for the officers.[15]

The phenomenal increase in the size of armies, as a result of the great wars, brought in its train a host of problems for both commanders and bureaucrats. Standing armies had to be supplied from regular magazines and depots; while on the march their every movement was dependent on the much more aggravated problems of supply. Logistics not only determined the strategy and tactics of war, but also increased enormously the numbers and authority of the civilian officials attached to the forces.

[13] C. E. Walton, *History of the British Standing Army, A.D. 1660 to 1700* (London, 1894), 451 ff.; Jany, *op. cit.*, I, 544 ff.; Girard, *op. cit.*, 16–20.

[14] A. Vagts, *History of Militarism* (New York, 1937), 49–76.

[15] J. W. Fortescue, *A History of the British Army* (London, 1899), I, 308–21; Girard, *op. cit.*, 39–40.

The development of new infantry weapons likewise affected tactics. The imperial armies in Hungary were the first (1687–1689) to abandon the pike for the bayonet, which by 1702 had become standard equipment for all European armies.[16] This change was due to the invention of the ring-type bayonet, which, unlike its predecessor, did not prevent the musket from being used as a firearm. At about the same time the flintlock musket replaced the firelock. Sporting guns had long been equipped with flintlocks, but conservative soldiers did not generally adopt the new weapon until the 1690's. The bayonet and the flintlock made possible the development of line tactics, and enabled the infantry to stop cavalry charges. The classic pattern of eighteenth-century warfare, with lines of soldiery delivering continuous volleys, was fully established by the War of the Spanish Succession.

With the abandonment of the pike the new era of fire power had arrived, and artillery necessarily became more important. By 1700 the artillery might decide an engagement. Better and more mobile guns allowed the artillery to keep up with the army, and made an increase in the number of cannon desirable. Gustavus Adolphus' "leather guns" were replaced by brass and iron cannon of almost equal mobility. In 1685 the standard of one gun for each thousand troops was rarely maintained; yet by 1709 the allied armies in the Netherlands commonly had from two to three cannon per thousand men, and often started the campaign with as many as four. Furthermore, experiments in multibarreled guns, although disappointing, reflect the effort to enhance the fire power of the artillery.

Though fire power did not outmode cavalry as the weapon for shock action, it did force a change in the armor and tactics of the mounted troops. Personal armor, effective at the opening of the century, ceased to be of value against musket volleys. On the other hand, by the use of a lighter, faster breed of horses, the momentum of the cavalry charge was considerably increased. The early seventeenth-century cavalryman attacked with horse pistols, wheeled before the pike line and fired; Marlborough's and Eugene's cavalry, on the other hand, depended upon heavy saber thrusts delivered by a galloping line. Cavalrymen still carried pistols, but used that weapon chiefly to break off action with other cavalry. The War of the Spanish Succession and the Northern War brought the fullest development of the cavalry charge, but the success of cavalry action had already become dependent upon a disciplined line of infantry to beat off counterattacks and hold the gains made by shock tactics.

---

[16] Jany, *op. cit.*, I, 590.

Fortress warfare loomed larger than field battles in the late seventeenth century. Bureaucratically minded statesmen, reluctant to stake success on brief battles, found sieges more to their taste. Louis XIV personally supervised the plans for a system of interrelated fortifications to cover the French frontiers, and the genius of Vauban made France practically invasion proof.[17] Vauban's fortresses were widely copied in the Lowlands, in Germany and elsewhere, so that Europe fairly sprouted fortresses by the end of the seventeenth century. These strong points reduced the art of war to the status of a dangerous chess game: rooks and bishops were strongly posted while the field armies (the queens and knights) maneuvered for attack. Though great soldiers like Marlborough and Eugene saw that the offer of a rook might lead to a checkmate, administratively minded statesman still preferred to play for an end game with the possibility of a stalemate.[18]

While the methods of land warfare were conditioned by the rise of standing armies, the development of naval weapons imposed new concepts of sea warfare and new standards for naval establishments. In the mid-seventeenth century naval conflicts opposing fleets came to grips through successive maneuvers that were anything but precise and orderly. Ships of all sizes, most of them well under 1,000 tons, locked in individual encounters which proved the valor of captains, but gave little indication of naval skill. By 1685 the conception of a squadron formation and a line of battle had developed as a counterpart to the orderly columns of infantry. This placed a premium upon trustworthy ships that could keep their place in line and deliver powerful broadsides. In 1660 the British navy had only 5 warships of 1,000 tons but by 1688 it had 59 of at least that size, some of them displacing 1,300 or 1,400 tons. Under Mazarin the French navy had been practically nonexistent; at the end of Colbert's life (1683) it boasted 120 vessels mounting 50 or more cannon. These large forces inevitably required the development of new administrative machinery, new technical skills, and new naval tactics.

Naval organization varied somewhat from state to state. In France Colbert and his son, Seignelay, presided over a council for marine that governed the navy through an elaborate bureaucratic apparatus. The commanders both at sea and at the bases were subject to close supervision

[17] G. Zeller, *L'organisation défensive des frontières du nord et de l'est au XVIIe siècle* (Paris, 1928), 119 ff.

[18] P. E. Lazard, *Vauban* (Paris, 1934), also L. Montross, *War through the Ages*, rev. ed. (New York, 1944 and 1946), 355.

by agents of the minister, whose reports went directly to Versailles. In England James II, first as heir apparent and later as king, was the moving spirit behind the navy. A naval commission, appointed in the last years of Charles II, virtually became a navy board to control both the construction and operation of the ships. With the Revolution of 1688 the navy again reverted to a lord high admiral, but the actual control was still exercised through a navy commission. In the United Netherlands there were five provincial admiralty authorities with almost coterminous powers. The admiral general was dependent on the co-operation of these provincial authorities. The Amsterdam and Maas admiralties were the most important, but the Zeeland, Friesland, and North Holland admiralties also collected tolls, regulated supplies, directed ship movements, and conducted admiralty courts.[19]

In France and England most naval officers were drawn from the gentleman class. The English system of education that sent cadets to sea at the ages of twelve to fourteen assured a supply of officers with practical experience. An English boy might take service on a ship commanded by a friend of the family, or be assigned to a ship by the "king's letter" to act as cabin boy and servant to the captain. At the end of three to five years of service, he became eligible for a midshipman's commission, and when he reached the age of twenty to twenty-one he became a lieutenant. His commission, however, was not a general one; it applied only to the ship on which he served, and when that ship was out of service both commission and pay came to an end. In the 1690's it became customary to place unemployed officers on half pay, but since there were more applicants than money, a system of seniority was devised that finally led to the navy list. In France the decay of the navy after 1693 created serious personnel problems; unemployed naval officers had to find fame and fortune as privateers when they were no longer able to put to sea in the king's vessels. In both countries influence and special talents were factors in promotion to higher ranks; the seventeenth century frankly faced the problem of favoritism by elevating it to a postulate.[20]

The crews of these navies were enlisted as far as possible from volun-

---

[19] There is a wealth of material on these late seventeenth-century navies. Cf. J. H. Owen, *War at Sea under Queen Anne, 1702–1708* (Cambridge, Eng., 1938), 1–70; J. R. Tanner, *Samuel Pepys and the Royal Navy* (Cambridge, Eng., 1920); W. L. Clowes, *The Royal Navy*, IV (7 vols., London, 1897–1903); René Memain, *La marine de guerre sous Louis XIV* (Paris, 1937); C.G.M.B. de la Roncière, *Histoire de la marine française*, VI (Paris, 1934).

[20] For an interesting discussion of the problem of officering the old navy, see Michael Lewis, *The Navy of Britain, a Historical Portrait* (London, 1948), 239–86.

teers, but this source of man power was never sufficient to satisfy the need. A popular captain could usually man his ship, but most vessels were sailed by men serving against their will. Press gangs in every harbor of Europe picked up sailors in taverns, brothels, and on the wharves to complete the crews, which consequently were of very uneven quality. The lack of volunteers for the navy was due in part to the fact that naval pay and service conditions were usually less attractive than those aboard merchant ships. However, in spite of the bad conditions and the system of impressment, there were relatively few mutinies in the period 1688–1713; it was reserved for the late eighteenth century to reap the harvest of mutiny provoked by the system.[21]

The quality of ship construction varied from country to country. French naval architecture was most advanced; both England and France built sturdier ships than the Netherlands, whose shallow coastal waters required vessels of less draught, length, and stamina than was standard in the English and French navies. Conditions worked further to the disadvantage of the Dutch when the 1,400-ton capital ship carrying a hundred or more guns became the backbone of the battle line. The fifty- to sixty-gun ship still did most of the fighting, but the new capital ships produced new standards of naval power. In the naval race between 1685 and 1715 England outbuilt both her enemy and her ally. By weight of numbers and by the skill of her seamen, England gained control of the seas.

When the War of the Spanish Succession came to an end, naval organization, naval architecture, and naval tactics had achieved the standards that prevailed through the eighteenth century. Like the standing armies and the diplomatic corps, the navies were institutions characteristic of the new great-power system. As the ancient dualism between crown and country broke down and states capable of mobilizing the political, economic, and military potentials of the community emerged, these new instruments of policy assumed the forms typical of the next two centuries. Out of three decades of war and revolution a new Europe was born, a Europe in which a balance of power, expressed in military, political, and economic terms, took the place of the dreams of universalism that had haunted Europe since the days of the Roman Empire.

[21] Owen, *op. cit.*, 15–16.

Chapter Two

THE WORLD WAR OF 1683–1699

I. THE FIRST STAGE, 1683–1684

On July 14, 1683, a Turkish army of approximately 200,000 men began to besiege Vienna. The defenders of the city, a small corps of regular soldiers and an improvised militia made up of artisans, merchants, students, and professional people, were pitifully weak compared to the hosts the Turks had drawn from Asia Minor, the Balkans, and North Africa. Beyond Vienna an imperial army under Charles of Lorraine was assembling its forces to raise the siege; out of Bavaria, Saxony, Swabia, and Franconia poured the contingents of the emperor's allies; to the north, John Sobieski gathered a Polish army; and from all Europe came a trickle of volunteers which soon became a stream of recruits for the last crusade. The Turks opened their trenches and began their bombardment. The Pope emptied his coffers to provide money for the defenders; the emperor from Ratisbon urged his allies to speed their assistance, and all Christian Europe offered up prayers to God. The stake at issue was the control of the European continent; at the moment no one could know that by September the Turkish army would be defeated and in full retreat down the Danube.[1]

Kara Mustafa, the Turkish commander, may have dreamed of himself as sultan of a new Moslem state in the heart of Europe, but Turkish power could probably never attain that objective. Had the Turks been successful, the fruits of their victory would have fallen to Versailles rather than to Constantinople, for the destruction of the imperial armies would have made Louis XIV the sword and shield of Christendom. Kara Mustafa had the assurance that French soldiers would not assist the emperor, but had the emperor's army been broken, only France and the Ottoman Empire would have remained as major military powers on

[1] O. Klopp, *Das Jahr 1683 und der folgende grosse Türkenkrieg bis zum Frieden von Carlowitz, 1699* (Graz, 1882), 220 ff. See also J. Maurer, *Kardinal Leopold Graf Kollonitsch* (Innsbruck, 1887), and A. von Thürheim, *Feldmarschall Ernst Rüdiger Graf Starhemberg* (Vienna, 1882).

the European continent, and France must then have become the core of a united Christendom against the infidel. Had the Turkish assault succeeded, there would have been little to stand in the way of Louis XIV's ambition to re-establish a universal monarchy and to rule Europe.

The events that led up to the siege of Vienna and the epoch of warfare that followed are a confused melee of conflicting and often apparently unrelated streams of action. Only under the unifying pressure of the sword were they finally channeled into a broad stream, but even so it is difficult to establish a unity that does not do injustice to the facts. In the west it was the treaties of Nijmegen [2] and the ambitions of the French king that seemed to be the driving forces behind events. In the east it was the inner pressures in the decaying Ottoman Empire and the arrogant ambitions of the grand vizier. However, to attribute the events of this stormy era solely to these forces is to do violence to the multitudinous nature of historical phenomena. All Europe was in ferment—the discontent in Hungary, the anarchy in Poland and Germany, the ambitions of princes from Italy to Russia, the business interests of merchants in London, Amsterdam, Calais and elsewhere, the aspirations of a sincerely devout pontiff in Rome, the hopes and fears of Protestants all over Europe, the ambitions that centered upon the Spanish inheritance—all these and many more were the eddies and currents that finally became a maelstrom sweeping across a large part of the continent.

At the very moment when the Turkish armies began their march up the Danube, western Europe was on the brink of war. After the treaties of Nijmegen, Louis XIV set forth a new rule in European public law by declaring that all territories and cities that had ever been dependencies of the lands he had acquired in the preceding half century belonged to the French crown. To implement this pretension he created courts of "Reunion" in the Rhineland to establish his "lawful" rights, and then proceeded to enforce the decisions of these courts by military action. France thus became plaintiff, judge, and executor of the judicial decisions that awarded her territory. Germany, at that time, was a morass of petty overlapping sovereignties, and German power was so dilapidated as a result of the settlements of Westphalia and Nijmegen that there was no force available to check French aggression in the Rhineland. One piece of land after another in Alsace and in the area we today call the Saar was adjudged to belong to the French crown. Seventeenth-century treaties

---

[2] The treaties of Nijmegen ended the Dutch War, 1672–1678. Cf. the preceding volume of this series.

never specified exact boundary lines, so the courts of Reunion had no difficulty in discovering that this village, this town, or that county was properly a dependency of the lands assigned to France by treaty. Were no halt called, it seemed as though these courts of Reunion might well annex the whole of Germany! On September 30, 1681, Strassburg in Alsace and Casale on the Po were both occupied by French troops; in Italy and Germany, French power was sufficient to make conquests in time of full peace. The rest of Lorraine and Luxemburg were obviously the next German victims, while the treatment accorded France's ally, the duke of Savoy, made it clear that northern Italy might suffer the same fate.

Nor were Louis's ambitions limited to the Rhineland and northern Italy. The great political fact of the day was the impending collapse of two empires, the Spanish and the Holy Roman. From the mid-seventeenth century onward these two empires had shown signs of rapid deterioration. The Holy Roman Empire had been greatly shaken by the Treaty of Westphalia; its emperor and diet were quite incapable of defending the frontiers. In Spain the degeneration of the reigning family had reached its end in Charles II, a sickly, dim-witted monarch, unable to beget an heir. The empire of Philip II, loose in every joint, obviously awaited a new master.[3] If both the Spanish and Holy Roman empires could be brought under Bourbon rule and reorganized in the spirit of the French government, Louis XIV could realize the universal imperium that had been the dream of Charles V.

Louis, the son of one Spanish princess and the husband of another, fully expected to see his family installed on the Spanish throne. He could not even await the death of his Spanish cousin to claim this inheritance. His first two wars, the War of the Devolution (1667–68) and the Dutch War (1672–78), had resulted in French annexation of part of the Spanish Netherlands and Franche-Comté. These acquisitions extended France to the Rhine-Alps frontier yet were intended only as a first step toward ultimate control of all the Spanish possessions.

In Germany Louis's policy was more complex. After the Thirty Years' War, the Holy Roman Empire was a political monster.[4] The imperial crown was practically impotent; the diet had become a political anachronism. But if the imperial dignity were united to the crown of France, it

[3] Cf. Chapter Five.

[4] Fritz Saloman, *Severinus de Monzambuno (Samuel von Puffendorf) De statu Imperii Germanici* (1910), Ch. VI, 3–9.

would be possible to revalidate its power and pretensions. Louis, like Mazarin before him, never lost sight of the fact that he or one of his sons might be elected emperor, and, with the power of France, rebuild the imperial power. By 1683, through subsidies and alliances, Louis controlled a majority of the votes in the electoral college, including that of Brandenburg, and not until the election of Joseph I (1688) as King of the Romans (German crown) did the possibility of a French emperor fade into the background.[5]

With the Spanish and the Holy Roman empires as ultimate goals of his policy, is it surprising that Louis concentrated his principal attention upon Leopold I? Many historians, impressed with the importance of trade and colonies, tend to overlook the fact that Louis's point of view, which led him eventually to neglect both his navy and his colonies, was predominantly continental and firmly rooted in the realities of European politics. Louis's alliances with Sweden, Poland, Turkey, Brandenburg, Saxony, and Bavaria, his assistance to the Hungarian malcontents and the Transylvanian princes were all directed against the principal opponent of his program, the Austrian Hapsburg ruler. If the power of Leopold I could be broken, the way to both the Spanish and the German crowns would be clear. Contemporaries never doubted that universal monarchy was France's ultimate aim. It could be accomplished only by the ruin of the house of Hapsburg.

Originally Louis's policy was not limited to the continent. A corollary to his ambition to control the Spanish Empire was his colonial, commercial, and naval program. Under the guidance of Colbert, France had become the foremost commercial and naval power in Europe, a threat to England and still more to the United Netherlands. The design of the Colberts was a grand one: they aimed at supplanting the Dutch staple markets and concentrating the commerce of Europe in French hands. To prevent interference with this program, Louis made both Charles II and James II pensioners of his treasury and bribed a large number of members of the general estates of the United Netherlands to block the anti-French program of William of Orange.[6]

Thus French policy faced in all directions. In Europe the Reunions were eating away the frontiers of Germany, and outright annexations

[5] B. Auerbach, *La diplomatie française et la cour de Saxe (1648–1680)* (Paris, 1888), 474–5, and *La France et le Saint Empire romain germanique* (Paris, 1912), 187–294; O. Hintze, *Die Hohenzollern und ihr Werk* (Berlin, 1915), 239.

[6] James II accepted Louis's money, but he also undertook to create a new navy for England.

established French power in Italy, while the prospect of a universal monarchy based upon the Spanish, French, and German thrones floated uneasily in the air. Europe had either to organize resistance or accept Louis XIV as her ruler. Only two statesmen might hope to oppose the Sun King: William III, stadholder of the Netherlands, and Emperor Leopold I. The one was the natural chief of Protestant Europe, the other, the obvious leader of the anti-French forces in Germany and Catholic Europe. Both of these men, however, seemed to be checked at every point. French gold and diplomacy obstructed the emperor's efforts in central Europe, roused his Hungarian subjects against him, and threatened his lands with a Turkish invasion. Since Louis was subsidizing a considerable number of its deputies, William III found the general estates hostile to him; the king of England and the more important Protestant princes of Germany were in French pay, and the king of Sweden was deeply involved in an internal revolution.[7] French military, political, and financial power seemed to hold all Europe within its grasp.

Hence, after 1680, resistance to France became daily more imperative. Many German princes realized that the "liberties" confirmed by the treaties of Nijmegen would become meaningless unless French aggression were checked. The courts of Reunion and the annexation of Strassburg, one German historian insists, gave the first impetus to German unity.[8] The imperial diet roused itself to protest against the Reunions, and in January, 1681, to pass a basic law for the creation of an imperial army of forty thousand men. This law proved unworkable, but it was the first time since before the Reformation that Germany seemed about to unite upon a policy. Charles XI of Sweden, too, became aroused when the courts of Reunion annexed the small Rhineland territory that belonged to his house, and the governments of both Spain and Denmark recognized that French annexations in time of peace must be stopped. After the seizure of Strassburg, Europe buzzed with projects of leagues and alliances against France; clearly another war was soon to be fought to check the imperious march of the Sun King.

In response to these war preparations Louis XIV attempted to divide and embarrass the incipient coalition. He tightened his alliance with Brandenburg-Prussia; his gold and his ambassador blocked a proposed alliance between Poland and Emperor Leopold; and he sent the Hungar-

[7] Cf. Chapter Five.
[8] U. Hölscher, *Die öffentliche Meinung in Deutschland über den Fall Strassburgs* (Munich, 1896).

ian magnates, who were in open rebellion against the emperor, greater aid in the form of munitions and money. In Italy, French ambassadors overawed the petty principalities with thinly veiled threats, to which the occupation of Casale added military pressure. In the Netherlands gifts and pensions to members of the anti-Orange party in the estates general practically paralyzed William's policy, and a subsidy to the debonair Charles II of England assured France's flank at sea.

Louis's trump card, however, was in Constantinople. He had no love for the Turks, but he recognized the Ottoman Empire as potentially a useful tool. After 1680, he became very accommodating to the sultan. He disavowed the action of his Mediterranean naval forces against Moslem pirates and the port of Chios, where a French bombardment had brought the two countries to the verge of war. He withdrew an ambassador who had been unable to get along with the arrogant grand vizier, and sent a new emissary to Constantinople with instructions to urge upon the Porte the advisability of a Turkish thrust up the Danube rather than in the Mediterranean. France, he assured the Porte, would gladly stand aside while the Turkish army overran the Hapsburg lands. At the same time, French agents in Transylvania and Toekeli's Hungary urged the princes to join with the sultan against the emperor. Thus French ambitions in the west stimulated and supported the Turkish forces that marched up the Danube in 1683.[9]

The new French ambassador arrived at Constantinople at a time when the policy of the Porte was still undecided.[10] At peace with Poland (1676) and Russia (1681), the Ottoman government was free for other adventures on its frontiers. Since the mid-seventeenth century Turkish power had made a spectacular recovery from its weakness at the opening of the century; strong viziers of the Kiuprili family had revived the martial spirit of the empire. The Kiuprilis had realized that war, and war alone, would hold the loose-jointed Ottoman state together, and unite the diverse interests struggling for control. Kara Mustafa, the current grand vizier, was practically an absolute ruler; Sultan Mohammed IV, interested in hunting, women, and family affairs, allowed his vigorous, arrogant ser-

[9] I. Hudiță, *Histoire des relations diplomatiques entre la France et la Transylvanie au XVIIe siècle (1635–1683)* (Paris, 1927), 382 ff.; J. W. Zinkeisen, *Geschichte des osmanischen Reiches in Europa*, V (Hamburg, 1857), 43 ff.; Kurt Köhler *Die orientalische Politik Ludwigs XIV* (Leipzig, 1907), 122.

[10] J. Hammer-Purgstall, *Histoire de l'empire ottoman, depuis son origine jusqu'à nos jours*, J. J. Hellert, Trans., XII (Paris, 1839), 1–120; J. W. Zinkeisen, *op. cit.*, V, 55, 97. N. Jorga, *Geschichte des osmanischen Reiches*, IV (Gotha, 1911), 135–182.

vant full control of the government so long as he could report regular Ottoman successes on the frontiers. But campaigning against a limited objective, a frontier fortress or town, and then holding an elaborate victory celebration, while satisfactory to the sultan, was not enough for Kara Mustafa. He was no Moslem fanatic, but he was ambitious for his own fame and for his family.[11]

In spite of the fact that the Turkish Empire was ringed with enemies, Kara Mustafa was planning to fight a new war. His arrogant demand upon foreign ambassadors for huge gifts of money, his obtuse treatment of their susceptibilities, and his unwillingness to redress the grievances of their merchants and religious protégés, indicated that the grand vizier was contemptuous of the power of Christian Europe. He vacillated between a plan to attack Sicily and Sardinia by sea, and one to campaign by land up the Danube. The fact that one after another of Emperor Leopold's ambassadors, sent to Constantinople to secure a renewal of the twenty-year truce, died before they could start negotiations, convinced many superstitious Ottoman leaders that Allah favored war with the emperor.

It was then that M. Guilleragues appeared in Constantinople with Louis XIV's assurance to the sultan that "there henceforth cannot be any understanding between me [Louis] and the Emperor that would oblige me to join my military forces with his for any reason whatsoever."[12] At about the same time, Count Toekeli, leader of the revolting Hungarian magnates, announced his willingness to become a vassal of the Porte in return for aid against Emperor Leopold. Thus from France and Hungary, as well as from Allah, came the suggestions that a campaign on the Danube be the next objective. The Porte ceased to treat the French ambassador with the studied, brutal disrespect his predecessor had encountered, and the pasha at Ofen (Buda), as well as the vassal prince of Transylvania, joined in giving aid to the Hungarian malcontents.[13]

By 1682 the court of Vienna was painfully aware of the possibility that it would have to fight a war on two fronts, and the emperor had to decide which was more important to him: Strassburg and the Rhineland, or Hungary. The Rhineland was an area rich in population, advanced in culture, and of vital importance to the defense of Germany. Were it to

[11] Indeed, it is said that he was an atheist. Jorga, *op. cit.*, IV, 172.

[12] Charles Gérin, "Le pape Innocent XI et le siège de Vienne en 1683," *Revue des questions historiques,* Vol. 39 (1886), 110.

[13] For a full-length study of Franco-Turkish relations at this period, see Kurt Köhler, *Die orientalische Politik Ludwigs XIV* (Leipzig, 1907).

pass into French hands, the possibilities of recovering it even in the distant future would be dim. Hungary, on the other hand, was less rich, less densely populated, and culturally as well as politically of less importance. A large part of the kingdom had been in Ottoman hands for over a century, and the provinces under Hapsburg rule had been unruly and turbulent for over a generation. They brought neither profit nor much prestige to the Hapsburg house. Furthermore, there was a deep-seated belief in Vienna that lands lost to the Turk would eventually be recovered, while lands lost to the French were permanently alienated. The Vienna court therefore decided to make peace in the east and war in the west. Leopold continued to co-operate with the papal nuncios in the effort to make a defensive alliance with Poland because he hoped thereby to detach John Sobieski from France, but he sent a strong mission to Constantinople to fend off the Turkish war and renew the truce of Vasvár.[14]

If the Turks could have been persuaded to renew the twenty-year truce, Leopold would have been ready to contest French aggression in the Rhineland, but the Turks could not be won over. The imperial ambassador, after being put off with ambiguous answers and impossible demands, was finally held almost a prisoner and was barely able to get word to Vienna that all negotiations had failed. Kara Mustafa had begun to assemble a great army in the fall of 1682, and by spring he was ready to move up the Danube. Before he marched, however, the grand vizier again sought assurance that France would not come to the aid of his victim. Without delay Louis XIV ordered the French ambassador to tell the sultan that, considering "the manner with which the Viennese court has conducted itself toward me [Louis], one does not need to fear that I would join them. . . ." "Be careful, above all things," he added, "to give these assurances in my name, and still more, not to put anything in writing."[15]

In the spring of 1683 the Turkish army moved north toward Hungary. Mohammed IV stayed at Belgrade, while the grand vizier and the army advanced to Esseg (June) and thence toward Vienna. Charles of Lorraine had about 30,000 men and 50 cannon with which to oppose the 200,000–250,000 Osmanli and their 300 cannon. There was nothing for the imperial army to do but to fight a delaying action and retreat. When

---

[14] Huber-Redlich, *Geschichte Österreichs*, VI (Gotha, 1921), 299–310; B. Erdmanns-dörffer, *Deutsche Geschichte vom westphälischen Frieden bis zum Regierungsantritt Friedrichs des Grossen, 1648–1740*, I (Berlin, 1892), 656 ff.

[15] Charles Gérin, *op. cit.*, XXXIX, 123.

it became evident that Vienna was the target of the invading host, the imperialists began frantically to prepare for a siege that might continue for months before aid could arrive. Count Starhemberg was named commander of the forces in the city; Kaplirs, a man of seventy-two, was appointed the highest civilian official. These two men, with the bishop of Wiener-Neustadt, Cardinal Kolonitsch, and the burgermaster Von Liebenberg were left with the destinies of Vienna and central Europe in their hands. The emperor and Charles of Lorraine with the imperial army withdrew just before the first Turkish horsemen appeared before the walls of the city. Kara Mustafa, advised by renegade Italian and French engineers and by a former Capuchin monk (Achmed Bey), began on July 16 to dig the trenches that, he hoped, would cut off and starve out the city.[16]

Even the appearance of Kara Mustafa's army before the capital did not convince Leopold that he ought to make peace with France. While Turkish horsemen ravaged Austria, he still insisted that France must submit her recent annexations to a general conference for a test of their legality. This, of course, was completely unacceptable to Louis; at a general conference France would be outnumbered by her enemies, and the flimsy legal arguments of the courts of Reunion would be exposed. To justify himself as well as to take full advantage of the political situation created by the Turkish invasion, Louis proposed that the western powers sign a long truce on the basis of the *status quo*. This truce, he argued, would allow central Europe to concentrate its efforts against the Turks; he did not add that it would also leave France in possession of the bridgeheads she had acquired in Germany. Despite the advice of French hirelings like the elector of Brandenburg and the Rhine bishops, Leopold adamantly refused to consider the proposal.

The French reaction was swift and brutal; Louis's armies invaded the Spanish Netherlands (September 1, 1683).[17] On the very day of the French advance, Bishop Bossuet in a sermon at Saint-Denis spoke of the terrible trials faced by the Christians in Austria, and exhorted his listeners to "do penance, to appease God by your tears." But Colbert de Croissy, Louis's foreign minister, replied to the papal nuncio's protests against French aggression by insisting that since the Spaniards contributed nothing to the defense of Vienna and actually prevented the emperor from

[16] There is a dramatic account of the siege in *Geschichte der Stadt Wien*, IV (Vienna, 1911–18), 40 ff., 136 ff.

[17] Jacques Hardré, *Letters of Louvois* (Chapel Hill, North Carolina, 1949), pp. 225–35.

coming to terms with France, the French action in Flanders and Luxemburg would serve the glory of God by enabling him to force an understanding in the west. This was double talk that deceived no one. Spain's power was so blighted by 1683 that her only defenses in the Netherlands depended upon the Empire and the United Netherlands, or upon general respect for public law and Christian obligations. The emperor had the Turkish knife at his throat; Louis informed the Dutch that any aid to Spain would mean war; and public law was of little avail in the face of predominant military power.

The defeat of Kara Mustafa's army before Vienna less than two weeks after Louis's action (September 12) emboldened the Spaniards to resist French aggression. In the hope that Leopold would make peace with the Turks, as he had in 1664, and would then be able to give assistance, the Spanish king bravely declared war on France (October 5, 1683) and called upon Europe to help him defeat the arch aggressor in the west. With no military strength to reinforce it, the declaration of war was an empty gesture. The Spanish fortress of Luxemburg fell to the besieging French army. Spain proper was invaded by land and harassed by sea while the French continued to press their occupation of the Spanish Netherlands. Unless Europe were willing to join Spain, there was no possible outcome of the war but complete victory for the French.

The problem in Vienna was vexing. To form a coalition against France with any chance of success, the whole force of the Empire and the Netherlands would have to be fully committed. But William III was unable to promise the co-operation of the Netherlands and the elector of Brandenburg held stubbornly to his French alliance. Thus Louis's gold and diplomacy practically assured a French victory even if Leopold made peace with the Turks. Furthermore, Louis himself seemed willing to be accommodating. He announced that France wanted peace, and again offered Spain and the Empire a twenty-year truce on the basis of the :tatus quo. This proposal was attractive both to the German princes who feared the consequences of another war with France and to the soldiers who had followed the defeated Moslem armies into Hungary and captured the Turkish fortresses of Gran and Parkány.

The clamor of the victorious Christian army for a chance to deal once and for all with Islam weighed heavily in the scale that balanced war and peace in the west. The new grand vizier asked for peace; but the men who had defeated Kara Mustafa demanded war. For a generation or more the politically wise had been certain that, despite its apparent vigor, the Ottoman Empire was in full decay; the golden opportunity to test this thesis and to win back the territory lost in the preceding generations seemed at hand. Furthermore, the advocates of war against Islam had another imposing argument. A widely circulated pamphlet argued cogently that the house of Hapsburg had everything to gain by following up its victories in Hungary. *Austria Holds the Trumps if She Would Only Play Them* [18] pointed out that Bohemia, Hungary, and the hereditary German lands would be capable of equipping and supporting an army of 200,000 men if they were effectively organized financially and administratively. They would then constitute a great power able to meet France on even terms, and, with the aid of Germany, to impose its will upon Europe. The *sine qua non* was, however, the reconquest of Hungary. In full control of the Danube the Austrian power would no longer need to fear France.

Leopold's advisers knew it would be folly to fight both France and the Turks. The truce that Louis offered promised victory in the east; the peace that the Turks offered could not assure victory in the west. Louis underlined this fact by the vigor with which he conducted his war with Spain: Luxemburg, Dixmude and Courtrai fell to his arms; cities and towns in Flanders were systematically destroyed by bombardment, and a French army invaded Catalonia. Furthermore, in spite of William of Orange, the general estates of the Netherlands decided upon neutrality, and the French bombardment of Genoa terrorized the Italian states into a desire to remain aloof from any conflict.[19] Reluctantly Leopold was obliged to recognize that his own best interests would be served by accepting the French offer of a twenty-year truce.

In August, 1684, in the Dominican convent at Regensburg, the truce was signed between France on the one side and the emperor and the Spanish king, on the other. Spain gave up Luxemburg and the emperor recognized the *status quo* of 1681, which meant that the French Reunions were accepted. It was not, however, a definitive peace, but only a truce for twenty years. Emperor Leopold thus salved his conscience with the hope that, when the term had expired, he would be able to force France to return the stolen lands. Louis, more realistically, recognized that twenty years is a long time, and that opportunity to translate the truce into a treaty of peace must certainly come within that span. Hostilities in

---

[18] *Österreich über alles wann es nur will* (1684), written by William von Hörnighk.

[19] A French naval squadron destroyed a large part of Genoa because the city had equipped naval vessels for Spain. There is a fine description of the action in C. Cantù, *Storia degli Italiani*, XII (1877), 76–83.

the west were thus temporarily suspended; Louis XIV had secured his hold on the German frontier, and Vauban, in preparation for the next move, proceeded to fortify the new position from Franche-Comté via Strassburg to Luxemburg.[20]

Once the decision for peace in the west had been made, the attention of Europe became concentrated on the crusade in Hungary. At the very center of this great military and political effort stood Pope Innocent XI, the crusading Pope who, more than any other, deserved credit for the expulsion of the Turk from Hungary. In 1664 his hopes for a crusade had been shattered by the truce of Vasvár, but he had never surrendered the idea that God had laid upon him the mantle of the medieval popes. He gave the crusade his entire attention, exhorting Christian monarchs to put aside their fratricidal strife, sending emissaries to Russia and Persia, collecting money and supplies to subsidize the Christian armies, and organizing the prayers of Catholic Europe for the success of the crusade. Innocent even attempted to temper the Machiavellian policy of Louis XIV and to induce him to behave like a Christian ruler. Several years later, when Ofen fell to the Christian army, James II remarked to the papal nuncio, "It is the Holy Father who has conquered Ofen just as he relieved Vienna. Not for centuries has such a pope sat on the chair of Peter." [21]

His Holiness was the guiding spirit behind the organization of the Holy League of 1684, for the promise of papal subsidies and the diplomacy of the papal nuncios defeated French efforts to detach Sobieski from the Austrian alliance, concluded in 1683 when the Turkish threat had become apparent. Likewise it was Father Marco d'Aviano, under papal orders, who negotiated with the Venetian government to secure its adhesion to the Austro-Polish alliance. The bitter memory of the unsatisfactory struggle that Venice had waged against the Turks a few years before, and the veiled threats of the French ambassador, had kept the

[20] The truce of Regensburg raises an interesting question. As Courtilz de Sandras, a clever contemporary observer, pointed out, Louis might have used the attack upon Vienna to destroy the Hapsburg house, since a determined thrust could not have been parried while the Turks were besieging Vienna. Gatien de Courtilz de Sandras, *Nouveaux intérêts des princes de l'Europe* (Cologne, 1685), 4. The fact that he did not do so seems to argue that Louis's actual policy stopped short of the dream of a universal empire. It must be remembered, however, that Louis expected the Bourbons to inherit the Spanish throne and to be *elected* to the imperial one; only thus could the universal Bourbon imperium be given a legitimate foundation.

[21] L. Pastor, *The History of the Popes*, XXXII (St. Louis, 1891–1940), 229. See also M. Immich, *Pabst Innozenz* XI (Berlin, 1900).

Venetians from heeding the papal exhortations in 1683, but after the relief of Vienna and the victories of the imperial armies in Hungary, a party had arisen in the senate in favor of joining Poland and the emperor against the traditional foe. Since Venetian sea power was necessary for any successful assault on the Turks from the south, Innocent XI had redoubled his efforts to make the league attractive to the Doge and the more timid members of the senate. His recent relations with Venice had been strained by other events, but Father d'Aviano and Senator Valiero, supported by the imperial victories on the upper Danube, finally persuaded the senate to join in a league with Austria and Poland.[22]

The treaty, signed at Linz in March, 1684, was christened the Holy League. The cardinal protectors of Venice, Poland, and the Empire administered the oaths for the observance of the treaty at a special congregation of the sacred college in Rome (May 24). Innocent XI and his successors were named protectors and guarantors of this Holy League. All these religious circumstances did not prevent the participants from securing their own political interests by the agreement. The emperor, in particular, insisted that the ancient lands of the Hungarian crown, when reconquered, should revert to the Hapsburgs. Poland's interest in the Ukraine and Venice's ambitions in the Adriatic Sea and Greece were also recognized. Finally, all Christian Europe was called upon to rally to the League and to help drive the Turks from Europe.[23]

The "War of the Holy League" opened an era of conflict that was to last for more than thirty years. In its wake it brought to consummation the European states system of the eighteenth and nineteenth centuries, and a series of reforms and revolutions which remade the internal structure of most states of the continent.

II. THE WAR IN THE EAST

Contemporaries regarded the War of the Holy League as a great crusade against the arch-enemy of Christendom. In Protestant as well as in Catholic Europe men toasted the victories and prayed for further successes. A flood of cheap prints depicting sieges, battles, and successful generals dramatized the conflict and advertised the progress of Christian arms. Only populations of the Morea and of Hungary, where the political implications of victory were patent, realized that the war was being fought

[22] L. Pastor, op. cit., XXXII, 192 ff.
[23] Baron Jean Dumont, Corps universel diplomatique du droit des gens (Amsterdam, 1726–1731), VII, 2, 71 ff.

to aggrandize Hapsburg and Venetian power as well as to regain territory for the cross. Not until the allied armies entered Athens and Belgrade did Europe begin to understand that victory over Islam had revolutionary implications for the political structure of the continent.

The general enthusiasm for the war undoubtedly contributed to the victory. Like all wars, this one required money, men, and more money, and all Europe contributed a share. Leopold's own lands on the upper Danube greatly increased their tax payment; the Venetian senate poured forth the profits of years of trade, and even Poland and the Empire raised additional revenue. But the greatest single contribution flowed from Rome and the church. Pope Innocent XI literally opened all gates of possible revenue and directed the flow toward Hungary, Poland, and Greece. Monasteries and convents throughout the Catholic world gave up their treasures; church lands were sold, papal taxes were raised to the limit. Many churchmen protested the impositions, for example the tenth laid upon the Spanish clergy, but Innocent XI and his cardinals overrode these complaints and collected the money. The huge subsidies that this vigorous old Pope directed toward the Venetian, the imperial, and the Polish treasuries leave no doubt that the victories in Hungary and in Greece were as much the fruits of Innocent's labors as of Christian heroism.[24] After the Pope's death, when French pressures reduced the flow of papal subsidies, the lack of Innocent's driving power and generosity was felt on every battlefield where Christian met Moslem.

The Osmanli had no such indefatigable leader to fill their war chest, but the financial machinery of their empire could and did produce the sinews of war. Special taxes were laid on the provinces from Egypt to the Balkans, and the ulemas (religious leaders) were made to give up much of their wealth. "You force us, who are devoted to the Sublime Porte, to sell all that we have acquired in the last sixty to eighty years," complained the kadiasker (governor) of Roumelia when faced by new demands for money.[25] But the worst feature was that the Ottoman seraskiers (commanders-in-chief) could not report victory. The Christians captured their guns, their horses, and even their money bags, and the grand vizier had to find more money to make good the losses. Thus, even though the Ottoman Empire was large and the sources of money were many, the Christian successes created heavy strains that eventually resulted in disorder, revolution, and defeat.

24 Pastor, *op. cit.*, XXXII, 198 ff.
25 Hammer-Purgstall, *op. cit.*, XII, 209.

The Christian armies were drawn largely from Germany and Bohemia, but all Europe contributed a share of the blood that reconquered Hungary. Religious fervor played the role later assumed by nationalism. The monks assured Christian soldiers that they were fighting the arch-enemy of their religion, and the recruiting officers held out hope of salvation as well as of gold and loot. Furthermore, the war was popular; the heroic defense of Vienna, followed by sensational victories in Hungary, captured the imagination of all Christendom. Great leaders like the duke of Lorraine, the dashing *Markgraf* of Baden, and the glamorous electoral prince of Bavaria became household names throughout Europe, and noblemen from many lands poured into Hungary to offer their swords for the crusade. Hammer-Purgstall has drawn a list of names which, though incomplete, indicates the quality of these noble recruits: from Spain came the dukes of Vexas and Escalona, the marquises of Valero, Gasp, Zuñiga, Almeida, Losana, Ottana, Rebolledo, and others; from England, a natural son of James II, and another of Prince Rupert, Lords Halifax, Granart, Monho, Cuts, and others; from Italy members of the houses of Piccolomini, Carminato, Caprara, Marsigli, and Rabatta; and even from France, despite the protests of the king, came representatives of the families of Suvri, Créqui, Chatellest, Longueval, Savoy, and Conti.[26] The last named was a prince of the blood, and Louis took pains to have his ambassador inform the grand vizier that Conti had joined the emperor without the king's permission. Though these names may mean little to twentieth-century readers, in the seventeenth century they were recognized as the highest nobility of Europe. They demonstrate that in this last great crusade the warrior estate of all Europe took part.

Along with the holders of proud names came humble men from all walks of life and from all parts of the continent. The exhortations of the Pope and his cardinals and monks transformed the struggle into a European movement that drew blood and muscle from all parts of Christendom for the battle against the infidel. Sixty Catalan artisans, most of whom gave up their lives at the siege of Ofen, comprised the largest single group, but at least six thousand other volunteers participated in the campaign of 1686.

The Turks drew their fighting men from the borders of Persia, from the Nile and North Africa, from Anatolia and Syria, as well as from the Balkans, but many of their recruits were of poor quality and incapable of handling modern weapons. Desire for salvation through fighting for Al-

[26] *Ibid.*, 198.

lah was not enough to make a man into a soldier. The core of the Turkish army continued to be the Janissaries and Spahis whom Achmed Kiuprili had reorganized a generation before; the provincial levies were at best only auxiliary forces, and at worst, became liabilities that drained supplies without contributing military power. It must not be thought, however, that the Turkish armies lacked valiant soldiers. The flag of the sultan was still a potent symbol for the descendants of the early Moslem conquerors. What the Turks lacked were officers competent to deal with the western tactics of the late seventeenth century. The few renegade Europeans in their camp were unable to make good this deficiency.

Volunteers were welcome in both armies, but the Christians wanted allies as well. Though the Holy League was formed under Catholic auspices and placed under papal protection, its members were quite willing to accept, indeed to seek, the aid of heretics, schismatics, and even Moslems. Leopold tightened his alliances with Catholic Bavaria and Lutheran Saxony; he secured the aid of Protestant Brandenburg for the war in Hungary, just as the Venetians obtained soldiers from Hanover for their Greek campaign. It was useless to seek assistance from Spain, for her navy could not put to sea and her army could not even defend the homeland. Innocent XI made unsuccessful efforts to obtain aid from France and from Persia. Louis, whom men were calling "the most Christian Turk of Versailles," refused to listen to the Pope's pleas, and the Shah of Persia contented himself with wishing the Christians luck in their enterprise.[27] After 1689, when the war became general, Leopold tried to enlist the sea powers against the Turks, but both England and the United Netherlands excused themselves for fear of damaging their commercial interests in the Levant.

The most enigmatic among the emperor's potential allies was Russia. For generations the Muscovite court had been politically and culturally isolationist, and both the Poles and the Swedes, regarding their eastern neighbors as barbarians, had maintained a sort of *cordon sanitaire* to keep them from obtaining western military techniques.[28] Russia, therefore, had never been considered seriously in the political arrangements of the west. But in the last third of the seventeenth century this isolation was about to break down. In 1672, when Mohammed IV captured the Polish fortress of Kamenets Podolsk, Tsar Alexis, awakened to the fact that the Turks

[27] Jorga, *op. cit.* IV, 203; M. G. Lippi, *Vita de papa Innocenzo XI, raccolta in tre libri*, ed. by G. Berthier (Rome, 1889), 168, *et passim*.

[28] It was actually easier for a Russian to go to China than to Rome. The Archangel route was the only one open; this placed Lisbon seven thousand miles from Moscow.

were neighbors more dangerous than the Tartars, naïvely sent ambassadors to the west to propose a coalition. He soon discovered that European
politics were not as simple as they appeared from Moscow.[29] Twelve
years later, after Innocent XI had convinced the Polish court that even
barbarians might be useful against the Moslem, emissaries from the Holy
League appeared in Moscow to enlist Russian aid against the Ottomans.

The first step was to arrange a treaty of "perpetual peace" between
Poland and Russia. The Poles opened their frontiers for transit to Moscow, and recognized Russian rule over Kiev. In return the Russians joined
the Holy League and agreed to send an army against the Crimea.[30] Russia's intervention in the war did not justify the hopes of her western allies,
but it was a decisive step toward Russia's entry into European affairs and
toward the westernization of the Russian army.[31]

The principal battlefields of the war were in Hungary and the Morea.
General Montecucculi, Austria's most successful general in the 1660's,
pointed out that all Hungary would fall if the Christian army could secure control of the Danube river system. The great inland fortresses like
Stuhlweissenburg and Temesvár depended upon the rivers for supplies as
much as did Ofen or Belgrade. This fact usually dictated the over-all
strategy of the war, even though at times purely political interests took
precedence over military considerations.[32]

The Turks had occupied Hungary for over a century, and had long
since prepared their defenses for an eventual Christian attack. The loss of
Gran and Parkány in 1683 was a serious blow to them, for with Stuhlweissenburg and Neuhäusel those fortresses were the outer defenses of
Ofen (Buda). In the south Esseg, Peterwardein, and Temesvár guarded
the approaches to the great fortification of Belgrade. The fate of all Hungary depended on these formidable positions, which could be taken only

[29] A. Brückner, Geschichte Russlands, bis zum Ende des 18 Jahrhunderts, I (Gotha,
1896–1913), 87–88.

[30] Dumont, op. cit., VII, 2. 125 seq.; cf. P. N. Milioukov, C. Seignobos and L. Eisenmann, Histoire de Russie, I (Paris, 1932–33), 265.

[31] Cf. Chapter Four.

[32] The imperative necessity of crushing the rebellion in Hungary as the Turks were driven
back, and the emperor's desire to reunite Transylvania to the Hapsburg holdings obliged the
commanders to move eastward before they had fully conquered the Danube-Drave river
system. These operations were facilitated by the support of a considerable
proportion of the population of the region. In Bosnia and Wallachia, where the Hapsburgs
had never ruled, Leopold's political ambitions were frustrated more because of the anti-
Roman Catholic feelings of the Greek Orthodox inhabitants than because of the military
power of the Turks. Already the Balkan peoples were beginning to look to the Orthodox
emperor in Moscow as their true leader, though the Russians were as yet quite unprepared
to play the role assigned to them.

with great difficulty. Ofen was besieged twice (1684 and 1686) before it fell, and the conquest of Belgrade proved to be at least as difficult a problem.

The Venetians at first hoped to attack the Turks through Dalmatia, but the emperor's contention that this region, with the exception of the commercial centers on the coast, belonged to the inheritance of the Hungarian crown (the Serbian crown had long since disappeared), induced them to turn their efforts southward. Since they had no interest in conquering territory for the emperor, the Venetians chose as their objectives the Morea, the isthmus of Corinth, Athens, and the island bases around Greece, all of which were of prime strategical and commercial importance to the mistress of the Mediterranean. The Poles were to operate in the Ukraine, Moldavia, and Wallachia, while the lands between the Bug and the Don were reserved for the Russians, but in neither of these theaters was the action significant.[33]

The first two years of the war, 1684–1685, did not produce the great results hoped for in Rome and Vienna, but they did soften the Turkish power to such an extent that in 1686 and 1687 practically all of Hungary could be liberated. Ofen was unsuccessfully besieged in 1684; in 1685 Neuhäusel fell and the imperial forces won a great victory in the field near Gran. The Hungarian rebels under Toekeli were crushed that same year and for the most part submitted to the emperor. In the south, a Christian army under General Leslie operated out of Croatia, and penetrated to Esseg, but without reducing the fortress. The war in Poland in these first years, as in later ones, was disappointing. Sobieski had great plans and was given substantial papal subsidies, but the results of his campaign were practically nil. His failure has been attributed both to the influence of a close relative of the queen of Poland, and to the king's inability to control the anarchical conditions in Poland. The Russians, on their part, made two assaults on the Crimea, in 1687 and in 1689, but their artillery was poor and their supply system even worse; though foreign advisers were in positions of command, both attacks ended in dismal failure. The second cost Russia twenty thousand men killed and fifteen thousand prisoners, and so undermined the position of Prince Golitsyn and the Empress Sophia that it opened the way for Peter I to assume sole power in Moscow. The Venetians, aided by the galleys of the Pope, Tus-

[33] On the opening of the great counterattack against the Turks, see Huber-Redlich, *op. cit.*, VI, 248 ff.; Fritz Salomon, *Ungarn in Zeitalter der Türkenherrshaft* (Leipzig, 1887), 363 ff.; J. W. Zinkeisen, *op. cit.*, V, 97 ff.; O. Klopp, *op. cit.*; G. F. Hertzberg, *Geschichte Griechenlands* III (1878), 129–157, contains an excellent account of the war in the Morea.

cany, and the Knights of Malta, as well as by an army of hired Hanoverian troops, established a beachhead at Coron (1685) and laid the foundations for the conquest of the Morea.

In 1686 Ofen fell to the Christian army, and the grand vizier was defeated in the field by Charles of Lorraine.[34] These victories were greeted with jubilation throughout the west. Since they had been won by troops from all Europe, they were Christian victories, even though the political advantages were all on the side of the emperor. During the same year (1686) the young Louis of Baden was awarded the rank of field marshal for his brilliant achievement in the south. In a single campaign he had captured the fortresses of Simontornga, Fünfkirchen, Dorda and Kaposvár, and had established a firm bridgehead at Esseg. The Venetians were also successful. Morosini took Naioplia (Napoli di Romania) in August of 1686, thereby earning the title "the Peloponnesian." A further series of victories enabled Königsmark, the commander of the land forces, to take Athens in 1687.[35]

The Turks then sued for peace (1687), but the allies were in no mood to listen. Mutinies in the Turkish army, a revolution in Constantinople that dethroned the sultan, and the obvious demoralization of the Turkish forces in the field, all pointed to the possibility of new and even greater Christian victories. The emperor put an army of sixty thousand men into the field. By the autumn the imperial forces had cut a line across the Danube and Theiss rivers and invaded Transylvania. The remaining Turkish forts in Hungary were isolated and incapable of sustaining themselves. Emperor Leopold was at last in a position to re-establish the ancient Hungarian kingdom.

The next year, 1688, saw the capture of Belgrade, the very key to the outer defenses of Constantinople. A scandalous dispute that had developed between Charles of Lorraine and Maximilian of Bavaria was solved when the former became so ill that the electoral prince had to assume full command of the army. The young general maneuvered his forces and managed the siege of the great Belgrade fortress so skillfully that he became the envy of his peers and the hero of a whole generation of young German noblemen. When the fortress finally fell to the ferocious assault of his storming parties, Maximilian was wise enough to resist Marco d'Aviano's plea for an advance southward toward Constantinople. As a

---

[34] F. V. Zieglauer, *Die Befreiung Ofens von der Türkenherrschaft, 1686* (Innsbruck, 1886), provides an excellent account of the two sieges.

[35] See J. M. Paton, *The Venetians in Athens, 1687–88* (Cambridge, Mass., 1940); Huber-Redlich, *op. cit.*, VI, 387–8.

soldier he realized that, even with the key fortress in his hands, the conquest of the Balkans would require much heavy fighting.

The Turks, thoroughly discouraged with the war, made another bid for peace (1688), but before it could be considered the French armies invaded the Palatinate, occupied Mainz, Trier, and Cologne, and laid siege to the fortress of Philippsburg. Louis XIV had decided that if he were to keep the Turks in the field against the emperor, he must furnish them immediate relief. His instructions to the French ambassador at Constantinople are revealing. After announcing his intention to send armies into Germany and Italy "to make a diversion of the forces of the house of Austria," so that the emperor "will be obliged to withdraw his troops from Hungary . . . ," he left it to the wisdom of his ambassador to utilize this information in his discussions with the grand vizier, who should "be able to profit advantageously by a conjuncture of events so favorable to him." He then went on to explain that William of Orange would soon depart for England to start a civil war, and that, if the Turks would make peace with Poland, the Poles could attack Brandenburg. "Thus," he concluded, "here is a general war in all Europe from which, I do not doubt, the Turks can draw a great advantage." [36]

With the outbreak of hostilities in the west, the Turks stiffened their peace conditions so much that Leopold could not accept them. His allies did not want peace, and he himself refused terms that did not completely underwrite the new status of Hungary, where he had recently had his son crowned as hereditary king, and Transylvania, where he had re-established Hapsburg control. Thus in 1688 the Empire was again, as in 1684, confronted with the problem of war on two fronts. But in 1688 Leopold's position was much stronger and France's position somewhat weaker, for in the intervening years the political ferment in the west had prepared the ground for a coalition against France that promised victory.

III. GENERALIZATION OF THE WAR

Between the truce of Regensburg (1684) and the French invasion of the Palatinate (1688) the political picture of Europe had altered greatly. In 1684 Leopold had been forced to sign the truce. Four years later the war in the east and the high-handed policy of the French king in the west had created a new situation. The Hungarian revolution had been crushed, the Turkish menace dispelled, and an imperial army of veteran of-

[36] Charles Gérin, "Le pape Innocent XI et l'élection de Cologne en 1688," *op. cit.*, XXXIII (1883), 121–2.

ficers and soldiers had come into being. In the west and north, William of Orange was fast becoming the leader of a coalition of Protestant states, anxious to join the emperor and Spain in order to end the hegemony of France. It was a change in the political climate that made it possible for Leopold to consider, indeed actually to decide upon, a war on two fronts.

At Regensburg in 1684 France had been in a position to impose her will upon Europe. Her armies had been the finest on the continent, her navy had been larger and better equipped than the combined navies of England and the United Netherlands, and her frontiers had been covered by strong fortifications. Furthermore, Louis's ambitions both in Spain and the Empire were at that time on the verge of fulfillment. A French princess was the wife of the sickly Charles II of Spain, and Louis, in anticipation of the king's death, had already prepared a manifesto claiming the entire Spanish inheritance for his family. In Germany, he controlled enough votes in the electoral college to have his son named King of the Romans, and many men expected that France would by military force make the German crown hereditary in the Bourbon family. The small states bordering on France were terrorized by the overwhelming power of their great neighbor. The duke of Genoa, after the destruction of his city by French naval bombardment, traveled to Versailles to make peace. The pirate states of Tunis and Tripoli, after a French attack, likewise sent envoys to Versailles to present their submission. These acts of terror, added to the ruthless manner with which France waged war upon the peaceful population of the Spanish Netherlands in 1684, deprived all Europe of a sense of security.

After 1685, however, France's splendid political and military position had begun to deteriorate. The revocation of the Edict of Nantes and the subsequent dispersal of the Huguenots was undoubtedly one of the great mistakes that led to the Sun King's downfall. By this measure Louis drove from France thousands of people who for the preceding five years had suffered severely for their faith. Many of these refugees were educated, articulate people: preachers, officers, businessmen, and artisans. They included one of Louis's best admirals (Duquesne) and one of his best generals (Schomberg). Many fled to England, the Netherlands, and Germany to spread tales of the brutality and persecution in France. All Protestant Europe was aroused against the bigoted monarch of Versailles, and when it was realized that this same ruler might, by combining the crowns of Spain and Germany with that of France, establish a universal imperium, Protestant Europe began to look to its defenses, or as Saint-

Léger describes it, to organize a Protestant crusade against France.[37] Actually the coalition formed against France after 1688 was anything but a "Protestant crusade." The emperor, the king of Spain, and a number of German Catholic princes were as much members of the alliance as were the Protestant rulers, and Pope Innocent XI himself was deeply involved on the side of the allies. The revocation of the Edict of Nantes played a part in affecting the political and military balance, but it was only one of several events that brought about a readjustment of forces unfavorable to France.

In the Netherlands the cautious burghers and those members of the states general who had accepted French gold were moved as much by Louis's suspension of certain trading privileges and by French interference with Dutch commerce with Africa as by the laments of Huguenot émigrés. Though shocked by French fanaticism and by stories of the brutal treatment of their coreligionists, they turned against France only when Louis also attacked their commerce. William of Orange and his party then gained the ascendancy. After years of frustration William was finally able to lay the groundwork for alliances with German princes and Sweden and at the same time to prepare military forces for the intervention in England that eventually brought that power into the Grand Alliance.

In Germany Louis' persecution of the Huguenots not only outraged the public, but also disabused the Protestant princes of the idea that the French king was their ally against the intolerance of the Catholic Hapsburgs. Frederick William of Brandenburg-Prussia answered the revocation of the Edict of Nantes by promulgating the Edict of Berlin, inviting the persecuted Huguenots to come to his lands. But there were additional reasons for the elector's change of front. The French navy was interfering with his colonial project in Africa, and Louis's pretensions to the Palatinate in the name of his sister-in-law threatened further French annexations in the Rhineland. Frederick William therefore ended his alliance with France, reached agreements with William of Orange and Emperor Leopold, and made an alliance with Sweden, though the latter treaty involved a temporary abandonment of plans for the acquisition of Swedish Pomerania. Once the vigorous old elector had convinced himself of the

[37] Many writers have assigned the beginnings of Louis' decline to the revocation of the Edict of Nantes. A. Saint-Léger and P. Sagnac, Le prépondérance française, Louis XIV, 1661–1715 (Paris, 1935), 303–321, present the thesis as convincingly as possible. The Huguenots have enjoyed the sympathy of liberal and Protestant historians, and thereby have probably attained an exaggerated importance in the eyes of posterity.

chances for success in a war against France, he began to talk of a march on Paris to dictate peace at Versailles.[38]

Catholic as well as Protestant Germany was upset by Louis's claims to territory in Palatinate. The Treaty of Westphalia had regulated the succession in the Pfalz-Neuburg house in case Prince Charles died without heirs. The duke of Orléans, brother to the French king, had married Prince Charles' sister, and when Count William of Pfalz-Neuburg inherited the electoral throne, Louis XIV at once laid claim to some of the best territory of the Palatinate for his brother's family. His argument involved an interpretation of the marriage contract, but the German princes of the Rhineland saw only the threat of further reunions. When Louis, with ostensible generosity, offered to accept the Pope's decision, the Germans were unwilling to consider even this proposition.

While Germany and the Netherlands were thus led to a conflict with France by Louis's commercial, religious, and dynastic policies, Spain was motivated chiefly by the anti-French feeling generated by the unprovoked attack of 1683 and the imposed truce of 1684. The French-born queen had been isolated and ill-treated. Deprived of her servants, she herself finally sickened and died. Rumors of poisoning were probably unfounded, but nonetheless prevalent. With her death French influence at Madrid virtually disappeared. The new star in Spain was Maximilian of Bavaria, the victor over the Turks, whose son was in the line of succession. Since there was reason to suppose that the Bavarian prince, rather than a Hapsburg or a Bourbon, might one day occupy the Spanish throne, Maximilian's house completely overshadowed those of France and Austria.[39] In the meantime, the Spanish government, itself incapable of initiating a war policy, was ready to join any coalition against Louis.

An opportunity to adhere to the anti-French alliance appeared in 1686, when the kings of Spain and Sweden were invited to participate in the famous League of Augsburg. The annexation of Strassburg had stimulated efforts to build up an imperial army. The military law passed by the diet in 1681 had proved to be unworkable, but the Luxemburg Alliance of 1682 had combined the forces of the Franconian and Swabian circles under the leadership of Count Waldeck, and had provided soldiers who were now hardened by the war against the Turks. With a view to extending this alliance, Count Hohenlohe, the imperial representative in

[38] J. B. Droysen, *Geschichte der preussichen Politik; Der Staat des grossen Kurfürsten,* III (Leipzig, 1870–1872), 518 ff.

[39] G. F. Preuss, "Oesterreich, Frankreich und Bayern in der spanischen Erbfolgefrage, 1685–89," *Historische Vierteljahrschrift,* IV (1901), 309–33, 481–503.

Franconia, promoted a new and more inclusive league for the defense of the Empire (1685). This League of Augsburg has attracted much more attention from historians than its actual military usefulness warranted, probably because Louis XIV made it an excuse for his invasion of the Palatinate in 1688. Actually, the League was militarily crippled by the reluctance of many petty princes to act for fear of French retaliation. A treaty signed at about the same time by Brandenburg and the emperor was of infinitely greater practical importance.[40]

While the revocation of the Edict of Nantes and the question of the succession in the Palatinate enhanced hostility to France in Germany and northern Europe, French colonial and commercial policy aroused the enmity and fear of the commercial powers. When the newly founded French Senegal Company attempted to cut off both the Dutch and the Brandenburg trade on the Guinea coast, the two threatened powers quickly reached agreement to submit their own differences to a joint commission and to present a common front to the French. At the same time, the conflicts between French and British commercial interests in the Americas made difficult the maintenance of the amiable relations between the two countries desired by their rulers. The French felt that the Hudson Bay Company and the New England colonies were encircling their North American possessions. The English, on the other hand, looked upon French pretensions in the Mississippi and Great Lakes basins as designed to surround their own possessions in the New World. Furthermore, there was continuous friction between the two countries in the sugar islands. Neither James nor Louis could control their subjects in America, while on the other side of the globe the British and French India companies had already embarked upon a conflict that was to continue into the eighteenth century. In 1686 Bonrepaus, a French special agent, negotiated a treaty to settle these Colonial questions, but it was easier to make a treaty than to get commercial and military agents far from Europe to comply with the terms.[41]

Although the French and English kings did not drift apart, the two governments were bound to feel the impact of growing popular hostility on both sides. James II, at the Pope's request and in order to allay the

<hr>

[40] M. Immich, *Zur Vorgeschichte des orleanischen Krieges* (Heidelberg, 1898); R. Fester, *Die augsburger Allianz von 1686* (Munich, 1893); and R. Fåhraeus, "Sverge och Forbundet i Augsburg ar 1686," *Historisk Tidskrift*, XVI (1896), 201–236.

[41] R. Durant, "Louis XIV et Jacques II à la veille de la révolution de 1688. Les trois missions de Bonrepaus en Angleterre," *Revue d'histoire moderne et contemporaine*, X (1908), 28–44, 111–126, 192–204.

public clamor, tried to induce Louis to soften his policy toward the Huguenots, and later felt obliged to open English ports to the refugees from French persecution. Louis, on his side, tried to brake James' attempts to force full recognition of Catholicism in England. Finally, James' rejuvenation of the English navy caused as much misgiving in France as it provoked enthusiasm in England. James, himself an old sailor, wanted to see England regain her lost naval status, but it was hardly to be expected that his policy would be agreeable to France, at that time in command of the seas.

In Italy, French policy terrorized the smaller courts and brought on an open conflict with the Pope. The occupation of Casale (1681) and the bombardment of Genoa (1684) showed clearly that France did not propose to abandon her pretensions in the peninsula in order to secure her position on the Rhine. Savoy was forced to embark upon a campaign to exterminate heresy in northern Italy, and her duke was treated like a mere servant of the French king. Even the Pope was not immune from French pressure. Innocent XI refused to recognize Louis's Gallican claims and indeed tried to induce the French ambassador to give up the extra-territorial privileges that made even the apprehension of criminals impossible in Rome. The dispute led to open warfare in the Holy City. The Pope excommunicated the French ambassador who maintained his position with the aid of French soldiers, while the king of Spain offered Innocent XI an alliance and aid against the "Eldest son of the Church" whose ambassadors behaved so badly toward the spiritual and temporal head of the church.[42]

Thus from Rome to London, from Vienna to Stockholm, the Sun King managed to offend or antagonize all of Europe, and to cause it to look to its defenses. Slowly the balance of power shifted against France. The victories of the Holy League in Hungary and Greece, the defection of France's allies in Europe, and the growing realization that force alone could foil Louis's program made France's position actually hazardous. By 1688 France was isolated in Europe and surrounded by powers anxious to bring Louis to judgment.

The news from the east, where a Christian army under Maximilian of Bavaria was besieging Belgrade, left little doubt that before long the Turks would be forced to make peace. Louis XIV and his ministers realized that they must salvage their gains and consolidate their position on the Rhine before the emperor could be released from the Turkish war.

[42] Pastor, *op. cit.*, XXXII, 246–325, 342–370.

They hoped to translate the twenty-year truce of Regensburg into a permanent peace for the Rhineland. Both Louis and Louvois believed they could achieve this by a military demonstration like the one of 1683–1684. France was actually unprepared for a long war. Neither the military nor the financial situation warranted a venture that might involve years of conflict, but the country was well able to mount a campaign such as Louvois believed would bring Europe to terms.

In the summer of 1688 there were two issues suitable as pretexts for such a demonstration. The first was the election of a new electoral bishop in Cologne, where the French candidate was opposed both by the emperor and by the Pope. The second was the plan of William of Orange for a military and naval descent on England.[43] William obviously intended his intervention to bring England into the anti-French alliance. Louis was well aware of his plan, and advised James II to take precautions, but James, believing William's preparations directed toward France, ignored the warning. Louis might have saved James his throne, but as the situation developed, it was believed at Versailles that this prospective invasion of England would be advantageous to France. To subsidize the English had proved insufficient for French purposes. Parliament could, and actually did in the previous war, force the king to change sides in a conflict. Furthermore Louis had little confidence in James II or his judgment. He had reached the conclusion that the Dutch invasion would result in a civil war that would paralyze both England and the United Netherlands long enough to enable him to win his objective in Germany.[44] So Louis ignored the preparations for the assault on England, and concentrated his attention on the Rhine.

The problem of Cologne provided a better gambit.[45] The old electoral archbishop, a member of the Bavarian house, had been so long in the pay of France that Louis regarded the electorate as an extension of his own kingdom. To assure his hold on the archbishop he had bought the election of one of his creatures, Bishop Fürstenberg of Strassburg, as coadjutor, but the bribery of the cathedral chapter was such a notorious scandal that the papal *curia* refused to recognize the election. While the question was in suspense, the archbishop elector died (June, 1688) and Louis immediately attempted to have Fürstenberg named his successor. But the emperor and the house of Bavaria had another candidate, Prince

[43] The problems of the English Revolution are discussed in Chapter Six.
[44] Rousset, *Histoire de Louvois*, IV, 152–4.
[45] C. Gérin, "Le Pape Innocent XI et l'élection de Cologne en 1688," *op. cit.*, XXXIII (1883), 76–127; Immich, *op. cit.;* and Pastor, *op. cit.*, XXXII, 376–384.

Joseph Klemens, the younger brother of Maximilian. The Bavarian Wittelsbachs had placed younger sons on the electoral throne for so long that the prince's election (although he was only seventeen years old) would have been a matter of formality had Louis not interfered. When the election was held, neither candidate secured the necessary two-thirds of the votes, and the problem was therefore referred to Rome for a judgment. Leopold announced that he would not allow a subject of the king of France to become an elector of the Empire, and Maximilian, in the very act of taking Belgrade, appealed to the Pope for his brother's appointment. Louis XIV, realizing that the Pope would support the imperial candidate, made a scandalous attack upon the career and motives of Innocent XI, which did not prevent His Holiness from in fact awarding the election to Prince Joseph Klemens (August 26, 1688).

Louis had decided upon war even before this news came from Rome. Four days before the papal decision was announced, he informed the French ambassador at Constantinople of his projected war on the Rhine and of William of Orange's probable invasion of England.[46] The war manifesto listing Louis's grievances was not issued, however, until September 2, 1688, when French troops entered the Rhineland and laid siege to the fortress of Philippsburg.[47] Louis complained of the hostile attitude taken by the emperor and the Empire in connection with his sister-in-law's inheritance in the Palatinate and with respect to the election at Cologne; he recited the fact that Leopold had not only refused to translate the truce of Regensburg into a permanent peace, but had also formed leagues and alliances obviously aimed at France. According to this manifesto, Louis himself was full of "sweetness and light," ready and eager to return Philippsburg and Freiburg and any other of the lands he had occupied, if only the emperor would make peace.

The French invasion of the Rhineland had immediate repercussions in the east as in the west. On the one hand the Turks advanced new proposals that precluded peace for Hungary. On the other, the commitment of Louis's armies in the Palatinate relieved the United Netherlands of French pressure and allowed William to embark for England. England itself became crucially important. If James II were to join Louis XIV, the French could be almost certain of victory. If, as was more likely, James attempted to exploit the continental war to strengthen England's commercial position and so rally the commercial classes in his own support,

[46] C. Gérin, "Le Pape Innocent XI et l'élection de Cologne en 1688," *op. cit.*, Vol. XXXIII, 121.

[47] M. Immich, *Geschichte des europäischen Staatensystems von 1660 bis 1789*, 135.

both the United Netherlands and France would suffer materially. Of William's objectives when he left for England only one was perfectly clear, and that was to involve England in the war against France. He already had treaties with Sweden, Brandenburg, and the emperor, while both the king of Spain and the Pope knew of and more or less approved his mission. It was imperative that England be added to the continental alliance to check the power of France.[48]

The phase of the great conflict of 1683–1699 that followed Louis's declaration of war has been called "The War of the League of Augsburg," "The War of the English Succession," "The Orleans War," "The War of the Palatinate," and, in American histories, "King William's War." This varying nomenclature reflects the fact that contemporaries, as well as later historians viewed the general conflict from particular—usually national or dynastic—viewpoints. The invasion of the Rhineland and William's descent on England were in fact only different aspects of the great political convolution that shook the continent. The conquest of Hungary and the rise of a powerful imperial army to counterbalance the French hegemony were undoubtedly more important than the alleged causes of the war. A new Europe was emerging, and a whole generation was to know no peace until two great wars had been fought and a new balance of power established on the continent.

The obvious hypocrisy of the French manifesto opening the hostilities and the war of frightfulness waged by the French armies aroused a protest in Germany resembling the outbursts of modern nationalist feeling. Louvois had ordered his generals to conduct the war on the destructive pattern of the Thirty Years' War, that is, to blow up or burn villages, towns, and cities, to disperse the population, and to make the country useless to the enemy. Refugees from the Rhineland carried tales of French brutality deep into Germany and stirred up the whole population against the invader. French warfare seemed to be the dragonnades against the Huguenots translated into international action.[49]

The so-called League of Augsburg was not strong enough to meet the situation, but on October 22 the powerful German princes, Frederick

[48] William apparently did not realize that his intervention would place him and his wife on the English throne. When he left the Netherlands he thought in terms of a regency through which he would control English foreign policy. Cf. Chapter Four.

[49] By 1688 Germany had already been flooded with pamphlets and books damning Louis's foreign policy. A good example was the telling attack of Monsr. L.B.D.E.D.E., *La cour de France turbanée et les trahisons démasquées* (Cologne, 1686), in which among other things Louis was revealed as Machiavellian, lacking in good faith, disdainful of law, breaking oaths and contracts, tyrannical, destructive of religion, and an ally of the Turk.

William of Brandenburg, John George III of Saxony, Ernest Augustus of Hanover, and Charles of Hesse-Kassel reached an agreement at Magdeburg that mobilized the military forces of north Germany. The emperor recalled the Bavarian, Swabian, and Franconian troops, as well as some of the imperial forces, from the Turkish war and sent them, under Maximilian of Bavaria, to defend south Germany. It was impossible to make peace with the Osmanli, but the Christian victories had been such that the imperial armies could go over to the defensive, holding the Ottoman forces below Belgrade. Before the imposing show of German force the French armies retired to the Rhine, leaving a broad belt of territory in smoking ruins.

During the next two years, as one power after another joined in the war, the alliances and agreements that preceded and followed upon the French invasion of the Rhineland hardened into a great confederation. When James fled from England begging aid for the reconquest of his throne, it was apparent that no civil war would distract that kingdom, and that under the influence of William, England would probably be enlisted for the coalition. Louis eased his enemy's problem by sending an expedition to Ireland to aid James, whereupon parliament promptly declared war on France. Spain and Savoy joined the coalition in 1690, and Sweden, allied with both Leopold and William of Orange, lent tardy assistance. Thus began the Grand Alliance of the Holy Roman Empire, the German princes, the Netherlands, England, Spain, Sweden, and Savoy, all banded together to force France to recognize Europe's rights and interests.

The war aims of the allies were nothing less than the re-establishment of the territorial settlements of the treaties of Westphalia and the Pyrenees, that is, to deprive Louis of all the gains he had made since his assumption of personal power. Leopold, by way of contrast, secured support for his dynastic ambitions, for England and the Netherlands pledged their support to the Hapsburg candidate for the Spanish throne. During the entire second half of the seventeenth century the question of the Spanish succession weighed heavily in all the negotiations of western Europe; it is therefore not surprising that the question should have been injected into the negotiations of the Grand Alliance.

The western phase of the war was fought in many theaters. It opened on the Rhine but, as might have been expected, the principal battles were fought in the Low Countries. The French landing in Ireland (1689) to support James II opened another theater and involved naval action in the

Channel and in Irish waters. When Savoy and Spain joined the Grand Alliance (1690), northern Italy also became a battleground, and a French army crossed the Pyrenees into Spain. The war spread also to North America, to the Caribbean, and to India. Considering that at the same time the Holy League, joined by Russia, was fighting the Turks in Greece, and on the Danube, Dnieper, and Don rivers, it becomes evident that the struggle was one involving all Europe and its dependencies.

Militarily the conflict was a dreary chronicle of sieges and maneuvers. Duke Charles of Lorraine, the ablest commander on the allied side, died early in 1690, leaving no first-rate strategist to succeed him. Maximilian was an adventurous, dashing warrior, but not a man to plan long-range strategy. William III, though a stubborn fighter, was not a general capable of forcing a decision. On the French side Luxembourg and Villars were both able commanders, but they were hampered by the fact that Louis and Louvois were administrators rather than warriors. The king and his war minister distrusted the issue of campaigns in the field; they preferred Vauban, the taker of fortifications, to the soldiers with grand notions of campaigns of movement. Even the successful sieges were not followed by vigorous action that might have imposed peace. None of the soldiers or statesmen of this period seem to have realized the simple fact pointed out to later generations by Clausewitz, namely, that the aim of war is to destroy the enemy's capacity to make war, and to force him to bow to the will of the victor. There was, therefore, no over-all strategy for the war in the west. The French were in possession of the disputed territory and defied their enemies to take it from them. This meant a war of position with only occasional field battles between the armies covering and attempting to relieve the sieges. In short, the war was one of attrition.

In the course of the very first year (1689) the French were forced to give up much of the German territory they had occupied at the outset. Even the fortresses of Mainz and Bonn were retaken by the Germans, largely because Louis's armies were overextended. The French fell back to a secondary line from which seven years of fighting failed to dislodge them. In the second year (1690), Luxembourg won a great victory at Fleurus that nullified all allied hopes of invading France, while at sea the French navy under Tourville covered a landing in Ireland and defeated the Anglo-Dutch navy at Beachy Head. The only bright spot for the allied armies in 1690 was William's victory over James II and his French and Irish army at the Boyne. Thus one theater of war was closed, and English efforts thenceforth could be concentrated on the war at sea and in the Netherlands.

In the east the Turkish war went badly for the imperial forces after the cream of the army was transferred to the French front. Louis of Baden, with insufficient forces and money, was able to protect Transylvania, but in October a powerful Turkish army retook Belgrade. Count Aspremont with eight thousand men defended the city until a Turkish fire bomb made a chance hit that exploded three powder magazines and blew a great hole in the walls. This catastrophe reminded the statesmen at Vienna that they could not neglect the eastern war without losing their dearly won gains. William of Orange pressed them to make peace, but peace with Turkey could not be had on acceptable terms.

In the years 1691–1693 the siege warfare continued, the French usually gaining the advantage. In 1692 Louis took the great fortress of Namur, but failed to follow up his victory. The battle of Steenkerke in the autumn of 1692 was almost a draw, though William of Orange abandoned some of his equipment in his retreat. The following year, at Neerwinden, Luxembourg won an imposing victory over the Germans and Dutch and sent so many captured banners to Paris that he was named the *"Tapissier de Notre-Dame."* However, none of these battles was of the "knockout" variety that could force a termination of the war.

On the seas the war of attrition at first concealed the fact that the French were losing their superior naval position. At Beachy Head (July, 1690) and in several chance encounters during the following year the Anglo-Dutch forces were beaten and forced to withdraw, but since they were not destroyed they continued to exert pressure as a "fleet in being." William III, himself largely uninterested in the navy, allowed his Whig supporters to pour money into the fleet at the very time when Louis and Louvois were starving the French navy to meet the ever-growing demands of the armies. Seignelay died in 1690 and his successor as director of French naval affairs had neither the vision nor the influence of the Colberts. The result was that by 1692 the balance of naval power was already tilted against France. The catastrophic defeat of Tourville's fleet at La Hogue in May, 1692, revealed dramatically the growing weakness of the French at sea. Tourville, implicitly following unrealistic orders, attacked an Anglo-Dutch fleet much larger than his own. The French acquitted themselves bravely, but the odds were too great and the French navy suffered a crippling blow. "La Hogue," wrote Michelet, "insignificant in appearance, changed the course of history." The French navy, forced on the defensive, had to abandon the high seas to its opponents.[50]

---

[50] De la Roncière, *Histoire de la marine française*, VI (1932), 60–123. R. Jouan, *Histoire de la marine française*, I (1932), Ch. 5; J. Tramond, *Manuel d'histoire maritime de la France* (1947 ed.), Chs. 8–9.

Louis XIV did not take this naval defeat seriously. He was continentally minded and Europe, rather than the high seas, impressed his imagination. As long as Colbert and Seignelay were alive they had been able to give French policy a commercial and naval orientation, but Louvois's continental point of view was closer to that of the king. Pontchartrain, who took over the navy in 1690, never had enough money to maintain an aggressive policy. Encouraged by Vauban, he contented himself with commerce raiding. Swarms of privateers preyed upon Anglo-Dutch commerce, while an occasional task force of navy vessels and privateers raided convoys or attacked isolated points. This type of warfare was damaging enough to cause concern both in England and Holland, but it did not affect the course of the war.[51]

The allies were slow to exploit their naval preponderance. As long as the French Channel fleet remained in being, the English commanders, adhering to Elizabethan concepts of naval strategy, concentrated their ships in the Channel to ward off invasion and control commerce. This left the French in command of the Mediterranean, even though the total French navy was considerably smaller than its opponents. In 1694, however, William conceived a plan whereby his control of the sea would count both in the Atlantic and in the Mediterranean. In face of the protests of his sailors and the refusal of his council to assume responsibility, the king sent an Anglo-Dutch fleet into the Mediterranean and maintained it there through the winter of 1694–1695. Cadiz became an English base to shelter and repair the fleet. The results were striking. The French Toulon fleet was confined to harbor just as were the French ships in the Channel ports. Louis's campaigns in Italy and Spain suffered and French commerce languished, while Anglo-Dutch merchantmen had free run of the Mediterranean.

The meaning of the Cadiz base was never forgotten in England. By controlling the Straits twelve months in the year the English navy could prevent the union of the French Mediterranean and Atlantic fleets, and at the same time ensure control over the western Mediterranean as well as over the Atlantic. In the War of the Spanish Succession the lessons of the campaign of 1694–1695 became basic to English naval strategy.[52]

With the exception of the Mediterranean campaign of 1694–1695, however, English naval action was largely confined to the protection of allied shipping and the destruction of French commerce. This commercial war-

[51] Cf. Chapter Six.
[52] Sir J. S. Corbett, *England in the Mediterranean, 1603–1713* (London and New York, 1904), II, 150–186.

fare was responsible for the first crack in the Grand Alliance. Sweden was obligated to contribute six thousand men and twelve warships to the common cause, but the government, in the midst of reorganization, found this a heavy drain on its resources. At the same time the efforts of the Anglo-Dutch navies to blockade France cut deeply into Sweden's principal exports—wood, pitch, and iron. The Stockholm merchants therefore petitioned Charles XI to alter Swedish war policy. Meanwhile the Danes, likewise suffering from the blockade but anxious to keep out of the war, were ready to sink their traditional difficulties with Sweden in an agreement to defend neutral trade. In March, 1691, the two kingdoms made a treaty of armed neutrality for the protection of their commerce and the prevention of the spread of the war to the north.[53]

Because of its commercial aspects, this war became the first European conflict that extended to the rest of the world. In earlier wars there had been occasional naval engagements in the New World and Asia, but these had been episodic. In the late seventeenth century the European stations in Asia were still mere islands in a sea of Oriental humanity, but from Madras to Pondicherry, from Ceylon to the East Indies, Frenchmen, Englishmen, and Dutchmen were staking out rival claims that were presently to develop into great empires. When the news of the war in Europe reached Asia, colonial governors and merchants quickly took up the struggle in their own areas. The French Admiral Duquesne-Guiton sailed into Madras (October, 1690) to bombard an Anglo-Dutch fleet and the shore installations. It proved to be a foolhardy attack, but initiated the extension of hostilities to the Far East. In September, 1693, the Dutch besieged the tiny French garrison at Pondicherry and forced its spice-merchant governor to surrender. Off the African coast and in the Antilles the war led to naval action. Saint Christopher changed hands twice; Jamaica, Martinique, and Santo Domingo became scenes of sporadic conflict. Anglo-Dutch control of the seas gave the allies an advantage in these isolated engagements, but in those days of sailing vessels and slow communications it proved impossible to keep the French from supplying their colonial forces.

The most serious fighting took place in North America. Even before the war broke out in Europe the governors of Boston and Quebec were preparing to attack each other. After 1689 war flared up from Hudson Bay to New England. The French and their Indian allies raided deep

[53] Rudolf Fåhraeus, *Sveriges Historia till våra Dagar*, VIII, *Karl XI och Karl XIII*. Ed. Emil Hildebrand and Ludwig Stavenow, 280–282.

into the English territory (Deerfield massacre) and hatched vague plans for an attack on New York. The English, on their part, retaliated by landing in Nova Scotia and capturing Port Royal. They also planned an attack on Quebec, but they lacked the power to mount the campaign. The French settlements in the New World were small compared with the English, but the vigor of Governor Frontenac, supported by his Indian allies, enabled the French to hold the initiative during most of the war.[54]

By 1693 both sides had come to realize that the war, despite its costliness, might prove indecisive and that perhaps the best course would be to seek a compromise settlement. The Emperor Leopold, to be sure, did his utmost to hold the members of the coalition in line, if only because of the all-important question of the Spanish succession. If Charles II of Spain were to die while his country was still at war with France, the Bourbon claims would be ignored and the throne would pass to Leopold's second son Charles, or to his grandson, the little prince of Bavaria. It was therefore to the emperor's interest to induce his allies to insist on the achievement of their war aims, namely, the return of all territory annexed by France since the mid-seventeenth century.

Louis, on his part, was certainly not blind to the dangers inherent in a prolongation of the war. Since Louvois's death (1691) the king bore the full burden of operations and was confronted by the problems resulting from heavy taxation and disastrous harvests. Yet France's position, while increasingly precarious, was not desperate and Louis could not bring himself to sacrifice the disputed territories over which he still had military control. He therefore still hoped that the coalition might fall apart. William III's hold on the English throne was still tenuous, and he was surrounded by malcontents who grumbled at the heavy cost of a war without victory. Many of the German princes, too, were weary of a war that promised no gains, and were prepared to form a "neutrality group" within the Empire. Leopold managed to detach the duke of Hanover from this group by awarding him an electoral hat in return for a money payment and increased help against the Turks, but this move only aroused the jealousy of other German princes, who thereupon joined the "third party." Louis XIV lost no time in exploiting this situation, reminiscent of the period of the Nijmegen settlement. He therefore opened secret negotiations in all directions in the hope of breaking up the Grand Alliance. By 1695 Europe was flooded with rumors of peace which in fact did much to undermine the confidence of members of the confederation.

[54] An excellent short account of the colonial wars is that of C. de la Roncière, *op. cit.,* VI, 232–395. See also his *Une épopée canadienne* (Paris, 1930).

IV. TURIN, RYSWICK, AND CARLOWITZ

The first breach in the alliance came in 1696 with the defection of Savoy and the neutralization of Italy. Once the solid front was broken, a general pacification in the west followed quickly. The duke of Savoy earned an unsavory reputation for his "treachery" and provided his former allies with an excuse for passing over his family's claims to the English succession, but actually Savoy's behavior was typical of the period. As a buffer state between France and the Hapsburg lands in Italy and central Europe, Savoy's independence hinged upon the political sagacity of her rulers. The duke believed his allies were negotiating with France and proposing to sacrifice his interests to secure their own. His objective, therefore, was simply to reach an agreement that would forestall a settlement at his expense.

The Treaty of Turin (1696), which ended the war between Savoy and France, was negotiated in deepest secrecy. Louis was willing to pay a high price. He agreed to allow the Savoyard army to "capture" Casale and Pinerolo, the two great fortresses that assured French power in northern Italy. Casale, after being dismantled, was to be returned to Mantua; Pinerolo was to remain in the possession of Savoy. In return Savoy agreed to join Louis, with military force if necessary, to secure the neutralization of Italy. Thus Louis XIV gave up the most important gains of half a century of French Italian policy, in order to free thirty thousand troops for use elsewhere.

Austrian generals were astonished at the ease with which the Savoyard army captured the two fortresses. They were soon dismayed to see their erstwhile ally transfer his forces to the French camp and demand a cessation of all fighting in Italy. Actually they had no alternative but to accept this demand. Since the allies could not find sufficient troops to make up for the loss of the Savoyard army, they had to agree to the neutralization of Italy. Savoy's prestige in the peninsula rose high, while the only advantage that accrued to the emperor derived from the transfer of Prince Eugene, now a general, from the Italian to the Turkish front.

The Treaty of Turin started a scramble for peace. William III, like others, was negotiating with France, and as soon as Louis expressed willingness to recognize the Revolution of 1688 (Protestant succession in England) and to satisfy English and Dutch commercial interests, the sea powers were ready to come to terms. This left Emperor Leopold and the Spaniards without support. They had to follow their allies and try to get the best possible terms. Since Louis was anxious to ingratiate himself in Madrid, Leopold had no choice but to scale down his expectations.

The Treaty of Ryswick was written at a villa belonging to the house of Orange. French negotiators occupied one wing and the allies the other, while in the center hall a Swedish diplomat acted as mediator by exchanging notes and urging compromises. Actually the major issues were ironed out by William III and Louis XIV in direct negotiations. When Louis recognized William III as king of England, agreed to allow the Dutch to garrison a line of fortresses in the Spanish Netherlands, and relaxed his commercial regulations to favor Dutch trade, William III found it easy to abandon the emperor's claim on Strassburg as well as to agree to a return of all colonial conquests. Louis generously returned Luxemburg and Barcelona to Spain, though his armies were in possession of both cities, so the Spaniards were satisfied and willing to make peace. Louis further agreed to give up some of the conquests of the courts of Reunion and to return Lorraine to the son of the hero-soldier, Duke Charles, but he was adamant about Strassburg and Alsace. Since none of his allies were willing to continue the war just for Strassburg, Leopold had to come to terms. His representatives signed on the last permitted day.

Germany alone fared badly at Ryswick. Not only was France allowed to retain territory demanded by the emperor and Empire, but even the retroceded lands became subjects of controversy. The French negotiators very cleverly inserted into the treaty the famous "Ryswick clause," which guaranteed against change in the religious status of the lands surrendered by France. Thus the Catholic party in Germany became the beneficiary and defender of the "gains" made by the revocation of the Edict of Nantes. By reopening the religious debate in Germany, Louis XIV divided the ranks of his opponents beyond the Rhine.

The total peace settlement, however, netted Leopold an enormous accretion of power. While the diplomats at Ryswick were making peace in the west, the Christian army on the Danube won a great victory over the Turks.[55] Augustus of Saxony had proved himself a mediocre commander, but a fortunate conjuncture of circumstances made him king of Poland at the very time when the Treaty of Turin released Eugene of Savoy from the Italian theater of war. The young Prince Eugene showed the world what the best of Charles of Lorraine's cadets had learned in the years since the siege of Vienna. He outmaneuvered the Turkish generals,

[55] Between 1694 and 1697 the war in the east had been practically a stalemate.

and, on the battlefield of Zenta (August, 1697) annihilated a large part
of the Turkish army under the very eyes of the sultan and grand vizier.
Immense quantities of loot, including the sultan's treasure chest of four
million gulden, fell into his hands. The Turks were then ready to make
peace.

Leopold, knowing that the question of the succession in Spain must
soon come to a head, resisted all temptations to follow up his victory in
the east and determined to liquidate the Turkish war in order to have a
free hand in the west. The sea powers also urged him to make peace so
as to end the commercial dislocations in the Levant. Peter's thirst for
military glory and Eugene's projected reconquest of Belgrade had to be
postponed. The much-vaunted crusade to drive the infidel from Europe
now appeared in its true light as part of the great struggle to establish a
balance of power among the emerging military states.

Leopold's peace with the Ottoman Empire was very different from his
settlement with France. His armies had conquered the territories he
claimed, his enemies were demoralized and beaten, and his representatives at the conference held the whip hand. Carlowitz, where the delega-
tions met, was a devastated town. The diplomats were housed in tents
surrounded by mute evidence of the ferocious struggle that was ending.
Four treaties were signed; the emperor, Venice, and Poland negotiated a
definitive peace, while the Russians signed a truce which was translated
into a final treaty the next year (1700) at Constantinople. By these treaties the Turks surrendered to the emperor Hungary, Transylvania, and
Siebenbürgen, except the Banat of Temesvár. The Morea went to Venice,
and Podolia and part of the Ukraine to Poland. The Russian agreement
with the Turks left Peter in possession of Azov, but did not give Russia
access to the Black Sea. Peter accepted this limitation in order to secure
peace; by 1699 his attention had turned toward Sweden, a termination of
the war in the south was essential to pursuance of his policy in the north.

The fact that the peace treaties of 1696–1699 were superseded within
two decades by the treaties of Utrecht, Passarowitz, and Nystad make the
treaties of Turin, Ryswick, and Carlowitz appear as truces that settled
nothing. Many writers have referred to the peace of Ryswick as a return
to the *status quo ante bellum,* while the treaties of Turin and Carlowitz
are sometimes omitted completely from general textbooks. Contemporaries, however, did not consider these treaties as evidence that the war
had accomplished nothing, and they cannot be dismissed if the part
played by war in the development of western civilization is to be properly

understood. Actually the results of this war, as embodied in the treaties of peace, were in many ways more significant than those that followed the War of the Spanish Succession.

In the general European setting of the time the emergence of Hapsburg Austria and England as great powers, capable of contesting with France the hegemony of Europe, was a fact of major importance. The development of Austria from the status of an outlying province of the old Empire to that of a military power in its own right changed the whole structure of European politics; the Danubian Monarchy was to be an essential element in the states system of the next two centuries. Even more significant was the fact that the Revolution of 1688 gave England a constitution and a government that allowed her to use her wealth and energy in world politics to the fullest advantage. Not since the death of Elizabeth had England been important in European affairs, but the next two centuries were to mark her development into a mighty world power. Beside the rise of Hapsburg Austria and England to their historic roles, the fate of Strassburg, Casale, Temesvár, or, indeed, of the Spanish Netherlands, became a minor problem in European politics.

Of equal importance were the limits set by this war upon the ambitions of France. Though the French armies could carry out raids into Germany, like the second destruction of Heidelberg in 1693, they had proved themselves unable to maintain advanced positions in the face of German counterthrusts, or to force the minor German states to accept a separate peace. Indeed, during the whole course of the conflict on the Rhine-Netherlands frontier the French had fought a defensive war; not once did they try to force a decision. This fact alone reflected an alteration in the military balance of Europe which in turn exercised a profound influence on political developments. The German crown was elective (King of the Romans), and the successful candidate was invariably the successor to the emperor. Louis XIV had the avowed ambition to have himself or his son elected to the German throne. Had the Turks won at Vienna, or the French on the Rhine, that ambition would have been within the range of possibility, and a Bourbon prince might well have occupied the throne of Charlemagne. The election of Joseph, eldest son of Emperor Leopold, as King of the Romans (1688) and the subsequent defense of the Empire against France ended that dream and left the future of Germany in the hands of the Germans.

Nor was this the sum of French reverses. In the sixteenth century a French prince had been elected king of Poland, but at that time the conditions of war, commerce, and politics were not such as to make the connection between France and Poland significant. By 1700, however, a French king in Poland would have been almost as meaningful as the later attempt of Napoleon to make Poland an extension of France. Indeed, the whole course of eastern European history might have been profoundly affected by such an election. Louis XIV had long watched events in Poland and had spent much money to maintain his influence among the Polish magnates. In 1696, when Sobieski died, the French ambassador poured out vast sums of money to assure the election of Duke Louis François de Conti, but when the election was over the electoral prince of Saxony and lately commander of the emperor's armies in Hungary became king of Poland as Augustus II. This opportunistic prince conveniently changed his religion to make himself acceptable to Catholic Poland. His election was an illustration of the fact that French power was waning beyond the Rhine. Conti, with a few French warships, sailed into the Baltic to challenge the election, but nothing came of his ill-advised venture. For better or for worse, and the latter was surely the case with Poland, the Saxon and the Polish thrones were joined, and France had suffered another defeat.[56]

In Italy, too, the war blunted France's military pressure. The surrender of the forts of Pinerolo and Casale was clear indication that French influence and power in Italy was declining. The Alps rather than the Po were to be the boundary of France in the southeast. In the east and the northeast the obstacles to French aggression had become more formidable. The Palatinate and Cologne were no longer at issue. The Dutch garrisoned a series of fortresses in the Spanish Netherlands as a barrier to French attack, and although Louis retained Alsace, he was forced to surrender some of his Rhineland annexations. The treaties of 1696–1699 set definite limits to Louis's expansionist ambitions in central Europe. Of his grandiose plans, there remained only the possibility of the Spanish succession as a means of recouping his position in Europe. At Ryswick the Spanish inheritance was not discussed. It therefore remained as the most important unsolved question of European politics.

[56] W. Konopczyński, "Early Saxon Period, 1697–1733," *Cambridge History of Poland* (Cambridge, Eng., 1941), 1–3 and ff.

Chapter Three

THE NEW BALANCE OF POWER

IN EARLY eighteenth-century Europe various wars could still be waged simultaneously without becoming merged in a generalized struggle. The Great War of the North and the War of the Spanish Succession actually remained distinct conflicts. To conclude, however, that they were unrelated, or to treat them separately, would mean to overlook the fact that the continent was already beginning to assume the political structure characteristic of the following centuries. In reality these two wars, by setting limits to the ambitions of France, by establishing Russia as a great European power, and by fixing the roles of England and the Austrian monarchy, completed the political system already outlined by the treaties of Turin, Ryswick, and Carlowitz.

The political complexity of these two wars accounts for the historical accidents that kept them apart. Both the maritime powers and France were antagonistic to the rise of Russia; their experience with the Russians led them to prefer Swedish control of the Baltic. Until the defeat of Charles XII at Pultava, both contestants in the west were pro-Swedish in the east. On the other hand, the two principal figures in the Northern War, Peter I and Charles XII, both had a deep dislike for and distrust of Louis XIV. Peter's prejudices arose from his naïve admiration for the Dutch, from the scornful treatment his envoys had received in Paris, and from Louis's pro-Turkish policy. Charles, with perhaps even less political realism, scorned the oppressor of the Huguenots as the enemy of Protestant Europe. His revered father had broken with the traditional French orientation, and Charles refused to reverse the policy until it was too late to secure effective aid from France.

On his first European tour Peter I visited Vienna, hoping to arrange the continuance of the war against the Turks. But despite Eugene's great victories, Leopold's attention was turned toward Spain rather than toward the lower Danube. Austrian preoccupation with the impending Spanish succession left Peter no alternative to making peace at Carlowitz. Deeply disappointed, he went to Poland, where he found a monarch who fascinated him and a cause which appealed to his restless energy. Augustus the Strong, with his multitude of mistresses, his lusty appetites, and his crafty statesmanship, was a ruler after Peter's own heart. In the midst of target shooting and drinking bouts, the two men planned the partition of Sweden.

The Swedish Empire, so blithely conspired against, had emerged from the Thirty Years' War and had ruled the Baltic during the second half of the seventeenth century. By 1700, however, it was having difficulty in meeting the standards for great-power status. Swedish historians maintain that cultural and religious homogeneity within the empire provided the cohesive force to make a modern state, but they tend to overlook the fact that neither the Germans nor the Baltic peoples showed any attachment to the Swedish crown and that commercial ties alone were too weak to ensure unity.[1] Provincial loyalties transcended the dynastic, and the core of the empire, the old Swedish provinces, was too poor and too sparsely populated to become a great power in the new era. This painful fact became apparent during the regency of Charles XI when Sweden, battered and beaten by her neighbors, was saved from partition at Nijmegen by her ally, Louis XIV. The reforms of Charles XI and the diversions created by France and the Turks allowed Sweden to maintain her role as mistress of the Baltic for a few more decades, but she had obviously reached the limits of her expansion, and her main interest was necessarily the maintenance of the *status quo*. Charles XII fully understood this; at the height of his military power and prestige, he categorically stated: "We have land enough." [2]

Even the maintenance of the empire in face of the hatreds, fears, and avarice of her neighbors was for Sweden a difficult assignment. A smoldering conflict with Denmark over Holstein-Gottorp threatened to flare into war on the slightest pretext. German rulers, like the Prussian and Hanoverian princes, watched expectantly for an opportunity to despoil Sweden of her German provinces. Poland, lost in political anarchy, was no longer as formidable a threat as before, but the new king, Augustus of Saxony, was ambitious, ruthless, and unscrupulous, and unlikely to overlook the advantages to be gained by Baltic conquests. Lastly, in the east,

[1] O. Siögren, *Sveriges Historia,* III, *Storhetstiden Vasaskedet* (Stockholm, 1925), 386–416; R. Fåhraeus, *Sveriges Historia till våra Dagar:* VIII, *Karl XI och Karl XII* (Stockholm, 1923), 316 ff.; F. Bengtsson, *Karl XIIs Levnad till Uttåget ur Sachsen* (Stockholm, 1935), 47–61.

[2] F. Bengtsson, *op. cit.,* 51.

the rising Muscovite state, ready to emerge from Oriental isolation, naturally looked to the Baltic as a likely field for commercial, political, cultural, and strategic gains. Even though Sweden may not have actually lost in power, her neighbors were growing so rapidly that she was relatively at a disadvantage. Nevertheless, the conspirators who formed the first coalition against her underestimated the military power inherited by Charles XII and quite mistook the character of the young prince who had ascended the throne.[3]

Charles XII was just eighteen when an unprovoked attack threatened the integrity of his realm. He was to spend the remainder of his life in the effort to defend his kingdom and to punish the aggressors. His career has always been something of an enigma because so little is known of his purposes and objectives. His madcap behavior, lust for fighting, and rigid morality provide only a partial explanation. Charles XII clearly identified himself with his father and with Gustavus Adolphus, and by patterning himself on these two men he became a statesman and warrior with fixed ideas about royal obligations and prerogatives, and with high standards of personal morality. He had been educated in languages and history, trained to be tough in mind and body, and disciplined to face fatigue and danger with stoical calm. Modern Swedish historians regard him as the champion of Protestantism and the defender of Europe against the Slavic barbarians rather than as a wild man who killed for pleasure, or a soldier who fought for the joy of conflict.[4]

Charles probably never understood clearly the high politics of his era. He was thrust into the responsibility of power before experience had ripened his understanding and, like many well-intentioned men, he entertained naïve ideas which he regarded as principles and which he tried to apply to all men and all circumstances. His early victories reassured him of his wisdom and invincibility, and made him reluctant to listen to advice. The dreary years in Saxony, the fiasco in Russia, the humiliating stay in Turkey, and the final climax of his career in the north all illustrate his stiff-necked adherence to fixed ideas regardless of the realities.

The evil spirit of the conspiracy against Charles XII was Johann Reinhold Patkul, a Lithuanian nobleman who had been exiled from his homeland because of his violent protests against Charles XI's land policy

[3] S. Ågren's, *Karl XIs Indelningsverk för Armén* (Uppsala, 1922), throws light upon the reforms that gave Charles XII an army feared throughout the north.

[4] For a discussion of the interpretations of Charles' role by Swedish historians, see Carl Hallendorff and Adolf Schück, *History of Sweden* (Stockholm, 1929), 314 ff.

(*Reduktion*).[5] Patkul has been variously pictured as a warrior for liberty and as a traitor to his king. His brutal execution by the Swedes has blinded some historians to the fact that he was at bottom a self-seeking adventurer typical of the sixteenth and early seventeenth centuries, but essentially anachronistic in his own age. Patkul interested Augustus of Saxony in an alliance with Denmark to despoil the Swedish crown, tried in vain to inveigle Prussia, and finally seized upon the Russian tsar's visit to Poland to complete the triumvirate that made war upon Charles XII.

The coalition was bent upon partition of Sweden's empire. Frederick of Denmark wanted Holstein-Gottorp whose duke, the brother-in-law of Charles XII, was commander in chief of the Swedish armies in Germany. Augustus coveted Lithuania, believing that control of that province would tighten his hold on Poland and enable him to alter the anarchic constitution of the Royal Republic. Peter desired an outlet on the Baltic that would facilitate commercial and political contacts with Europe. These were war aims that bespoke international piracy on a scale theretofore unknown in Europe. The alliance was formed in deepest secrecy. Peter could not go to war until his ambassador at Contantinople had transformed the truce of Carlowitz into a treaty of peace. Indeed, he even went out of his way to assure the Swedish government of his friendship until he received news that the Treaty of Constantinople had been signed. Augustus and the Danish king attacked first by invading Lithuania and Holstein and Peter's army did not get under way until after the Danes had been forced to sue for peace.

Frederick of Denmark and Augustus of Saxony-Poland suffered a disagreeable surprise when they invaded Charles' empire. General Dahlberg drove the Saxons across the Dvina River before Patkul could rally the Lithuanian gentry. Frederick's punishment was even more severe. Confident that Denmark's naval superiority would prevent a descent upon his kingdom, he had concentrated his army against Sweden's German provinces. Only a year before, however, William III of Orange had made an alliance with Sweden guaranteeing the *status quo* in the north in return for Swedish aid in case of a war with France. Thus the Danish declaration of war brought an Anglo-Dutch fleet into the Sound. Admiral Rooke, with instructions to maintain "peace and tranquillity" even at the cost of naval action, turned the balance of sea power in Sweden's favor. With the Sound under their control, the Swedes quickly moved eleven thousand troops into Zeeland. Copenhagen was at their mercy, and King

[5] Cf. Chapter Five.

Frederick of Denmark was forced to surrender. On August 8, 1700, he signed a treaty with the duke of Holstein-Gottorp whereby he recognized the independence of the duchy and agreed to withdraw from the alliance with Saxony and Russia. The Anglo-Dutch squadron sailed home, and Charles, flushed with easy victory, prepared to turn on his antagonists in the east.

Both Peter and Augustus, impressed and sobered by the fate of the Danes, offered to negotiate, but Charles XII refused adamantly to listen to any proposals until he had avenged the "unjust and treacherous invasions" with "lawful weapons." Hastily gathering supplies, he transported a tiny army across the Baltic to Pernau (October, 1700). The Russian threat to Narva seemed greater than the Polish threat to Riga, so he decided to move first against Peter. Since the road from Wesenberg to Narva was boggy and desolate and the Swedish forces greatly outnumbered, Charles' thrust northward appeared foolhardy. The French ambassador and Charles' own best generals advised against it, but he would not be dissuaded. He had well taken the measure of the Russians. Neither Peter nor his generals knew enough to fortify the approaches to Narva, and the tsar lost his nerve when the Swedish force was one day's march away. On the eve of the battle he turned over the command to an observer in his camp, General Charles Eugene de Croy, who hardly had time to study his position before the Swedes were upon him. In a blinding snowstorm Charles launched his little force like a thunderbolt at the left center of the Russian camp. De Croy believed the attack a mere feint, having no idea that Charles commanded so few men.

The Swedish soldiers were well-trained and ably led; furthermore, they had seen the plundered villages, the murdered peasants and the ruined churches left by the Russian troops, and they burned with a desire to punish the semibarbarous invaders. Their assault carried them into the heart of the Russian camp and the Russian cavalry fled without firing a shot. De Croy and the other foreigners surrendered to escape butchery by their own soldiers. The Russian forces of over forty thousand were either dispersed, captured, or killed. In the west it was reported that six thousand Swedish soldiers had defeated eighty thousand Russians. The actual odds were closer to five to one, but even those figures were enough to win acclaim for the hero king and his gallant army.[6]

The battle of Narva made Charles XII the most courted ruler in

[6] F. Bengtsson's chapter "Narva" (*op. cit.,* 131–165) is a brilliant, colorful story of the battle.

Europe. In view of the impending conflict over the Spanish succession, a man of such military talents inevitably became the object of solicitous attention. Charles, however, spent the winter of 1700–1701 hunting elk, amusing himself at snowball fights, and keeping his own counsel. He had resolved to invade Poland and punish Augustus. Only after this was accomplished would he be willing to discuss Sweden's role in the west. In the spring of 1701 the Swedish army fought its way across the Dvina River, winning a victory as brilliant as the one of the preceding fall, and for the next seven years Poland and Saxony were to provide the stage for the Caroline saga. Lured by hopes of early victory, Charles sank in the mire of Polish politics while in the west the War of the Spanish Succession moved toward its climax and while in the east Peter was busily teaching his people to look and to fight like Europeans.

II. THE WAR OF THE SPANISH SUCCESSION: DIPLOMATIC BACKGROUND

The last Hapsburg king of Spain died on November 1, 1700, bequeathing to Philip of Anjou, grandson of Louis XIV, the entire Spanish inheritance. In the event of Philip's declining the throne, Archduke Charles, second son of Leopold I, was nominated as next in line. On November 24, 1700, Louis XIV proclaimed Philip V king of Spain; within two years all western Europe was at war to challenge the succession of the Bourbons.

The background for these events was complex. In 1685 Louis had fully assumed that the Bourbons would inherit the Spanish throne, while in the years between 1688 and 1697 Leopold had had every reason to expect that a member of his family would become king of Spain. But after the Treaty of Ryswick it was clear that a question as important as the disputed succession to the Spanish throne could be solved only with the approval of all Europe. Not only France and Austria with their dynastic rights, but also the sea powers with their commercial, strategic, and political interests claimed a voice in the decision regarding the Spanish inheritance. England and the United Netherlands held the balance of power between French and Austrian pretensions. Neither would accept a solution that involved French domination of the Spanish Netherlands; neither wished to see the lax Spanish commercial and colonial system supplanted by more effective administration. Nor were they willing to stand by while French commerce usurped the place won by their own merchants in the Spanish markets. As soon as the Treaty of Ryswick had been signed, William III therefore began to negotiate with the rival claimants in the effort to find a mutually satisfactory solution.

Leopold, believing that right was on his side and that the German wife of Charles II would be able to arrange for a Hapsburg succession, showed himself singularly unwilling to co-operate, but Louis, somewhat shaken by the outcome of the recent war and anxious to avoid another until his kingdom had recovered, willingly joined the stadholder-king in seeking a compromise solution. There were two possible formulas: the Spanish Empire might be divided among the rival heirs, or it could be awarded to one of them on the understanding that it should never be united with the crown of either France or the Danubian Monarchy. The three possible heirs were a Bourbon prince, a Hapsburg prince, and the young Wittelsbach prince of Bavaria.

Of the three heirs Joseph Ferdinand of Bavaria was least objectionable to all parties. His house did not threaten to seize the hegemony of Europe, and his father, a hero of the Turkish wars, was admired by the Spaniards. The mere fact that his mother had many times renounced her rights to the Spanish throne impressed only Leopold; most European statesmen held easy views about renunciation. Thus in October, 1698, England, the United Netherlands, and France had signed a treaty agreeing that on the death of Charles II, Prince Joseph Ferdinand should inherit Spain, the Spanish Netherlands, and the Spanish colonies. As compensation, Milan was to be awarded to Austria and Naples and Sicily to France. This first partition treaty was signed while Leopold was still involved in the Turkish war. One month later (November, 1698) Charles II made a testament leaving the entire Spanish inheritance to Prince Joseph Ferdinand, since the Spaniards were altogether averse to any partition.

In February, 1699, to the consternation of all, Joseph Ferdinand died. Thereby the choice was narrowed to the French and the Austrian claimants. William resumed negotiations. Leopold intransigently insisted that his son was the sole rightful heir, while Louis, dreading a war, proved reasonable beyond all expectations. A second partition treaty, between France, England, and the Netherlands, awarded Spain, the Spanish Netherlands, and the colonies to Archduke Charles of Austria, while France was to receive Naples, Sicily, and Milan on the understanding that the latter was to be given to the duke of Lorraine in exchange for his province, which was already almost wholly in French hands.[7] With

---

[7] H. Reynald, *Succession d'Espagne, Louis XIV et Guillaume III, histoire des deux traités de partage et du testament de Charles II*, 2 vols. (Paris, 1883).

amazing obstinacy, Leopold refused to accept this generous settlement. "He preferred," writes Trevelyan, "to fight for the whole without a chance of success." [8]

In Madrid rumors of the second partition treaty were received with angry consternation. The Spanish grandees, whose arrogant pride outran the realities of their situation, apparently cared little who became king so long as the inheritance was not divided. They knew that militarily their country was at the mercy of neighboring France and that Austria, lacking sea power, could not hope to validate her claims. Headed by Cardinal Porto Carrero and armed with a letter from Pope Innocent XII, the grandees pushed aside the dying king's wife and played upon his superstitions and fears until he agreed to sign a will giving the whole inheritance to the grandson of his lifelong French enemy. The pride of the Spanish nobility and the weakness of Charles II rather than the flattery of Louis XIV or the machinations of his ambassador won Philip V the Spanish throne.[9]

Why did Louis discard the second partition treaty and accept the throne for his grandson? A host of arguments have been advanced, some legal, some political, some psychological. The bare facts of the case, however, reveal that Louis had no real choice unless he were willing to allow a Spanish mission to proceed to Vienna to offer the throne to Archduke Charles. Leopold had not signed the partition treaty and the Spaniards had not recognized it. For Louis, implementation of the treaty would have meant war with Spain and Austria, with little likelihood of aid from the sea powers. To accept the testament of Charles II meant war with Leopold, but with Spain as an ally and, as Louis's ambassadors assured him, with the sea powers probably as neutrals. Charles II had deprived the French king of his freedom of action; Louis could not allow his enemy to acquire the throne that had been willed to his grandson.

As Louis had foreseen, Leopold prepared for war, while the sea powers were willing to negotiate for the recognition of Philip V. The English

[8] G. M. Trevelyan, *England under Queen Anne*, I (London, 1930), 129.

[9] Macaulay's description of the intimidation of Charles II is a classic. *History of England*, V (Am. ed., 1901), 445–49. Prince Adalbert von Bayern's, *Das Ende der Habsburger in Spanien*, II (Munich, 1929), 156–269 is more complete and merits careful study. Another scion of the Bourbons, Prince Sixte de Bourbon, argues that "no one in 1700 sought to derive the rights of Philip V from an act of royal power of Charles II," for Philip was the legitimate heir. He quotes Harley, member of the Parlement of Paris, "God . . . has reflected the spirit of His wisdom and His justice in the heart of the late king" when he recognized Philip as his successor. Sixte de Bourbon, *Le traité d'Utrecht et les lois fondamentales du royaume* (Paris, 1914), 19–36, 31–32. This doctoral dissertation is an interesting example of a legalistic argument divorced from political realities.

Tories and the Dutch oligarchy had had enough of war; they both agreed to recognize the new Spanish king providing their commerce were not molested and the crowns of France and Spain not united. In December, 1700, however, Tollard warned Louis from London: "Your Majesty cannot take too great pains to exhort the Spaniards not to make any changes in their commercial relations with England and Holland nor to behave too circumspectly with regard to the security of the Lowlands." [10]

The sea powers actually recognized Philip V as king of Spain before success turned Louis's head and committed him to policies that provoked a new coalition against France. Apparently Louis had forgotten the lesson of the previous war and again thought of himself as the Sun King, the arbiter of Europe. Arrogantly he sent his troops (February, 1701) into the Spanish Netherlands and disarmed the Dutch soldiers who garrisoned the barrier fortresses. [11] This move not only deprived the Dutch of their defenses, but put French forces in control of fortresses and harbors from which both England and the United Netherlands could be attacked. Louis hastened to announce that the measure was taken only to "protect" the Spanish provinces, and that his soldiers would retire as soon as Spain was able to perform that task herself, a point in time sufficiently remote to justify the worst suspicions. Actually Louis immediately began negotiations for the annexation of the territory to France. This was the first act that forced the sea powers toward war.

Before long French influence on Spanish commercial policy presented a new and serious threat to England and Holland. Louis could not resist the temptation to press Spain for special privileges to French subjects. French slavers took over the lucrative trade between Africa and South America while English and Dutch merchants were harassed out of business. The trade in cloth, hardware, leather, and staple commodities that the English and Dutch had carried on in Spain, the Spanish Netherlands, and Spanish Italy was transferred to the French by administrative regulations. Faced with probable loss of their pre-eminent position in international trade, the merchants of the maritime states petitioned their governments for aid and loudly proclaimed their grievances in the effort to arouse popular support. Without doubt, the new Spanish commercial policies convinced an important segment of opinion in both England and the United Netherlands that peace with France was impossible. [12]

[10] H. Reynald, *op. cit.*, II, 339–340.

[11] The Dutch troops were unable to oppose the French invasion since their commander, Maximilian of Bavaria, was party to a plot to surrender the fortifications to France.

[12] J. O. McLachlan, *Trade and Peace with Old Spain, 1667–1750* (Cambridge, Eng., 1940), 30–45.

In June, 1701, Louis added yet another threat by arranging a treaty of alliance between Spain, Portugal, and France. Seeing French power in the ascendant, the Portuguese had no apparent alternative to joining the alliance, though King Peter II feared becoming a French vassal. The treaty had far-reaching implications. In the preceding war the wintering of the Anglo-Dutch fleet near the Strait of Gibraltar had given the Allies control of the Mediterranean. By this new treaty all Iberian ports were closed, and France could easily dominate the Strait and the whole western Mediterranean. By July, 1701, William III had ample support both in the United Netherlands and in England for a war policy. He therefore proceeded to negotiate with Emperor Leopold to rebuild the Grand Alliance.

William had waited patiently until Louis's folly had stirred England to war. After the peace of Ryswick his relations with Parliament had embittered him and made him cautious. Parliament had disbanded the army, sent away William's "Blue Guards" as foreigners, attacked the integrity of his government and the prerogatives of his crown. Had William been of another stamp, he might well have followed in his uncle's footsteps and accepted the thinly veiled subsidy that Louis XIV offered him, for there seemed little chance that he could make the economy-minded, fox-hunting English squires understand the dangers that threatened. In Arbuthnot's fable John Bull (England), tailor to the Spanish king, and Nicholas Frog (Holland), his majesty's runaway servant, were slow to take up the cudgels against Lewis Baboon (France), with whom they had conspired, inkhorns and measuring poles in hand, to partition the king's lands. The injured characters in the *History of John Bull* became aroused only when they finally realized that Lewis Baboon intended to make the whole of the Spanish inheritance his own.

From the beginning Emperor Leopold had refused to accept the will of Charles II, but the immense expenditures of the last war had left the Hapsburg treasury ill prepared to sustain another life-and-death struggle. Furthermore, despite the prestige won by victory over the Turks, the Hapsburg government was far from popular in Hungary, where there was danger of a new revolt once the imperial troops were engaged elsewhere. In Germany, too, although the emperor's position was much stronger than it had been fifteen years before, there was dissatisfaction over the award of the electoral dignity to Hanover and over the "Catholic provisions" of the Treaty of Ryswick. Furthermore, the invasion of Poland by Charles XII and the subsequent involvement of the Saxon army not only deprived Leopold of an ally, but created a real danger of a diversion in the northeast. Nonetheless, Leopold prepared for war. Prince Eugene organized an army for the invasion of Italy; Brandenburg-Prussia's aid was secured by the recognition of Frederick III as Frederick I, king in Prussia; [13] the agreements with the petty German states were tightened; and the imperial ambassador joined William III in his efforts to rebuild the Grand Alliance.

On September 7, 1701, England, the Netherlands, and Austria concluded an alliance. The terms were not altogether to Leopold's liking, for the maritime powers refused to assume responsibility for driving Philip V from the Spanish throne, but Naples, Sicily, Milan and the Spanish Netherlands were awarded to Austria, and the crowns of Spain and France were to remain forever separate. The maritime powers reserved the right to conquer their enemies' colonies, and the Dutch were promised vague but extensive military and commercial advantages in the Spanish Netherlands. This treaty, the third of the partition treaties, was to be implemented many years later at Utrecht, but not until more ambitious policies had led to attempts to put Archduke Charles upon the Spanish throne at enormous cost in blood and treasure.[14]

When it became evident that war was inevitable, both sides engaged in a scramble for the aid of the lesser states. Most of the German states were brought into the coalition by fear of the French, by the gold of the Dutch and the English, and by the skillful diplomacy of the emperor. Only the two Wittelsbach princes, the electors of Cologne and Bavaria, joined Louis. The bishop of Cologne led the way; his brother held back until the military situation favored intervention. Maximilian, hero of the Turkish wars, had hoped in turn for the throne of Spain and for sovereign ownership of the Spanish Netherlands; he now began angling for the imperial crown. In Italy the principal figures, the Pope and the duke of Savoy, gravitated from one side to the other, the one as a neutral, the other as a belligerent, in response to the fortunes of war. The duke of Savoy broke his alliance with Louis only after allied victories indicated a probable French defeat. In the east, the Turks were deterred from intervention by Anglo-Dutch influence in Constantinople and by memories of

---

[13] Cf. Chapter Six.

[14] Louis's recognition, upon the death of James II, of James Edward as James III of England had nothing to do with this alliance. He did not definitely know of its existence at the time he so defiantly legislated for the island kingdom, and the alliance was made before England received news of his act. Recognition of the Pretender as king did, however, make the English more wholeheartedly favorable to the war.

Eugene's destruction of their army. The Venetians, in turn, remained neutral so long as the Turks were willing to stay at peace.

III. THE CAMPAIGNS IN THE WEST, 1701–1706

The general adoption of the flintlock musket and ring bayonet, the abandonment of the pike and the cuirass, and the increase in the fire power and mobility of artillery had modified but not changed the accepted pattern of warfare. Wedded to the idea that sieges were safe and sure, the bureaucratically minded rulers still distrusted adventurous generals. Nonetheless, a new kind of warfare was gradually developing. Charles XII's impetuosity, Eugene's calculated daring, and Marlborough's cold-blooded willingness to accept casualties signaled a new type of command while improved weapons and better discipline provided a new type of army. The successors of Turenne and Charles of Lorraine, unwilling to be tied to fortress warfare, prepared the way for the great Frederick of the mid-century.

Even before the Grand Alliance was concluded, Prince Eugene had given Europe an intimation of things to come. Emperor Leopold had declared war, but before his armies could move, Marshal Catinat, the French commander, occupied Milan with a large army, and proceeded to close the main passes into Austria so effectively that the French party at Rome assured the Pope that the imperials would have to turn into birds to get into Italy.[15] Eugene, however, crossed the Alps by "impassable" passes, with artillery and baggage, and debouched into northern Italy behind the French. The mere fact that he was outnumbered three to one did not daunt him, for Catinat's forces numbered ninety thousand only when united. Eugene forced his opponent to defend a half-dozen places simultaneously, and proceeded to defeat him in detail. Louis replaced Catinat with Villeroi, instructing him to annihilate the "Little Abbé."[16] The new commander, confident of his overwhelming force, attacked Eugene at Chiari on a field of the latter's choosing. The imperials held their fire until the French were within a few paces of their earthworks; their first salvo, when it came, blasted Villeroi's hopes for a speedy conclusion

[15] O. Klopp, *Der Fall des Hauses Stuart und die Succession des Hauses Hannover in Grossbritannien und Irland* (Vienna, 1875–1888), IX, 252.

[16] Louis had refused to consider Eugene for an army command, and assumed that he would enter the church. Eugene never forgave the French king. After his victory over the Turks in 1699, Louis offered Eugene a Marshal's baton, which the latter refused disdainfully.

of the campaign. He, rather than Eugene, retired from the field. The inferior imperial army then proceeded to raid French supply lines, harass the outposts, and destroy reconnaissance parties. Villeroi's cries of rage, pain, and indignation were relayed to Versailles. When the French settled down to winter quarters in Cremona, leaving Mantua and the supply routes to central Italy and Germany in imperial hands, Eugene planned a daring raid, forced his way into Cremona itself and captured the French marshal.[17] A contemporary epigram gave the French what consolation was possible:

> *Français rendez grâce à Bellone*
> *Votre bonheur est sans égal*
> *Vous avez conservé Crémone*
> *Et perdu votre Général.*

But neither the genius of Eugene nor the valor of his soldiers could alter the fact that the total French position was much stronger than it had been at the end of the previous war. Only at sea could the coalition muster more powerful forces, and even this advantage was more or less counterbalanced by the French possession of bases in the Mediterranean and in the two Americas. On land the French and Spaniards not only controlled all the disputed territories, but were strongly posted on the principal avenues of attack. The occupation of the Spanish Netherlands and the bishoprics of Liège and Cologne gave the French a practically unbroken line of fortifications from the Channel to the lower Rhine and up that stream to Switzerland. Vauban strengthened this position by building earthworks and water barriers covering the area from the Channel above Ostend to the Meuse below Namur. Behind this so-called Line of Brabant were two other lines of fortresses, the erstwhile Dutch Barrier and the forts on the French frontier. Thus, the north was practically impregnable. Only the isolated but powerful Dutch fortress of Maestricht broke the chain in the Meuse valley. The great fortresses on the Rhine from Rheinberg and Kaiserworth to Strassburg blocked any invasion by way of the Meuse or Moselle valleys and the Vosges Gap. Breisach defended the Belfort Gap on the upper Rhine. Similarly Spain and Savoy protected the south and the east. With an army of 400,000 men to garrison her fortresses and put in the field, France seemed immune from in-

[17] A. Arneth, *Prinz Eugen von Savoyen* (Vienna, 1858), I, 138–162.

vasion; her alliance with the Bavarian elector was, in fact, soon to give her access to the very heart of Germany.

While Louis had appreciably strengthened his position in the years between Ryswick and the outbreak of the new war, his enemies had not only lost many of their gains from the late treaty, but were also threatened with the dissolution of their alliance by the death of William III (March, 1702). William had not been a brilliant soldier, but his experience with coalition warfare and his position as king and stadholder had made him a key figure. If the alliance did not dissolve, it was chiefly because Leopold was committed to war, because Dutch politicians of all parties closed ranks in the face of the foe, and because the new government in England announced its intention to continue the late king's policy. In place of William III two great statesmen-soldiers, Eugene of Savoy and the duke of Marlborough, assumed direction of the war against France.

English historians often call the War of the Spanish Succession "Marlborough's War against France," because Turenne's handsome pupil was indeed the guiding genius of the conflict. Both as soldier and statesman Marlborough played the part of King William better than that ruler himself had played it. He was admirably placed to control English policy. He and his wife had been friends of Queen Anne in her adversity. On Anne's accession, Sarah Churchill became her confidante and John [18] her favorite. The new government was Marlborough's creation. His friend and relative by marriage, Godolphin, controlled finances and occupied a position similar to that of a modern prime minister; his brother was in the admiralty; and at one time or another his two sons-in-law occupied positions of trust. The Marlboroughs, with the exception of Sarah, leaned toward the Tories, but the Marlborough-Godolphin governments worked with members of both parties. Their principal objective was the defeat of France, and Marlborough would co-operate with anyone willing to aid in attaining that goal.

Since Marlborough had been associated with William in framing the Grand Alliance, it was easy for him to assume leadership of the Anglo-Dutch forces. Dutch politicians would not accept Queen Anne's husband, Prince George, as commander in chief, but, in spite of his limited fame as a soldier, they readily accepted Marlborough as captain general. As commander of the Anglo-Dutch armies and leader of the English government, Marlborough directed the course of the war until his enemies at

[18] John Churchill, Duke of Marlborough.

home overthrew him, and by that time his victories in war and diplomacy had given England a commanding position in Europe.[19]

The first two years of the war passed without decisive action on land or sea. The conflict seemed to be merely a renewal of the desultory war of the preceding decade. The north German princes besieged and took Kaiserworth on the east bank of the Rhine, while Marshal Boufflers, unable to cross the river, attempted to raise the siege by invading Cleves and threatening to overrun the Dutch Republic from the rear. As soon as Marlborough had assembled an army, he assured the Dutch that he would deliver them from their "troublesome neighbor." Over the protests of his timorous confederates, the captain general invaded Spanish Brabant and threatened Boufflers' communications. The French retreat was precipitous and disorderly, but when Boufflers' columns passed in front of the Anglo-Dutch army, the Dutch field deputies vetoed Marlborough's plans to destroy them in open battle. A few days later, when they saw with their own eyes the disorganized retreat of the French, they admitted their error, but even then would not approve a battle in the open field. They preferred to hail Marlborough as the winner of "bloodless victories."

This cautious attitude resulted in the prolongation of the war for ten year. Timid politicians and conservative generals did not understand that the purpose of war was to destroy the enemy's will and ability to resist. Their satisfaction at reducing a fortress or winning a few square miles of territory as cheaply as possible was a gauge of their psychology. Such men could only fight on until one side or the other collapsed economically. Prince Eugene and Marlborough envisaged a different type of warfare; when finally they freed themselves from the politicians, they demonstrated dramatically how war should be waged, but for years their violence made timid·men even more timid and more determined to hold such dangerous soldiers in check.

While Marlborough overran the corner of the lower Rhine (1702) and Eugene held off Vendôme in Italy, the spread of the war to southern Germany and Hungary greatly increased Louis's advantage. Armed with money and promises from France, a Hungarian revolt under Prince Rákóczy spread quickly throughout the kingdom. At the same time Prince Maximilian of Bavaria joined the French. The emperor's position became perilous early in 1703 when Marshal Villars led a strong force

---

[19] Like all men, Marlborough had his faults, but the two recent monumental studies of his era, G. M. Trevelyan, *op. cit.*, and Winston Churchill, *Marlborough, His Life and Times*, 6 vols. (New York, 1933–1938), leave little question of the importance of his career or of the skill with which he threaded his way through the problems of war and diplomacy.

through the Black Forest to link up with the Bavarians. Germany was thereby cut in two, and had Maximilian followed Villars' advice, the Hungarian rebel and the Bavarian prince might well have shaken hands in Vienna and forced Leopold out of the war.

Maximilian, with the French king's assurance that he should retain all the territories he could conquer, ignored Villars' plan for a direct assault upon Vienna and instead invaded the Tyrol. His aim was to make contact with Vendôme in Italy, and then with Vendôme and Villars to attack the Austrian capital. In the meantime Villars was left to guard the rear of the Bavarian army—an assignment that made a naturally irascible general even more difficult to deal with. In the Tyrol the Bavarians encountered a hornet's nest. Peasants and hunters took to the rocks with their long guns and showed Maximilian what marksmanship was necessary to kill the chamois. By this upsurge of loyalty to the Hapsburgs, the Tyrolese made impossible the projected contact between Bavaria and Milan. The Bavarians withdrew too late to attack Vienna before winter set in, and Villars proceeded to make himself so disagreeable that Louis was obliged to replace him with Marsin, a soldier with a softer tongue but fewer talents.

While the French were unable to make capital out of the Hungarian revolution and Bavaria's adherence to their cause, the naval war in 1702 and 1703 brought the allies important assistance, but at the same time saddled them with a policy that proved unrealizable. In an effort to secure an advanced base in the Mediterranean Admiral Rooke made an unsuccessful attempt to take Cadiz. But on its way home the Anglo-Dutch navy entered Vigo Bay and destroyed the Spanish treasure fleet in the inner harbor. Most of the gold had already been removed, and many of the goods that went down belonged to Dutch merchants; nonetheless, it was a daring exhibition of sea power. The king of Portugal, uneasy in his alliance with the French, took this naval action to mean that he might safely join Louis's enemies and escape from the invidious position in which his French alliance had placed him.[20]

It was an allied triumph to detach Portugal from her French alliance. With Lisbon as an advanced base, the allied fleet could dominate the Strait of Gibraltar and cripple French action in the Mediterranean. William had shown how decisive naval power could be when the fleet did not have to winter in the Channel ports.[21] But the Methuen Treaty

[20] J. H. Owen, *War at Sea under Queen Anne* (Cambridge, Eng., 1938), 71 ff.

[21] Cf. Sir J. S. Corbett, *England in the Mediterranean, 1603–1713*, II (London and New York, 1904), 187 ff.

(1703) did more than provide a naval base. King Peter II of Portugal insisted that the allies place Archduke Charles on the Spanish throne so that Spain would be in friendly hands when the war ended. This involved an important change in the war aims of the alliance. Neither England nor the United Netherlands would agree to such an ambitious policy when Emperor Leopold had proposed it two years before, but it was the price of Portuguese adherence to the coalition.[22]

The arrival of the allied fleet in the Mediterranean paid immediate dividends. The duke of Savoy found it possible to desert his French alliance and the Huguenot "Camisards" [23] took hope that the allies might aid them in their revolt. The Huguenot rebels were too few in number and too poorly armed to exert much influence on the war, but their insurrection, even though unsupported by English aid, did occupy Villars throughout 1704 when his talents might have been used in Bavaria. A few hundred of their number, including their best leader, escaped to join the English army in Spain. Savoy's adherence to the allies was a more serious loss to Louis. The French succeeded in disarming part of the Savoyard army before it could join the Austrians, but Duke Victor Amadeus II proved to be as vigorous a soldier as he was a crafty politician. By keeping the French out of Turin, he retained the key position from which, later in the war, Eugene was to expel Louis's armies from Italy.

However, neither the adherence of Savoy and Portugal to the allied cause nor the Camisard revolt in Cévennes saved Vienna from the double offensive of the Hungarian rebels and the Franco-Bavarian armies in 1704. At the critical moment when the specter of a Bourbon universal monarchy arose again, Marlborough marched his army into Bavaria, joined forces with Louis of Baden and Eugene, and won a decisive military victory at Blenheim that reduced the French to the defensive. The march of the redcoats into southern Germany and the battle of Blenheim, as the English earned the right to call it, are among the most dramatic episodes in the annals of warfare.[24]

---

[22] This policy, responsible for the disastrous Spanish campaign and the prolongation of the war, was not dropped until the Tories gained the upper hand in English politics. The Methuen treaties also had other implications: from them dates the profitable Anglo-Portuguese trade in cloth, fish, and wine, and perhaps the high incidence of gout among England's upper classes.

[23] The "Camisard" revolt is one of the tragic stories of the war. Made desperate by French religious intolerance, the Huguenots in Cevennes appealed to arms, only to be crushed by military force; cf. Issarte, *Des causes de l'insurrection des Cévennes* (Montbéliard, 1899).

[24] Many myths have grown up about the Blenheim campaign. See Trevelyan, *op. cit.*, *Blenheim,* I (1930) and Churchill, *op. cit.*, Vol. II (English ed.). The two hundred pages

The Blenheim campaign was conceived and initiated in utmost secrecy.[25] Marlborough's own officers knew nothing of their destination until the columns turned eastward from the Rhine. The advance up the river pinned down every French army from the Channel to Bavaria, for if the move proved a feint, and the French armies in the north followed it, the redcoats might be shipped down the Rhine before the French could march back to meet them. There was nothing to do but wait to see whether the English meant to move up the Moselle, into Alsace, or into the Neckar valley. By the time Marlborough's destination became apparent, it was too late to move against him in force. Above Ulm, Marlborough met Louis of Baden and Eugene; the latter moved back to Stollhofen to guard the Rhine, while Marlborough and Louis advanced on Bavaria. Since their enemy held all the fortified places and their own army was short of siege guns, it was imperative to establish a base on the Danube to which they could draw supplies from central Germany. Donauwörth, on the road to Nördlingen, suited the requirements, but before the allied army could reach it, D'Arco, a Bavarian general, seized the town and began to fortify the hill, Schellenberg, that dominated the crossing.

Marlborough, recognizing that the hill must be taken before D'Arco could complete its fortification, mounted a furious assault on the center of the Bavarian lines. The attack was repulsed, but it drew most of the defenders to the bloody angle so that Louis of Baden found almost no opposition when his forces attacked on the right and turned the Bavarian flank. The destruction of the defending forces was almost complete (of D'Arco's fourteen thousand men scarce five thousand rejoined the main army), but the Anglo-Imperial losses were also heavy—six thousand casualties, of whom fifteen hundred were dead. This was a bill larger than men were accustomed to pay; vicious tactics won victories, but at the price of precious blood.

At Donauwörth the allied armies stood between Maximilian's army

---

on this campaign in Churchill's book are perhaps the best of an unusually well-written work; they are exciting, dramatic, and reasonably accurate. The *Feldzüge des Prinzen Eugen von Savoyen,* edited by the Royal and Imperial War Archives in Vienna, Vol. V, 460 ff.; Hans Delbrück's *Geschichte der Kriegskunst* (Berlin, 1900–1920), IV, 364 ff.; and O. Klopp, *Der Fall des Hauses Stuart und die Succession des Hauses Hannover in Grossbritannien und Irland.* Vol. XI should also be consulted.

[25] Actually Marlborough was accused at the time of stealing the English army. So little was understood about the basic problems of the war that, when the army disappeared into Germany, many Dutch and English politicians believed their captain general had gone off to fight for the emperor instead of staying at home and guarding their towns.

and Bavaria, but the elector would not give battle even when the allied cavalry ravaged his country, because he knew that Louis would send him aid. Late in July, Marshal Tollard with an army slipped by Eugene and joined the forces of the elector and Marsin. Eugene, with a third the number of men, followed him and joined Marlborough and Louis of Baden. The two armies were now approximately equal, but the Franco-Bavarians held all the fortresses. Tollard knew that his enemies had either to win a victory or retire, so he tried to avoid a battle. For the same reason Eugene and Marlborough, who had become fast friends, were determined to fight. Louis of Baden, cooler about a battle, settled down to besiege Ingolstadt, while the rest of the allied army moved up the river. The Franco-Bavarians barred the way at Höchstädt, where they established a camp which they considered unassailable. Little did Tollard measure the genius and the daring of the men who opposed him.

The battle of Höchstädt-Blenheim was a large-scale repetition of Schellenberg. This time Eugene made the holding attack on the right while Marlborough's forces struck on the left and annihilated Tollard's army. The elector and Marsin were able to break off the battle in reasonably good order, but Tollard was taken, the flower of the French cavalry destroyed, and many famous regiments either captured or so shattered that they had to be completely reformed. Blenheim was the first of a series of great reverses that ended the military superiority of France.

The results were immediate and far-reaching. The French withdrew over the Rhine, leaving Bavaria in the hands of the allies. Vienna was saved, Germany cleared of French troops, and France rocked back on the defensive. The allies took new heart; even the English squires admitted that at last they had value received for the tax of four shillings on the pound.[26]

While the redcoats invaded Bavaria, the Anglo-Dutch navy, supported by marines and Hanoverian troops, captured Gibraltar. French and Spanish pride could not accept the loss without attempting to drive out the invaders. A French task force, approximately equal to the allied fleet, offered battle off Málaga, the only significant general naval engagement of the war. The battle was a slugging match; both fleets lined up and let loose their broadsides, so that ability to give and take punishment rather than skill of maneuver became the critical factor in the fight. The Anglo-Dutch casualties were over twenty-seven hundred; the French admitted

---

[26] Later when Marlborough's political star was on the wane, they called him the Butcher of Blenheim, whose victory was won by Eugene's military genius.

only fifteen hundred, but the figure was probably an understatement, for the French admiral refused to renew the engagement and withdrew. Admiral Rooke recognized the valor of his enemy and probably thanked God that the French were unaware that his ships had only eight to ten rounds of shot left for each gun. In the fall and winter of 1704–1705 the Franco-Spanish forces attacked Gibraltar by land, but the nature of the terrain, the bravery of its defenders, and English control of the sea frustrated the attempt.[27]

The campaigns of the next year (1705), like those of the first two years of the war, were relatively fruitless. The stalemate war of maneuver and siege could not be broken by a field battle. The great battles of 1704 seem to have unnerved the allies as much as the French. At the end of the campaign of 1705, Marlborough had finally broken through the Lines of Brabant by a trick maneuver, and was preparing to give battle near Waterloo, but the Dutch generals and field deputies vetoed the plan and the only significant allied gain was the destruction of a section of Vauban's fortified line—the section that covered Ramillies. An invasion of Spain from Portugal and a landing in Catalonia opened another theater of war and produced the most colorful and controversial figure of the war, Lord Peterborough, whose competence and responsibility have been matters of dispute ever since. But the allied armies, unable to win a decision, did little more than unite most of Spain behind Philip V.[28]

The year 1706 brought allied victories in the Netherlands and in Italy and thereby roused hopes for a speedy end of the war. After Marlborough's comparative inactivity in 1705, the French lost some of their fear of him, and even began to scorn his talents. Sound strategy would probably have required that the French remain on the defensive in the north and make an effort to clear their enemies from Italy and Spain but Louis, sharing the optimism that beclouded the court, decided for offensives in all theaters in the hope of concluding the war. He gave Villeroi a fine army and encouraged him to attack Marlborough while Villars was to invade Germany, Vendôme to clear north Italy, and Berwick to win Spain.

French optimism was soon shattered. The campaign had hardly begun when Villeroi and Marlborough fought a great battle at Ramillies (May 12, 1706) that decided the fate of the whole Spanish Netherlands.

[27] J. H. Owen, op. cit., 90 ff.
[28] A. Parnell's War of the Succession in Spain (London, 1905) is too hard on Peterborough; Trevelyan's summary is more just.

As at Blenheim, the French had the choice of position. Ramillies was a few miles inside the destroyed section of the Lines of Brabant, and the fact that Vauban's engineers had ignored it in planning their fortification system suggests that it was not the best position in the neighborhood. The extreme right of the French line ran perpendicular to a small marshy stream, while their left faced another stream almost impassable for horsemen. Between the stream on the right and the village of Ramillies lay an open field admirably suited to cavalry action. The defense of this exposed position was entrusted to the famous *Maison du roi,* the cream of the French cavalry. Villeroi disposed the rest of his horsemen in the conventional manner, on the other flank. Marlborough, fully conversant with the terrain, made his dispositions in the same way: half his cavalry on either flank, the massed infantry and artillery in the center.

At the opening of the battle, Marlborough detached a strong force, supported by two cannon, to drive the French out of two small settlements along the stream, at the limits of the French right. The success of these troops partially unhinged the French line and paved the way to catastrophe. As a feint, Marlborough also attacked across the marshy ground on the left, but at a critical moment the entire allied cavalry was massed between Ramillies and the stream on the French right. This transfer of cavalry from one side to the other gave Marlborough better than a two to one advantage over the *Maison du roi.* The French commander had dismounted some dragoons and sent De la Colonie's Bavarian cavalry to retake the little villages on the right. These troops were literally swept off the field into the marsh, leaving the *Maison du roi* to meet the full weight of the allied attack. The Frenchmen fought like fiends, but each time they repulsed their assailants Marlborough's horsemen would retire behind advancing infantry which poured volleys into the French counterattack. At last the line was penetrated and the entire allied cavalry formed on a line perpendicular to the French. It was probably the most spectacular cavalry action in all military history. The French infantry was in a hopeless situation: it could not meet the allied attack on its front while cavalry charged its flank. The whole French army was soon in full flight; even the fifty squadrons of horsemen who faced the marshy creek on the left of the line, and had not struck a blow, were seized with panic and fled the field.[29]

[29] One officer had a ringside seat for the whole battle. De la Colonie, whose Bavarians and dragoons were pushed off the field, watched the conflict from high ground beyond the marsh: his description, that of a competent, though partisan, eyewitness, is a classic commentary on the art of war in this period. De la Colonie, *The Chronicles of an Old Campaigner* (trans. by W. C. Hosley, 1904), 309 ff.

The results of Ramillies were quickly apparent. Villeroi lost his artillery, his tents, his baggage, over thirteen thousand men, and, worst of all, the morale of his army. The unnerved fugitives threw away their weapons, and were generally so shaken that they were useless for battle for a long time to come. The entire Spanish Netherlands quickly fell into Marlborough's hands; some of the cities opened their gates without further ado; others submitted after sieges which no French field army could hope to relieve. Villars' plans for an invasion of Germany were canceled, and Vendôme was recalled from Italy to attempt to reform an army for the defense of France. England and her allies were jubilant, and Marlborough's reputation rose to new heights. Eugene was in Italy when Ramillies was fought, so the English commander could show that he knew how to win victories without the Savoyard's assistance.

In Italy the French armies were almost three times as numerous as those of Eugene and the duke of Savoy. The French, under La Feuillade, besieged Turin, but the warlike duke left the defense of his capital to the imperial general, Count Daun, while he, with a small but mobile force, harassed the besiegers' lines. Almost two hundred miles away Eugene faced Vendôme on the Adige River with an army half the size of the French, but determined to break through and relieve Turin. After Ramillies, when Vendôme was replaced by Marsin and the Duke d'Orleans, Eugene crossed the Adige and the Po (July 17), and pushed through Ferrara toward Turin. Marsin followed him to the north, but was forced to leave a part of his army behind because imperial reinforcements had crossed the Alps and moved upon his rear. By the time Eugene joined the duke of Savoy, he was convinced that the French were already half beaten. At one point in the outer line of circumvallation at Turin the besiegers had not completed their fortification, since the danger of relief had seemed remote. Eugene struck at this gap with all his forces (August 7). A sortie from the city completed the disorganization of the French, and Eugene made good his boast that Turin would be his headquarters that evening.

Marshal Marsin, mortally wounded, was captured, and the young Duke d'Orleans ordered a retreat toward France. This move sealed the fate of Italy, for even though French garrisons controlled all the important fortresses save Turin, these places could not be held without a field army. Eugene's victory at Turin did for Italy what Marlborough's battle at Ramillies had done for the Netherlands.

IV. CHARLES XII: POLAND, SAXONY, RUSSIA

At this stage of the war, when operations in Italy and the Netherlands pointed to a collapse of French resistance and opened prospects for peace, the war in Poland, which had thus far been little more than a smoldering fire, turned into a conflagration that threatened to destroy all the advantages gained by the allies. Charles XII with his ragged but effective army appeared in the heart of Germany. Momentarily, the balance of power in Europe was in his hands.

The arrival of the Swedish army in Germany was the high point of Charles XII's career. After crossing the Dvina (1701) the young king had marched from one end of Poland to the other. Victories crowned his arms wherever he met the enemy, but somehow he was never quite able to destroy the Saxon forces. His devastation of Poland made men wonder whether the Swedes were a reincarnation of the Huns or merely a band of knights-errant roaming the land. After campaigning in Poland for five years, Charles finally struck boldly across neutral Silesia to attack the center of Augustus' military and economic power, Electoral Saxony. Augustus was soon forced to accept Swedish terms.

Actually the Polish king had been willing to negotiate from the very moment when Charles defeated the Russians at Narva. He had sent diplomats with arguments for Charles and gold for his advisers, and had dispatched his most talented and beautiful mistress, Aurora von Königsmark, the mother of two of his 365 children, to attempt other methods of persuasion. Aurora's mission was fruitless, but it captured the imagination of posterity: Voltaire made much of her beauty and charm, and of the resistance of the monkish king, while a Swedish poet wrote succinctly:

Nu snart på ottomanen skall
Aurora bringa Karl på fall.

Neither love nor money could deter Charles: Augustus had treacherously and without cause attacked Sweden and must be punished. The retribution decided upon by Charles was Augustus' dethronement in Poland.

To depose a duly anointed Polish king was no easy task, but to find a successor was even more difficult. The Polish magnates had no great love or loyalty for their monarchs. Under the constitution they could and did ignore their commands and even organized armed rebellion against them. But they could not legally dethrone them, for had that been permitted, the organized anarchy of the Royal Republic would have lost the last trace of a system. The kingdom of Poland was a dual monarchy consisting of Poland and Lithuania. The two states had a common king and diet, but separate governments and administrative systems. When Charles occupied Lithuania (1701), he established Swedish control over the province by an alliance with the powerful Sapieha family, but he was unable to convert a single palatine of Poland to his program. The Poles insisted that their kingdom was not involved in the war at all; that Augustus had made war as elector of Saxony, not as king of Poland. They therefore refused to deal with the Swedish king.

By his victories Charles secured the power to call a diet, but he could not force the important Polish nobles to attend. The great magnates regarded the imperious demands of the young Swede as offensive and odious, and only those who hoped to benefit from the invasion responded to his call. Charles' diet dethroned Augustus and elected a successor (1704), but since it was boycotted by most of the important personages in the realm, including the cardinal-primate, its action was of questionable validity. Stanislaus Leszczynski, Charles' candidate for the throne, was a stout, good-natured young man with little force of character and not much real ambition. His Polish peers did not want him as king and he was not the man to fight for power. Elected to the Polish throne by Swedish arms, he occupied it only so long as the Swedish king continued victorious.

The mere presence of a rival did not drive Augustus out of the war. Saxon and Swede prowled the Polish countryside, fighting on occasion, but mostly making more miserable the wretched existence of the Polish population. Both sides had Polish soldiers to assist in this destructive work, but their propensity to disappear when it came to fighting earned them the name "butterfly soldiers" from the Swedish king. On the Saxon side at least one battle was lost through their pride and ignorance. The war dragged on inconclusively until Charles finally turned his army into Germany to force a decision in Dresden itself.

The Swedish invasion of Saxony brought temporary peace. By the treaty of Altranstädt (1707), Augustus renounced his right to the Polish throne and gave up his alliance with Russia. Stanislaus Leszczynski, as party to the treaty, was recognized as legitimate king. Thus the Saxon ruler was, like his Danish ally, forced out of the war by an invasion of his homeland. Russia alone held the field against Sweden.

The Swedish army in Saxony was a terrible threat to the emperor and his allies. If Charles were won to the French cause, his forces, joined with the insurgent Hungarians, might upset all the victories won by Eugene and Marlborough. Altranstädt became a Mecca for European diplomats; even the duke of Marlborough appeared with an autographed letter from Queen Anne and flattery for King Charles. But Charles kept his own counsel. He had come to Saxony to punish Augustus; he remained in Saxony almost a year to be sure that the terms of the treaty were loyally fulfilled and to right certain "wrongs" that had been done to German Protestants.[30] He had no intention of intervening in the war in the west. Neither Marlborough's diplomacy nor the gold he distributed freely to Swedish officials decided the king's policy. Tsar Peter was the last remaining member of the trio that had lightheartedly agreed to partition the Swedish empire; it was now his turn to feel the full force of Charles' vengeance.

While the Swedish armies campaigned in Poland, the Russians had conquered a large part of the Swedish Baltic, leaving a trail of burned villages and towns, raped women, and fresh civilian graves wherever they went. Swedish captives were treated like slaves, forced to labor at the building of the new capital on the Neva, St. Petersburg, and at other menial tasks, quite contrary to the customary treatment of prisoners of war. Reports of these doings reinforced Charles' determination to wreak vengeance and hastened his advance to the east.

Unfortunately for himself and Sweden, Charles had not been following the developments in Russia. He had only contempt for the army he had met at Narva. He either did not know or refused to believe that Peter had created a new Russian army, with more modern equipment than the Swedes possessed, and outwardly, at least, in accord with western standards. The building of St. Petersburg, the construction of a Russian navy on the Baltic, and the new army of 100,000 men were the work of the years spent by Charles in Poland.

Sweden probably lacked the physical resources to exclude Russia from the Baltic area for any great length of time, but Charles' decision to invade Russia and to dictate terms in Moscow hastened the end of Swedish domination and facilitated the establishment of Russian hegemony in northeastern Europe. Like later generals, Charles was to learn that invaders of Russia are apt to be outnumbered, and obliged to combat cold,

---

[30] Emperor Joseph, who complied with his wishes, assured the papal legate that, had Charles demanded it, he probably would have been obliged to become a Protestant himself as well as to grant relief to his Protestant subjects.

space, and time, as well as to face a blind hostility from peasants and landlords, prepared to destroy their all rather than leave it to the enemy.

Indeed, Charles' decision to invade Russia rather than to expel the enemy from the Baltic was rash beyond belief. He was apparently misled by his success in battle even though the odds were two to one, as at Holowczyn (1708), but he should have noticed that on that occasion the Russians withdrew in good order. He also counted on General Lewenhaupt to bring reinforcements and supplies from Sweden and expected the Hetman Mazepa to rally the Ukraine against Peter. However, when Lewenhaupt failed to keep the rendezvous on the Dnieper, Charles pushed on without him. The Russians waylaid the Swedish reinforcements and, though they failed to capture them, forced Lewenhaupt to burn his stores and sink his cannon in a morass, so that finally he joined Charles with only eight thousand of his eleven thousand men. Mazepa proved to be an even greater disappointment to Charles, for Peter foiled his projected treason, and Mazepa appeared in the Swedish camp with fifteen hundred instead of thirty thousand horsemen. Even these setbacks did not deter Charles; obstinately he marched on into Russia to make Peter pay the penalty for his treachery.

The winter cold of 1708–1709 did the Swedish army more harm than did Russian bullets. It was an unusually severe season and the invaders, ill-clothed, ill-fed, and ill-sheltered, suffered from frost and hunger till the army was decimated and demoralized. Only the stubborn courage of its leader and the raiding Cossack horsemen, who cut off stragglers, held it together. Nonetheless, despite its reduced numbers and scanty stores, Peter hesitated to attack this famous army. The Swedes pushed on to Pultava in the spring of 1709, and prepared to besiege the fortress.

This siege precipitated the battle that broke the power of Sweden. Charles was unable to command in person because of a severe foot wound, but his soldiers, knowing that their leader was watching them from a litter, fought with their usual ferocity. It is said that Peter would have retreated had he not suddenly realized that the odds were so greatly in his favor that he could hardly lose. Finally the Swedish resistance collapsed. Charles, with a small party, managed to escape to Turkey, but most of his army surrendered and joined their comrades in the Russian labor camps. Only a few of them ever saw Sweden again. Pultava ended Swedish ascendancy and undid the work of nine years of arduous but successful campaigning. Though Europe's sympathies were with the hero king, whose army had gone down before odds of four to one, and though the western world smiled at the boasts of the naïve barbarian who had defeated him, Pultava secured Russia a permanent place in the European political structure and made possible Russian hegemony in the Baltic.[31]

V. WAR AND DIPLOMACY, 1707–1712

As soon as it became apparent that Charles XII did not propose to interfere in the western war, the effects of the victories at Ramillies and Turin began to make themselves felt. The French retreat left the Spanish Netherlands in allied hands, and the inhabitants welcomed the victors as deliverers. However, as soon as the Dutch moved into the barrier cities, they proceeded to milk them of their wealth. The war had placed a terrible strain upon the Dutch purse, and despite Austrian protests, the Hollanders felt justified in recouping their losses at the expense of their Roman Catholic cousins. In Italy, officials from Vienna moved into Milan and organized the duchy for permanent occupation even though the sea powers regarded it as part of the Spanish inheritance. They also pushed southward to Naples to reward the participants of the abortive revolt of 1701. This procedure brought the new Emperor Joseph I into conflict with the Pope. Less respectful of ecclesiastical authority than his father had been, Joseph treated His Holiness so roughly that the *curia* became definitely pro-French.

Allied discord developed in other areas as well. The emperor refused to listen to Anglo-Dutch suggestions that he compromise with the Hungarian rebels and resented such interference in his domestic affairs as ignorant presumption. At the same time, the close political relationship between England and the Netherlands began to cool as soon as the Dutch learned of the commercial concessions accorded the English by King Charles III of Spain, and discovered England's intention to retain Gibraltar and Port Mahon.

While the allies were beginning to quarrel over the spoils of victory, Louis prepared for a campaign which, he hoped, would force his opponents to accept a compromise peace. With an army outnumbering Marlborough's six to five, Vendôme operated in the Lowlands and kept the terrible "Malbrook" in check. Meanwhile Villars made a raid into central Germany where his soldiers pillaged, burned, exacted ransom, and in general frightened the Germans into a desire for peace. In Spain, Berwick

---

[31] F. Bengtsson, *Karl XIIs Levnad Från Altranstädt till Fredrikshall* (Stockholm, 1936) is the most dramatic as well as one of the more complete accounts of this period of his life.

showed himself a worthy grandson of Marlborough's father by roundly defeating the Anglo-Portuguese forces and driving them back to the coast. At the same time the allied "grand project" for an invasion of France failed despite Eugene's leadership. An imperial army from Italy, supported by the British fleet, reached the outskirts of Toulon only to be forced to embark its wounded and its equipment and itself retreat over the Alps. The year of victory had been followed by a year of frustration.

In the spring of 1708 Vendôme, emboldened by the superior size of his army, the failure of his enemies to act the year before, and the assurance that he would find friends in the barrier cities, moved aggressively into the Spanish Netherlands. The allied forces were divided into three armies: Marlborough's in the Netherlands, Eugene's on the Moselle, and the electoral prince of Hanover's (the future George I of England) on the upper Rhine. Eugene and Marlborough made plans to unite their forces and bring Vendôme to a battle.

Th opportunity came after Vendôme had surprised the allies by taking Bruges and Ghent without striking a blow, the reward of Dutch exploitation of the Spanish Netherlands. In the maneuvers that followed, both armies arrived at the Scheldt River just below Oudenarde. As soon as Cadogan's cavalry had crossed the river, Marlborough opened an attack that might have proved foolhardy had Vendôme thrown his forces into the fray before the rest of the allied army had established itself beyond the river. Unlike Ramillies and Blenheim, the battle of Oudenarde developed from field maneuvers rather than from an attack upon a fortified position. Both armies moved onto the field under hot fire, each attempting to outflank the other with fresh columns.

As the battle took shape, Vendôme failed to bring a large part of his army into action before Marlborough succeeded in getting Overkirk's infantry and cavalry through Oudenarde. These troops outflanked the French from the left while Eugene's forces succeeded in enveloping them on the right. By nightfall the French found themselves inside a horseshoe of fire. Had the allies had modern weapons, Vendôme might have suffered a catastrophe comparable to that inflicted on the Russians by Hindenburg two centuries later.

The French were outgeneraled and outfought. The English redcoats and the Prussian blues cleared the orchards, hedgerows, and cabbage patches with a raking fire that justified Louis's warning to his commanders against becoming engaged in an infantry battle. It was now too late to obey the king's instructions. When darkness, shattered by yellow flashes of gunfire, enveloped the field, Marlborough ordered his men to cease fire, while French Huguenot officers in the allied army, beating French retreats on their drums, rallied hundreds of French soldiers to the allied prison camps. Vendôme, angry and frustrated, yielded to the advice of his officers and ordered a general retreat. He lost twenty thousand men killed, wounded, or captured. The remnants of his army were fit only for fortress duty.

Confident that Oudenarde had opened the road to Paris, Marlborough was eager to advance and impose peace at Versailles, but the preponderant allied opinion deemed an invasion of France too hazardous unless Lille, the most powerful of Vauban's fortresses, were first reduced. Lille was believed to be almost unassailable, but with Eugene in charge of the siege and Marlborough in command of the covering army, the fortress was doomed despite Boufflers' defense and Vendôme's harassing action on the supply lines. The fall of Lille heralded the first serious negotiations for peace. The allies had established themselves on the "sacred soil" of France.

By 1708 the war in the west had become really two wars: one against Louis XIV for the hegemony of Europe, the other against Philip V for the Spanish throne. The allies had won the first and lost the second. Louis was ready to admit defeat and pay a heavy penalty, but his grandson was firmly established on the Spanish throne and in command of a victorious army. But Whig politicians in England and the emperor's advisers hoped to use their victory over France to secure their pretensions in Spain. This hope proved fatal to the chances of peace.

Louis was ready to make great concessions: to recognize the Protestant succession in England; to abandon the Spanish colonies to the allies; to restore to the Dutch their barrier in the Spanish Netherlands, including Lille with Menin and Maubeuge; to surrender Strassburg, Luxemburg, and Kehl along with most of Alsace; and to dismantle the privateers' base at Dunkirk. He was even willing to request his grandson to quit Spain. But there was one allied demand which he would not accept, namely the right to reopen hostilities from the advanced bases to be surrendered by France in case Philip failed to leave Spain within two months. Thus peace became impossible. Philip was no longer his grandfather's pensioner; he was at the head of a Spanish army and enjoyed the full support of most Spaniards. Since Louis could not compel him to leave Spain, the terms offered would not assure peace. There was nothing to do but to renew the war.

The *Tatler* taunted the French king with a poem that ended:

> Then, sir, the present moment chuse
> Our armies are advancéd
> These terms you at the Hague refuse
> At Paris won't be granted.
>
> Consider this and Dunkirk raze
> And Anna's title own
> Send one Pretender out to graze
> And call another home.

The peace party in France was almost as pessimistic about the future as was the *Tatler;* it seemed that God had withdrawn His protection from the kingdom.[32] Defeats in the field and disasters at home called imperiously for peace. After a decade of good harvests, frosts and drought combined to produce the most disastrous crop failure in the memory of living men. The maritime powers could draw grain from the Baltic and, at the same time, prevent all but a trickle from reaching France. Besides crop failures, France suffered from the cumulative effect of more than twenty years of almost uninterrupted warfare. The fiscal structure of the kingdom was tottering, while tax collectors were harassing both peasants and merchants and France was beginning to look like a land occupied by a ruthless foe. While Godolphin, supported by the Whigs and the London "money men," could borrow millions at reasonable interest, the bankrupt French treasury had to resort to unorthodox and irregular expedients that proclaimed the king's distress to all the world.[33]

For all her need, however, France was not yet finished. Louis, rejecting the idea that he call the estates general to rally the country for a final effort, issued a manifesto explaining to his subjects the enormity of his enemies' demands and the extent of his own concessions to secure peace. It was the cry "the fatherland in danger" which both before and after

---

[32] After Blenheim a peace party had arisen at Versailles including by 1708 Madame de Maintenon and many other influential people. Madame de Maintenon wrote: "How can you say that God has not declared war against us . . . ? He sent a winter the like of which has not been seen for five or six hundred years." In another place she wrote: "It is necessary to give in . . . the arm of God is clearly against us . . . our king was too glorious, He wishes to humiliate him. France has extended herself too much, and perhaps unjustly. Our nation was insolent. . . . God wishes to punish her." P. Gaxotte, *La France de Louis XIV* (Paris, 1946), 367–368.

[33] Cf. Chapter Seven.

Louis's time aroused the French people to action. Money and men again became available; the nation responded with an *élan* not unlike that of modern nationalism. Many a sturdy peasant boy may have joined the army because there was bread for soldiers and none in the villages, but the response of all classes to the king's needs cannot be explained solely in terms of food. It was a mighty upsurge of loyalty to king and country that brought a new army into being.

Marshal Villars, an outspoken critic of military incompetence and court generals, a blunt, irascible fighter whose tongue, tastes, and manners were out of place at Versailles, was given command. His army was less brilliantly clad than its predecessors, had fewer cannon and much less food than its opponents, but under Villars the French regained confidence and lost some of their fear of the terrible "Malbrook."

Villars was too good a soldier to risk another Ramillies or Oudenarde. Combining courage with caution, he built a line of field fortifications from Aire to Douai, just inside the French frontier, that was soon too formidable to invite direct assault. Eugene and Marlborough, finding the road to Paris blocked, began the siege of Tournai.[34] Tournai was only slightly less powerful than Lille, and its underground mines and tunnels made its siege one of the most difficult problems of military art. The sixty-four hundred defenders of the city inflicted five thousand casualties on the besiegers before the fortress fell. Thereupon the allied commanders moved on Mons. Villars had extended his lines to nearby Condé. As soon as the enemies' intention became clear, he moved his army into the wooded area southwest of Mons near Malplaquet, and began to fortify that position. This challenge to battle Eugene and Marlborough were quick to accept.

The two allied commanders planned to put heavy pressure upon the wings of the French army to force a weakening of the center, and then to launch a blow at the middle of the line that would disorganize the whole French position. But Malplaquet was not a Blenheim. The French were better posted, better commanded, and inspired with a new spirit. When the battle was over, the allied armies held the field and claimed the victory, but after counting the casualties it became clear that they could not afford to win many such victories without risking the loss of the war.

[34] Had the allies been able to assemble an army early in the spring, an invasion of France would have been feasible, but by the time they were ready, Villars had his army and his lines.

The battle was the most complicated of the Marlborough-Eugene combinations. The allied infantry, supported by artillery, attacked fortified redans across a narrow front on both sides of the field. The young prince of Orange led the flower of the Dutch army on three desperate charges only to have it cut to pieces by infantry volleys and the murderous fire of a twenty-gun battery. On the other flank the Hanoverians and Prussians suffered almost as severely when they attacked the earthworks at the edge of the wood; only the presence of artillery saved them from being thrown back over the marshy ground already covered with their dead. But pressure on the flanks did force a weakening of the French center and finally the allied infantry succeeded in penetrating the redans in the middle of the field. This marked the critical point in all battles of the war: cavalry could now come into the fray for a decisive action. Fortunately for the allies, a mixed force of cavalry and infantry had succeeded in scouting the Sars Wood and now appeared behind the enemy left flank, thus obliging the French to divert from the center part of the forces required to ward off the allied cavalry attack. In this scrimmage Villars was severely wounded and old Marshal Boufflers assumed command.

The French cavalry gave a good account of itself. The *Maison du roi,* burning to avenge defeats on other fields, repeatedly repulsed the allied horsemen. Indeed, only the presence of well-trained infantry saved the allied cavalry until the weight of the attack finally broke through the French center. Boufflers ordered a general retreat, which was so well executed that the allies did not follow. A century was to elapse before Europe was to see another battle like that of Malplaquet. Not until Borodino (1812) was so bloody an engagement to take place. In an area of approximately ten square miles there were almost forty thousand men dead, dying, and wounded.

Accustomed to victory, the allies were jubilant at the first news of the battle; hardened to defeat, the French received the tidings glumly. Within a few days, however, reports of the high casualties appalled the victors and heartened the vanquished. In England particularly the peace party began to make converts. Both sides were willing to reopen negotiations, but when the conference met at Gertruydenberg in the spring of 1710 the French were confronted with demands exceeding all previous ones: they were now to agree to drive Philip from Spain. The Grand Alliance presented a solid front. The Dutch ardently supported the Anglo-Austrian policy with respect to Spain because the Whig government held out great promises: not only had it agreed to give up the commercial and territorial advantages secured from the Hapsburg pretender to the Spanish throne, but it had freely signed a treaty assuring the Dutch extensive control over the fortresses of the Spanish Netherlands. Louis had no possibility of dividing his enemies, nor would he agree to fight his own grandson. Once again the peace negotiations collapsed.

After 1710 the armies could do no better than the diplomats. Prospects of a decisive victory had vanished. On the Rhine and Italian frontiers the operations languished, the armies moodily watching each other during the summer and then going into winter quarters. On the Netherlands-French frontier Marlborough had to content himself with the capture of a few fortresses. In Spain, after two striking victories, the Anglo-Imperial armies under Stanhope and Starhemberg were defeated by Philip with the aid of Vendôme and a few thousand French troops. Only in the New World was there any decisive action. Throughout the war the North American frontier was the scene of periodical Indian raids, massacres, and ambushes, but none of these were more than hideous reminders of the conflict in Europe. In 1710, however, an English expedition to Acadia resulted in the capture of Port Royal and in English control of the whole coast. The expedition against Quebec in 1711 ended in fiasco, but Acadia, or Nova Scotia, remained in English hands till the end of the war.

But successes in the colonies could not win the war, and victories on the continent failed to bring peace. The chief obstacle was still the Anglo-Imperial slogan: "No peace without Spain." Until the allies were able to put an army into Spain strong enough to impose their political aims or until they were willing to readjust their demands to correspond with Spanish realities, there could be no agreement. Marlborough and his Whig colleagues would not face this dilemma, but when Queen Anne dismissed the Marlborough-Godolphin government, the Tories lost no time in concluding a compromise with the enemy.

In the early years of the war, Marlborough had co-operated with the Tories. This suited the pious, narrow-minded Queen Anne, for she feared and hated the Whigs. But as the war progressed, the Whigs proved the better allies of the crown: they favored the war, their friends in the "city" provided loans, and they easily won victories in parliament. The Whigs entered and finally dominated the government, despite the protest of the queen. Each new Whig addition cost Marlborough some of his influence with Anne. So long as Sarah remained Anne's confidante, these "victories over the queen" could be safely won, but when Sarah fell from grace, her husband's position as commander of England's armies was in danger.

Harley, St. John, and a group of their Tory friends started the political maneuvers that finally ruined Marlborough. Mrs. Masham, a red-nosed, unattractive lady, who became Anne's confidante, was their creature. She played upon the queen's feelings and prejudices, which were legion, and persuaded her to listen to the Tory schemes. It all resembled an old-fashioned court intrigue, curiously mixed with elements of a modern ministerial crisis. The queen was estranged from the Marlboroughs and fed large doses of malicious gossip. Old Shrewsbury, once a famous Whig whose Italian wife had been offended by Sarah, was slipped into the ministry to help discredit his Whig colleagues, while in the back staircases of the palace plots and conferences luxuriated as in the days of old. The conspirators played upon the religious and social prejudices of the ignorant squires and country parsons. The squire-rousing slogan, "The church is in danger," was revived, and stories of corruption, money men, and military incompetence were babbled in the back lanes of England. The nation was war weary, and suffering from drought, the four-shilling land tax, and heavy excises. The Tories charged that Whigs could not bring peace and played up the isolationist ideas that fitted so completely the mentality of the country folk. By these methods they won support for their party and program.

The destruction of the Marlborough-Godolphin ministry was cleverly contrived. Had the Tories attempted a frontal assault, the Whig parliament would undoubtedly have frustrated their plans. But the idea of ministerial solidarity was at that time unknown, and it was possible to attack the government piecemeal. First Sunderland, Marlborough's Whig son-in-law, was dismissed, and then, after parliament had adjourned, Godolphin received a note from the queen commanding him to burn his staff of office. With the great treasurer out of the way, the rest could be given short shrift. Once the ministry had been remade, the appointment of sheriffs, justices of the peace, and lords lieutenant prepared the way for the election of a new parliament. Control of the government assured victory at the polls and the new parliament was in fact full of ardent Tories, who naïvely believed all the malicious stories that the more urbane Harley had put about as election propaganda.

Marlborough's position was difficult. The scurrilous attacks upon his family and himself were clear evidence that his days were numbered, but he could not resign his command without being classed as a traitor. His was an unenviable position for a soldier; he could not name his subordinates or reward his friends. His opponents ascribed his victories to luck and his defeats to incompetence. For a whole year Marlborough operated in this uneasy political climate, suffering insults and slights, yet winning several fortresses within the French frontier and breaking through Villars' lines, yet finally receiving dismissal as his reward. His foes blackened his reputation, enlarging upon his weakness for money, position, and fame, and playing down the military talents that had served the nation so well.

The fall of the Marlborough-Godolphin government, coupled with the death of Emperor Joseph, at last made possible the termination of the war. The emperor died of smallpox and was succeeded by his brother Charles, the pretender to the Spanish throne. The allies obviously no longer had an interest in backing his Spanish claim. In England the new Tory government in fact had declared that England would not fight to re-create the empire of Charles V. Charles VI refused to recognize that his succession to the crowns of the Danubian Monarchy and of the Holy Roman Empire had changed the political problem in Spain, but the Dutch and the German princes agreed with the English Tories. Peace was therefore possible, indeed inevitable, but the peace that was made was an English, not an allied peace.

VI. THE PACIFICATION OF THE WEST

The settlement negotiated by Viscount Bolingbroke has been the subject of controversy from his day to the present. English Whigs as well as continental politicians regarded the Anglo-French agreements as little less than treason, while historians, if they have not condemned it, have gone to great lengths in their efforts to explain and excuse the Tory policy. Bolingbroke himself wrote eloquently if not always honestly in defense of his actions, and time, which consecrates accomplished facts and cancels alternatives, has seemed to justify the treaty. Bolingbroke's negotiations with Torcy and the subsequent betrayal of England's allies were probably unavoidable if peace was to be secured in 1713. The diverse and unrealistic attitudes of England's allies, the emperor's stubborn unwillingness to recognize the impracticality of the war aims of 1710, and the war weariness of Europe in 1711 and 1712, made a showdown and settlement imperative.

The Tories made contact with Louis XIV as soon as they came to power, and indicated a willingness to deal with France if England's interests could be assured. Bolingbroke and Oxford (Harley) decided to outdo the Whigs in securing economic privileges for English merchants and thereby to silence criticism of their negotiations with the enemy. As for the allies, the Tories had no love for any of them: their hatred of the Dutch, and their contempt for the Empire were alike boundless, and they had no compunction about negotiating behind the backs of those powers.

Bolingbroke's peace might not have been so criticized had it not been for the famous "restraining order," which seriously compromised the honor of the English army. The Tories had hoped that Marlborough's successor, the duke of Ormonde, would win a military reputation glamorous enough to make Englishmen forget the victor of Blenheim, Ramillies, and Oudenarde. Ormonde himself had assumed command with the full intention of co-operating with Eugene and winning further victories for the allied arms. In May, 1712, however, he was ordered to avoid combat, to enter into correspondence with Villars, and to refrain from telling his allies of his instructions. Villars was informed, but not Eugene! The result was a defeat of the allied army and Villars' recapture of several fortified places lost in the preceding year. Many English soldiers felt bitterly humiliated by their enforced inactivity, and when Bolingbroke and Torcy contrived an armistice, they were galled with shame. "With nobler feelings," writes Trevelyan, "was mingled bitter disappointment at missing the rich plunder of France. . . ." [35]

The Anglo-French negotiations had reached an advanced stage when a series of tragic deaths raised the possibility that Philip V of Spain might inherit the throne of France. The dauphin died in 1711, to be followed in February, 1712, by Louis, duke of Burgundy, next in line, and less than a week later by the young duke of Brittany, Burgundy's eldest son. Only a sickly boy, the future Louis XV, stood between Philip V and the throne of France. Just as the succession of Archduke Charles to the imperial throne had made his candidature to the Spanish crown unacceptable, so the possibility that Philip might wear the French as well as the Spanish crown raised the very specter which England and her allies had fought for ten years to exorcise. It was suggested that Philip abandon Spain and await the death of the sickly Louis, but instead Philip renounced his rights to the French throne. All possible legal provisions were made to keep the two thrones separate, but as Louis warned the English, the French parlement would probably recognize none of them in the event of the young heir's demise.

The conference between the British and French delegates at Utrecht laid the foundation for the pacification of western Europe, other treaties dealing with special problems being fitted into the framework established

[35] *Op. cit.*, III, 220.

by Anglo-French diplomacy. The guiding principle of the negotiations was the reaffirmation of the balance of power in Europe. The English took for themselves the lion's share of the colonial, commercial, and strategic spoils; they assigned to their allies those territories that could not safely be left under French or Spanish control; and they created legal barriers to separate the Bourbon thrones of France and Spain. By under-lining the balance of power, the peace consecrated the new states system of Europe, based upon the dominance of the great military and commer-cial powers, as it had been hammered out in decades of almost uninter-rupted war.

The peace might be called the last of the partition treaties. Even though the emperor refused to participate in the negotiations, the agreement al-lotted the Spanish Netherlands, Milan, Sardinia, and Naples to the Aus-trian Hapsburgs; Philip V retained Spain and the overseas empire; Sicily was awarded the duke of Savoy. England also shared in the partition. She received Gibraltar and Minorca, small but important acquisitions that enabled the British fleet in war or in peace to dominate the western Mediterranean and its entrance.

The United Netherlands reacquired the right to garrison a string of fortresses in the "Austrian" Netherlands. This barrier was important to the Dutch both as a line of defense against France and as a method of controlling and exploiting the profitable trade of the area. The Dutch wanted to assure themselves firstly, that their Catholic cousins could not compete with them in the world markets, and secondly, that the com-merce of the Lowlands would be organized to their own advantage. The barrier acquired in 1713 was by no means as extensive as the one prom-ised them by the Whigs in 1709, when England needed Dutch support at Gertruydenberg, but it was large enough to give them economic control of the Austrian Netherlands.[36] The king of Prussia, despite an earlier English commitment to the Dutch, received Upper Guelderland, and his royal title was recognized by all Europe. Maximilian recovered his lands and titles in Bavaria, including the tiny principality of Mindelheim, which had been given to Marlborough when he became a prince of the Empire.

England required the French to dismantle the privateering base at Dunkirk, to cede Acadia, Newfoundland, and Saint Kitts' Island, and to recognize the rights of the Hudson's Bay Company. Canada itself re-mained in French hands until later in the century. England's client,

[36] R. Geikie and I. A. Montgomery, *The Dutch Barrier, 1705–1719* (Cambridge, Eng., 1930).

Portugal, secured full recognition of her rights in Brazil and the Amazon basin by the restriction of France's Guiana colony. Fishing rights off Newfoundland were left so vague that for two centuries they were to provide an irritating issue of Anglo-French diplomacy. The *Asiento* contract for the slave trade with Spanish America and the commercial treaty between England and Spain opened vistas of commercial gain comparable to that secured by the Anglo-Portuguese treaties concluded early in the war. Though these trading privileges proved disappointing, it was evident in 1713 that the commercial advantages secured by England would assure her a paramount position in world trade.[37]

Emperor Charles VI refused to sign the treaty because it left Alsace to France and ignored Hapsburg rights in Spain. His father had fought for Strassburg, he had fought for Spain; he was unwilling to surrender them without further conflict. Villars and Eugene fenced all through 1713; the great Savoyard, who was fast becoming the most important statesman of the Hapsburgs, was at a disadvantage without English, Dutch, and Prussian aid. Despite his military skill, he could not prevent Villars from invading Germany. Louis XIV, however, was in no position to continue the war even though his marshal might win victories. The Peace of Utrecht had set limits to his possible gains, and the terrible economic distress in France made peace imperative. Charles, too, had to listen to reason in spite of his romantic attachment to his title, King of Spain. The Danubian Monarchy, after three decades of international and civil war, required peace.

The negotiations were left to Villars and Eugene. These two soldiers sparred diplomatically with the same *élan* they showed in the field. Midst compliments and intrigue, frankness and bluff, they carried on their negotiations. Since the Peace of Utrecht had already established the main lines of the settlement, only details remained for discussion. The treaty, signed at Rastatt in 1714, left Alsace to the French, but in return France surrendered all conquests east of the Rhine and confirmed the terms of the Peace of Utrecht.

In recounting the long wars that stretched from the siege of Vienna in 1683 to the peace of 1713–14, an effort has been made to keep the story on the general European plane. Yet there was one personality whose life was completely bound up with the story and who, like the sinister character in a tragedy, seemed at times to exemplify human fate. Louis XIV, the Sun King, the arbiter and warlord of Europe, the visage of

[37] Cf. J. O. McLachlan, *Trade and Peace with Old Spain, 1667–1750* (Cambridge, Eng., 1940), 46–77.

Jove with smiles for his friends and thunderbolts for his enemies, unwittingly played the part of midwife to the birth of the new great-power balance. He himself had envisaged the situation quite differently. Proud and ambitious for his family and his kingdom, Louis had aimed at hegemony in Europe and even at a universal empire in the tradition of classical antiquity. Yet at the end of his reign the balance of power had become firmly established. His biographers either praise him for his magnificence, his style, his court, or damn him for his extravagance, his pretensions, his wars. But Louis's role for good or for evil was not of his own making. It was inevitably part of the great historical structure inherited from the Middle Ages. The last thirty years of his reign gave the west a new conception of political destiny and hastened the development of new political institutions.

VII. THE END OF SWEDISH HEGEMONY

After the defeat of the Swedish army at Pultava, Russia was obviously the leading power in the north. Her armies occupied the Baltic provinces, captured Riga, and invaded Finland; her rapidly growing navy ruled the Baltic, and even raided the coasts of Sweden. The Danish king and Augustus of Saxony re-entered the war, and the Polish diet reinstated Augustus on the throne. This second coalition had every reason to hope for success. In north Germany, Hanover and Prussia were preparing to join the coalition in order to profit from the impending partition of Sweden's empire. Had his foes fully understood the weakness of Charles' kingdom, they would probably have overwhelmed it at once, but a single reverse was not enough to shatter Sweden's military prestige. The tiger and the jackals who hoped to devour the wounded Swedish lion still feared his claws.

The caution of the allies seemed justified when Stenbock, with an army clothed in goatskins and wooden shoes, defeated the Danes at Helsingsborg (1710) and drove them out of Scania, but Sweden's resources and strength were almost exhausted even though this fact was not recognized either by Charles XII or his enemies. The Swedish empire could still fight, but without powerful allies it was doomed.

The new situation in the north was embarrassing to England and Holland. They were obliged by treaty with Sweden to keep Denmark at peace, but Denmark had hired to the western powers a strong contingent of soldiers, including some of the best cavalry in Marlborough's army, and the Prussian and Hanoverian force were almost indispensable to the opponents of France. The maritime powers could therefore hardly afford to offend Denmark or to provoke the north German princes into recalling their troops. A Saxon-Polish-Russian attack upon Charles' German territories, or the adherence of Hanover and Prussia to the coalition against Sweden, might seriously affect the outcome of the War of the Spanish Succession. To prevent this, a treaty was drawn up at The Hague (March 20, 1710) which neutralized Sweden's German possessions. The Stockholm government willingly signed, for it was unable to defend these territories. Charles haughtily repudiated the treaty, but it nevertheless served to isolate the Northern War until the war in the west was over.

Meanwhile Charles lived at Bender as a guest of the sultan. He did more, however, than write letters, practice his religion, and review his own small band of troops and the Janissary guard supplied by the sultan. Old "Ironhead," as his Janissaries affectionately called him, worked hard to bring the Ottoman Empire into the war against Russia. As a diplomat and intriguer in the Oriental fashion he showed himself hardly less brilliant than as a commander of troops. One vizier after another fell into disgrace when Charles found him hostile or lukewarm. To be sure, he was ably supported by the French ambassador, but the involvement of the Ottoman Empire in war with Russia was largely his own achievement.

After unseating two viziers, Charles persuaded Sultan Achmed III to declare war on Russia. Early in 1711 Tartar irregulars ranged as far as Kharkov and Voronezh, while a regular Turkish army under the grand vizier moved northward into the Danubian principalities. Peter, overconfident and trusting in the aid of the governors (hospodars) of Wallachia and Moldavia, arrived at the Pruth River early in summer with an army of about 60,000. His opponent had a plan of campaign devised by Charles himself and designed to trap the Russian bear. By the first week of July, the trap began to close. The Turks on one side and the Tartar kahn on the other surrounded the Russian forces with about 200,000 men. Peter's allies drifted from the scene, and supplies were simply not to be had. With a little artillery fire or by merely waiting until the Russians ran out of food, the grand vizier could have compelled an unconditional surrender.

Peter's plight was almost exactly that of Charles at Pultava. His first impulse was to flee, leaving his army to look out for itself, but flight itself had become impossible. Apparently at the instigation of his empress,

Catherine, Peter offered the grand vizier an advantageous peace and a huge bribe. Mehemet Baltadji was a man of unheroic disposition and slight ambition; he had the Russian bear by the throat and might have saved both Islam and Sweden considerable future difficulty had he strangled him. But he decided that the sultan's interests would best be served if he forced the tsar to give up the territory he had recently acquired on the Black and Azov seas. He could then return to Constantinople, a victor who had spilled no blood. He therefore agreed to the Treaty of Pruth, which at least temporarily frustrated Russia's march to the Black Sea.[38]

Charles was furious. He arrived at the Turkish camp before the Russians had escaped from the trap, but the grand vizier refused to let him take over the command. In November, 1711, Mehemet Baltadji was deposed, the third vizier to fall victim to Charles' rancor. Jussuf Pasha, a Janissary officer, thereupon assumed the high office and promptly repudiated the treaty of the Pruth, which, however, was reaffirmed in the spring of 1712 through the influence of England and Holland.

Once the sultan had definitely decided upon peace, he wished to be rid of his troublesome guest at Bender, but Charles would take no hints, accept no suggestions. There seemed no choice but to expel him. Charles preferred to fight rather than allow himself to be "escorted" to the fron-tier, thus provoking the *Kalibalik,* the most disgraceful and foolish episode of his life. His Janissary guards, who had come to love old "Iron-head," tried unsuccessfully to persuade him to accept their protection. When ordered to attack him they mutinied, but only to have twenty of their leaders executed. In the "battle" that followed the Swedish king and forty of his followers stood off twelve thousand Turks and Tartars for eight hours. The Swedes lost fifteen men, the besiegers two hundred. The Janissaries, convinced that Allah had driven "Ironhead" mad, exhibited the utmost forbearance, without which Charles could hardly have escaped alive.

Charles remained in the Ottoman Empire for a whole year after the *Kalibalik* before he finally persuaded himself that nothing was to be hoped from the sultan. His return to Sweden through central Europe was another dramatic saga. Since recognition might have been fatal, he traveled as a Swedish officer. But his features were as well known as his

[38] Lord Eversley points out that Baltadji was probably empowered by the sultan to make peace if Peter would surrender his recent conquests. The Turks could not hope to conquer part of Russia. The Peace of Pruth, therefore, was not unwise from the vizier's point of view, the more so as Peter scrupulously respected its terms. Lord G. J. S. Eversley, *Turkish Empire 1288 to 1914* (2nd ed., London, 1923), 196.

fame; almost every inn in Europe had a picture of the Swedish lion, and almost anyone could tell tales of his severe austerity and his physical vigor. With the aid of a wig and by adopting an unpuritanical behavior that must have distressed him, "Captain Peter Frisk" crossed central Europe and arrived at Stralsund on November 11, 1714, without having been recognized.

The last years of Charles' life were as stormy as the first. Prussia and Hanover, supported by England, joined the coalition against him, and one defeat after another haunted his footsteps. His kingdom was bled white by extraordinary financial measures invented by his new friend Görtz, the "grand vizier," as he was maliciously called in Sweden. Swedish historians have described this German favorite as a ruthless man who encouraged the king in the only policy he would adopt. Nonetheless, Görtz was a diplomat of rare ability. He prevented an impending invasion of Sweden by separating Peter from the allies and, had the king not been killed, it is not at all certain that he might not have succeeded in extricating Sweden from her difficult situation with less loss of prestige and territory than actually occurred.

Charles was killed on December 11, 1718. It is not known whether the shot was fired by an assassin, an outraged peasant, or a soldier on the walls of Frederikshald, but his death brought peace to the north.[39] Görtz was immediately arrested, and executed shortly after. Charles' sister, Ulrika Eleonora, became queen under conditions that severely limited the royal prerogative exercised by her father and brother. Sweden entered a period during which the nobility regained much of its power, while the nation was given an opportunity to recover from the disastrous strain of the wars.

Peace negotiations were not fully concluded until 1721. By the treaties of Stockholm and Frederiksborg in 1719 and 1720 Hanover received Bremen and Verden; Prussia, Stettin and part of Pomerania; Denmark, though failing to get Stralsund and Rügen, obtained the Gottorp share of Schleswig and Swedish resignation of free passage in the Sound. Augustus of Saxony had to content himself with the recognition of his right to sit on the unstable Polish throne. The Treaty of Nystad (1721), forced upon Sweden when England, Hanover, and Prussia refused to intervene

[39] Rudolph Fåhraeus, *Karl XI och Karl XII*, 495 ff.; Oswald Kuylenstierna, *Karl XII Hans Öden och Hans Personlighet*, p. 263 ff. (Stockholm, 1925), Major Kuylenstierna was present when Charles' tomb was opened in 1917. The king was killed by a short-barreled firearm at close range; the direction of the shot could not be determined. Since no plot was ever discovered, the question of assassination is still moot.

in her behalf, marked the great disaster to the Swedish Empire. By it Russia acquired Livonia, Estonia, Ingria, Karelia, and the fortress of Viborg. Sweden retained Finland and received an indemnity of two million thalers, but the great Swedish Empire was definitely destroyed. By twenty-one years of war Peter had acquired a firm grip on the eastern Baltic, given his empire a dominating position in northern Europe, and earned for himself the title, "the Great."

VIII. CONCLUSION

To the Treaties of Utrecht (1713), Rastadt (1714), Stockholm, Frederiksborg (1719–20), and Nystad (1721) should be added the Treaty of Passarowitz (1718), which ended Eugene's last war with the Turks and marked the farthest southward advance of the Danubian Monarchy. These treaties ended an epoch which began when French power seemed irresistible. At Nijmegen and in the years immediately following, the prospect of a Bourbon imperium stared Europe full in the face, while the centers of resistance in Madrid, Vienna, London, Stockholm, and The Hague appeared paralyzed. A French Europe, more or less patterned after classical models, was definitely within the realm of possibility. But by the second decade of the eighteenth century the threat had disappeared, and the organization of Europe as it was to continue for two centuries was already crystallizing. Limits had been set to the expansion of France, and the three established empires, the Spanish, the Swedish, and the Ottoman, had given way to the new powers of Europe. At Zenta, Blenheim, Ramillies, Pultava, Lille, Gibraltar, and other battlefields, at Ryswick, Utrecht, Nystad, and other conferences, Europe's political structure was assuming its modern shape.

This important change affected European life profoundly. It was not merely the massed cavalry charge, or the smoking broadside of a line of ships, or the bellowing blast of the mine blowing a gap in a fortress, or the insinuating manners of statesmen at the conference table that were transforming Europe. With war came revolutions and reforms. The Richelieuian reforms had made possible the mobilization of the latent power of France in the service of a central authority. The Glorious Revolution in England, the reforms of Peter in Russia, the Leopoldian development of Ferdinand's reforms in the Hapsburg monarchy, and a series of similar reforms elsewhere in Europe provided bases for the organization characteristic of Europe from 1700 to 1914.

Chapter Four

THE SHIFT OF POWER IN WESTERN EUROPE

I. THE ADMINISTRATIVE MONARCHY IN FRANCE

In 1680 France was the only great military power in Europe; medieval survivals in the organization of the other states prevented them from mobilizing their full military and political power. But within a generation England, the Danubian Monarchy, and Russia all reached great-power status, and fundamental alterations had occurred in the internal structures of most other states. As a result of these internal changes, the constitution characteristic of European states during the next two centuries had begun to emerge. It would be an exaggeration to ascribe this development solely to the three decades of warfare that filled the period, for the process that changed the weak medieval kingdoms into powerful military states began even before 1500. Nonetheless, it is true that these wars, with their insistent demands for the mobilization of power, accelerated the process and at the same time fixed the form of the new states system.

The system of balance between the great military powers as it emerged from the dust and smoke of war and revolution marked the end of the medieval political synthesis. Medievalism continued to survive in many areas, but the rise of standing armies and centralized administrative systems doomed the loose-jointed federalism of old Europe. When Hobbes hailed the Leviathan state, early in the seventeenth century, the beast was still little more than a husky tadpole, but by the opening of the eighteenth century it had grown wondrously. The authoritarian state had become typical of western political organization, and had developed a complicated system of international relations.

The obedience enjoyed by the government of Louis XIV had not been accorded to earlier French kings. When Henry IV died in 1610 the provincial governors and the great lords behaved like quasi-independent sovereigns, the walled towns largely managed their own affairs, the Huguenot community practically constituted a Protestant republic within the Catholic kingdom, and every gentleman with a sword regarded himself as sovereign in his own affairs. Maria de' Medici could assure herself

97

a measure of obedience by bribery, but she did not possess either the moral or the physical strength to make her commands respected throughout the kingdom. Louis XIII and Richelieu were the real architects of the France that obeyed Louis XIV; they broke the forces capable of opposing the central authority, and elevated the power and prestige of the kingdom to the place left vacant by the decline of Spain. The revolution they began was extended and consolidated by Mazarin and the advisers of the young Louis XIV during the first two decades of his reign. The old federalism of the French constitution gradually disappeared, to be replaced by the centralized power of the royal government.[1]

In the process the role of the king was sensibly altered. French monarchs had long preened themselves on their divine-right absolutism, but there was a great difference between the absolutism of Henry IV and that of his renowned grandson, the Sun King. Henry had ruled the kingdom informally. His whole administration, with the exception of the treasury and the parlement, could conveniently follow the king on his travels. When his grandson moved the government from Paris to Versailles, the bureaucracy had already grown so numerous that it occupied all the rooms on both sides of the great court of the ministers and spilled over into other parts of the palace. Henry's secretaries of state had written the king's letters; Louis's had become chiefs of elaborate bureaus with deputies, clerks, and archives. Henry could and did know about all the problems of his government; his grandson's secretaries referred only important papers to the king and even with these burdened him more heavily than Henry had ever been burdened. From despot by divine-right, the French king was being transformed into the chief of a vast administrative machine.

The king's officials, too, were changing character. In the two generations between Henry IV and Louis XIV the victory of the men of the pen over the men of the sword became complete. In place of soldiers and great noblemen, the king came to rely upon men of affairs, the so-called nobility of the robe, to execute his will. These men, the Colberts, the Louvois, and their successors, developed a loyalty to the kingdom that

[1] There are several recent books on Louis XIV's France; but none is particularly novel. Volume VIII of E. Lavisse's *Histoire de France* (Paris, 1911) is still the standard account for the last years of the reign. See also P. Gaxotte, *La France de Louis XIV* (Paris, 1946); G. Pagès, *La monarchie d'ancien régime en France* (Paris, 1946); P. Sagnac, *La formation de la société française moderne* (Paris, 1945), and the new edition of Sagnac and Saint-Leger, *Louis XIV 1661-1715* (originally called *La prépondérance française 1661-1715*) (Paris, 1949).

transcended even their personal loyalty to the king. They were ministers of state and their letters and memorials reveal them as men who could have served a Napoleon or a Clemenceau as easily as a Louis XIV. After the deaths of Colbert (1683) and Louvois (1691), however, none was any longer able to grasp the whole problem of French government. Even Colbert's brilliant nephew, Torcy, was a bureau chief rather than a statesman of vision. This was perhaps as much the result of the bureaucratic character of Louis's government as it was of the king's insistence upon keeping personal control over the conduct of the wars.

The extension of the administrative organization inevitably affected all parts of the country. In the two or three decades before 1680 the office of *intendant* with an authority and power that made its incumbent a little king in his *généralité,* had become standardized and, despite Colbert's efforts to check the process, the *intendants* were already represented on the parish level by *sous-intendants* whose authority, too, was seemingly unlimited. After the stress of war had made imperative the collection of as much revenue as possbile, there was no longer any attempt to check the multiplication of *sous-intendants*. Since administrative law was either nonexistent or in an embryonic stage, and since there were no administrative courts to interpret decrees and to rule upon competence, this extension of royal power on the parish level increased enormously the impact of the king's government upon the population, and gradually insinuated a bureaucratic hierarchy between the king and his people.

The emergence of the standing army involved further revolutionary changes in the government of the kingdom. Under Henry IV the army had been negligible in size except when the king went to war. The constable, the admiral, the colonel general of the infantry, and the superintendent of ordnance were usually important noblemen whose private position as great lords and whose public status as governors of provinces outweighed their military importance. By 1680 the revolutionary work of Richelieu, Le Tellier, Colbert, and Louvois had altered the picture. The army and navy were under bureaucratic administration and were controlled by councils dominated by officials completely dependent upon the king. The soldiers, who a half century before had often acted like independent agents, were completely subject to the king's command. It would have been unthinkable for one of Louis's generals to comport himself as had the great soldiers of the first half of the century. An elaborate bureaucratic machine supplied arsenals, fortifications, hospitals, ships at sea, and regiments on the land, and reported directly to the central government on all matters, from the needs of the troops to the loyalty and efficiency of the officers.

The enormous expenditures for the wars and for the elaborate court of the king involved a sensational increase in the number of treasury officials as well as an almost unbearable rise in taxation. Louis's treasury, however, suffered from the same evils that haunted his grandfather's. Neither Sully nor Colbert had been able to achieve a thoroughgoing reform of the French financial structure. Thus, at the end of Louis's reign, the routes to the king's strong box were beset by hosts of tax officials, tax farmers, and special agents. This extension of the treasury's activities greatly enhanced the impact of the king's government, and added its bit to the growth of the administrative monarchy.[2]

The rise and extension of the bureaucratic state inevitably brought social implications in its train. The great of the land, whose fathers had behaved like sovereign princes, were stripped of most of their power and brought to court to contribute to the king's grandeur. Hardly fifty years before "to leave the court" meant a declaration of civil war; by 1680 "to be sent from court" was a sign of personal disgrace. Moreover, the new government had no significant role for most of the courtiers. Policy was made in secret by the king and his officials; the great noblemen were neither admitted to the councils nor given an opportunity to discuss the king's projects. A few found outlets for their energy in the army, but even in the military service high commands were likely to go to professionals who, like Villars, were awarded high titles for their services. At the same time the sale of titles of nobility cheapened the social position of the second estate. By increasing the number of noblemen, the king reduced the significance of all.

The lesser nobility likewise suffered diminution of status by the rise of the royal power. In former days they had ruled the countryside in the king's name, but the *intendants* and their deputies steadily encroached upon their powers and gradually stripped them of their political influence. Like the great noblemen at the court, the country gentlemen retained their privileges, economic interests, and rights, but lost their place in the political hierarchy. This divorce of the economic and social status of the nobleman from his political and military responsibilities created an imbalance that made the aristocracy a parasitic class. Their privileges became meaningless when stripped of the corresponding obligations.

The development of the French bourgeoisie, too, was determined by

[2] Cf. Chapter Seven for discussion of French finance.

the rise of the bureaucratic monarchy. Louis's government imposed royal officials upon the municipalities at precisely the moment when the townsmen were attempting to create a large-scale commerce and industry, and thereby deprived them of control over their own enterprise. Moreover, the pressing need for money led to a great increase in excises and tolls which burdened commerce, while the creation of new offices (for sale) enlarged the bureaucracy and led to unnecessary regulation of both commerce and industry.

In addition to these discouraging measures, psychological factors came into play. The French bourgeoisie accepted at face value the nobility's evaluation of commerce as ignoble. The sons of merchants, therefore, strove to rise in the social world by becoming lawyers, notaries, officials, and even tax farmers (selling salt was somehow more honorable than selling cloth!). The sale of offices provided the opportunity for satisfying their aspirations. Since government posts carried prestige and the possibility of hereditary tenure, both investment and social position were secure. Naturally not all French commoners were lured away from commerce, but a sufficiently large number entered the bureaucracy or became lawyers, notaries, and tax farmers to justify the belief that commerce and industry were impaired by this office-seeking penchant of the rising middle class.

The peasantry may have received some protection against their feudal lords through the extension of the power of the *intendants,* but any such gain was nullified by the mounting burden of taxation. Throughout the seventeenth century stories were prevalent of misery in the villages, but in the last twenty-five years of Louis's reign the distress wrought by bad harvests and excessive taxation passed all bounds. Even if a peasant managed, somehow, to rise above the level of bare existence, he did not dare use his money for fear of an immediate increase in taxes. The French peasantry hardly could have suffered more had Louis's enemies occupied the country.[3]

Louis, the administrator, was a state builder in that he recognized that a united kingdom required common loyalties, but his vision was medieval and egotistical, with the result that he introduced controversy and antagonism rather than unity to his realm. In the Middle Ages the church was regarded as the cement of society, the arbiter of good and evil. Louis, perhaps unfamiliar with the literature of the *politiques* of the late sixteenth century, failed to realize that there were other values that could and

[3] Cf. Chapter Seven.

should transcend religious unity when a large section of the population insisted upon dissenting from the church of the majority. Thus ignorance, arrogance, and perhaps the flattery of ministers led to the attempt to drive the Huguenots back into the Roman Catholic fold. Lacking the wisdom and subtlety of his father or of Richelieu, Louis could not see that the Huguenots might be converted by skillful use of argument and political preference, and that force would only harden their attachment to the reformed church. The revocation of the Edict of Nantes (1685) not only failed to convert the Huguenots but cost the kingdom dearly. The exiles placed their skills in manufacturing, commerce, and war at the disposal of France's enemies, and as propaganda agents they stirred up antagonism against France abroad. Instead of uniting France under one God, the revocation undermined the authority and power of the king.[4]

Louis's quarrels with Pope Innocent XI over the Gallican Articles, the archbishopric of Cologne, and the immunities of the French embassy at Rome were almost equally disastrous to his reign.[5] His objective was clear; to identify God and His church with the throne of France. But Louis's *Kulturkampf* was bound to fail when his armies met reverses in the field and when the Pope refused to recognize his pretensions. The quarrel with Rome, like the expulsion of the Huguenots, aided France's foreign foes and provoked criticism of the regime at home.

The sensational rise of enemy powers, and the ensuing military disasters, the disorder in the fiscal system and the impoverishment of the population, the failure of the crops and the haunting specter of famine, and finally the deaths of his son and grandson led Louis and his court to believe that these trials and misfortunes were God's punishment for his arrogance, his pretensions and his transgressions. At the end of his life the future of his house and throne was insecure. The peace of Europe and the safety of the kingdom depended upon the life of his sickly great-grandson, who alone stood between a union of the French and Spanish crowns which, in turn, would have inevitably brought a reopening of the war. But even if the child lived, the kingdom was bankrupt, its people discouraged, and its enemies triumphant. Twenty-five years of warfare had finished the work of creating an administrative monarchy, but they had also wasted the kingdom and enhanced the power of its opponents. The period that engendered this disastrous situation has been called by one French historian the *déformation,* because it reduced the glory and

[4] Cf. Chapter Ten.
[5] Cf. Chapter Three, Chapter Ten.

power of the country.[6] This judgment may be too severe. Although
Louis's last years were haunted by disasters, they were also marked by the
consolidation of the reforms begun by Richelieu and by the consummation of the bureaucratic system.

II. ENGLAND: THE "GLORIOUS" REVOLUTION

Generations of English politicians and an array of English historians
have stood in almost superstitious awe before the work of their forefathers in 1688–1689. Those days have seemed to them as important as the
days of creation, and altogether worthy of the most minute study. The
"Glorious" Revolution was important: it solved the constitutional problem of England and released the energy and power of the nation to such
an extent that within a generation England could seize the hegemony of
Europe and lay the foundations of her great colonial empire.

Throughout the seventeenth century England had seethed with political unrest. The Stuart parliaments had been quite unwilling to play
the role assigned them by the Tudors. The result was conflict—conflict
that cost Charles I his head and the country two decades of turmoil. The
return of the Stuarts in 1660 did not really solve the problem, for Clarendon and the Restoration statesmen failed to understand that no solution
could be lasting unless it removed the probability of conflict between king
and parliament. The constitution of 1660 established an equilibrium between the rights of the throne and the rights of parliament, but it was
not the acme of political wisdom its creators conceived it to be, for it
would work only when king and parliament were in essential agreement.

Such agreement and trust did not prevail. The parliaments of Charles
II and James II had little confidence in the foreign policies and not much
more in the domestic policies of their rulers. As a result both kings were
kept on relatively short rations. Parliament would, at the beginning of a
reign, grant the king revenues for life, but not more than enough for the
ordinary expenses of the court, and certainly insufficient to allow the king
to pursue an independent policy. Both Charles II and James II gladly accepted subsidies from Louis XIV in order to escape royal poverty.

Even if they had enjoyed more ample revenue, these rulers were further
limited by parliament's distrust of a standing army. Parliament not only
restricted appropriations for the army but refused to pass a Mutiny Act
that would enable the king to maintain discipline. Were a soldier to

[6] G. Pagès, *op. cit.,* 182 ff.

desert, he could be punished in the civil courts under the Apprentices Act; were he to strike an officer, he could be brought before a civil court for assault. But neither of these laws made possible the enforcement of discipline like that of the new continental armies. James II was probably right when he pointed out that the English militia and trainbands would have melted like snow before a determined thrust by a continental army, but parliament distrusted James and his intentions. The English squires looked upon the redcoats as at worst a menace to themselves, and at best as an instrument of a foreign policy of which they did not approve. They would grant money for a navy to prevent an invasion; they refused to consider a large army.

A second problem was the religious settlement. The Restoration was both anti-Puritanical and anti-Catholic. Religious services other than those of the Anglican Church were illegal, and John Bunyan found himself in jail, like the Jesuit priests, for violation of the Clarendon Code. But popular antagonism to the Catholics was greater than to the dissenters. To exclude Catholics from office, the Test Act (1673) required every officeholder to give evidence that he had received the sacraments in the Anglican Church. Catholics might take an easy view about an oath, but they would not endanger their souls by heretical practices. The act prevented James, the brother of the king, from ruling over the admiralty; it did not prevent him from becoming king.[7]

In 1685 James II mounted the throne.[8] The new king, with little of his brother's political astuteness, was a devout Roman Catholic convinced of his mission to bring England back to the Roman fold. To achieve this end as quickly as possible, James ignored the advice of the Pope, of most of the Catholic rulers of Europe, and of the Catholic aristocrats of England. A firm believer in divine right, he refused to compromise, as much because he felt he was carrying out the will of God as because of his conviction that compromise had cost his father his head. James II was

[7] For the most recent full-length portrait of the Restoration see David Ogg, *England under Charles II*, 2 vols. (1934).

[8] Any historian writing about the fall of the house of Stuart must acknowledge the excellent work that has been done on this subject. Macaulay's *History of England* (Am. ed., 1901), G. M. Trevelyan's *England under Queen Anne* (London, 1930–34), and O. Klopp's *Der Fall des Hauses Stuart* (Vienna, 1875–1888) so completely cover the internal and external history of the period that every subsequent writer must stand in their shadow. But these three monumental works are not the only ones. Distinguished historians like Ranke, Feiling, Clark, Firth, and others have also found in the Glorious Revolution alluring subjects for their pens. Inevitably "corrections" of Macaulay, of Ranke, and of Klopp abound in the subsequent literature, further to humble the modern student approaching the subject.

obviously unsuited to be king; he was narrow, bigoted, and stubborn, and in spite of his undoubted administrative talents, he had no clear conception of his role as king of England.

The new ruler was greeted enthusiastically by the Tory party. A decade before, in the controversy over the Exclusion Bills, these gentlemen had taken an extreme position as defenders of divine right. Actually they, like the Whigs, were neither willing to re-establish Catholicism nor to support royal absolutism, but they had given the impression that they were ready tools of the royal will.[9] The Tories dominated James' first and only parliament, willingly voted him revenues much larger than his brother had enjoyed, and gave him money for an army to put down a rebellion headed by the late king's bastard son, Monmouth. But once the rebellion was crushed, they soon found themselves in conflict with James, for they were not willing to betray their church and their country to Roman Catholicism.

Monmouth's rebellion was a foolhardy adventure carried out by a reckless, stupid young man. The fact that the Whigs had, during the succession controversy, mentioned Monmouth as a possible heir to the throne led him to believe that he could count upon their support. Actually only a few country boys and a handful of the militia rallied to his cause. Professional soldiers, some of them loaned to James by William of Orange, quickly put down the revolt. Monmouth was beheaded, and the harsh reprisals taken against the hapless lads who had joined his standard were a warning to future rebels. Judge Jeffreys' "bloody assizes" resulted in wholesale executions, banishment, and even slavery for the victims. The grisly reminders of the king's justice, hanging on trees and gibbets in Hampshire, Dorset, and Somerset, were a shock to Englishmen even though they had not sympathized with the rebellion.[10]

The rebellion armed the king, but James made a mistake when he thought he could easily convert his soldiers to Catholicism and use them to suppress the liberties of the nation. Neither the priests nor the Catholic officers could convince the rank and file that papists should not be hanged along with rebels, and there was not time to rebuild the army with Irish recruits. Indeed, the introduction of Irishmen only further alienated the Protestant soldiery, who regarded their neighbors as an inferior race. On the other hand, parliament looked upon the army (and would have

[9] K. Feiling, *A History of the Tory Party, 1640–1710* (Oxford, 1924).

[10] Macaulay's description of the "bloody assize" makes one's blood run cold, but even though it was a terrible butchery, Macaulay overstated the case. Cf. Sir Charles Firth's *A Commentary on Macaulay's History of England* (London, 1938), 285–286.

done so even if it had not been illegally officered by Roman Catholics) as an unmitigated evil, and urged its disbandment. Despite the fact that the militia had proved to be practically useless in the rebellion, parliament proposed a militia reform in lieu of the standing army. James dismissed parliament rather than disband his army, and tried to rule the kingdom by himself.

The conflict between king and parliament ranged far beyond the simple question of the standing army. Ever since the civil wars the army had been under suspicion, but even more disconcerting was the fact that James had begun to install Catholics in high political as well as military places. With dismay the Tories saw their leaders deprived of office, and replaced by Catholics. This was in direct violation of the Test Act, but the courts decided that, in particular cases, the king could disregard even acts of parliament. Armed with this ruling, James used his royal power to excuse Catholics on a large scale from the requirements of the Test Act. In the army, in the municipal councils, and in the royal government officeholders were confronted with the choice of conversion to Catholicism or dismissal.

The crisis became acute when James issued a general Declaration of Indulgence according freedom of worship and opening the public service to Catholics and dissenters alike. The dissenters, who had as little use for Catholicism as the high-church Anglicans themselves, were thus invited to become allies of the king. In response to this move both the Tories and Whigs also began to talk toleration. The king could give the dissenters immediate relief; but only parliament could promise them permanent, legal toleration. The dissenters were in a seemingly favorable position, but they were reluctant to turn either way. The Church of England and parliament had not been generous to them in the past, while the Church of Rome had a record that promised little for the future.

The king's attack upon the established church not only relieved Catholics and dissenters of the disabilities of the Test Act, but led to war between James and the Anglican Church. When the clergy refused to read the Declaration of Indulgence to their parishioners, James imprisoned seven bishops and put them on trial for seditious libel. The sight of these men, God-fearing servants of the church and zealous supporters of divine right (five of them were Jacobites in later years!), as prisoners before the bar of justice seemed like monstrous evidence that no man was safe. The king's own soldiers asked their blessing and two of the royal judges advised the jury to find them innocent. Finally, the jury unanimously pronounced them "not guilty."

The birth of a male heir to the throne brought the issue to a climax. So long as James' Protestant daughters, Mary, the wife of William of Orange, and Anne, the wife of the prince of Denmark, were his legitimate successors, there was reason to assume that the effort to make England a Catholic country would end with the death of the king. But when James' second wife, Mary of Modena, gave birth to a son (June 10, 1688), the prospect of a Catholic succession and the eventual triumph of Catholicism became a perilous reality. The queen had so long been childless that the birth of the little prince, James Edward [11] seemed incredible. Professor Clark has aptly remarked, "In the seventeenth century people would believe anything. The Catholics thought it was a miracle, and the Protestants said it was an imposture. It was neither." [12]

James' army, his efforts to place Catholics in power, his attacks upon the church and the university,[13] and finally the birth of a male heir, made England ripe for revolt. Leaders of the opposing parties sank their differences, and strict advocates of divine right agreed to close an eye while the revolution was being accomplished. But James had an army of more than thirty thousand men. Its discipline had been stiffened in spite of the parliament's failure to pass a Mutiny Act, and the presence of Catholic officers and numerous Irish companies made it a formidable instrument. Without outside aid the opposition would have found it difficult to stage a successful insurrection. It was one thing to throw one's hat in the air and shout, "Hurrah," when William appeared with an army of continental veterans; it would have been quite a different thing to face the volleys of the royal redcoats led by resolute officers. Thus, though the crisis had come to a head when the seven bishops were brought to justice and when a Catholic male heir was born to the throne, it was in Holland, and ultimately in Europe as a whole, that the decisions for the English Revolution were made. Protestant England was unable to act alone. On June 30, 1688, the very day the bishops were acquitted, a group of leaders from both parties, including the bishop of London, sent an invitation to William of Orange requesting his aid against James.

The invitation to intervene in the English crisis came as no surprise to William, for he was fully informed about the situation in his father-in-law's kingdom. But William too was a firm believer in the prerogatives

[11] James III, the Old Pretender.

[12] G. N. Clark, *The Later Stuarts, 1660–1714, Oxford History of England* (Oxford, 1934), 121.

[13] He converted two Oxford colleges into Catholic seminaries. His policy was an attack on all ecclesiastical freeholds, a sure way to alienate the clergy, which had been willing to support him.

and rights of princes and, through his experience with the general estates, had become thoroughly distrustful of the wisdom of parliaments. He apparently hoped to wean James from his French and Catholic orientation and, if necessary, to force him to renounce them, and thereafter to secure the adherence of England to the coalition against France. Like James II, William fully believed that God had given him a mission, in his case to defend Protestantism and to check France. His intervention in English affairs was the result of European politics rather than of the domestic conflict in England.[14]

Protestantism was decidedly on the defensive in 1688. The revocation in 1685 of the Edict of Nantes, the succession of a Catholic prince to the Palatinate, the imperial victory over Hungarian and Transylvanian Protestants as well as over the Turk, all pointed to the continued vigor of the Catholic Church. If England were to become Catholic, Protestantism would be driven back to its last defenses. Even these were in danger, for Louis XIV had not yet given up hope of realizing his political ambitions in Europe. Sincere Protestants could not contemplate the ultimate victory of the persecutor of the Huguenots without fear for the future of their churches. Thus Protestantism as well as the balance of power, threatened by French aggression, could be served by Dutch intervention in English affairs. After July, 1688, William began seriously to raise an army and to prepare a fleet for a descent upon England. At the same time he protected his European flank by diplomatic negotiations extending from Rome to Stockholm. The Catholic emperor and the Catholic Pope, as well as Protestant princes of Germany and elsewhere, were brought within the scope of operations which culminated in the landing of an army composed of Swedes, Swiss, Germans, French Huguenots, Dutch, and Englishmen on the English shores.

It was the war in Hungary and the threat of war in western Europe that made possible the organization and eventually the embarkation of this army. Europe, including the Pope, knew that William planned to intervene in England, but Europe did nothing to prevent the invasion because Protestants approved of all measures that might keep England Protestant, while the Catholic enemies of France hoped to see William bring England into the great coalition. France did not move because Louis XIV believed the invasion would provoke civil war which would

---

[14] The correspondence with his two best friends and confidants provides a striking picture of William's political thinking. N. Japikse, *Correspondentie van Willem III en van Hans Willem Bentinck*, 3 vol. (1927); P. L. Muller, *Wilhelm III von Oranien und Georg Friedrich von Waldeck*, 2 vol. (Haag, 1873–80).

effectively eliminate both England and the Netherlands from high politics until he had achieved his objectives in central Europe. As soon as Louis marched his forces into the Rhineland [15] William persuaded the Dutch estates to let him sail for England. With French military pressure temporarily removed, it was deemed safe to send the army abroad in the hope that the stadholder could bring England into alliance with the United Netherlands.

It was a fateful decision that William had made. The stakes were high and the risk was great. The balance of power in Europe, the crown of England, and the cause of Protestantism were all at issue. A victory would mean a decisive check to French hegemony as well as a reform of the English constitution. Historians whose interest had been centered upon the development of parliamentary institutions in England have tended to forget that the constitution of Europe itself was determined by the revolution following William's landing on English soil, for with the wealth and military power of England behind the alliance against France, Louis XIV was forced to accept limitations to his ambition and power.

The English Revolution of 1688–1689 had about it an atmosphere of theatrical unreality which has not been dispelled even by the brilliant historical analyses it has evoked. James' last-minute attempt to regain his subjects' loyalty; the "Catholic" and "Protestant" winds that first impeded and then greatly aided the invading armada; the polyglot Protestant army marching through the muddy lanes of Devon in finery wilted by rain; the switch of plans made necessary when William did not land where he was expected; the hesitation with which men, already committed, joined his army; the indecision of the king, his attempted flight to France, his ludicrous hope of creating anarchy by throwing the great seal into the Thames, and his apprehension by Kentish fisherfolk; the disorder in London; the arrival of the Dutch blue guards to take the place of the redcoats; and finally the successful escape of the king across the Channel—all these events flitted through the last months of 1688 like a kaleidoscope and blur into confusion even in Macaulay's masterly account. Clear it is that William landed with the words "The liberties of England and the Protestant religion" added to the motto of the house of Orange, "I will maintain," and that about nine-tenths of the people were ready to welcome him as soon as they understood that Monmouth's unhappy experiment was not to be repeated. The king, betrayed even by his trusted commander Churchill (later Marlborough), sent his queen

15 Cf. Chapter Two.

and his son to France, and then followed them as soon as he could. James apparently feared his father's fate, and William did nothing to disabuse him, but rather facilitated his escape. With the king gone, there was nothing more to do but establish a government to replace him.

The Whigs were jubilant over this turn of events. Their theory was that the illegal conduct of the king had nullified the contract between people and sovereign and justified a rebellion. From this doctrine it followed that a new king, who would abide by the law, must be put in the place of the lawbreaking king. The Tories were not so happy. About half their chiefs had come around to the Whig position because they feared James might call a parliament, pack it with his own people, and force through laws that would legalize all his illegalities and make absolutism the recognized basis of the English constitution. The less conscientious Tories thought it expedient to make their doctrine fit their political needs. The more tender-minded of the party had accorded the tyrannical king the passive obedience taught by St. Paul, but they did not defend the tyrant when his enemies overwhelmed him. Now they were confronted with a political fact that made nonsense of their theories. If the baby James Edward were James II's son, then it was sacrilegious to place another on the throne, yet obviously neither James nor his infant son could be king and at the same time be exiled and at war with the kingdom. Some of the Tories met the dilemma by piously repeating the story that the child was an impostor, introduced into the queen's chamber in a warming pan; others by ignoring his existence; and others yet by becoming Jacobites and awaiting a legitimate restoration. The bulk of the nation, however, saw in William and his wife Mary the solution to the problem, and enthusiastically accepted the plan to make them king and queen of England.

It appears that William, when he set sail for England, did not foresee that his invasion would win him a crown. Both he and his English friends envisaged some sort of parliamentary regency that would compel James to govern the nation as it desired. Such a solution would undoubtedly have given the English constitution a turn toward parliamentary republicanism, for parliament could never again have trusted James, and it undoubtedly would have enthroned itself in both the executive and legislative spheres of government. James' flight and the decision to vest the crown in William and Mary made necessary a radical change in the Restoration constitution, though probably not so radical as it would have been had James remained king, for parliament was willing to trust

William and Mary with powers that could not have been safely given to a Catholic prince.

The "convention parliament" was a highly irregular body. In the first place, the elections were almost completely free, since there was neither a king nor a regular government to influence them. Secondly, the two parties had become accustomed to working together, and were not yet ready to split apart for partisan purposes. Finally, a considerable number of the members belonged to neither party; they were simply stout Protestants elected to parliament to save religion and the country. All this may help explain the fact that the "convention parliament" decided issues by common sense rather than by party prejudice.

The fundamental question of the Revolution of 1688 was the constitutional one: is the law above the king or the king above the law? Since James had been dethroned for altering the law, the answer was clear. Parliament, that is king, lords, and commons together, alone had the right to alter the law, and so constituted the supreme power in the state. Never again could a king hope to govern without parliament. At first sight this parliamentary change seems like a revival of the medieval *Stände* constitution of England; actually, by shifting the focus of real power from court to parliament, it provided a base for a strong central authority.

To prevent the abuses that Charles II had introduced by the Triennial Act of 1661, a new act of 1694 limited the duration of any one parliament to three years. Under the old law the king had been required to summon a new parliament within three years of the dissolution of its predecessor. Charles II had prolonged a "good" parliament indefinitely with the result that it ceased to represent public opinion. The new law made the electorate politically conscious, for every three years the politicians had to campaign for votes and defend their policy before their constituents. Thereby it contributed also to the development of political parties, and eventually to parliamentary government.

Two other problems ranked in importance with the constitutional one: the dynastic question and the religious question. The first was solved along Whig lines, the second, largely in a Tory manner.[16] The formula for the first, arrived at despite the conscientious scruples of the Tories, ran thus: ". . . King James the Second, having endeavored to subvert the Constitution of the Kingdom, by breaking the Original Contract between

---

[16] See the excellent brief discussion of the Revolutionary Settlement in G. M. Trevelyan, *The English Revolution, 1688–1689* (London, 1938), 143–187.

King and people [Whig political theory], and by the advice of Jesuits and other wicked persons having violated the fundamental laws and withdrawn himself out of the kingdom, hath abdicated the government [he did no such a thing, of course, but this thesis salved many Tory consciences] and that the throne is thereby vacant." This last statement completely ignored the baby, James Edward, but both parties conspired to ignore him because ". . . it hath been found by experience to be inconsistent with this Protestant Kingdom to be governed by a Popish prince." This, in effect, extended the Test Act to include the wearer of the crown as well as his servants.

If James Edward was an impostor, then Mary was the legitimate heir, but William, who had no personal claim to the throne, refused to be a prince consort, for his notions of the relationship between husband and wife precluded his ever playing a secondary role subordinate to any woman. Thus, when the crown was given to the couple jointly, the whole theory of divine right was scrapped. Tender-minded Tories did not accept William as their "rightful king," but rather as their *de facto* king." The Whigs, however, gladly accepted the opportunity to underwrite their doctrine that the king's position was dependent upon the contract between ruler and people. A considerable number (four hundred) of the clergy, including five of the bishops whom James had placed on trial, refused to take an oath to the new king. Churchmen stuck to the idea of divine right even though the "rightful" king appointed by God had shown no sympathy for their religious ideals.

The religious settlement was made largely according to Tory desires. Toleration was granted to dissenters, but the word "toleration" did not appear in the new law. The "Act for exempting their Majesties' Protestant subjects, differing from the Church of England, from Penalties of certain Laws" allowed all who would take the oaths of allegiance and supremacy and the oath against transubstantiation to absent themselves from church and to attend public worship in their own conventicles. Dissenting clergymen were given relief from the existing oppressive laws if they signed thirty-four of the thirty-nine articles of the Prayer Book. Special clauses made provision for Quakers and Baptists. Only Catholics and Unitarians remained beyond the pale: the first as dangerous to the state, the second as heretics. "To the modern mind," Trevelyan remarks, "this all seems silly and ungracious. Yet a more liberal bill . . . would either not have passed or would soon have been repealed . . . it would have

1. Louis XIV
From a painting by Mignard, Frick Art Reference Library

2. Leopold I
From a contemporary engraving by Jacob Gole,
Fogg Museum of Art

3. Innocent XI

From a contemporary engraving,
Metropolitan Museum of Art

4. John Sobieski, King of Poland

From a contemporary engraving by Peter Schenck,
Boston Public Library

5. The Siege of Ofen (Buda), 1686

From a contemporary engraving by Romeyn de Hooghe, Nationalbibliothek, Vienna

6. Print celebrating the victory of the Christian army at Belgrade, 1688

From a contemporary engraving in the style of Romeyn de Hooghe

7. Spahis and Janissaries

From a contemporary print,
University of Minnesota Library

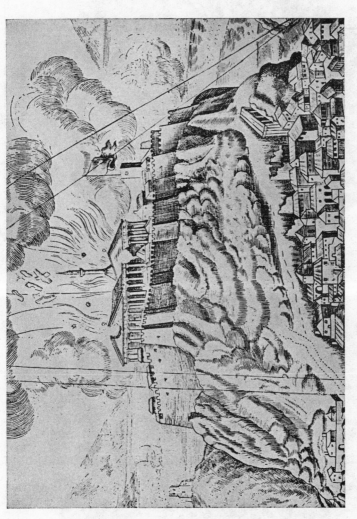

8. Destruction of the Parthenon, September 26, 1687

From a contemporary Venetian drawing

10. Anne of England

From a contemporary engraving of a Kneller portrait by
John Smith, Minneapolis Institute of Arts

9. William III

From a contemporary engraving by Peter Schenck,
Boston Public Library

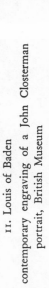

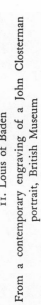

11. Louis of Baden

From a contemporary engraving of a John Closterman portrait, British Museum

12. Eugene of Savoy

From a contemporary engraving of a portrait painted by Jacques van Schuppen, Fogg Museum of Art

13. The Battle of Zenta,
1697

From a contemporary
engraving by Jan van
Huchtenburg, National-
bibliothek, Vienna

15. Charles II of Spain
From a contemporary engraving by Peter Schenck,
Boston Public Library

14. Maximilian-Emanuel of Bavaria
From a contemporary engraving by Hubert Spiess,
Metropolitan Museum of Art

16. Marlborough

From a contemporary engraving of a Kneller portrait
by Bernard Picart, Fogg Museum of Art

17. Marshal Villars

From a contemporary engraving of a Rigaud portrait by Pierre Drevet, Minneapolis Institute of Arts

18. The Battle of
Blenheim, 1704

From a contemporary
print by T. C. Marchant,
Albertina, Vienna

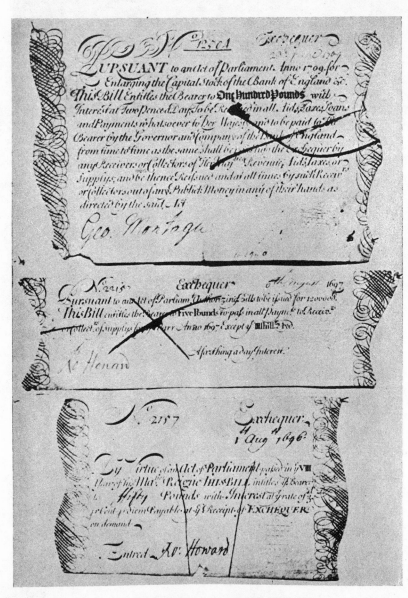

19. Exchequer Bills, Used for Tax Payments

20. The Battle of Malplaquet, 1709

From a contemporary print by Jan van Huchtenburg, Nationalbibliothek, Vienna

21. Charles III Landing at Barcelona
From a contemporary engraving by Paul Decker from the collection of
Dr. and Mrs. Dwight Minnich, Minneapolis

22. View of Stockholm
From a contemporary print, University of Minnesota Library

23. The Harbor at Amsterdam
By Ludolf Backhuyzen, Boston Museum of Fine Arts

24. Peter I

From a contemporary French print (Mariette) showing what Paris thought a well-dressed Russian monarch should wear. Metropolitan Museum of Art

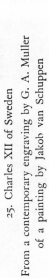

25. Charles XII of Sweden

From a contemporary engraving by G. A. Muller
of a painting by Jakob van Schuppen

26. Augustus the Strong of Saxony-Poland

From a contemporary engraving of a painting by
Anton Schoonjans

Prop. XXXIV. Prob. XIV.

*Invenire Variationem horariam inclinationis Orbis Lunaris ad
planum Eclipticæ.*

Defignent *A* & *a* Syzygias; *Q* & *q* Quadraturas; *N* & *n* No-
dos; *P* locum Lunæ in Orbe fuo; *p* veftigium loci illius in pla-
no Eclipticæ, & *m T l* motum momentaneum Nodorum ut fupra.
Et fi ad lineam *T m* demittatur perpendiculum *P G*, jungatur *p G*,

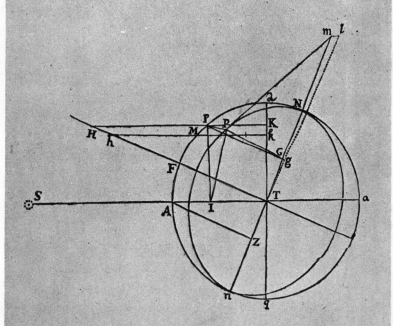

& producatur ea donec occurrat *T l* in *g*, & jungatur etiam *P g*:
erit angulus *P G p* inclinatio orbis Lunaris ad planum Eclipticæ, ubi
Luna verfatur in *P*; & angulus *P g p* inclinatio ejufdem poft momentum temporis completum, adeoque angulus *G P g* Variatio
Hhh   mo-

28. Sir Isaac Newton
From an engraving of a Kneller portrait,
New York Public Library

29. John Locke
From an engraving of a Kneller portrait by Robert Graves,
New York Public Library

30. Leibniz
From an engraving of a contemporary portrait,
New York Public Library

31. Fontenelle in his old age
From a contemporary engraving,
New York Public Library

32. Fénelon

From an eighteenth-century engraving by
J. B. Grateloup of a portrait by Vivien

33. Pierre Bayle

From a contemporary engraving by
E. Desrochers, New York Public Library

34. Bishop Bossuet

From a contemporary engraving by Gerard
Edelinck, adapted from a Rigaud portrait.
Minneapolis Institute of Arts

35. Antoine Watteau
From a contemporary drawing by Boucher

36. Jean Mabillon
From a contemporary engraving,
Nationalbibliothek, Vienna

37. Arcangelo Corelli
From a portrait by Hugh Howard,
Nationalbibliothek, Vienna

38. Versailles

From a contemporary engraving by P. Menant, New York Public Library

39. Versailles: The Fountain of Saturn
From a contemporary print by Maurice Baquoy, New York Public Library

40. Versailles: The Theater of the Waters
From a contemporary print in the collection of Dr. and Mrs. Dwight Minnich,
Minneapolis

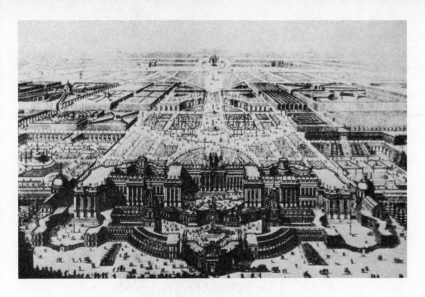

41. A Plan for a Royal Palace
Paul Decker's "Fürstliche Baumeister," 1711-1716

42. A Plan for a Palace Garden
Paul Decker's "Fürstliche Baumeister," 1711-1716

43. Tomb of Mazarin
Antoine Coysevox

44. Stage Setting for an Italian Opera
From a contemporary print by Antoine Buffagnotti, Metropolitan Museum of Art

45. Lady at the Clavier

From a contemporary print by N. Arnoult, Metropolitan Museum of Art

46. Sketches of Soldiers
By Antoine Watteau

47. Suzanne in the Bath
Painting by J. B. Santerre, Louvre, Paris

been impossible to induce either Tories or Whigs . . . to grant legal re-lief to Roman Catholics." [17]

The Revolution also marked a significant step in the development of an independent and impartial judiciary. One of William's first acts was to make judges irremovable—so long as they behaved properly. This practice was put on a statutory basis in the Act of Settlement of 1701, which came into force with the accession of George I in 1714. Thus the old Tudor idea that judges were "lions under the throne" gave way to the modern conception of the judge as the impartial arbiter of the laws. The new status of the courts led to the law of treason of 1695, which required two witnesses to an overt act of treason. "Henceforth," writes Trevelyan, "for the first time in our history, judicial murder ceased to be an ordinary weapon of politics and government." [18]

Important for the history of England and of all Europe were also the military and financial institutions that sprang from the Revolution. The Declaration of Right laid down the proposition that "the raising and keeping of a standing army within the Kingdom in time of Peace, unless it be with the consent of Parliament, is against the Law." But parliamen-tary control over the army was greatly extended by the passage, at first for only seven months, of the Mutiny Act of 1689. Thereafter it became customary to re-enact the law annually. Thus, so long as parliament ap-proved of the king's policy, his soldiers could be kept under discipline; if parliament disapproved of the royal course, there would be no sanction.[19] Parliament never again had to claim the right to control the army, be-cause it knew that for all practical purposes the army's existence de-pended upon its will.

The financial arrangements of the Revolution laid the foundation for the mobilization of England's wealth in the national interest. A specific sum was given to William for his personal use, the beginning of the mod-ern "civil list." The rest of the budget was appropriated on an annual basis, after examination by parliament of the needs of the government. William, who entertained continental notions about the rights of princes and never quite understood or sympathized with the English constitution as it was developing, wrote to his friend Waldeck in the Netherlands, "I

[17] *Ibid.,* 168.
[18] *Ibid.,* 182.
[19] It is true that parliament neglected to pass a Mutiny Act for two years after the Peace of Ryswick, and that discipline was not broken in the army. But that same parliament had also greatly reduced the size of the army, sent home William's Dutch soldiers, and to all intents and purposes controlled, financially at least, the remaining military establishment.

am persuaded that you and I have on our hands the most troublesome affairs in all Europe." [20] Nonetheless, the new system produced important results: when the treasury officials each year presented their budget, they educated the squires so that parliament, in full sympathy with their policy, freely granted the necessary funds. Furthermore, when the costs of war mounted beyond the income, the resulting debts were national debts, which, though they would have bankrupted a king, did not endanger the solvency of the state. The parliaments of the two great wars (1688–1714) made grants of money which proved decisive in the contest of power provoked by Louis XIV.[21]

Like all constitutional provisions the legal innovations of the Revolution of 1688 provided only a frame within which the form of government could be fitted. Neither William nor his successor Anne was a monarch who willingly surrendered the right to rule, and there was nothing in the settlements of 1689 that deprived them of control over administration. Parliament's consent was necessary, but parliament neither formulated policy nor named the king's officials. The ruler, therefore, retained much power, for England at the end of the seventeenth century was governed in the counties by royally appointed lords lieutenant, justices of the peace, and sheriffs who were all in a position to exert considerable influence upon parliamentary elections. These county officials, however, were not bureaucratic servants of the king; they were local lords and squires who owned land in the counties which they administered. Thus, so long as the king's ministers appointed country gentlemen who approved their policy, the government could reasonably expect to control parliament. Nonetheless, it remains a fact that English rulers in the early eighteenth century had to consider the interests and opinions of many more individuals than does a prime minister of the twentieth century.

William and Anne called men to their government who were in sympathy with their policy, but these men, in turn, had to secure the support of parliament. The system worked two ways. On the one side the ministers influenced elections to assure a parliamentary majority; on the other the king chose men who had a following in parliament. In the course of time the party system, which had been developing for a half century, became established in English politics. The old idea that the representatives in parliament must be either of the court party, which supported the

20 Firth, *op. cit.,* 342.
21 Cf. Chapter Seven for a discussion of England's fiscal system.

king, or of the country party, which suspiciously watched the doings of the king's placemen, gave way to the Whig and Tory dichotomy of political opinion.

The Whigs, still associated with the Roundheads of the previous generation, had a clean-cut political philosophy, cogently expressed by John Locke, which gave the bankers, merchants, dissenters, and Whig lords who organized and supported the party an advantage over the squires, parsons, and Tory lords. The Tories, with their Cavalier background, were weakened by the very facts of the Revolution. Practically all of them believed in divine right and had Jacobite leanings, more emotional and religious than political, which placed them in an ambiguous position. For, combined with Jacobitism, went a bigoted defense of the church that James II and his son had repudiated. The Tories never could love William; Anne they could accept by assuring themselves that she *was* the heir and that James Edward was an impostor. The Hanoverian succession, which alone could save their church, was a break with divine right that continued to bother their consciences.

Both William and Anne attempted to govern by calling ministers from both parties. William acted as his own first minister; Anne tried to rule through her friends, Marlborough and Godolphin. The Whigs, however, were more fully committed to the wars than the Tories. The fox-hunting squires were isolationist and antiforeign in their attitudes, while the financiers, merchants, and soldiers in the Whig camp better understood the great international issues and the interests of England. Therefore, both William and later the Godolphin-Marlborough government ended by installing the Whig party in office. But when Anne lost sympathy with the policies of the Marlborough-Godolphin ministry, the residual royal power became clearly manifest. The queen had never liked the Whigs whom Godolphin, Marlborough, and Sarah Churchill had forced upon her to assure the success of the war. When she became convinced that her kingdom's interests demanded a change, she was able, in the face of a Whig majority in both lords and commons, to dismiss the ministry and give the staff of office to the Tories. The latter, after changing officials and using pressure and propaganda in the counties, called new elections and secured a Tory majority in commons. The queen appointed enough new peers to give them control of the house of lords as well. There is no better illustration of the functioning of the political process under these last Stuarts than the fortunes of this Marlborough-Godolphin ministry. It began largely Tory; the needs of the war made it Whig; the will of the queen ended its life and its war policy.[22]

Yet the role of parliament in government was considerable, and gradually parliament, rather than the court, became the center of political activity. Lobbyists, petitioners, and all the tribe that hoped for favor from government had formerly fawned upon the king's favorites and ministers, but after 1688 they buzzed around parliament. The result, considering the nature of parliamentary elections, was just what one might expect: corruption on a broad scale. Bribery and peculation had always been common at court, and in the eighteenth century, under the new system of government, venality settled in parliament. Such corrupt practices shocked later generations who had other standards of political morality, but in an age when diplomats and soldiers did not blush to take bribes from the enemy, when ministers assumed that money would cross their palms for a political favor, when the surest road to great wealth was to become a minister of state, political morality in England was evidently not out of line with that of other European countries.

When England accepted a new king and queen, with a revised constitution, a question immediately arose concerning the other lands formerly under James' rule. In the American colonies, particularly in Massachusetts and New York, where James had curtailed the activity of elective assemblies, the colonists revolted against the authority of the governor and reestablished their "liberties and rights," after which they recognized the new government in England with the tacit understanding that it would not reassert the late king's royal prerogatives. In a sense, the flight of James II postponed the American Revolution, for the colonists had been in open conflict with his officials, and had already voiced claims that savored of independence.

In Ireland, the deposition of a Catholic king meant the return of religious persecution as well as economic enslavement. The Irish had little reason to expect much from William and they were therefore willing to try to re-establish James even if it meant war. The result was that William and the "Orange" party reconquered Ireland with military force and subjected the population to an oppressive regime that drove a steady stream of Irish youth, filled with hatred of England, to enlist in the French army.

[22] The Tory attitude toward the war was partly economic. The country squires paid the land tax (cf. Chapter Six) while the city Whigs loaned money, received interest from it, and presumably would eventually recover their principal. Cf. Chapter Three.

In Scotland the outcome of the Revolution was more fortunate. James II of England was James VII of Scotland, the two kingdoms forming a dual monarchy bound together by the person of the king and by common reliance upon the navy. Although there was no legal reason why his dethronement in England should have cost James his Scottish throne, the same forces that provoked rebellion in England were at work in Scotland also. In England the Reformation had left the old church organization intact; both Puritan and Anglican understood and accepted the proposition that the state controlled the church, and that therefore parliament decided religious issues. The Revolution of 1688 merely established the right of parliament to control the religious structure. The Scottish Reformation, however, had set the kirk free of both king and parliament and had thereby erected a third power in the kingdom that was at once democratic and tyrannical. The Scots, unable to control the crown, had created a Calvinist church under the control of laymen and ministers, more or less free from the episcopal power. The Scottish parliament never developed the vitality of the English, so the Scottish kirk had to fight for its rights or submit to the king. The kirk claimed to represent the people. The crown, on the other hand, built up support for itself by defending the individual against the inquisitorial kirk. The Scottish Tories were tolerationists and anticlericals, who resisted the attempts of preachers and elders to dictate their lives. Had the later Stuart kings played their religious cards well, they might have succeeded in establishing their authority on the grounds that the crown alone could defend the individual's rights against the stiff-necked Calvinistic clergy, but Charles II re-established an episcopal organization that showed little more humanity than did the Presbyterian zealots, and James II tried to reintroduce Roman Catholicism, thereby antagonizing both Episcopalian Tories and Presbyterian Whigs.

The Tories were unwilling either to defend or to resist James, but the Whigs, with less tender consciences, imitated their English neighbors by dethroning him and then calling William and Mary to the throne. All Scotland, however, did not accept the Revolution. The highlands, inhabited by wild, militant clans whose taste for war and plunder was mixed with primitive conceptions of loyalty to their chiefs and king, refused to submit. In the summer of 1689, at the pass of Killiecrankie, an army of wild swordsmen from the hills hacked William's troops to pieces. Only the death of Dundee, their leader, prevented them from following up their advantage. It was many years before the power of the new government extended beyond the highland line to the clans whose chiefs decided what their allegiance should be. In the eastern lowlands the abolition of the Episcopal Church organization created a substantial minority that provoked unrest for over a generation.

The Scottish Revolution created a difficult problem for government on the British island. For the first time in generations the Scottish parliament had achieved an independent and active status. From time immemorial the king had been able to control its business, but in 1689, parliament freed itself of royal influence and assumed the right to discuss and pass any law—subject to royal veto—that it wished. This greatly weakened the political dependency of Scotland on England, and Scotland thenceforth adopted policies different from those of its neighbor. Indeed, early in Queen Anne's reign, the Scottish parliament announced that the succession to the Scottish crown would be decided in Edinburgh, and that the Hanoverian successor to the English throne would not be recognized in Scotland. It was not improbable that the Scots might choose the Pretender.

This manifesto of Scottish independence was a decisive factor in promoting the union of England and Scotland. William had suggested union before he died, and several times early in Anne's reign the issue had been raised, but in neither kingdom was there sufficient support for it. Faced by the prospect of the Pretender's mounting the Scottish throne, the English parliament therefore passed an act declaring that all Scotsmen would be treated as aliens in England and that the importation of Scottish goods would be prohibited unless the succession of the Scottish crown were settled by Christmas, 1705 in a manner satisfactory to England. In the same act, the queen was empowered to appoint commissioners to negotiate for the union of the two kingdoms. The threat had the desired result: the Scots had no real alternative to the treaty of 1707 which united the two kingdoms under one crown and one parliament. Scotland's religious institutions, her courts of law, the privileges of her royal burghs and the feudal jurisdiction of her nobility and landed gentry were guaranteed against English interference, and freedom of trade was assured for the whole kingdom. In spite of the obviously favorable nature of this agreement, it met vigorous opposition in Scotland. The clergy petitioned; the city populace rioted; the treaty was publicly burned. Nonetheless, it did pass, and Scotland and England became the United Kingdom. This was not the least important of the results that flowed from the Revolution of 1688.

The "Glorious Revolution" of 1688 was not completely fixed in the

English system until George I mounted the throne in 1714. The death of
the young duke of Gloucester (1700), the only surviving son of Princess
Anne, left the succession in doubt, since it was obvious that Anne could
not bear another child. There were three possible heirs: James Edward,
son of James II; the duke of Savoy, grandson of Charles I; and Electress
Sophia and her son George, issue of a daughter of James I. To take the
"warming pan" prince, James Edward, was impossible. The Whigs would
not hear of it, the Tories could not do it, and in 1701 neither William
nor Anne would tolerate it. The Savoyard prince was out of favor because of his shifty policy in the late war, while both Electress Sophia and
her son were in high favor as trustworthy allies. Sophia had at first sided
with James II for, like most of her contemporaries, she believed in divine
right. But the philosopher Leibniz and William III had eventually persuaded her to become a candidate for the throne which parliament alone
could offer her and her family.

In 1701 the English parliament passed the Act of Settlement. The Tories, looking forward to Anne's reign, were no longer actively Jacobite
and the Whigs were anxious to assure the retention of their formula. The
act bound not only the succession, but also the new dynasty. Future rulers
were obliged to join the Anglican Church, to agree not to engage England in a war without parliament's consent, and to promise not to leave
the British Isles without parliamentary permission. Foreigners were excluded from parliament, the privy council and certain civil and military
offices, and were not to be granted land. No pardon under the great seal
could prevent impeachment by commons; judges were to have life tenure
and fixed salaries, and to be removable only by an address of both houses
of parliament. Members of the house of commons were forbidden to accept offices or pensions from the crown, and all business was to be trans-
acted before the privy council. These last two conditions were repealed
before Anne's death; they would have prevented the development of the
cabinet system that was already customary in her time. The fear and suspicion of the "court" entertained by the "country" broke down with the
further evolution of the party structure.

It was one thing to regulate the succession, another to assure it. As
long as Anne lived she would not agree to any of the Hanoverians being
invited to England, and there was a strong group that was committed to
James Edward as the rightful heir. Even Anne herself entertained doubts
about the "warming pan" theory which allowed her conscience no rest
while she ruled England. Furthermore, at the critical moment, that is

during Anne's last illness, the government of England was in Tory hands, and at a time when the Tories were shifting rapidly in a Jacobite direction. Bolingbroke was in communication with the Pretender and had placed Jacobites in high military and civil offices, so that the restoration of James' son might be easily accomplished. But James Edward stood in his own way. Unlike so many of the unscrupulous rulers of his age, the Stuart Pretender refused to forsake his religion. On his part Bolingbroke realized that he could not place a Catholic on the English throne.

The crisis and a possible civil war was averted when, in the last days of Anne's illness, the middle party members of the privy council secured the appointment of the duke of Shrewsbury to the treasury and, together with the Whig lords who were members of the privy council, prepared orders for the defense of the realm against invasion. Half the members of the privy council were to some degree Jacobite in their feelings, but when Queen Anne died, George I was proclaimed king of England, and a civil war was averted. The new government immediately took control, and the reign of George I opened a new era. From the Revolution of 1688 and the two great wars that followed it, Hanoverian England inherited both a stable government and a powerful position in the world.

III. THE DUTCH REPUBLIC AND THE VENETIAN OLIGARCHY

The Republic of the Netherlands suffered from the wars of this period to an extent that seriously impaired its power and prestige. For over a century the republic had played a major role in European affairs: its ships had sailed the seven seas, its armies and navies had crossed swords with those of Spain, England, and France, and its bankers and merchants had made Amsterdam the economic capital of Europe. With its colonies and trading posts in Asia, Africa, and America, the republic had been a formidable competitor for power throughout the seventeenth century. After the Treaties of Utrecht, however, this proud position was never regained. With a navy rotting in harbor, a treasury overloaded with debt, a people burdened with taxes, and markets sharply contested by rivals, the republic of the dykes had to adjust to a more modest role in the councils of Europe. The Dutch continued to be important as bankers, merchants, and diplomats, but they could no longer deal with the great powers as equals.[23]

Fundamental to the weakening of the republic's international position were the revolutionary changes that raised the requirements for great-

[23] C. Wilson, *Anglo-Dutch Commerce and Finance in the Eighteenth Century* (1941).

power status. With less than three million inhabitants and a tiny strip of land painfully held against the sea, even the ingenuity of Dutch craftsmen, merchants, and bankers, the stubbornness of Dutch soldiers, sailors, and statesmen, and the liberalism of the Dutch constitution could not maintain the republic's pre-eminence. Internal problems, too, contributed to the decay of the republic's power. The great wars between 1688 and 1713 left the country with a crushing debt that weakened its credit, while politically the death of William III left the nation divided.[24]

The United Netherlands was a federation of provinces, born of Renaissance political theory and quite out of keeping with later conceptions of the Leviathan state. Its political life rested upon an oligarchy of patrician families whose position and power were founded upon wealth. Each municipality of the seven provinces elected a panel of regents who, when assembled at the provincial level, constituted the provincial estate. The provincial estates, in turn, sent representatives to the states-general, which governed the affairs of the federation. The states-general appointed an executive council, but most business was referred to the states-general itself. In each province a salaried officer, the pensionary, acted as governor, the pensionary of Holland being the grand pensionary who, with the stadholder, was one of the most important men in the state. The role of the stadholder himself was not clearly defined. Each province, theoretically, had its own; in several of them the office was hereditary in the house of Orange, while in the rest of the provinces the prince of Orange was usually elected to the office. The stadholder was captain general of the army and navy, and his authority overlapped that of the pensionary at many points. In times of stress he became virtually an uncrowned king.

From the time of his triumph over the De Witts (1672) until his death in 1702, William III, as stadholder, ruled the Netherlands almost without opposition. "William III," writes Blok, "monarch without a title, had during his absence allowed his trusted friends or creatures to rule over the country. The 'republicans' had not ventured to lift their voices against the abuses of the prince's favorites. . . ."[25] Nonetheless, opposition to the house of Orange, which was almost traditional, had not been entirely exterminated. The proud patrician "republicans" submitted to William's *coup d'état* and to the imperious necessities of the wars, but the spirit of the De Witts was still active. Upon the death of the great stadholder the "republicans" proceeded to take their revenge, and for a

24 E. Baasch, *Holländische Wertschaftsgeschichte* (Jena, 1927), 174 ff.
25 P. J. Blok, *History of the People of the Netherlands* (New York and London, 1898–1912), Am. ed., V, 3.

whole decade the cities and provinces of the Netherlands were subject to sporadic outbursts of party strife and violence.

The "republicans" were unwilling to elect another stadholder. William's heir, the prince of Orange-Nassau, was too young to aspire to the honor in 1702, and even though his prestige as a soldier grew during the War of the Spanish Succession, all efforts to install him as stadholder failed, and his untimely death in 1711 prevented the king of Prussia and others from imposing him upon the states-general. The republic fought the great war and governed itself for a whole generation without a stadholder. During the conflict Marlborough acted as captain general of the combined Anglo-Dutch armies, the Dutch politicians allowing him command over their troops so long as he respected the wishes of the political commissars attached to them. The states-general thus asserted its right to be the policy-making body of the state and re-affirmed the power of the bourgeois oligarchy.

In the years following the peace of Utrecht, the posthumous heir of Orange-Nassau was again too young to influence policy, and the republican faction was unwilling to change the constitution to meet the requirements of eighteenth-century politics. Lacking a stadholder to build up military power, loaded with debt and oppressive taxation, and unable to maintain its commercial hegemony the United Netherlands sank to the position of a second-rate power, dependent upon England for the defense of its empire beyond the seas.

The Venetians were even less fortunate than the Dutch in adapting themselves to the new conditions of the late seventeenth century. The ancient constitution of the republic had worked well in less highly organized times, when the center of economic gravity was still in the Mediterranean, but it was badly suited to the era of great bureaucratic military powers. Moreover, like the Dutch, the Venetians found themselves weighed down with the debts incurred by their seventeenth-century wars. Their enemy had been the Ottoman Empire, rather than the French, and even though they were ultimately victorious, their triumph was to be short-lived. Venice had lost her commanding naval position and much of her commercial power and was therefore unable to maintain her conquest of the Morea or her dominance in the Levant. The republic lasted out the eighteenth century, but her antiquated constitution, her unstable economic situation, and her military weakness doomed her to a minor role in the political structure of Europe.

IV. SPAIN IN DECLINE

Spain had been the great power of the sixteenth century, but within a hundred years had become practically impotent. Pedro de Valencia had written to Philip III in the mid-seventeenth century: "The greatest need of kings is men, not land and much less gold. Since the population has fallen by more than half, Your Majesty has lost more than half your realm." [26] This contemporary judgment was exaggerated but was nevertheless in line with the trend of development; in the mid-sixteenth century Spain had had a population of seven to seven and a half millions; by the end of the seventeenth century it had fallen to four or four and a half millions. The kingdom had lost its vitality and its power.

The reasons for this dramatic failure of the population to reproduce were economic, biological and moral, as well as political. Disastrous monetary practices corrupted the currency so that commerce, agriculture, and industry all suffered severely.[27] High taxes both on agriculture and on manufacturing forced the inhabitants of whole villages to abandon the land, and ruined one industry after another. The Spanish fiscal system was vicious, complex and crippling, yet the yield to the king's treasury was too small to meet ordinary expenses. At the death of Charles II there was hardly enough in the treasury to pay the funeral expenses and the usual masses.

The biological decline in the Spanish branch of the Hapsburg family was a factor of paramount importance because of the role played by the king in the whole imperial system. Charles I had been both a king and a soldier; Philip II had been a king; Philip III and Philip IV had at least looked like kings; but Charles II was hardly a man.[28] Throughout the seventeenth century the royal family had showed a progressive deterioration in virility and intelligence, and the court reflected the decay of the ruling family. A mad march of loose women, priests, grandees, and adventurers, all apparently moved by selfish aims, preyed upon the progressive weakmindedness of the monarch.

The nobility showed no more vigor than the court. Most of the grandees managed somehow to retain enough wealth to support their preten-

[26] R. Konetzke, *Geschichte des spanischen und portugiesischen* (Leipzig, 1939), 260–61.
[27] Many Spaniards welcomed the fact that the War of the Spanish Succession brought foreign armies into Spain because the soldiers brought good coins with them. E. J. Hamilton, *War and Prices in Spain 1651–1800* (Cambridge, Mass., 1947), 36 ff.
[28] The most recent biography of Charles II is by L. Pfandl, *Karl II, Das Ende der spanischen Machtstellung in Europa* (Munich, 1940). It leans heavily upon Prinz Adalbert von Bayern, *Das Ende der Habsburger in Spanien* (Munich, 1929), 2 vols.

sions but the lesser nobility vegetated in pride and poverty. Their status forbade their engagement in trade, for even though royal edicts proclaimed their noblemen might enter business without loss of social position, they failed to break the prejudice against the market place. With openings in the army and the government becoming fewer with every decade, and with the decline in the agricultural population upon which they relied for their income, poor noblemen therefore found no opportunity to recoup their fortunes. Some of the grandees were caught up in this same net of circumstance and, like their poorer brethren, maintained their pride, though little else. Furthermore, the economic decadence of the ruling class brought in its train a moral crisis. The grandsons of the conquerors of the New World and the rulers of Europe either became adventurers seeking their outside chance, or moodily despaired of reestablishing their position.

The political structure of Spain was yet another factor in its degeneration. Charles I had not really united the kingdom. The laws, constitutions, and customs of the feudal kingdoms of the Iberian peninsula had been left intact, and the Hapsburg government had merely added a central authority to what remained a federal system. So long as the kings were strong men, the councils of the royal government functioned smoothly, but by the end of the seventeenth century the several states were in process of regaining independence from the royal authority.

This development was one of the principal problems confronting the first Bourbon king. The grandees and nobility had welcomed the grandson of Louis XIV because they believed that French armies would defend the Spanish empire. When Philip V introduced French centralization as well as French troops, many of the ancient families who had benefited from the loose structure of the kingdom joined the Austrian pretender, Charles III. The kingdom had become used to a weak central government, and although that government was responsible for many of the evils that beset them, the great ones of the land wanted no master who would really rule.

The death of Charles II only aggravated the problems of the kingdom, for during the next decade two kings, each supported by foreign troops, attempted to validate their claims to the inheritance. Under such circumstances no real recovery was possible. Philip V and his vigorous queen succeeded in winning for themselves substantial support in all classes of society and, with the aid of French arms, to gain the military and political victories that excluded Charles III from the throne. It was not, however, until after 1713 that the centralizing tendencies, inherent in the Bourbon tradition, could make significant progress. Philip's French advisers laid the groundwork for reform and recovery, but the changes that enabled Spain to maintain itself in the eighteenth century came only after 1714.

Chapter Five

THE HAPSBURG MONARCHY AND MIDDLE EUROPE

I. THE RISE OF THE DANUBIAN STATE

THE wars with France and the imperial victories on the Danube strengthened the power of the Hapsburg emperor without rejuvenating the Holy Roman Empire. The treaties of Westphalia and Nijmegen had endowed the German princes with sovereign powers and had thereby destroyed the old ideas of the federal empire. Though the imperial crown still carried with it a complex of honors, perquisites, and privileges, it had lost all real power. By the turn of the eighteenth century Voltaire's description of the Empire as neither holy, nor Roman, nor empire was a reasonably accurate characterization of the ineffectual political structure that supposedly ruled central Europe. But out of the ashes of the old were arising new political institutions. The decay of the imperial power had revealed the basic weakness of the federal structure: each land [1] had its own constitution, its own institutions, and, to a surprising degree, its own laws. In the old feudal empire these differences had been reconciled by the loose confederation, which vested in the emperor and the diet powers sufficient to deal with defense and common policy. But by the seventeenth century these powers, emasculated by successive treaties, were no longer sufficient to meet the problems of the age.

Since physical geography influenced but slightly the organization of political units in central Europe, it is not surprising that new political forms should have reflected purely dynastic interests. The territorial sovereigns who emerged in the seventeenth century quite naturally responded to the tendencies of their age and attempted to consolidate their powers into princely absolutism. The more important of them ruled over several lands, each of which had its own constitution and laws. This meant that their first problem was to co-ordinate and integrate the territories to which God had appointed them. At first glance this would not appear to have been difficult, but in reality it proved to be the key problem of Germany. The populace of the various lands recognized the divine right

[1] The word *land* is perhaps the best English equivalent of the German term *Land*.

of their prince, but the landed aristocracy and the *Landtage* (diets), representing the *Stände* (estates) of the province vigorously opposed princely encroachments upon their traditional rights. The princes who defended "German liberties" against the sixteenth- and seventeenth-century emperors later met corresponding opposition to their own rule in the name of the traditional "liberties" of their lands. It was difficult to teach provincials to see their destiny in terms of interests that transcended their own birthplaces.

Englishmen and Frenchmen had long since been taught to identify their loyalties to the ruling house with allegiance to the entire kingdom. The lesson had, to be sure, been only imperfectly learned even in seventeenth-century England and France, but it was sufficiently rooted in the articulate classes to give those kingdoms unity. Germans, on the other hand, were called upon for loyalty to political units that had no rational geographical or cultural basis, that were mere segments carved from the mass of central Europe by the accidents of inheritance. The concept of the Prussian state, of the Bavarian state, or of the Hanoverian state corresponded neither to the old tribal unities of Franconia, Swabia, etc., nor to any geographical features. Such states were nothing but the expression of dynastic interests, supported by the efforts of the civil and military bureaucracy.

The formation of organic political units from the minute particularism of central Europe was only imperfectly accomplished in most of the lands. The dynastic cast of politics led to impossible experiments, like the attempt to combine the Saxon with the Polish crown. In many smaller lands the territorial base was too narrow to permit more than a brutal absolutism or a freakish political structure. Only in Prussia and the Hapsburg lands could the ideas and the aims of central European statesmen reach their fullest development, and it was the rise of these two united states (*Gesamtstaat*) that created the dualism which dominated central European history in the eighteenth and nineteenth centuries.

The complexity and heterogeneity of the political structure ruled over by the German house of Hapsburg makes its history difficult to expound. The chief problem arose from the fact that there was no inner urge, no natural community of interest, no common outlook underlying the political union of the ancient kingdoms of Hungary and Bohemia and the German inheritance of the Hapsburgs. From the fateful battle of Mohács (1526), when the frightened Bohemian and Hungarian nobility looked to the Hapsburgs for salvation, to the catastrophic *Götterdäm-*

merung of 1917–18, pressures from without rather than cohesive forces within dictated the development of the Danubian Monarchy. The historical connection between the house of Hapsburg and the imperial dignity further complicated the problem of government, for no small part of Hapsburg prestige came from the imperial crown, and yet the imperial prerogatives, such as they were, were constantly challenged in Germany and in Europe. Yet out of a heterogeneous collection of provinces and kingdoms with different languages and cultures, and out of their shadowy pretensions to imperial dignity the Hapsburgs created the state that defended central Europe successively against Turkish, Swedish, French, German, and Russian aggression, and was overwhelmed only by the avalanche of 1914–1918.[2]

Ferdinand I (1503–1554) had begun the work of shaping a state from the kingdoms, lands, counties, and towns that depended upon his house for protection, but in the later sixteenth century the persisting idea that these territories were a patrimonial inheritance rather than a single political complex had led to their partition among several heirs. With the Turkish danger somewhat relaxed, the imperative necessity for unity had disappeared; it was not until the opening of the seventeenth century, when a historical accident endowed Ferdinand II with most of the titles and crowns of his forefathers, that the ideal of a Hapsburg state, in contradistinction to a patrimonial inheritance, again emerged. Ferdinand II (emperor 1619–1637), the conqueror of Bohemia and the champion of the Counter Reformation, was in fact the founding father of the Danubian Monarchy. Leopold I and his sons, whose reigns fall within the scope of this book, came chronologically halfway between the emperor who fought the Thirty Years' War and the great reformers Maria Theresa and Joseph II, who consolidated the Hapsburg state in the later eighteenth century. Leopold reconquered Hungary, and his son, Charles VI, proclaimed the Pragmatic Sanction. These two events were significant links in the chain of development that made the Hapsburg inheritance a great power.

In 1680, however, there was no reason to believe that Leopold I would achieve the great political and military victories that were to be the foundation of the new state. The dignity of the imperial crown was threadbare, and whatever prestige it still enjoyed seemed destined soon

[2] The best modern discussions: H. Hantsch, *Die Entwicklung Österreich-Ungarns zur Grossmacht* (Freiburg, 1933), and J. Redlich, *Das Werden einer Grossmacht; Österreich von 1700 bis 1740*, rev. ed. (Leipzig, 1942).

to pass to the house of Bourbon, for Louis XIV practically controlled a majority in the electoral college and planned to name a prince of his own family as the next King of the Romans. With a Hungarian revolt and the threat of Turkish invasion in the east, and with French annexations in the Rhineland, the position of the Hapsburgs was decidedly insecure. Even the birth of a son in 1678 did little to reassure Leopold, for he had already buried a wife and several sons and had no reason to believe that the child Joseph would necessarily reach maturity. It is small wonder that the Leopold of 1680 was a moody, morose, irresolute, priest-ridden character, convinced that God had withdrawn protection from the imperial house. A few years later, when his armies had reconquered the Danube basin and contained the marshals of France, when he saw his son crowned hereditary king of Hungary as well as king of the Romans, and when, allied with England and the Netherlands, he was fighting a great war to place his second son on the throne of Spain, Leopold the pious and stubborn presented a less lugubrious figure to the world.

The victory over the Turks and the subsequent conquest of Hungary reversed dramatically the fortunes of the Hapsburgs. Leopold's predecessors had reduced Bohemia and the German lands to submission; now he himself subjugated Hungary and imposed changes upon that kingdom's ancient constitution. The battle of Mohács and the pressure of Islam had united Germans, Bohemians, and Hungarians under Hapsburg rule, but it was not until Hungary was effectively integrated with the other Hapsburg lands that the political complex on the Danube emerged as a great power. Just as in France Richelieu and his successors, in England, the Glorious Revolution, and in Russia the Petrine Revolution struck heavy blows at the medieval constitutions of those states and fortified the central authority, so the revolution in Hungary destroyed much of the antiquated constitution of that kingdom and laid the foundation for its incorporation in the larger unity of the Danubian Monarchy.

When Leopold came to the throne, Hungary was more of a liability than an asset to his government. The Turkish conquests of the preceding century had split the kingdom into three parts: Hapsburg Hungary, Turkish Hungary, and Transylvania, of which the two latter were lost to the crown of St. Stephen. In Turkish Hungary the pashas had been content to rule and collect taxes, without attempting to colonize the land or convert the population to Islam. Many of the old families, it is true, had lost their properties as the result of unsuccessful revolts, but most of the land was still held by Christian noblemen, while in the cities and towns the Christian and Jewish populations greatly outnumbered the Moslem. Turkish rule was generally mild and it is quite probable that there was less unrest in Turkish Hungary than in either of the other parts.[3] Transylvania enjoyed a large degree of autonomy under Turkish overlordship; its diet elected a native prince, but the real power remained in the hands of the great landed magnates.

The organization of Hapsburg Hungary suggested a frontier province, unable to develop stable institutions because of the proximity of the enemy. While the politically articulate elements recognized their dependence upon the Hapsburgs for protection, they were fiercely proud of their traditions of liberty and resentful of any display of absolutism. Ancient custom as well as the military organization of the kingdom made revolt easy and relatively safe until Leopold showed a seventeenth-century tendency to take severe reprisals. But even Leopold encountered difficulties in a land where Turkish raiders made fortification and military preparedness imperative. The whole kingdom was interlaced with forts, most of them simple stockades similar to the outposts which nineteenth-century Americans built against the Indians, but reinforced at strategic points with formidable towers capable of sustaining a prolonged siege. The key fortifications were garrisoned by more or less disciplined soldiers, drawn from the western lands of the Hapsburgs, but the simpler forts were manned by local noblemen and a kind of primitive militia, leading a life not unlike that of the robber barons of the Middle Ages. These troops defended the frontier and staged raids—retaliatory, of course—into Turkish Hungary. Furthermore, they were always on hand to defend Hungarian "liberties" against the Hapsburgs, especially if rebellion promised monetary reward. They called themselves "Kuruz" or crusaders, but their unruly habits, their passionate defense of their "rights," and their almost complete lack of political responsibility made them more like characters in a Hollywood "western" than soldiers of the cross.

The Hungarian problem was further complicated by the identification in that kingdom of Protestantism with rebellion. Since the Hapsburgs posed as leaders of the Counter Reformation, religious differences served as a cloak to cover revolt against the dynasty or as an excuse for foreign intervention in Hungarian affairs. There had been severe reprisals

[3] Theodore Mayer, *Verwaltungsreform in Ungarn nach der Türkenzeit* (Vienna, 1911), 7.

against Hungarian Protestants in the years immediately preceding 1680. Leopold reluctantly granted an amnesty in 1681, after his officials had hanged, exiled, or otherwise persecuted thousands of Hungarian Protestants, but even this did not give real security to the survivors. The Protestants were therefore as ready as ever to supply rebellious leaders with military and financial aid against the king.

Toekeli's revolt, which finally brought the Turks to the gates of Vienna, was deeply tinged with religious dissatisfaction. The rebels demanded religious as well as political freedom, and were willing to risk an alliance with both the French and the Turks to achieve their end. Thus Leopold's victory over the Turks was also a triumph over the Hungarian Protestants. It was at the same time a conquest and a liberation, and the reprisals against Toekeli's followers were swift and terrible. Hungary was a conquered kingdom, which Leopold was free to recognize. He could treat it both as a land "liberated" from Islam and as a kingdom in which he had successfully repressed a revolt.[4]

Leopold's chief aim was to have Hungary recover and become a source of strength to his dynasty. Early in 1684 he appointed a special commission to lay down policy and prepare for the restoration of order. Stratmann and Kinsky, the chancellors for Austria and Bohemia, were the guiding spirits of this commission. As able representatives of the new bureaucratic school arising everywhere in Europe, they threw their entire influence on the side of absolutism and centralization, at the expense of feudal liberties. Like Richelieu earlier, they regarded the "liberties" of the nobility as tantamount to anarchy, and as obstacles in the path of effective administration.[5] Leopold, perhaps less of a statist and more responsive than his state-building servants to the age-old relationships of lord and vassal, accepted the idea that Hungary was a conquered kingdom as a temporary expedient, but left all final arrangements to the Hungarian diet. This reservation was more formal than real, but it did prevent an open break with the past. The Hungarian revolution was to be accomplished legally and with due reverence for the ancient laws of the kingdom.

Immediately following the soldiers, however, came the commissars of the *Hofkammer* (imperial council) to rebuild civil society and restore the land economically. In the seventeenth century it did not occur to men that they could construct a political system with new bricks and mortar;

---

[4] Cf. Chapter Two.
[5] The most complete account is in T. Mayer, *op. cit.*, 15–43.

that was to be the illusion of a later age. Therefore the commissioners vested the authority of the emperor in the traditional ruling classes. The noblemen in the country and the councils in the towns retained power, but had thenceforth to look to Vienna for instructions. Along with the civil commissioners came the clergymen, especially the Jesuits, to seize Calvinist churches, to open schools, and to preach salvation through the Church of Rome. The toleration act of 1681 was not repealed, but the suspicion of treason that attached to religious dissent gave the missionaries a strong argument for conversion.

The enthusiasm with which several of Leopold's officers eradicated "treason" produced many martyrs and almost provoked a new, if hopeless, rebellion. Anyone who had supported Toekeli, even though he might later have changed sides and fought valiantly under the emperor's banners, was regarded as a potential traitor. If Protestant, he was on principle not to be trusted. General Caraffa's hot-blooded Neopolitan suspicions provoked him to wholesale tortures and executions that made his name, like that of Judge Jeffreys' in England, synonymous with ruthless, bloodthirsty suppression. Leopold finally removed him from his post when the palatine and a group of Catholic magnates convinced him that the choice lay between retaining his general and facing a new rebellion.

By 1687 Turkish power in Hungary had been practically eliminated and the time had come to incorporate the kingdom in the emerging Hapsburg state. Stratmann assembled a group of Hungarian magnates in Vienna to explain to them the emperor's wishes: the martyrs had paid for the conquest with their blood, and the nobility would now have to pay for it with their liberties. The great statesman's language showed clearly that in Vienna men were no longer thinking in terms of the feudal era, that Hobbes, Grotius and Pufendorf had inspired a new politics based upon natural law and political reality, while the onward march of the imperial armies had underlined the futility of resistance.

The Hungarian diet met at Pressburg on October 12, 1687. The proceedings were not quite as brutal as those of Ferdinand in Bohemia after the battle of the White Mountain (1620), for Leopold was not prepared to liquidate the old families. Nevertheless, the elective crown of Hungary was doomed along with the ancient right to resist the king. The crown was made hereditary in the Hapsburg house and the Golden Bull of 1222 was "corrected" in such a way as to place all real power in the hands of the king. On December 19, 1687, Leopold's eldest son, Joseph, was crowned king of Hungary by the ninety-five-year-old bishop of Gran with

all the ancient pomp and ceremony. The boy swore to maintain the freedom, laws, and goods of the kingdom and accepted the "corrected"
Golden Bull of King Andrew.

Only after the ceremonies were over did the real meaning of the conquest begin to appear. Even though the diet had ratified his demands,
Emperor Leopold was master of the land by military right, "a strong
point of departure for the creation of a truly monarchical and effective
regime for all of Hungary." [6] The Hungarians might, indeed did, again
take up arms against their king, but the chances of success as well as the
legal basis for their action had disappeared. In July, 1688, a high commission "for the organization of Hungary" met under the presidency of the
Oberhofmeister, Dietrichstein. Stratmann, Kinsky, and especially Cardinal Kolonitsch were the moving spirits of the group which, significantly, did not include a single Hungarian.[7] It was packed with Austrian
statesmen convinced of the absolute necessity for bringing order to the
heterogeneous lands under Hapsburg control and determined to introduce
the administrative and fiscal machinery developed elsewhere in the Hapsburg lands into the Hungarian government.[8]

It should be noted, however, that the changes were primarily political.
Although Hungary was a conquered kingdom, many of the Magyar nobility had participated in the war against the Turks and could claim a
share in the victory. Despite all administrative, financial, judicial, and
military innovations the established families were therefore left in possession of the land. Only in Turkish Hungary was there much property
to be disposed of by the king, and even there the rights of ancient families dispossessed by the Turks had to be given some consideration. These
old families were represented in the diet and, since it was not the Hapsburg practice to destroy the estates (*Stände*), the latter lent strong support to the traditions of the kingdom. More than any charter or legal
document, the fact that the old nobility continued to rule their estates, to
control their peasants, to represent government on the local level, and to
influence policy by representation in the diet, accounts for the dualism
that developed within the Hapsburg state between Hungary on the one
hand and Austria-Bohemia on the other. Leopold and his advisers
thought in terms of federal rather than unitary organization. They prob-

---

[6] Huber-Redlich, *Geschichte Österreiches*, VI (Gotha, 1921), 537.

[7] J. Maurer, *Kardinal Leopold Graf Kollonitsch* (Innsbruck, 1887), provides an interesting account of the Cardinal's relationship to Hungary. T. Mayer, *op. cit.*, gives the best
description.

[8] O. Zarek, *The History of Hungary*, trans. by Prince P. P. Wolkonsky (1934), 266.

ably had no alternative, but that fact, added to the inner tensions in Hungary after the conquest, helps to explain the further evolution of the Danubian Monarchy.

Many of the reforms in Hungary were revolutionary. The creation of a Hungarian section of the *Kanzlei* (chancellery) in Vienna, the reorganization of the tax system so that Hungary paid a proportionate share to the Hapsburg war chest, the reshaping of both the judiciary and the administrative systems, and the settlement of Croats and Germans in the depopulated areas all date from the period of the conquest. Furthermore, when Transylvania was incorporated into the Hapsburg state it was definitely severed from Hungary, and came to be ruled from Vienna through a separate *Kanzlei*. That wild province presented certain obstacles to the centralizing pressures from Vienna, but the presence of imperial troops as well as the constant threat from the Turks was enough to bring it to heel.

The conquest of Hungary did not end the era of Hungarian revolts. What Ireland was to England or Catalonia to Spain, Hungary was to the Danubian Monarchy. When the crisis arose over the Spanish succession, the French found no difficulty in stirring up a Hungarian revolt that kept about thirty thousand of Leopold's soldiers busily engaged.[9] The leader, Rákóczy, was the son and stepson of famous rebels, a man whose family traditions, wealth, and influence with both the magnates and the masses gave promise of success. But in the last analysis the issue was decided on the battlefields of Bavaria, Italy, the Netherlands, and France, rather than in Hungary. Rákóczy had no difficulty finding in religion, high taxes, and Hungarian "liberties" issues that would draw supporters to his banners, but Hungarian malcontents were no match for the emperor once Louis XIV was defeated in the west. The rebellion was no more than a pawn on Louis's chessboard, a pawn that lost its power when the king was cornered and confronted with the possibility of a mate.

At one point, the rebels controlled Transylvania and most of Hungary, but under Joseph I, who succeeded his father in 1705, when allied victories were already undermining French prestige, the rebellion gradually collapsed. Joseph had no intention of destroying the social fabric of the kingdom, nor was he willing to surrender the claims of the crown. Rákóczy's followers were gradually won over to the Hapsburg side, and finally even the rebel chief himself was offered full pardon and the return of his estates in exchange for submission. Rather than yield, Rákóczy went into exile, but Hungary returned to Hapsburg control. The Treaty

[9] Cf. Chapter Three.

of Szatmár (1711) granted liberty of religion, but also re-established the authority of the king and reaffirmed the constitutional reforms of 1687.[10]

Imperial policy in Hungary was typical of the methods by which the Austrian *Gesamtstaat* was created. The Hapsburgs did not destroy the local political institutions of the lands they ruled; on the contrary their method was to reconcile local differences wherever possible, and to reform the traditional institutions to fit a loose framework of centralized administration. Ferdinand I had recognized the problem in the mid-sixteenth century and had created the *Geheime Rath* (privy council), the *Hofkriegsrath* (war council), the *Hofkammer* (treasury), and the *Hofkanzlei* (chancellery) to centralize control over the multitudinous political agencies of his dominions. Ferdinand II had endowed these institutions with varying degrees of power and prestige. It remained for Leopold I, with his bureaucrats and soldiers, to make these institutions the organs of an indivisible federal state, and to further extend their power over the many subordinate administrations.[11]

During Leopold's reign, the *Geheime Rath* became purely honorary through the emperor's creation of the *Geheime Konferenz,* a board of four or five members, and of a number of special commissions to expedite matters at the highest level. The chancellors and the *Hofkanzlei,* which came to be divided into sections corresponding to the larger political areas, at the same time attained greater importance, since the learned jurists and bourgeois statesmen who staffed the chancellery not only had knowledge superior to the courtiers and clerics, but also disposed of an organization for discovering facts and implementing decisions. Thus the *Hofkanzlei,* originally a drafting and recording office, assumed control over both foreign and domestic affairs, except those specifically related to finance or war. The chancellors, writes Hintze, "from the Thirty Years' War onward, became the tools of monarchical centralization." [12]

The *Hofkammer* and the *Hofkriegsrath* administered finance and war, but the peculiarities of the Hapsburg political structure prevented their developing into a *Kammer und Kriegs Kommissariat* like that of Prussia. The *Hofkammer* administered the domain revenues and excise taxes, acted as a central treasury and even established a bank to finance loans. In the various lands, however, direct taxes remained within the control of the collegial governments associated with the *Stände* (estates). The *Hof-*

---

[10] The best short account of the rebellion is in J. Redlich, *op. cit.,* Ch. IV.

[11] An excellent short discussion of this problem is to be found in O. Hintze, "Der österreichische under der preussische Beamtenstaat," *Historische Zeitschrift,* LXXXVI (1901), 402–444.

[12] *Ibid.,* 86, 418.

kriegsrath was a war ministry, but it, too, shared some of its powers with the collegial governments of the lands, which, for example, retained the right to recruit and quarter troops. The *Hofkriegsrath* also acted as a high command and a commissariat. Its prestige in part came from the fact that its president was usually a distinguished soldier like Eugene of Savoy or even a sovereign prince like the *Markgraf* of Baden.

The shortcomings of the Austrian federal monarchy were less apparent at the center than at the lower levels of administration. Each of the kingdoms, lands, and provinces retained its ancient constitution, based upon representation of the estates. In Hungary there was a bicameral diet but in most other territories a three-chamber organization was the rule. The diets or *Landtage* represented the interests of the clergy, the nobility and the bourgeoisie and it was extraordinarily difficult to force them to think in terms of the larger political unity of a federal state. Several times between the sixteenth and eighteenth centuries attempts had been made to establish a *Generallandtag,* a sort of estates-general, for all the lands under Hapsburg rule, but always the divergencies in culture and privileges prevented any permanent action.[13] The federal structure, therefore, depended upon the prince and his government rather than upon any organic development of representative institutions.

The forms of government in the component parts of the Hapsburg state had much in common. The representatives of the *Stände* had the right to assess, collect, and administer all direct taxes (contributions); they regulated the enlistment and quartering of troops; and they had extensive police powers. Each government was under an official—the palatine in Hungary, the *Oberhauptmann* in Silesia, the *Landesoffizier* in Bohemia—who was at once responsible to the *Landtag* and to the prince. The administration was in the hands of a collegial government, usually appointed for a limited period by the *Landtag.* County government (the *Viertel* in the German lands, the *Kreis* in Bohemia, the *Komitat* in Hungary) was left almost entirely to the nobility, sometimes represented in a county *Landtag,* sometimes directly appointed by the collegial government of the land. This decentralization of power imposed an effective barrier between the inarticulate masses and the royal government at Vienna.[14]

The central authority, however, was in a position to exert considerable political pressure upon the nobility and thereby to enforce its policy. Elec-

13 J. Redlich, *Das oesterreichische Staats-und Reichsproblem* (Leipzig, 1920), Part II, 4.
14 *Ibid*. The first chapter of Vol. I gives a valuable analysis of this problem.

tions to the diets could be influenced, just as were the elections to the English parliament at this same period. The influx of nonnoble bureaucrats into all strata of the administration provided the imperial authorities with willing tools, for these men depended upon the emperor's favor for advancement.[15] Furthermore, in Bohemia and to a lesser degree in parts of Hungary, the old nobility had been replaced by nonnative families of different language, culture, and traditions, which owed properties and position to the emperor. These men could usually be expected to support the imperial policy. Furthermore, Leopold and his sons were able to subdue revolts and centralize much of the governmental machinery in Vienna by a judicious use of political persuasion and force. Thus by the end of the War of the Spanish Succession, the political pattern of the Danubian *Gesamtstaat* had become fairly well established, despite the essentially decentralized nature of the monarchy.

Emperor Charles' Pragmatic Sanction (1713) was a public manifesto proclaiming the fact that the German, Bohemian, and Hungarian lands of the Hapsburgs had become a single state. It had proved impossible to establish a common diet (*Generallandtag*) to demonstrate this organic unity, but even before Leopold's death a family pact (1703) had established the principle that the Hapsburg domains were indivisible. The Pragmatic Sanction was merely another affirmation of this ideal. The basic reforms of Ferdinand and Leopold had given the monarchy the form of a state; the problem of resolving the conflicting cultural, institutional, and moral aspirations of its peoples remained the task of later generations.[16]

The strengthening of the monarchical power in Austria permitted the emperor to act more effectively in Germany also. The imperial dignity in itself no longer carried much power, but, when added to the crowns of the Danubian Monarchy, it enabled both Joseph I and Charles VI to maintain an imperial party in Germany and thereby materially to strengthen their position in Europe.[17]

[15] Viktor Thiel's "Die innerösterreichische Zentralverwaltung, 1564–1749," *Archiv für österreichische Geschichte,* III, 497–670, provides an instructive study of centralization in the German lands as well as an indication of the type of men who were being recruited for government service.

[16] Cf. G. Turba, *Die pragmatische Sanktion mit besonderer Rücksicht auf die Länder der Stephanskrone* (Vienna, 1906), 2–31, and *Die Grundlagen der pragmatischen Sanktion* (Leipzig, 1921), V, passim; J. Redlich, *Das oesterreichische Staats-und Reichsproblem,* Part II, 4; Hantsch, *op. cit.,* 1–88.

[17] H. Hantsch, *op. cit.,* 86–88.

II. THE GROWTH OF BRANDENBURG-PRUSSIA

The Brandenburg-Prussian state eventually became a challenge to the Danubian Monarchy, but its sensational rise to great power did not come till the mid-eighteenth century. Yet the true founder of this north German state was Frederick William, the great elector (1640–1688) who forced the *Landtage,* nobility, and towns of his domains to sink their provincial interests in the larger interest of the Hohenzollern state. Neither geography nor tradition made this assortment of lands, scattered from Mark-Cleve to East Prussia, into a *Gesamtstaat.* On the contrary, it was the Prussian army that performed that function.[18] In order to build an army that would provide a measure of security in the disorder of post-Westphalian Germany, Frederick William and his successors had been obliged to create institutions that in turn united all their territories.

Of transcendent importance in this development were the agencies established to organize the army and administer the finances. The war *Kommissariat (Generalkriegs Kommissariat)* began as a general intendanture for the army: its officials provided housing, supplies, food and forage for the troops and served as the prince's commissioners in handling the relations between soldiers and civilians. By the end of the seventeenth century it had become as well a tax-collecting agency and a police organization with wide power throughout the Hohenzollern lands. The *Amtskammer,* in turn, began by administering the crown lands and collecting the prince's revenues, but by 1683–1698 it had become a general finance bureau managing most of the income and disbursements of all Brandenburg-Prussia. Under the reign of King Frederick William I (1713–1740) these two bureaus were consolidated into a single agency which became the characteristic administrative organization of the eighteenth-century Prussian state.

These bureaus and the special commissions, set up to handle specific problems, inevitably came into conflict with the ancient provincial governments of the separate lands, but complaints about the encroachments of the *Landräte* (governors) in the country, the *Steuerkommissare* (tax commissioners) in the towns, and other agents of the central administration fell upon deaf ears. It has been aptly remarked that while by the end of the seventeenth century the old provincial *Stände* (estates) governments still existed, they had in effect been already subordinated to the

---

[18] H. Delbrück, *Geschichte der Kriegskunst* (Berlin, 1920), IV, 281.

central administration to such an extent that when Frederick III proclaimed himself King in Prussia, the *Gesamtstaat*, Brandenburg-Prussia had already become a reality.[19]

This important change was effected largely by the new officials who identified themselves with the *Gesamtstaat*. The great elector's privy council was staffed by jurists and newly created aristocrats whose devotion was to the state rather than to any specific province. In the army and in the bureaucracy Prussians, Brandenburgers, Pomeranians, Rhinelanders and others found common loyalties that transcended the old provincial boundaries, while at the same time the new institutions provided unity to the whole of the Hohenzollern inheritance.[20]

The great elector, however, did not himself fully appreciate the meaning of his own labors. When he came to make his testament in 1686, he divided his lands like a feudal baron between the sons of his first and second marriage. Even the involved arguments of modern historians cannot alter the fact that Frederick William regarded his domains as a family estate which he could dispose of at will. This is highly instructive as reflecting the persistence of antiquated political concepts. Though Frederick William had labored all his life to give organic unity to his lands, he obviously did not fully accept the idea of a *Gesamtstaat*, an abstraction transcending both provincial barriers and the person of the ruler.[21]

The great elector's testament was, as a matter of fact, out of line with the family tradition, for the Hohenzollerns had for two hundred years consciously attempted to prevent the splintering of the inheritance. Frederick III, the new elector, had no trouble in securing support from his privy council to put aside his father's will. He was not a strong man, but reason of state and perhaps jealousy of his stepbrothers easily outweighed filial piety. In 1710 and again in 1713 royal decrees reaffirmed the unity of the Hohenzollern lands. On his succession to the throne in 1713, Frederick William I proclaimed: "The lands, peoples, goods, and revenues . . . are forever incorporated in the crown and the electorate." Never again was the integrity of the state to be threatened with partition by testament.

[19] C. Bornhak, *Geschichte des preussischen Verwaltungsrechts* (Berlin, 1884), I, 252 ff.

[20] The best short discussion is to be found in M. Braubach's *Der Aufstieg Brandenburg-Preussens, 1640 bis 1815* (Freiburg, 1933), 169–212.

[21] J. G. Droysen, *Geschichte der preussischen Politik* (Leipsig, 1870–72), IV, 150–161; L. Tümpel, *Entstehung des brandenburgisch-preussischen Einheitsstaates im Zeitalter des Absolutismus* (Berlin, 1915), 18–28.

The young Elector Frederick III, who had succeeded to the throne in 1688, has been dwarfed historically by his father and his son. All his display of pomp and circumstance failed to conceal the deep feeling of inadequacy that haunted him all his life. Lacking a vigorous will, he bowed to a conception of fate that excused him from making decisions. He listened to the advice of favorites, indulged his taste for luxury, and watched the prestige of Brandenburg-Prussia sink without being able to check the process. The most important achievement of his reign was the acquisition of the royal title for the Hohenzollern family. Other German princes were trying to become kings in Poland, in Spain, in England, and elsewhere, so Frederick III's ambition to be king was at bottom a modest one. At first the imperial court at Vienna was cool to the suggestion, but with the Spanish war in the offing the emperor was only too glad to arrange for the recognition of the royal title in exchange for military aid. On January 18, 1701, Frederick placed the crown upon his own head and called himself King in Prussia. His allies in the War of the Spanish Succession recognized his new dignity and at the end of the war all Europe did likewise.[22]

Despite the new dignity, the prestige of the kingdom declined. Frederick I proved himself a patron of the arts and letters: he adorned Berlin and Königsberg with new buildings and statuary and founded the Royal Academy and the Berlin Academy of Art. But he did little to repair the damages of war and not much more for the military and political position of his realm. As long as his father's trusted servants survived, all went well, but as time went on his own bad judgment led him to undo much of his father's work. Yet Prussia was destined to play a grand role in Europe. Frederick's son, Frederick William I, continued the great elector's program and left behind him the kingdom which Frederick the Great was to raise to the status of a great power.

III. THE COLLAPSE OF THE SWEDISH EMPIRE

Twice within a century Swedish kings blazed a trail of glory and destruction across northern Europe and left their people a heroic tradition. Yet Swedish historians recognize not Gustavus Adolphus nor Charles XII, but Charles XI as the ruler who laid the foundations of modern Sweden. This shy, awkward prince, whose education had been neglected and whose personal rule had begun under most adverse conditions, broke the power of the great barons, created an effective bureaucracy, and forged

[22] M. Braubach, *op. cit.*, 216–20.

the weapon with which his famous son staved off ruthless and powerful enemies for two decades.

Charles XI was only four years of age when his father died (1660), so the first years of his reign were dominated by a regency composed of the great landed aristocrats whose families had traditionally shared the government of the kingdom with the king. This regency continued to rule even after Charles XI was declared of age, partly because of the traditional organization of the kingdom, but also because the young king showed no interest in affairs. Unfortunately for themselves, however, the regents involved the kingdom in Louis XIV's war against the Dutch without adequately considering the possible consequences. Louis XIV succeeded in maintaining the offensive, but his Swedish ally suffered one catastrophe after another and by 1678, when peace was made at Nijmegen, the Swedes were denouncing those responsible for the disaster. During the last years of the war, Charles XI had aroused himself and, with the aid of Johan Gyllenstierna, had saved what he could from the debacle. This assured him a position of leadership in the years to follow, and the opposition of the powerful barons soon rallied around him. The discredit of the regency provided an ideal opportunity to set up a new government in the interest of the state.

The *Riksdagar* (parliaments) of 1680 and 1682 were packed with the king's men, enemies of the great landed barons, who promptly granted Charles XI plenary powers to reorganize the kingdom. The king, according to their formula, had received his fief from God and "only to God [was he] responsible for his actions." [23] The *Riksdag* even relieved the king of dependence upon itself, an abdication of power that left him free to act at his own discretion. The *Riksdag* further consolidated his personal power by authorizing him to take punitive action against the members of the late regency and, even more important, to reassume ownership over lands that had been alienated from the crown. In 1686 this right was extended to cover all property that had changed hands since the original alienation, although some compensation was provided for innocent third parties. Since much of the land had originally been crown land, this act in effect cast doubt upon every land title in the kingdom, and assured the crown a substantial increase in wealth. Charles used the authority granted him so effectively that the *Riksdag* members of 1686 were taunted by a popular verse tacked on the milestones around the capital:

[23] R. Fåhraeus, *Sveriges Historia till Våra Dagar VIII Karl XI och Karl XII* (Stockholm, 1923), VII, 215.

Vad göras skall, är alloredan gjort,
I herredagsman, reser icke så fort.[24]

The old aristocratic families suffered the hardest blows of the king. A royal commission investigated the conduct of the regency during the late war. If guilt there was, it consisted largely of bad judgment and political ineptitude, but the commission, supported by the country, found excuse to fine the members over four million silver taler. Even this was only the beginning of trouble for the late rulers of the land. The *Reduktion* commission began the investigation of the land titles with the view to recovering all lands properly belonging to the crown, and continued its work throughout Charles XI's reign. It forced one landlord after another to show title to his property, and ruthlessly reoccupied all lands that had formerly belonged to the crown. *Reduktion* broke the economic power of the great lords and brought hardship and some injustice to most of the landowners, for the commission was ruthless in its application of the law. But it also secured for the crown an independent economic position, free from the poverty that had haunted Charles XI's immediate predecessors. The *Reduktion* process was then extended to all territories under the king's rule, with considerably less justification than in Sweden proper. In the Baltic states, lands that had been in aristocratic hands before the Swedish conquest were "reoccupied" on the grounds that they had been crown lands under earlier rulers of those provinces. Patkul's plotting with the tsar of Russia and the kings of Denmark and Poland was the result of that Baltic baron's failure to obtain relief from the *Reduktion* commission's rulings.[25]

Reduktion and the resultant alteration of the government personnel accomplished a social and political revolution in Sweden. The income of the state increased enormously and allowed the king to carry through reforms, but at the expense of public trust. Part of the reclaimed land had been granted in compensation for legitimate and worthy services, but the *Reduktion* classed all lands alike and assumed that the original transfer had been made by chicanery. The great families which had ruled the land were thus reduced to poverty and impotence. "The country," writes a distinguished Swedish historian, "may not therefore have lost any particularly brilliant coming statesman, but it was deprived

---

[24] What's to be done is done already.
  Mr. Riksdagsman, don't travel so speedily. Quoted by Fåhraeus, *Ibid.*, 219.
[25] Cf. Chapter Three.

of the tradition of public service . . . which those who were to replace them did not possess." [26] A new nobility, dependent upon the crown, took the place of the old families which theretofore had considered the government as their patrimonial inheritance.

Reduktion was the key to Charles XI's regime. His authority was firmly grounded so long as he did not have to turn to the *Riksdag* for further funds; the reacquisition of the crown lands provided just the economic relief that he needed. Freed from restraints, he could establish a new corps of civil servants devoted to the interests of the crown and the state. These new servants, both civil and military, were paid from lands assigned for their maintenance. It was an old-fashioned way of providing salaries, but the only one possible at the time, and one that continued in use for a century after Charles XI's death. The new men who took over the government were typical of the bureaucratic officials who came to power elsewhere in Europe. They were drawn largely from the lesser nobility and the learned professions, and were almost completely dependent upon the throne for their livelihood and status. They were, therefore, the king's men, subservient to his wishes, and unable effectively to criticize or correct his errors. This situation was accentuated by Charles' very low opinion of men, which led him to insist that he himself should supervise all their acts. It would be unfair to call the new bureaucrats bootlickers or timeservers, for many of them were hardworking, conscientious officials. But none of them rose to be statesmen capable of directing the fortunes of the empire. Their greatest weakness was their inflexibility in carrying out the king's orders.

Charles XI's government was very successful in giving relief from the disorders that had plagued Sweden in 1680. The crown debt of over forty-four million silver mint taler was reduced to less than twelve million. This miracle was accomplished without rigorous taxation because *Reduktion* and fines had filled the royal coffers. Perhaps an equally great achievement was the establishment of a regular budget and the creation of an efficient collegial administration. Charles XI took a gloomy view of human integrity; few men, he believed, were honest unless carefully supervised. This belief, applied to the finance and *Kammer* administration, resulted in a businesslike government that became a model for all central and eastern Europe.

Charles XI's reorganization of the military forces gave his son the power to stand off his enemies in the early years of the eighteenth

[26] C. J. H. Hallendorff and A. Schuck, *A History of Sweden* (Stockholm, 1929), p. 283.

century. His first care was the construction of a system of fortification in the modern manner, to prevent a recurrence of recent disasters. The new forts were manned by regular mercenary troops. The main army was organized on a provincial basis whereby each province raised a quota of troops. Officers were provided with royal lands for their maintenance; soldiers were made the responsibility of the provincial landlords. The result was a standing army whose members divided their time between agriculture and military exercise; in times of peace the farmer was more important, but in time of war a reservoir of soldiers was available at an inconsiderable cost to the king.[27] Charles XI also rebuilt the navy and founded the naval base at Karlskrona. How careful he was with his forces can be seen from Sweden's limited role in the great war that raged throughout the last years of his reign. He was unwilling to risk the military power that made his kingdom strong; his son was to enjoy no such opportunity to husband this strength.

When Charles XI died (1697), the nobility hoped his successor would return to the earlier aristocratic pattern of government, but they misjudged the boy whom they declared king at the age of fifteen. Charles XII adored his father and was resolved to continue his policies. He refused to regard the fire that practically destroyed the castle while Charles XI's body lay in state as an evil omen. The system of government was to remain unchanged. The first few years of the new reign were disturbed only by intriguing mothers with marriageable princesses. The handsome young king would have been a fine catch, but he was shy and timid, and the intriguers could not bring him to the altar. In 1700 grimmer business occupied Charles and the kingdom when the coalition of Denmark, Russia, and Saxony-Poland attempted to prey on his provinces. The rest of his life was spent in his campaigns of vengeance against these enemies.[28]

While Charles XII was victorious and courted by both belligerents of the War of the Spanish Succession, the system he had inherited from Charles XI worked with reasonable efficiency. But after Pultava the situation became desperate. The king's long exile in Turkey failed to achieve the diplomatic and military diversion necessary to relieve his position in northern Europe, and on his return he was everywhere confronted with misery and desolation. Sweden simply did not have the

[27] S. Ågren, *Karl XI's indelningsverk för Armån, bidrag till des Historia éren 1679–1697* (Upsala, 1922).
[28] Cf. Chapter Three.

money and the men necessary to meet the forces arrayed against her, but Charles XII, with mad stubbornness, bled the nation white rather than admit the facts. The results were catastrophic. The regular system of finances could not produce the needed funds, so temporary committees assumed the responsibility. Forced loans were imposed, trust funds belonging to minors were absorbed, money was debased by recoinage, commerce came under crown management. Even these measures did not supply enough money to stave off the catastrophe. The wastage of men in the military campaigns was fantastic for so small a country. Fresh drafts and foreign troops kept Charles' ranks filled, but for a generation Sweden was to be a land with a surplus of unmarried women.

The hero king has been damned by some as a foolhardy man who ruined his kingdom, and by others praised as a great and gallant captain. It was his fate to stand in the way of the Muscovite power, and not to see until it was too late that Russia was his greatest and most dangerous enemy. It is improbable that Sweden, with her limited economic resources and her sparse population could have hoped to stop the expansion of her neighbor. Charles XII threw Sweden's whole force into that task, and in his catastrophic failure left a kingdom that could never again fight a major war. The disaster, however, left the nation intact, and gave it a national tradition that has persisted ever since in the folklore of the people.

Chapter Six

THE RESHAPING OF THE EAST

I. THE ACHIEVEMENT OF PETER THE GREAT

THE rise of Russia to the status of a great power was the most significant development in eastern Europe in the early eighteenth century. Peter's wars, his exuberant, sometimes childish, sometimes brutal personality, and his avid desire to make his country look like western Europe accelerated tremendously the process of bringing Russia into the orbit of European affairs. His vigorous assault upon traditions and institutions at best prepared Russia, perhaps prematurely, to play a role in Europe, and at worst interrupted a more orderly development that might well have accomplished the same ends without so much violence and suffering.

Peter was able to revamp his empire because the ancient institutions of the country had already lost so much of their vigor that effective resistance was not possible. The Russian church, which in the past had often played a vital role, was demoralized by the schism of the late seventeenth century. When the "Old Believers" split off from the church rather than accept the revision of the Russian Scriptures by competent students of Greek, the religious community was rent and its authority weakened. The patriarchs had never been able to maintain for long an ascendant position over the tsars; much less could they hope to do so after the schism. The boyars (landed nobility), in spite of their recovery of prestige in the Time of Troubles, were politically and culturally decadent. The people did not trust their leadership, for they had shown themselves as a class to be venal, selfish, and oppressive, and there was so little cohesion within their ranks that they could not hope to oppose a tsar who could command an effective military force. The service nobility and the landed gentry were culturally even lower than the boyars. The former held their lands and positions directly through the tsar's benevolence, while the latter vegetated in indolence, ignorance, and irresponsibility, concerned only with the exploitation of the peasants, whose reduction to slavery was almost complete. When called upon for military service, their usefulness was vitiated by their undisciplined behavior and by their unwillingness to expose themselves to the dangers of battle. The merchant classes had long since come under the tsar's authority through their management of monopolies for his government. The richest of their number were, for practical purposes, servants of the state, since most of the wholesale business of Russia was handled through the tsar's treasury. Like their brothers in the various grades of the nobility, they were in no position to challenge the tsar's authority.

In 1682, the *streltsy* (guards) had played a role in the *coup d'état* which established Sophia as regent for her two brothers, but this undisciplined corps of soldiers, a Slavic version of the Turkish Janissary corps at its most decadent period, could not even enforce its will upon the regent. Even before Peter's "pleasure regiments" appeared, the Russian rulers had been building up two regiments of troops organized and trained on the European model, with foreigners as officers and mercenaries in the ranks. The *streltsy,* with their antiquated conception of war, their rank and file dependent for support upon petty trade and land grants, and their officers lacking in education and *esprit de corps,* could not hope to oppose a duly anointed tsar, endowed with the symbols of power, and supported by mercenary forces.

While native institutions were in decline, Europeans and European ideas had taken root in Russia even before Peter's accession to the throne. For about two centuries Europeans had been trickling into Russia as merchants, envoys, craftsmen, and advisers to the tsars. Their position was an ambivalent one, for though their services were valued, they were forced to live in a kind of ghetto, the German quarter, quite apart from the mass of the population. They were invited to settle in Russia, but once there they found it difficult to obtain permission to leave. Culturally the Russians were obviously their inferiors, but Russian racial and cultural pride, born of ignorance and superstition, assumed a superiority over the foreign unbelievers. Some of the earlier tsars and many of the people washed themselves carefully after contact with westerners.

Nonetheless, these Europeans made an impression. As merchants they brought Russia into contact with western markets and helped the tsars to organize foreign trade as state monopolies. The overland trade with Asia in furs, leather, linen cloth, and many other articles, was likewise controlled by the tsar's treasury, often by foreigners in his service. Even a regular postal service between Moscow and Europe had been established before Peter's reign. Many Russians looked upon it as a window for spies, as a scheme to make foreigners rich and Russians poor, but it proved a useful service to the government.

Despite the decadence of their traditional leaders, the Russian people were a vigorous race. Thinly scattered over the plains and steppes of Eastern Europe, they had been increasing in number for two centuries, had by 1700 already driven back Tartars, Cossacks, and other nomad peoples and had begun the colonization of their lands. Moveover a thin stream of trappers and fur traders, followed by a few emigrants, had trickled across Siberia and had reached the Amur River and the Pacific Ocean. This expansion brought contacts with Asia as well as with Europe and stimulated Russian commercial and manufacturing activities. Marxist historians are probably wrong in describing this commercial capitalism as the motive power behind the revolutionary policy of Peter the Great, but it would be equally mistaken to dismiss it as insignificant.[1]

Thus far, however, the Russians had succeeded in expanding only at the expense of unorganized or decadent societies. From the Caspian to the White Sea, as in the wastes of Siberia, Russian colonists, merchants, and soldiers had encountered no peoples capable of resistance. In the west and the southwest, where Russia's frontiers met Sweden, Poland, and Turkey, the Russians had made no comparable progress. Indeed, in the Time of Troubles the encroachments of their western neighbors had despoiled the tsars of part of their "patrimony." Russia's military power, an exterior expression of her cultural status, was quite unequal to the forces of civilizations more tightly knit and technologically more efficient than her own. Before expansion toward the west became possible, Russian society had to undergo drastic reforms.

By the end of the seventeenth century only very few Russians realized that this reorganization must be undertaken. Golitsyn and Sophia had already made overtures to the west in the 1680's, but they found it difficult to overcome the inertia of the country. Russians knew very little about the west. Europeans might come to Russia, but Russians did not visit Europe. It was frightfully expensive to travel and difficult to obtain foreign money. At any rate the Russians rationalized their isolationism by proclaiming that they feared the contamination of foreign lands and dreaded the thought that death might overtake them far from an Orthodox priest.

Thus when Peter seized power by the *coup d'état* of 1689 the process of orienting Russia westward had already begun, but hardly any appreci-

[1] M. N. Pokrovsky, *History of Russia* (New York, 1931).

able progress had been made. The government, the army, the church, and even the economic institutions of the realm resembled those of Asia rather than of Europe. Russia was still far from the "modern culture" as understood in the west. Her scholars did not comprehend fourth-grade arithmetic, to say nothing of higher mathematics; her craftsmen were unable to build ships, work metals, or finish cloth with western proficiency; her soldiers knew nothing of the western art of war. Cultured Poles, who regarded their neighbors as barbarians, saw only too clearly the gulf that existed between Russia and Europe.

The *coup d'état* of 1689 was a palace revolution. In 1682, with the aid of the *streltsy,* Sophia had made herself regent for her two brothers, on the plea that one of them, Peter, was too young and the other, Ivan, too feeble-minded to govern. The taste of power prompted her to consolidate her position as actual ruler of the land. Though her regime was on the whole enlightened, the failure of Russian campaigns against the Turks branded her as a usurper and so weakened her hold upon the people that Peter's supporters were able to encompass her downfall. Peter's own role in the *coup d'état* was probably only that of a bystander, but his "pleasure regiments" provided the needed military power and his position as anointed tsar gave legal status to the banishment of his sister and her advisers. The whole affair, were it not for the serious consequences to Sophia and several of her friends, was almost like a comic opera. Peter, in terror for his life, fled to a monastery and then ordered the army and the government to join him in his retreat. The regent, apparently unaware of the "danger" Peter was facing, was astounded to see her followers desert to her brother and was finally forced to go herself to receive the order for her incarceration in a convent.

The new government gave no indication of Peter's future regime; it was conservative, mildly anti-European, and completely dominated by Peter's relatives, his favorite boyars, and the patriarch. By many the new regime was regarded as a reversal of Sophia's program for introducing western customs into Russia. However, the military instrument of the *coup d'état* and the personality of the young Peter had within them many of the seeds of the coming revolution. Peter was a ruler of a new type. His formal education had been neglected, but his play as a child and an adolescent had prepared him for his historic mission. As a boy he had organized his playmates in military companies; as a youth he had developed these companies into two regiments of soldiers, armed with modern weapons and trained in the art of war as practiced in the west. Peter had early discovered that the foreigners of the German quarter knew more about fortifications, sieges, maneuvers, and weapons than did the Russians, and he drew heavily upon their advice in organizing and drilling his troops. The young tsar was by turns serious and boisterously riotous; his temperament seemed always to drive him to extremes. But beneath it all he was a wide-eyed, naïve, bubbling individual, anxious to learn and ambitious to play his part. His training and temperament led him to discard the traditional ceremonial, semireligious role of his predecessors. He took his court into the streets and onto the highways, dressed himself as a workingman, labored with his own hands, and ruled the land in a rough-and-ready, unceremonious fashion.

In the first years of his personal reign, however, Peter lived as he had before, save for the fact that he spent more time in the German quarter, where men like General Gordon and Lefort taught him much about Europe and the role of a ruler. His war games became more and more extensive until they were field maneuvers on a large scale, realistically simulating actual warfare. Such preparation could have only one ending: a real campaign against real enemies. The Turkish war was still in progress, though for years there had been nothing more spectacular than border raiding, so a real enemy was at hand. Furthermore, Peter's friends had pointed out to him that the capture of Azov from the Turks would put his government in a stronger position to share in the commerce that came from the south. Thus an attack on the enemy would exercise the army and might pay dividends to the tsar's treasury.

The first campaign against Azov (1695) was a complete disaster. Although some of the Russian troops were armed and organized on the western model, the bulk of the army was old style. It lacked discipline, cohesion, and drive, and the handful of European advisers were unable to make up its deficiencies. Furthermore, without sea power it was impossible to make an effective assault on the fortress. After a long, disappointing adventure, the Russians withdrew, and Peter returned to Moscow bitterly aware that real war was much more serious business than the maneuvers of his "pleasure regiments."

It was this campaign that launched Peter on his reforms. Gordon, Lefort, and other European advisers pointed out to him that European technique and equipment were essential for success. Peter probably did not realize that to achieve these things he would have to turn Russia upside down, but he did understand that without them he could not fill the role of soldier tsar. His reaction was immediate and violent. He set up a

naval yard at Voronezh for the construction of warships that could reduce Azov. About fifty sons of the highest nobility were ordered to go
west to learn seamanship and to study ship construction. The order sent
a shudder down the spines of the superstitious Russians. They complained of the expense, of the humiliation, of the dangers, but their sons
obeyed. While the river fleet was being built, the army underwent a new
course of training. The old *streltsy* regiments and the unruly semifeudal,
semi-Tartar levies were beyond reform, but the western-style troops were
increased and drilled, and officers for them were hired abroad.

With this preparation, a second assault was launched against Azov
(1696). The Turks, curiously unaware of Peter's activities and intentions,
had made no effort to organize defenses; they had failed even to fill in
the trenches dug by the Russians the year before! Furthermore, the Turkish naval forces, apparently commanded by inept and irresponsible officers, allowed themselves to be driven off by inferior power. This second
siege was conducted in the old Russian and the European styles combined. A great mound of earth, characteristic of traditional Russian procedure, was thrown up against the walls, and, after the arrival of
European artillery officers, guns were so disposed as to bombard the fortress most effectively. Assaulted by land and by sea and inadequately
garrisoned for defense, the fortress finally surrendered. Peter made careful
note of the lesson of this first triumph. He realized that victory over even
so feeble an opponent as the Turk at Azov could be won only with modern instruments of war. In order to hold this conquest and extend his
power, further development of western techniques was clearly necessary.

Thus by the end of the seventeenth century the scene had been set for
revolutionary changes. Commerce and war had brought Russia within
the orbit of western Europe, and the tsar's government was strong
enough to brush aside the criticism of boyars and priests. It remained only
for the architect of the revolution to go to Europe and see for himself
how things were done.

Peter's first western tour introduced that young barbarian to a totally
different world. His manners and morals and those of his suite contrasted
painfully with those of the people he met, for Russian society, grounded
upon ancient rites sanctified by religious taboos, was a vivid contrast to
that of the west. From life in the German quarter of Moscow Peter had
gotten his first inkling of another world, but his trip to Holland, England, and Germany impressed it indelibly upon his mind. He directed his
attention primarily to the workaday world of crafts and skills, and he

worked as a laborer in a shipyard; he traced with his own hand the pattern of an etching. But the life of a free, self-respecting, ambitious people, whose interests were secular and whose lives were framed by a culture undreamed of by the average Russian, left a deep mark on his imagination. Although Peter's sensitivity was well below that of the cultured people he met, he could not help seeing that his followers and his people could hope for recognition from Europeans only if they drastically altered their society to conform to the western pattern.

This first western trip, then, was fraught with consequences. Peter and his suite learned much of Europe, and engaged many Europeans to return with them to Russia to teach their arts and crafts. Peter also got his first real conception of European politics. He visited princes and kings from Poland to England, and laid the first plans for the great war against Sweden. Undoubtedly his experiences in Europe induced him to attack the ancient customs of his countrymen. He had contacted a secular culture, he had acquired political ambitions, and he was resolved to introduce a new regime in his home land.

During his absence the *streltsy* had revolted. They knew full well that Peter bore them no love, for they had served Sophia in her maneuvers against her brothers. They had murdered several of Peter's relatives before his very eyes (1682), and they had been the last to submit when in 1689 Peter overthrew his half sister. In the Azov campaigns, their role had been inglorious, and when the victory was celebrated in Moscow, the Europeanized regiments took part while the *streltsy* were sent off on frontier duty. Palace revolutions and popular revolts had forced important decisions in Russia in the past but the *streltsy* uprising was a foolhardy affair. Its leaders did not succeed in enlisting the entire corps, nor were they prepared to fight against Europeanized regiments. General Shein, with the westernized soldiers, quickly suppressed the rebellion, hanged some of the leaders, and placed the entire corps under arrest until Peter's return.

News of the revolt cut short Peter's tour; instead of visiting Venetian shipyards, he hastily started for Russia, resolved to root out all possibility of another uprising and to collect evidence that would justify action against his half sister, who would undoubtedly have benefited had the *streltsy* been successful. A veritable army of torturers examined the unfortunate men, using all the refined cruelty of an oriental ruler. When the last bit of information had been extracted, the victims were hanged or beheaded. To later generations this orgy of executions seemed like unmitigated savagery, but it must be remembered that in England, Hungary, and France, all of them highly civilized countries, "bloody assizes" and wholesale political executions had been common almost until Peter's time. But Peter, it must be admitted, proceeded on a grand scale. Thousands were killed and their bodies left hanging around the city for an entire winter as grim reminders of the tsar's justice. The extent of the savagery and Peter's personal participation in the executions, rather than the act of judicial murder, shocked even his contemporaries.

Upon his return from Europe, Peter inaugurated a series of reforms in the hope of breaking down the ritualistic life of his people and giving them the western, secular point of view. Instead of going to church to give thanks for his safe return, he went to the German quarter, indulged in a wild, drunken feast, and began the clipping of his boyars' beards. He had returned to his capital dressed like the king of Poland, and he let it be known that he expected his subjects to follow the same mode. Even before his visit to the west, he had authorized the sale of tobacco; upon his return he tried to put a pipe in the mouth of every one of his subjects. In 1702 he ordered Russian women to leave the *terem* and join the society of men. Later in his reign, when he discovered that there was no "society" for people to enjoy, he ordered periodical "receptions" or "assemblies" and prescribed how his subjects were to conduct themselves—an act probably unparalleled in history.

Peter's eagerness to remake the externals seems ludicrous until its deeper implications are examined. As aforesaid, Russian life was conditioned by religious rites. The Orthodox Church stressed ceremonial rather than spirituality, and hence set its face squarely against changes such as Peter desired. The patriarch had forbidden the use of the razor on the plea that man was made in God's image, and since God was always portrayed with a beard, He obviously intended that man should have one. It may seem trivial to us, but it was grim business for the superstitious boyar when the tsar clipped his beard, and a shock to the common man when ordered to do the same or pay a tax. The use of tobacco, too, had been condemned on scriptural grounds, and the calendar was almost as sacred as the Holy Books themselves. When Peter introduced the western calendar, it was objected that God could not have created the world in winter, when the apple trees were bare of fruit, so New Year's Day could surely not come at that season. When the days from the creation of the earth were counted, it was discovered that Peter had stolen eight years from God!

The abolition of the flowing robe was even more immediately serious. Peter, in his anxiety to have his people look like Europeans, forgot that Russia is not warmed by the Gulf Stream. The short robes, so stylish in Holland and England, were hardly appropriate in the severe climate of Russia. Nonetheless, the old garb had to go. Peter personally clipped some gowns, while others were pulled off, even from women, at his orders. And yet the western dress was not universally adopted. The tsar's entourage, the officers and the people who wished to curry his favor, shaved and wore German or Hungarian styles, but the mass of the people held back and continued to dress as before. Spasmodically they were harassed by their tsar, but Russia is a large country and Peter soon had more important things to do.

The outcome of these attempts to change the outward forms of the society was the creation of a rift between the ruling class and the people. Razors, tailors, and tobacco were the marks of the foreigner. When Peter's soldiers, courtiers, and officials adopted them, they began to alienate themselves from the people. Before long their sons, returning from Europe, were to make German, French, and English the languages of the upper classes, while foreign tutors and teachers propounded ideas of good and evil quite at variance with those of the people. This cultural revolution transcended all military or governmental reforms. It drove a wedge between the rulers and the ruled that was to be fundamental for the entire subsequent history of the nation.

The people naturally distrusted innovations. Peter's neglect of his religious duties, his friendship with foreigners, and his unreasonable demands upon their personal habits all disturbed and troubled them. Rumors—the only news available in a land without regular sources of information—spread rapidly. The real tsar, it was said, had died and the throne was occupied by an impostor—perhaps Lefort's son. He was anti-Christ; if one letter were dropped from the new title, "Emperor," the remaining letters would correspond to the Slavonic figures totalling 666, the number of the apocalyptic beast and a sure sign of the approaching end of the world.[2] However, with the *streltsy* dead, Sophia carefully guarded, and Europeanized troops at his command, Peter could afford to ignore this discontent. When the patriarch died, the tsar was careful not to fill his position. Stephan Iavorski became "the temporary guardian of the pontifical throne," and a layman was given the management of the monasteries. Prokopovitch, a highly educated, urbane prelate of western

[2] P. Miliukov, *Russian Culture* (Philadelphia, 1942), I, 46.

orientation, declared that any pretension by priest or monk to independence of the tsar's will was a "popish delusion." Thus, though there were distrust and fear of Peter's work, it was impossible to translate opposition into action. The dead bodies of the *streltsy* and the tsar's control of the church insured against any organized revolt.

Though the Azov campaigns had opened the era of reform, the defeat of the Russian army at Narva (1700) greatly increased the tempo. The Northern War made demands first upon the army, then upon the treasury, and finally upon the whole of Russian society. When Peter, almost innocently, declared war upon Charles XII, he had at his command the two more or less Europeanized regiments and the *poteshnye,* the two "pleasure regiments" of his youthful war games. The *streltsy* were dead or disbanded, so these regiments had become the core of the Russian army, supported by Cossacks and miscellaneous auxiliary troops. Peter ordered each section of the country to supply a quota of troops and these levies were then incorporated with the old regiments, which were transformed into divisions by this influx of new soldiers. About 28,000 new recruits were thus added to the original 4,000 soldiers to fight the battle of Narva. The problem was to make the raw levies into seasoned soldiers and to find officers with skill and knowledge enough to handle them. Naturally it was impossible to secure Europeans in the numbers necessary for this task, so Peter entrusted his new army to Russian noblemen, suddenly elevated to officer rank. The new army did, in fact, look reasonably well on parade, so much so that Peter exclaimed, "Why should I spend money on foreigners when my own subjects can do so well?"[3]

But wars are not fought on the parade ground, and Peter's first army only superficially resembled a European army. The troops were green, and the officers too often drunken illiterates without any notion of war. The artillery's value was largely confined to the noise it made, while the supply and commissary departments were in chaos. After the battle of Narva[4] it was perfectly clear that this was no weapon to use against the greatest captain that Sweden had ever produced. Only Charles XII's contempt for the Russians and his decision to turn south against Poland saved Peter from complete disaster.

The rout of 40,000 Russians by 8,500 Swedes was a humiliating catastrophe. But to Peter it meant simply that he must reorganize his political and military forces. Though a man of many trades, Peter re-

---

[3] E. Schuyler, *Peter the Great,* I (New York, 1884), 374.
[4] Cf. Chapter Three, pp. 58–9.

garded himself as first and foremost a man of war. Defeat taught him that he must learn the art of war, but as Miliukov says, "he did not acquire this 'art' at a single stroke!" [5] In the next nine years he tried to teach the Russian bear to walk like a European. He had to fight against the slovenliness, indolence, and stupidity of his people; he had to drive from their thoughts the national proverb, "Flight is not a very noble thing, but it is a very safe one." He had to reorganize old agencies and create new ones to collect and distribute money, forge arms, and maintain discipline. The four original regiments were expanded into an army of about 100,000 men. No ukase or law fixed its form, but between 1700 and 1707 various levies (eleven in all) established the obligation of each region to furnish a quota of troops to replace the fallen. Thus the Russian soldier became "immortal," for a replacement was always at hand to repair the wastage of war. In the nine years between Narva and Pultava the losses were over 100,000, victims of illness, bullets, and desertion, but the levies kept the ranks full. During the same period the soldiers were clothed in European dress, deprived of their beards, and taught how to handle muskets, cannon, and bayonets.

These years saw also the rise of the Russian Baltic fleet. Once Charles' preoccupations in Poland had allowed the Russians to establish themselves upon that sea, Peter lost interest in the shipyards at Voronezh and Archangel, and concentrated his attention on the Baltic. The first steps were halting and unsatisfactory, but gradually a Russian sea power, capable of challenging the Swedish fleet and even of landing raiding parties on Sweden's coasts, came into being.

To carry on the business of war, an effective diplomatic machine had to be developed. Peter established embassies at the principal courts of Europe and spent considerable money on their upkeep. He also instituted the practice of subsidizing foreign journals to advertise, favorably of course, Russia and her ruler. The problem of finding suitable diplomatic agents was a difficult one. No matter what the first Russian students had learned in western Europe, they were conscripted into the diplomatic service because they could use western languages and understood the ways of Europeans. Not until the end of Peter's reign, however, did Russia's ambassadors look and behave like Europeans.

Peter was not an administrator, but a man of action, bubbling with ideas, his own and others'. When confronted with a crisis, he flailed out on all sides at once. There were taxes to collect, materials to procure, troops to administer, and government to organize and direct. During the first decade of the eighteenth century Peter produced a welter in Russia that almost deserved the description "chaos." The war was upon him, and he fought it on all fronts. He had no time to find a logical system, and he probably would not have understood it, had one been submitted to him. Institutions sprang up, foliated, absorbed other, older institutions, and were in turn absorbed or crippled by new ones. In the process the capital moved from Moscow to the posting stations on Peter's line of march, and finally settled at St. Petersburg, a new city, built on a swamp.

To organize the military effort a whole series of new *prikazy,* or bureaus, were set up helter-skelter so that conservative Russians must have been as confused by them as later Americans by the New Deal. *Prikazy* for war, for the cavalry, for the artillery, for the admiralty, for the marine corps, for the arsenal, for the *preobrazhensky* (guards), and for the diplomatic service all sprang up on Peter's orders. Each had the right to allocate revenues; some, like the *prikaz* for the cavalry, were empowered to raise new taxes; all of them appropriated whatever they needed from the older governmental institutions. Not until years later, when the senate and the colleges were set at the apex of the administrative system, was anything like order introduced into the new bureaus.

Tax collection and the discovery of new revenues presented even greater problems. While Peter was abroad the first time, an effort had been made to introduce a new system of municipal government which would permit the wealthiest merchants to shift some of the burden of taxation to other shoulders. Most of the cities, however, were unable or unwilling to take advantage of the new charter which authorized them to elect a burgomaster and "free" themselves from the old military governors, the *voevody,* because with the gift of the charter came an order for double taxation. Peter finally canceled the double tax and made the reform obligatory, because of the "waywardness and excessive ingatherings of our *voevody.*" [6] The elected *burmistry* (burgomasters) could be held responsible for the collection of taxes more easily than the feudal barons and landlords and, as bourgeois, their position, economic and social, was dependent upon the tsar's good graces. Peter attempted to extend the system of bourgeois control over tax collection to the countryside, where the landlords, great and small, acted like semi-independent rulers. The

[6] V. O. Kliuchevskiï, *A History of Russia* (London, 1911–1931), (Eng. trans., 1926), IV, 155.

attempt failed, for the new collectors alone could hardly invade the domains of the nobility, and the police system was too primitive, the tsar's soldiers too distant to be of much use. The landlords continued to raise taxes and recruits and to dispense justice and maintain order; they would not tolerate the interference of bourgeois, bureaucratic officialdom.

Closely connected with this municipal reform was the reorganization of the grand treasury as a ministry of finance with a Europeanized title, the *ratuša* (Rathaus). For a few years this institution gave a semblance of unity to the financial structure till the rise of the governments again decentralized tax collection. The *ratuša* for the first time created something like a budget, and its records reflect the chaos and difficulties of the first period of Peter's reforms. In 1701 the *prikazi* were ordered to present a statement of their needs to the *ratuša*. This and subsequent statements reveal an ascending curve of demand and an ever-growing difficulty in meeting requirements. Miliukov has shown that the income of the Russian tsars before Peter's time was about 1,200,000 rubles a year. A little over one-half of this came from government trading operations (the tsars were always the first merchants of the country); the rest came from various direct and indirect taxes. But this sum was not enough to meet the rising demands of war. The ordinary budget for the army, fleet, artillery and diplomatic service rose from 1,107,000 rubles in 1701 to 2,206,000 in 1706 and to 2,455,000 in 1710, not including the extraordinary nonbudgeted items appropriated each year. In 1702, these "extraordinary expenses" ran to 781,000 rubles, in 1705 to 1,475,000. Nor did the regular budget include the subsidies granted to Poland, or the ordinary expenses of governing the country. Each year's costs increased: the fleet, for example, received only 81,000 in 1701, but by 1710 absorbed 440,000 rubles. The two guard regiments cost 99,000 in 1701, but 144,000 in 1710. The diplomatic expenses rose from 24,000 to 121,000 rubles in the same period. When one recalls that Peter could not borrow money either at home or abroad, it became clear that these expenditures necessitated heroic, or at least drastic, measures. "Money," said Peter, "is the heart of war. Do ye gather in all that ye may."

Neither the tsar nor his advisers were sufficiently versed in problems of finance to devise a rational taxation system to meet the emergency. Peter's financial measures were a direct assault upon all the wealth in the country, an attempt to sop up any and all money that could be squeezed from his subjects. He took suggestions for new revenue-collecting devices from all sorts of people. Klîuchevskiï, after describing the ingenuity shown by the *pribylshchiki,* or "projects men," who proposed taxes on marriages, births, beards, stovepipes, bees, ice cuttings, fountains, etc., etc., exclaims that somehow these *pribylshchiki* overlooked "the idea of a tax on funerals . . . it was, surely, a financial inconsistency to tax a Russian for having dared enter the world whilst letting him leave it tax free." In his enthusiasm for a witty remark, the eminent historian forgot that Peter had all oaken caskets seized at the joiners' shops and sold at four times the original cost, and that he also instituted a tax upon graves; neither the living nor the dead escaped the tsar's treasury!

Waliszewski has dubbed Peter's fiscal policies, "financial brigandage." [7] The tsar resorted to all sorts of questionable practices. The greatest temporary relief to the treasury came from reducing the weight of coins. Over a period of six years this devaluation realized a profit of almost three million rubles. The disadvantages that resulted, however, canceled the benefits, for the new coins swiftly lost value in terms of goods and a situation analogous to modern inflation began to plague the regime. Need for more money led Peter even to undo the reform that had created the *ratuša.* The rise of the chancellery of Izhora, under Menshikov initiated a decentralization of the system that was not to be realized until late in Peter's régime. The Izhora chancellery reorganized the administration of the state "farms," created a monopoly on fishing, and collected new taxes on taverns, inns, and bathhouses. These moneys, separate from the *ratuša* budget, were used for extraordinary expenses.

In an attempt to broaden the base of taxation, Peter's government ordered a new census of taxable households (hearths). The assumption that there had been an increase in the number proved to be completely unfounded. The actual count showed a decline of as much as forty per cent in some districts. The requirements of the army and the forced drafts of labor to build ships, guns, and all manner of things had taken men from the villages, while the ever-increasing taxes had provoked a general flight of population to Siberia and the southeast. The government, of course, ignored the disappointing census and assessed the tax on the basis of the 812,000 households of 1680 rather than the actual 791,000 of 1710.

The victory at Pultava and the subsequent release from Swedish pressure gave Peter a breathing space and an opportunity to bring some order into the chaos of his government. It was to be a long process, not completed even at Peter's death. Various reforms were effected, among them

---

[7] *Peter the Great,* trans. by Lady Mary Loyd (New York, 1897), 472.

the establishment of the governments (*gubernii*) as a new form of provincial organization, and the creation of the colleges and the senate for centralized administration. The governments were set up largely because the central government was unable to administer from Moscow the thinly settled, enormous territory. Peter made his friend Menshikov governor for the conquered Baltic lands (1705), and finally centered his authority at St. Petersburg (1707). A revolt in Astrakhan, the Swedish invasion of the Ukraine, and other crises then led to the creation of further governors. These new officials had more authority than the old *voevody*, and were more responsive to the tsar's will. They gradually absorbed many of the functions of the *ratuṧha* by appointing officials, the *Oberkommandant and the Landrichter*, to perform the principal administrative and tax-collecting duties in their areas. By 1711 Russia was divided into eight *gubernii* and the Moscow district itself had been reduced to the status of a provincial government. The practice of calling a congress of the governors at least once a year began at this early period, but it took a full decade to fix the administrative system of the *gubernii*.[8]

The centralization of the work of the *prikazy* under a series of colleges, more or less modeled upon a Swedish prototype, came after 1712. Over a hundred and fifty foreigners, many recruited in Slavic-speaking Bohemia, were brought to St. Petersburg to institute the reform. Some of the colleges, for example the college for foreign affairs, absorbed only one of the old *prikazy;* others were a combination of several. Under the new system the government became more compact and flexible by introducing more rational methods for transacting business.

The administrative senate, which came to be one of the characteristic institutions of post-Petrine Russia, was originally intended merely as an *ad hoc* commission of the *boyarskaya duma* (assembly of the nobility), but the *duma,* which had held both administrative and legislative powers, disappeared, and the senate's role as the interpreter and administrator of the tsar's will became one of considerable importance. The personnel of the senate was drawn from the upper administrative cadres consisting of men who could be held responsible for their acts, and who could be depended upon to concentrate on the purely administrative work assigned to them. As a directorate to interpret the cryptic wording of Peter's hastily framed *ukazi*, the senate became Peter's *alter ego*. Its most important task was the supervision of the administrative system. By a ukase of 1711 Peter created the office of *oberfiscal* under the senate. This brought

[8] Kliuchevskii, *op. cit.*, IV, 157 ff.

into being the secret police, empowered to scrutinize the acts of all officials, not excluding the very highest. It was in consonance with Russian traditions that one of Peter's *oberfiscals,* Nestorov, brought men as highly placed as the governor of Siberia, Prince Gagarin, to the gallows for peculation, only in the end to be himself broken on the wheel for accepting bribes!

These institutions were not fully developed until the closing years of Peter's reign,[9] but it is important to note that they all sprang from the problems created by the wars. The development of war industries, the establishment of the capital at St. Petersburg, where a secularized culture could be developed, the attempt to provide schools and academies, the regularization and centralization of administration, and the host of minor reforms all derived from the soldier-sailor-mechanic into whose hands fate had delivered Russia—all were products of his attempt to reorient Russian society so as to heighten its military potential and enable it to play a role in European politics.

Peter's revolutionary changes were fraught with social implications. Like his illustrious predecessor, Ivan the Terrible, Peter had to deal with established classes which no longer fitted his requirements and which obstructed his program. Ivan had struck a mighty blow at the powerful boyars; Peter combined the boyars, the service nobility, and landed military aristocracy in the *dvoryanstvo,* or nobility, all of which owed service to the ruler. Peter's plebeian-born statesmen had no respect for ancient names or traditional rights, and Peter himself was interested only in securing soldiers and officials, no matter what their origin. The hereditary nobility were forced to send their sons for review and impressment into the tsar's service. "No state of birth, however eminent, absolved them from liability to inspection," [10] and there were no tasks, however menial, that these young men were not expected to perform. The unfortunate *dvoryané* were rounded up and put to work; those who sought to escape by hiding on their estates were hunted down and forced into service. It is no wonder that many of them prayed that they might be wounded enough to be sent home, but not seriously enough to be fatal! A tsar who would compel princes of the Galitzy and Gagarin families to do sentry duty and the brother of the Grand Admiral Apraksin to drive piles in the Moika canal was after a type of *dvoryané* unknown to Muscovite society.

Nor was that all. A prince was whomsoever Peter called prince. The

[9] Cf. Roberts, *The Quest for Security,* in this series.
[10] Kliuchevskii, *op. cit.,* IV, 75.

tsar did not hesitate to elevate men from the lowest ranks of society to the highest positions in the nobility. The members of his *prikazy*, the administrators, soldiers, and comrades who surrounded him and helped him fight the wars, all had to be or had to become *dvoryanin* in status. Thousands of new names appeared in the ranks of the nobility, while the old hierarchy of *boyare*, *okolnichii*, *stolniki*, and *striaptchie*, based on the rule that no one could serve under a man of lesser origin than his own, broke down under the weight of Peter's program. Peter's "table of ranks" of 1722 was but a rationalization of the fact that rank had become dependent upon services to the state.

The same pressures that fused the old gradations of the nobility into one class transformed the vast majority of the peasants into serfs. For over a century the peasants had been subjected to varying forms of bondage. Peter needed a tax-paying peasantry, and one that could be impressed into the army. Therefore, his legislation merged the existent forms of serfdom in a single homogeneous category, *kriepostnyie liudi*. The peasant serf owed services to his lord, taxes to the state, and sons to the army. In the north, where the great hereditary estates were not common, the peasants remained free men, but the great mass of Russian farmers became serfs. In the towns, the nondomiciled elements of the population were assigned to the lesser civil guilds, "to the end that thereafter all such wanderers may be led to seek a trade, and cease to walk abroad without any sort of labor." [11] These measures, according to Kliuchevskii, were designed to simplify the complexities of individual status and specify the obligations and liabilities of the individual by forcing him into a clearly defined class. The *dvoryané* youths were obliged to go to school and then were drafted for the state service or the army. The *krestianin* (peasant) youth were bound to the soil, drafted into the army, and forced to pay taxes to the treasury. The urban population, through civil guilds and the tsar's monopolies, was compelled to provide the money and goods that supported the state's political and military program.

Yet Peter's efforts failed to make Russia into a European society, or even to alter basically the superstitions, the ideas of good and evil, and the patterns of life of the overwhelming majority of the people. They did, however, make Russia into a European power, endowed with an army and a navy with which Peter's successors were to conquer the borderlands to the south and the west, and with which they were able to play a role in high politics. At the same time, by reorganizing and at least super-

11 Quoted by Kliuchevskii, *op. cit.*, IV, 219.

ficially westernizing the government, and by forcing the nobility to adopt European manners, Peter's revolution brought a vast new land under the influence of western civilization. It is true that Russian culture "russified" the culture it adopted, but it is also true that European culture gave Russian civilization new directions.

II. THE POLISH REPUBLIC AND THE OTTOMAN EMPIRE

In the borderlands between Russia on the one side and Prussia and the Danubian Monarchy on the other lay two states which proved unable to adapt their political institutions to the forces that were shaping the Europe of the future. The one, Poland, was destined to disappear from the map; the other, the Ottoman Empire, found internal expedients and external friends to assist in staving off complete disintegration. In both these states the internal weaknesses that spelled destruction appeared as soon as their neighbors had developed their political and military organization to the point of becoming great military powers.

In Poland the disintegrating forces proved fatal because they ran directly counter to the dominant tendency of European political evolution. While neighboring states were centralizing governmental authority and devising machinery for mobilizing society in the interest of the state, the Poles romantically clung to feudal decentralization. The Polish kingdom was actually a dual monarchy, comprising the kingdom of Poland proper, and the grand principality of Lithuania. Over this kingdom presided an elective king. On extinction of the Jagellon dynasty, in the early seventeenth century, the nobility had reasserted the elective principle of the constitution; thenceforth both native and foreign princes competed for the throne by the time-honored methods of bribery and concession and, once elected, found themselves bound by coronation agreements, *pacta conventa,* as well as by a constitution that made them figureheads rather than rulers. The "golden liberties" of the Polish nobility, whether of the great lords or the petty squires, were completely secure. The nobility elected the king, monopolized the national and the provincial diets, and controlled the high offices of state. The national diet met biennially, and its activities were dependent entirely upon the whims of the least responsible of its members. The *liberum veto* (free veto) allowed any deputy not only to block legislation, but to render inoperative all work already accomplished in that session. Of the fifty-seven diets between 1652 and 1764, forty-eight were rendered futile by this *veto*—in one case simply because a country squire wanted to see what would happen if he exercised his right! The senate, composed of the great political and religious officials of the country, ruled the land along with the king when the diet was not in session. The venality and political irresponsibility of these officials were only slightly less flagrant than those of the members of the diet itself.

The weakness of Poland was further aggravated by the fact that in each of the palatinates the provincial diet had the right to reject any measures taken by the king or the national diet. Moreover, every Polish nobleman had the right of "confederation," that is, the right to organize military opposition. In any other country such military confederations would have meant civil war, but in Poland legalized revolt was a constitutional device to safeguard the liberties of the nobility.

By the end of the seventeenth century the task of ruling the country was increased by the intervention of foreign powers in Polish affairs. The disgraceful behavior of the "French" and "Austrian" factions during the reign of John Sobieski was matched in the early eighteenth century, when Swedes, Russians, Saxons, and Prussians all interfered in Polish politics. Even a popular cause like the crusade against Islam or a national disaster like the invasion of the Swedish army failed to unite the Polish factions; on the contrary, they made for further disunion.

The last great king of Poland was John Sobieski.[12] His career as a warrior against the Turk secured him the throne, and his heroic relief of Vienna in 1683 won him a European reputation. But even in his pursuit of the defeated Turks Sobieski was hampered by breaches of discipline and lack of obedience in his army. Polish noblemen, great and small, would not accept the authority of their king, no matter how great he might be. The "French party," whose protagonists extol Sobieski's exploit at Vienna as an act of heroic simple-mindedness,[13] did all they could to prevent the king from following up the victory. In the following decade this party, aided by Sobieski's French-born queen, made it impossible for him to reap the advantages which Christian victories in Hungary and Greece undoubtedly entitled Poland to expect. Sobieski's campaigns diverted enough Turkish military power from Hungary to facilitate the reconquest, but they netted neither the king nor Poland any gains.

At Sobieski's death (1696) the usual maneuvers led to the election of

---

[12] The biography written by J. B. Morton, *Sobieski, King of Poland* (London, 1932), is very readable.

[13] Older Polish historians blamed Sobieski for saving Vienna because almost a century later the Danubian Monarchy participated in the partitions of Poland, but modern historians, while condemning the partitions, admit that Sobieski was acting in the interests of Poland as well as of Europe.

two kings: the French candidate, François-Louis de Conti, and Frederick Augustus, Elector of Saxony. The latter's prompt appearance with military forces gave him the throne and two years later he was universally recognized as the rightful king. Bribery, foreign pressure, a cynical willingness to change his religion, and a rather questionable record of achievement as commander of the imperial army against the Turks had tipped the scales in Augustus' favor. Once on the throne, he dreamed of making himself a Louis XIV of the east, of establishing a hereditary monarchy that would give Poland an authoritative regime. But Augustus, with his women, his drunken feasts, and his luxurious living, was not the man to tame the Polish squires, and his fanciful foreign policy led him to cross swords with Charles XII, with disastrous results.

The Great Northern War accelerated the disintegration of Poland, because that unfortunate kingdom became its chief battlefield and because Russia emerged from that conflict as a great power. Poland was ruined; cities were pillaged and countryside was ravaged by Swede, Russian, and Saxon alike. The kingdom's economy, already backward compared with that of western Europe, fell even further behind. Charles XII's formation of a pro-Swedish government under Stanislas Leszczynski; the organization of confederations and counterconfederations; and the demoralizing effect of the abdication of a "legitimate" king under military threat of a foreigner, all these completed the political disorganization. On Sweden's defeat at Pultava (1709) the Poles secured nothing but the doubtful advantage of Augustus' return to his vacated throne. Even before the war was over, the Prussian king and the Russian tsar were discussing the partition of Poland; only Peter's belief that he could gain more by controlling an "independent" Poland postponed the partitions for a later generation.

While the disintegrating forces within Polish society were strengthened by this era of war and revolution, the Ottoman Empire, repulsed and crippled by its enemies, was able to recover and present again a brave face to the world. Predictions of the early demise of the Ottoman Empire seemed vindicated when the Holy League drove the Turkish army out of Hungary, established Christian control over the Morea, and initiated the Russian march to the Black Sea. To many sanguine observers Turkey in 1688 seemed already in the last stages of decay. And yet the Ottoman Empire succeeded in weathering the storms of military disaster.

The decline of Ottoman power had set in shortly after the death of Suleiman the Magnificent (1566). The old empire had been dependent upon the sultan's vigorous leadership, and under Suleiman's weak successors it no longer functioned effectively. In the mid-seventeenth century a new principle had been introduced when the first of the Kiuprili grand viziers transformed his position from that of a mere executor of the sultan's commands into that of a real director of the Turkish government. A succession of Kiuprili viziers then revived the waning strength of the empire, but without altering the fundamental principle that made the effectiveness of government dependent on the intelligence and vigor of a strong leader. The Kiuprilis re-established military discipline, and for a generation after 1650 Islam, in the guise of the Ottomans, again became a threat to the security of Europe. Kara Mustafa's invasion of the Danube valley in 1683 was the high point of this first recovery.

Under the heavy blows of the Holy League, Ottoman power again melted away. Such decisive reverses in war were a new experience for the Turks, and one for which they were quite unprepared. The soldiers dethroned the sultan, the first of many to fall victims to the Janissaries and Spahis. Another member of the Kiuprili family was made grand vizier (1690) and in the two remaining years of his life injected new vigor by Spartan measures. Corrupt and dishonest officials were executed; the wealthy, including the sultan, were obliged to give up their silver plate, and discipline was restored in the army. The recovery, however, was incomplete. Because of the distraction of the imperial armies by the war against Louis XIV, the Turks reconquered Belgrade and reinvaded Hungary, but Eugene of Savoy nullified most of these gains and revived the Turks' desire for peace by annihilating the Ottoman army at Zenta.[14]

The defeat of Kara Mustafa at Vienna and the subsequent Christian victories made a deep impression upon the subject Christian populations of the Ottoman Empire. Behind the conquering armies of the Holy League came Jesuits and Franciscans representing Roman Catholicism, and merchants representing western capitalism.[15] French, English, Venetian, and Dutch traders had already introduced western business methods in the Levant, and Roman Catholic missionaries had long since stirred up religious issues, but Christian victories in the field made both of these instruments of western society more active.

The religious issue was at once racial and cultural. The Roman *curia* was willing to make concessions to secure the reunion of the Greek Or-

14 The best short account is to be found in K. Ritter von Sax, *Geschichte des Machtverfalls der Türkei* (Vienna, 1908), 77–88. Cf. Chapter Two.

15 J. W. Zinkeisen, *Geschichte des osmanischen Reiches in Europe* (Hamburg, 1840–1863), V, 303 ff.

thodox Church, but in return it demanded an obedience to Rome that the Greeks were unwilling to give. The Slavic Orthodox Christians, with no traditional allegiance either to the German or the Hungarian crown, preferred to look beyond the emperor in Vienna to the tsar in Moscow, who could re-establish the Byzantine Empire, while the German emperor could only make a conquest. The tsar's prestige grew in direct proportion to Greek Orthodox fear of Jesuits and Germans. The Serbs who, at the emperor's invitation, migrated to Hungary after the liberation, were soon disillusioned. More and more the Greek Orthodox Slavs looked to the tsar as the "true emperor," the protector of the Orthodox Church. Thus the Austro-Russian rivalry, which was to come to a head in Catherine's time, began in the last decade of the seventeenth century. It presented racio-cultural problems that set limits to the German conquests to the southeast.

Professor Jorga's studies [16] led him to believe that the activity of the British and French Levant companies and the merchants who came in the wake of the Venetian victories played a perhaps even greater role than the politicians and priests in arousing the antagonism of the Greeks. Western commercial capitalism, with its monopolistic forms, cut into the trade of the Greek merchants who were the most important economic element within the Ottoman Empire. For two hundred years the Greeks had dreamed of the re-establishment of Byzantium; when it became likely that the western powers might replace the Turks, the Greeks apparently decided that under Ottoman rule they might fare better than they would as a colony of the west. The Venetian occupation of the Morea confirmed their opinion.

The Greek merchants and bankers formed an elite community within the empire. Their sons, educated in Italy, France, and England, understood western as well as Levantine languages, and through their business enterprises had become accustomed to large affairs. While the ignorant Serb or Bulgar might confuse the barbarian at Moscow with the successor of Constantine, the educated and refined Greeks made no such error. They concluded that Greek interests could be better served by rejuvenating the Ottoman Empire than by encouraging its disintegration.

The infiltration of Greeks into the Ottoman administration began in the last half of the seventeenth century, and before long Greek bureaucrats and diplomats practically controlled the Turkish state. Two men de-

[16] N. Jorga, *Geschichte des osmanischen Reiches* (Gotha, 1908), IV, 273–399, is the most complete account of the attitudes and problems of the subject peoples in the Ottoman Empire.

serve special mention in this connection: Panageotes Nikusios and Alexander Maurokordatus, both of whom occupied the office of grand interpreter of the Sublime Porte. Nikusios began his career under Mohammed IV and before his death (1673) had made his position one of the most important offices in the state. Maurokordatus, who succeeded him, continued to hold office despite the violent changes occasioned by revolts and palace revolutions. He became the indispensable man: he controlled the Orthodox Church, he had his children installed as vassal princes in Moldavia, he staffed the sultan's government with his fellow nationals, and he firmly established the phanariot tradition. These prosperous Greeks became a new aristocracy within the old empire, drawing their wealth, prestige, and power from government, the church, and business. In view of the Oriental traditions of the Turks, the Greeks could not, of course, revamp the empire on the western model, but the new phanariot diplomats and bureaucrats reformed at least the government in the spirit of the western state builders.

The Greek statesmen and civil servants found able allies in the new effendi class, which began to emerge in the later seventeenth century. The Ottoman Turk had come to Europe as a soldier and a conqueror; beside the subtle Arab, he had been an uncouth barbarian. But power, wealth, and leisure had softened the martial instincts of the upper classes and by the opening of the eighteenth century an intellectual awakening was taking place in the upper strata of Turkish society. Schools and tutors gave the Turks, even some of the women in the harems, interests that their forefathers would have little understood. History, philosophy, theology, mathematics, and medicine were studied, discussed, and written about, so that the Christian as well as the Moslem elements were affected by the movement. Inevitably men touched by these new interests rose to places of power. The process was slow, but eventually scholars tended to displace soldiers as rulers of the state. They and the educated Greeks appeared none too soon.The Turkish army no longer had the advantage over the Christians that had facilitated the conquests of the fifteenth and sixteenth centuries; what the empire needed now were diplomats and statesmen able to exploit the rivalry of the great powers in the interests of Turkish defense.

The recovery of Ottoman power in the early eighteenth century was neither spectacular nor complete, but when Charles XII involved the empire in war with Russia, the Turks managed to regain their hold on the Black Sea by trapping Peter's army at the Pruth, and in the following decade they reconquered the Morea and dislodged Venice from the Balkan mainland. But they were unable to match the genius of Eugene of Savoy on the Danube. The peace of Passarowitz (1718) left Belgrade in Austrian hands, though the settlement proved ephemeral. The emperor failed to secure the allegiance of the Orthodox Slavs and before the middle of the eighteenth century the whole south bank of the Danube was again under Turkish control. Even though the Turks were unable to accommodate their political institutions to the historic processes of Christian Europe, the injection of new blood, Turkish and Greek, into the old structure saved the empire for the time being from the catastrophe that overtook Poland.

Chapter Seven

ECONOMICS AND WAR

I. THE DEMANDS OF WAR

THE almost complete absence of statistics makes an appraisal of the impact of warfare upon the economic life of the late seventeenth century a difficult and frustrating enterprise. Economic historians have not as yet uncovered the evidence that would make possible a satisfactory quantitative or qualitative analysis of the economy of Europe in that period. Obviously the military action of the three decades, 1685–1715, made demands upon the economy, but it is not equally clear that the wars were a predominant factor in the total economic life.

Warfare in this age had reached a point about halfway between the feudal conflicts of medieval kings and the total involvement of twentieth-century leviathans. In earlier days the subject could be forced to pay the bill for his sovereign's military activities, but he could not be obliged to regard the war as a holy cause. Neither the leading intellectuals nor the common people, whose lives leave but small marks upon the pages of history, believed it necessary to stake life, liberty, and future happiness upon the foreign policies of their rulers. Those of the mercantile classes who financed the king's public debts, those who felt their religious convictions endangered, and finally the military and political officials might be anxious for victory, but the masses received the news of war with mixed feelings. They grumbled at increased taxation, deplored the wastage, and perhaps enjoyed the satisfaction of a spectator at a game, but only when the tax burden became unbearable, as it did in France, Russia, and Sweden, or when their prosperity was threatened, or when their towns and villages were destroyed, as they were in Hungary, the Rhineland, southern Spain, the Baltic, and Bavaria, did they become directly interested in the conflict. The prince might send a man's purse to war, but not his son; the war might interrupt trade, but often it did not seriously interfere even with postal services between belligerents.

The economy of Europe, however, was deeply involved, perhaps even strained, by these wars. Defoe's observation that his age spent less blood and more money on war would indicate that the late seventeenth century had begun to experience a modern phenomenon, namely, the steadily increasing cost of killing men. Furthermore, warfare may not have increased in ferocity, but it had come to include larger numbers of men. The recognition of the right of rulers to tax their subjects and to organize and maintain large bodies of troops led them perhaps inevitably to test the limits to which their military establishments could be pushed before problems of matériel or finance checked further development of their armies. The costs of war were not, however, limited to the take of the prince's tax collections. Seventeenth-century warfare was waged against commerce as well as against fortresses. The predatory actions of soldiers and statesmen wreaked havoc with shipping, agriculture, and cities, and therefore could not but affect the entire economic civilization.[1]

Even without exact statistics, it is not difficult to demonstrate that the costs as well as the materials needed for war were increasing at a prodigious rate. Colbert financed the Dutch War (1672–1678) largely out of current income, but the war of 1688–1697 practically doubled the already large public debt, while the War of the Spanish Succession increased the funded and unfunded debt of France sevenfold. England's fiscal machinery was better organized, yet between 1688 and 1697 its debt rose to £53,283,000. In the Netherlands, where public debts had been high throughout the seventeenth century, the two wars laid enormous charges upon central and provincial treasuries. Elsewhere in Europe, where public credit was not as good, mounting and often ruinous taxes, huge deficits, and ever-increasing demands for subsidies indicate that every treasurer in Europe had to find sums undreamed of by his predecessors.[2]

The end of cheap wars, if such there ever were, and the era of ever-increasing military establishments, was at hand. In the first half of the seventeenth century, even a wealthy nation found it burdensome to keep 80,000 men under arms in time of war, and the famous captains of the mid-century still believed that 50,000 men constituted as large an army as could be practicably handled. By the War of the Spanish Succession France had about 400,000 men under arms, while her enemies deployed

---

[1] Professor J. U. Nef's interesting and provocative articles, "War and Industrial Civilization, 1640–1740," *Review of Politics*, VI (1944), 275–314, and "Wars and the Rise of Industrial Civilization, 1640–1740," *Canadian Journal of Economics and Politics*, X (1944), 36–78, are the most recent attempts to explore the problem.

[2] E. Hamilton, "Origin and Growth of the National Debt in Western Europe," *American Economics Review*, XXVII (1947), 121, 127; E. Baasch, *Holländische Wirtschaftsgeschichte* (Jena, 1927), 190 f.; A. Vühner, *Histoire de la dette publique en France* (Paris, 1886), Chapters VI and VII.

even more. Faraway Russia had an army of 100,000, little Prussia had 40,000, and it was not unusual for a single general to command 100,000 men. Navies, too, had grown in ships, the size of ships, and the weight of broadsides. In the Dutch War, a first-class ship of the line carried 80 guns, of which 12 were 24 pounders; by 1689, a similar ship carried 100 guns, of which 28 were 36 pounders. The total number of projectiles carried by a first-class ship in 1674 was 5,800; in 1689 it was 9,260.[3] When Colbert took over the French navy in 1661, it boasted a total of 30 warships of all classes, but at his death it had risen to 176 and an additional 68 were either planned or under construction. The British navy began its period of rapid growth under James II, and by 1715 was the largest fleet in the world.

Nor was the expense attributable merely to multiplication of numbers of soldiers and ships. The new armies were more costly to operate because the state undertook to furnish more services. By 1700, practically all the soldiers of Europe were uniformed at state expense. The *condottiere* soldier of the earlier period had often furnished his own weapons and all his own equipment. He had provided his own food, and brought his woman along to cook his meals and nurse his wounds. By 1700, these disorderly hordes were gone, their place taken by a much more disciplined, better-organized army. The soldier now received his weapons from the prince, either loaned or deducted from his pay, for only thus could standards of quality and caliber be maintained. His food was provided by the commissary, in some armies as a free issue, in others as a charge against his pay. His wounds were cared for by a primitive field-hospital service, and in his old age or convalescence he could live in a hospital provided by his king.[4] All this made armies costly, but also assured better discipline and morale.[5]

New weapons and installations also raised the expense. Vauban's fortresses, which guarded the French frontiers, set a new pattern for fortification that was studiously copied everywhere, with varying degrees of success. The amount of money and the number of man-hours spent on these works have not been tallied, but they must have been impressive. The increasing use of artillery likewise brought financial drain. The ornate guns of earlier periods gave way to plainer, functional types, but the number required by warships, fortresses, and field armies had greatly

---

[3] René Mémain, *La marine de guerre sous Louis XIV* (Paris, 1937), 816.

[4] The establishment of the Greenwich Naval Hospital in 1694, presumably at the insistence of Queen Mary, is an example of the new attitude toward veterans of the services. W. L. Clowes, *The Royal Navy*, II (London 1897–1903), 237.

[5] W. Sombart, *Krieg und Kapitalismus* (Leipzig, 1913), Chapters 3–5.

increased. The more general use of iron cannon in place of the expensive brass weapons, despite the justified preference of soldiers and sailors for the latter, is probably an indication of the fact that more guns were needed than could be afforded if made of brass.

The introduction and general acceptance of the flintlock musket in the last quarter of the seventeenth century put a more complex and therefore more expensive weapon in the hands of the infantry. Furthermore, in these same years the pike disappeared and the ring bayonet was generally adopted. The earlier plug bayonet had been too difficult to attach and when fixed had made the weapon useless as a firearm; [6] the ring bayonet, on the other hand, gave the musketmen a pike as well as a gun. Flintlocks, bayonets, and the increased demands for powder and ball meant more money and materials and artisans to meet the demands of Mars.

The introduction of these new weapons did not greatly enhance the tempo of warfare. Battles in the first decades of the eighteenth century were perhaps a little more ferocious than those of the preceding wars, but the new weapons did not particularly encourage shock action. Armies volleyed at each other, bayonets were used to stop cavalry charges, and on a number of battlefields the soldiers actually engaged in hand-to-hand combat. For the most part, however, the Earl of Orrery's remark, "We make war more like Foxes than Lyons," accurately characterized the conduct of operations. As we have seen, there were generals like Luxembourg, Eugene, and Marlborough who entertained grim ideas about destroying their foes, but their theories were held in check by civilian statesmen, who insisted upon safer and less costly ventures.

In this connection the suggestion has been made that tactics in the field were dictated by the capabilities of the economic structure. Complaints about the deforestation due to the rapid consumption of wood by the furnaces, the frantic efforts of governments to secure adequate supplies of saltpeter, the difficulties encountered in finding suitable ship timber, the quest for tar, pitch, and hemp, and many other signs of raw material or production "bottlenecks," all seem to point to the conclusion that "wars were increasingly mild in the late seventeenth and early eighteenth centuries . . . partly because of the scarcity of indispensable materials." [7]

[6] The defeat of William's army at Killiecrankie by the Highlanders was attributed in part to the fact that the troops could not fix their clumsy plug bayonets before the wild Scotsmen were upon them with their swords. John W. Fortescue, *History of the British Army* (London, 1899–1930), I, 341.

[7] J. U. Nef, *op. cit.*, 67.

There can be no doubt that economic considerations were constantly in the minds of the men who directed the wars, but it is not equally clear that the lack of raw materials was serious or that there was a real crisis in war production. Recent studies of price trends discount the thesis that soldiers were hampered by a scarcity of metals, except gold. The latter half of the seventeenth century and the first of the eighteenth was an era of declining prices.[8] If the wars had actually created a crisis in the market, this declining price trend should have been dramatically reversed. The years of the two great wars did show measurable rises in price levels, but most of the changes were in agricultural commodity prices and are explicable in terms of unfavorable weather rather than of inflationary war.

The Dutch market was the commercial center of Europe at the turn of the eighteenth century, and prices quoted there for commodities in world trade serve as a satisfactory price index, if not for all Europe, at least for the states allied with the United Netherlands.[9] The prices of metals during the years 1680–1715 were astonishingly stable; indeed, when one remembers that there were no price controls, it is difficult to believe that they applied to a society at war. The following table gives an indication of the fluctuations of the metal market between 1685 and 1715.

Dutch Market Prices in Gulden between 1685 and 1715 [10]

COMMODITY	HIGH	LOW
Common iron	6.25	5.63
Swedish iron	6.25	6.00
Steermark steel	23.50	22.00
Gar copper	59.00	51.60
English tin	47.50	42.00
English lead	7.35	6.50
Bullets	10.00	10.00

[8] Cf. Paul Hasin, *Les doctrines monétaires et financières en France du XVIe au XVIIIe siècle* (Paris, 1928), 88–93.

[9] Actually the price curves discovered in the French, English, Austrian, Spanish, Swedish, and South German markets underline the fact that the Dutch prices were fairly standard for Europe.

[10] These prices are taken from N. W. Posthumus, *Inquiry into the History of Prices in Holland* (London, 1946), 363 ff.

The most surprising thing about these figures is the fact that after an initial rise at the opening of war, the prices actually declined during subsequent years.[11]

The prices for saltpeter and gunpowder are equally interesting.

	GUNPOWDER IN DUTCH GULDEN	SALTPETER IN DUTCH GULDEN
1683	24.50	21
1688	23.50	—
1693	38.50	34
1701	24.50	19.50
1705	33	31
1708	30	28.75
1710	26.75	20.38

Unfortunately, Professor Posthumus was unable to determine prices for the years 1695–1700, so it is impossible to say whether or not prices dropped during the later stage of the first war as they did during the closing years of the War of the Spanish Succession. Whether or not a more rapid consumption of gunpowder would have completely exhausted available supplies we cannot say, but a price rise of less than fifty per cent surely does not indicate a serious shortage.

Although it is impossible to get a complete picture of shipbuilding problems, it seems that this industry experienced more of a raw-material shortage than did any other. Ship construction involved many and varied requirements: rope, sailcloth, hardware, anchors, pitch, sheet lead, tar, timber of all kinds, and numerous other commodities had to be assembled to build the vessels and keep them at sea. A first-class ship of the line required eleven anchors to operate, and eleven more for reserve, to say nothing of spare rope, sails, pitch, tar, spars, and masts. Even the little coasters that shuttled between English and Dutch ports consumed large quantities of naval stores. Holland was the greatest shipbuilding center in Europe, while England and France followed close behind. Yet Holland had no suitable native timber, England's supplies of oak and pine proved inadequate in the 1680's, and France was forced to make extensive forestry surveys of the coastal areas, especially along the great rivers.

Despite the complaints of the shipbuilders and of statesmen interested

[11] The English admiralty prices for sheet lead show the same variations. Sir W. Beveridge, *Prices and Wages in England from the Twelfth to the Nineteenth Centuries*, I (London, 1939).

in naval power, the timber problem did not prove insurmountable. The Dutch floated logs down the Rhine from Germany and imported them from the Baltic. The English established a regular trade with Courland, East Prussia, and the Scandinavian peninsula, where lumber was actually cut to English specifications. Demands for lumber actually forced a modification of the Navigation Laws, for English ships could not always be spared for the trade, but there is no indication that the English shipbuilding industry was seriously or chronically hampered for lack of wood. The French in Colbert's time assured themselves of an adequate supply by careful inventory of the trees within about twenty miles of all rivers suitable for floating tree trunks to the shipyards. Some of the measures adopted to secure the supply provoked complaints from the peasants who were drafted into the lumbering service, but there is no evidence that lack of timber checked French naval development. The fact that neither England nor France seriously attempted to tap the vast resources of their New World colonies until after the Treaty of Utrecht, would suggest that the problem, while admittedly a difficult one, had not yet reached a critical stage.

Pitch and tar, like timber, came largely from Scandinavia and the Baltic. Whether France suffered from Anglo-Dutch interference with this trade is not known, but it is probable that the country was self-sufficient or could import these items from Spain and the Mediterranean. English price figures suggest that at times these commodities were scarce, for they reveal violent fluctuations, which, however, may have been due to Swedish commercial policy and the Great Northern War, rather than to absolute shortages. There is no indication that English or Dutch ships stayed in harbor because of lack of pitch.[12] The price of hemp rose about thirty per cent with the beginning of the war in 1688, and continued to rise until 1696. The price remained relatively high during the years of peace, and then in 1705 dropped off to below the 1688 price.[13] Toward the end of the war (1710) it reached a level more than twice as high as that of 1687, but then again dropped off by about a third. This, however, may be explained, as in the case of grain, by weather conditions as much as by war.

France's inability to maintain her position as the dominant sea power

12 *Ibid.*, I, 739; Albion, *Forests and Sea Power, the Timber Problem of the Royal Navy 1652–1862* (1926), 159–160; G. N. Clark, *The Dutch Alliance and the War against French Trade, 1688–1697* (1923), 92 ff.

13 The index numbers are: 1687, 74; 1688, 103; 1696, 137; 1700, 128; 1705, 91; 1710, 152; 1713, 87.7. Beveridge, *op. cit.*, I, 739.

after 1692 does raise the question whether or not "bottlenecks" in raw materials could have accounted for the changing relationship between English and French naval power. There is no doubt that the French navy was handicapped by lack of timber, harassed by the problem of securing anchors, guns and projectiles, and embarrassed by shortages in cordage, sailcloth and pitch. Nonetheless the basic difficulty with respect to these items seems to have been not so much the inadequacy of French production as the starvation of the fleet by government policy. The wars on land were a severe drain upon the French treasury; lack of *livres* rather than shortages of oak determined the king's naval policy.[14]

There were, of course, complaints of shortages of weapons in all armies. Time and again generals reported lack of guns, projectiles, and explosives, but it is impossible to determine whether these grievances reflected inadequate transportation, official negligence, lack of funds, and manufacturing "bottlenecks," or were merely the habitual laments of soldiers. Undoubtedly all these factors were operative. The Rochefort arsenal, for example, could not cast bronze guns in 1688 because of lack of tin and copper, but between 1684 and 1688, when both items could have been obtained easily, no supplies had been stockpiled because of insufficient funds. The French army was unable to meet the standard requirement, set by its opponents, of two to four cannon to every thousand soldiers, but the explanation lay in part in French efforts to equip the army with bronze guns, while the enemy used the heavier and less serviceable iron as well as bronze cannon.[15] Iron was both cheaper and more plentiful than copper and tin. Lead, tin, and copper must have been less abundant in France than in England and Holland, for a brisk, if illegal, trade in these metals continued throughout the entire period of the two wars. English and Dutch patriotism were not strong enough to deter smugglers from supplying the enemy with goods, provided a profit was to be made.

The industrial apparatus behind the war machines seems to have grown apace with the demands. It is evident that the iron industry, for example, expanded considerably in the second half of the seventeenth century. The technical problems connected with large furnaces had been largely solved in the two preceding generations and, as Beck's study of the geographical distribution of forges clearly indicates, a reasonably "modern" iron industry was well established in almost every part of

[14] Mémain, *op. cit.*, 617–61 *et passim.*

[15] F. Reboul, *Des croisades à la Revolution*, in Hanotaux, *Histoire de la nation française*, VII (Paris, 1925), 442.

Europe.[16] The quality varied from place to place, but iron suitable for guns, muskets, and other weapons was not hard to find. The armament industry, too, was highly developed. Great war plants were, of course, fewer in number than the forges, but there seems to have been no lack of arms manufacturers, some of whom employed several hundred workmen and used machinery for boring, turning, and hammering the metal into guns. The basic techniques had been largely worked out in the first half of the century, and the benefits derived from a division of labor were already understood. For the limited means and needs of the seventeenth century the armament plants were quite adequate.

Certain areas were famous for the quality of their products. Suhl, Nürnberg, Milan, Tåburg, Rochefort, Sussex, Dauphiné, Tula, Solingen, Toledo, Brescia, and Pistoia, to mention a few, were renowned for their weapons for over a century. The production of weapons was not, however, limited to the famous armament centers. Practically every town in Europe boasted gunsmiths, whose workshops could and did produce muskets. There were over seventy enterprises in Germany alone making weapons with distinctive trademarks that have become collectors' items in our times.[17] Towns like Freiburg had about a dozen small factories with the necessary equipment for boring muskets.[18] It is clear that these small shops contributed substantially to the armaments of the great wars of the period.[19]

The ownership of these establishments varied from state-owned arsenals to purely private enterprises. Naval installations like Toulon and Rochefort were close to the sea and drew much of their raw material from the hinterland; army arsenals were close to the frontiers so as to obviate the need for long-distance transportation. Behind the state-owned arsenal and serving it directly were the forges and workshops of private ownership to which the French government granted many privileges. At Rochefort, for example, privately owned forges made all the iron cannon, a large part of the anchors, and most of the muskets.[20] In England and

[16] L. Beck, *Die Geschichte des Eisens in technischer und kulturgeschichtlicher Beziehung* (Braunschweig, 1893–95), 1036–1304.

[17] August Demmin, *Die Kriegswaffen und ihre geschichtlichen Entwicklungen* (Leipzig, 1893).

[18] Konrad Knebel, "Die Gewerken der Schmiedehandwerke besonders der Waffenkunste Freiburgs," *Mitteilungen des freiburger Altertumsvereins*, XLIV (1908), 120–128.

[19] See Wilhelm Wick, "Die landesherrlichen Eisenhütten und Hämmer im ehemaligen Kurhessen bis zum Ende des XVII Jahrhunderts," *Verein für hessische Geschichte und Landeskunde*, Suppl., XVI (1910); Arthur Salz, *Geschichte der böhmischen Industrie in der Neuzeit* (1913), p. 160 ff. and 197 ff.

[20] C. W. Cole, *Colbert and a Century of French Mercantilism*, I (1939), 457–8; II, 336–41; Mémain, *op. cit.*, 782–872. Mémain's discussion is most illuminating.

Scotland, king and parliament favored the iron manufacturers with charters and special grants. The Sussex industry caused some misgivings because of its rapid consumption of wood that might otherwise have been used for shipbuilding or for the fuel supply of London; eventually it did move to Shropshire, where the forest of Dean could be drawn upon for wood as well as iron.[21] Germany, northern Italy, and, in the mid-seventeenth century, Sweden, were most renowned for their arms factories, the majority either privately owned or under princely protection. In Russia, after Peter became seriously involved in war, over five hundred families were attached to the Tula arsenal, while the Sestrorecker gun factory employed about seven hundred workers by 1729.[22]

Professor Mémain's careful and exhaustive study of the Rochefort arsenal has revealed the problems of some of these war plants. The Landouillette brothers, for example, supplied the arsenal with iron cannon, muskets, anchors, and projectiles. It is not unlikely that their problems were those of armament makers elsewhere: recruiting agents lured away their best workingmen; they needed advance payments and loans to enlarge their plants and purchase raw materials; they encountered shortages that threatened to force suspension of activities. The government was obliged to grant them the right to use wood from the royal forests, and secured for them "priorities" on iron ore. Some of their activities vaguely suggest "lobbying" and corruption of the king's officials. Furthermore, surprisingly large numbers of their cannon blew up on the arsenal testing grounds, yet the brothers became rich and eventually acquired titles of nobility. Possibly their story was unique, but Louvois's relationships with the Keller establishment would seem to indicate that it was not.[23]

Curiously enough, neither the demands of war nor the desire of manufacturers to become rich through war contracts was responsible for any significant technological progress in the metallurgical industry. Indeed, in the last half of the seventeenth century technology in this industry seems to have been almost at a standstill.[24] The boring machinery that made possible the large-scale manufacture of muskets and the new retorts that reduced the iron ore to pig iron had been developed almost a hundred years earlier, while many other processes were even older. The two

---

[21] Cunningham, *Growth of English Industry and Commerce*, I (Cambridge, Eng., 1912), 523; Bremner, D., *The Industries of Scotland* (1869), 40 ff.

[22] Tugan-Baranowski, *Geschichte der russischen Fabrik* (German edition, 1900), 14; W. Sombart, *op. cit.*, 85–116.

[23] Mémain, Chapter XXII *et passim*.

[24] Hans Ehernberg, "Die Eisenhüttentechnik und der deutsche Hüttenarbeiter," *Münchener volkswirtschaftliche Studien*, LXXX (1906), 29.

great inventions that came about 1700 were not applied to war production. The Newcomen steam engine, the outcome of half a century's efforts to reconstruct Hero's classical engine, was largely employed to pump water from mines. It was highly inefficient and clumsy by modern standards, but it did come into fairly wide use in England by the middle of the eighteenth century. The other great discovery, namely the production of malleable iron by use of coke and limestone rather than charcoal, came after almost a century's experimentation in preventing the "humors" in coal from contaminating the iron. The successful experiment of the Coalbrooksdale ironmaster, however, had only a slight effect upon the production of iron in England until the latter eighteenth century and was not generally adopted on the continent until the mid-nineteenth century. Defoe tells us that the wars stimulated "projects," but these were obviously commercial rather than technological.

The textile industry, as well as the metallurgical, felt the demands of war. By the end of the seventeenth century uniforms had become the rule for soldiers of all nations. The English redcoats, the Prussian blue and the French green, yellow, white, and blue regiments won fame on a dozen battlefields. As Sombart has pointed out, this fact suggests an expansion of the textile industry. Quantities of cloth of standard quality and color had to be woven and worked into uniforms. The manufacturers of rough woolen cloth were prosperous in France when most of the textile industry languished under the strain of taxes and low demand, and there was a lively trade in woolen cloth from Saxony, Silesia, and England to Hamburg, Frankfurt, and Holland, where elaborate equipment for dyeing and finishing adapted the material to military use. An estimate of the demand can be derived from the fact that an army of 100,000 men required 20,000 pieces of cloth every two years. Considering that all Brandenburg consumed in this period only 50,000 pieces a year for civilian use, and that 100,000 troops used about half of the textile production of West Riding, this figure assumes its proper proportions. Though these figures do not imply that war necessarily strained the cloth industry, they do demonstrate that the demands were substantial.[25]

With regard to the grain trade it has been argued that the regulatory legislation of the period was dictated by the needs of war. This thesis has not been proved and most writers on the subject are agreed that it was the needs of the city populations, the ever-present threat of famine, and

[25] Brandenburg's cloth came largely from Moravia, Saxony, and England. G. Schmoller, *Umrisse und Untersuchungen* (Berlin, 1898), 514; W. Sombart, *op. cit.*, 166.

the exigencies of fiscal policy that occasioned the grain trade regulations. Likewise, there is little evidence to support the thesis that prolonged wars of the time determined grain prices. The Netherlands market came close to being an international market and Amsterdam prices generally reflected the major price fluctuations. In the decade and a half from 1681 to 1695, the years 1682, 1686, and especially 1694 were periods of high prices. Since these years coincided with the years of crop failure due to bad weather, the war can hardly be held responsible for the high prices. French grain prices in 1693–1694 undoubtedly suggest that the Anglo-Dutch blockade provoked something like a crisis, but even though the fall of prices following the arrival of a Baltic convoy is evidence that the fortunes of war could affect the cost of wheat, it must be remembered that in England and Holland prices were also high. The years 1701–1706 were good harvest years everywhere in Europe and resulted in a drop of about twenty per cent in grain prices, but from 1708 to 1710 crop failures again sent grain prices everywhere to heights not reached for thirty years on either side of 1710. Acts of God, therefore, rather than the needs of the armies, created the scarcities.[26]

It is impossible to say how much the limitations of war production affected military operations. The mutiny and license of unpaid troops caused more difficulties than the lack of shot and powder. Again and again shortages of funds rather than industrial "bottlenecks" checked the ambitions of generals. Fiscal problems, involving the bankruptcy of the nation, were the ever-present threats to Louis XIV's regime, while British statesmen won some of their greatest triumphs in the field of finance. Credit and cash seem to have controlled the balance between defeat and victory; men and materials were available to the power that could pay for them.

II. THE FINANCIAL CRISIS

"To pay for the majesty of the king, his pleasures, his glory, his victories and his reverses, the government of Louis XIV developed a financial administration, multiplied the number of fiscal laws, and in the end attempted great innovations without being able to escape bankruptcy." [27]

[26] The studies of prices are most significant. Cf. H. Hauser, *Recherches et documents sur l'histoire des prix en France de 1500 à 1800* (Paris, 1936); Wm. Beveridge, *op. cit.*; A. F. Pribram, *Materialien zur Geschichte der Preise und Löhne in Österreich*, I (Vienna, 1938); M. J. Elsas, *Umriss einer Geschichte der Preise und Löhne in Deutschland* (Leiden, 1936); N. W. Posthumus, *Inquiry into the History of Prices in Holland* (London, 1946); E. J. Hamilton, *War and Prices in Spain* (Cambridge, Mass., 1947).

[27] Lavisse, *Histoire de France* (Paris, 1900–1911), VIII, 1, 164.

In this generalization Professor Sagnac has summed up the tragedy of the Sun King's reign without specifying the fundamental problem behind the fiasco. The expenditures of the king for glory, splendor, and war undoubtedly overwhelmed and bankrupted the French treasury, but it was the financial system of France, based upon age-old practices and upon outdated social and political ideas, that faltered and broke under the strain of victory and defeat. The fatal weakness of Bourbon France was not the inability of its people to produce wealth, but rather the inability of the French treasury to fill its needs without hampering commerce and ruinously taxing the poorest elements of society. England under William III and Anne, with a much smaller population and an inferior productive capacity, sustained much heavier burdens to carry on the wars, yet emerged at the end of the period as not only a great military, but also a great financial power. France, unlike England, was unable to organize her fiscal structure in a rational manner, and eventually was defeated and ruined as much by her own failures as by the will to victory of her enemies.[28]

From the days of Henry IV to the overthrow of Louis XVI, France contended uninterruptedly with financial problems. None of the Bourbon kings was strong enough to carry through the needed fiscal reforms. Sully and Colbert earned great reputations as watchdogs of the king's treasury, but they were not imaginative financiers nor had they plans for reorganizing the archaic and unequal system of collecting the royal funds. Neither Louis XIV nor his ministers had the courage to attack the chartered privileges, class rights, and age-old practices that had become the very essence of French society.

The medieval kings of France had financed their government from the returns of crown lands, dues, tolls, and fees that came to them as feudal lords, and a limited subsidy granted by the estates. By the seventeenth century these private sources of revenue had become woefully inadequate to meet the demands upon government, and in France as in other countries direct taxes of various kinds had become the rule. Nonetheless, the idea of government as a public charge was still but imperfectly accepted, and the notion that a tax system should weigh equitably upon all subjects and at the same time cause a minimum of friction in the economy had not yet arisen. As revenue demands increased, new taxes were intro-

---

[28] P. Harsin, "Comment le gouvernement de Louis XIV a-t-il financé la guerre de la succession d'Espagne?," *Bulletin de la société d'histoire moderne*, 7th Ser. No. 38 (1932), 11–13.

duced without serious consideration of their relationship to the whole tax structure, with the result that fiscal systems all over Europe were chaotic. Ancient taxes tended to become stereotyped, and cumulatively formed layers which only a historian with an archeologist's turn of mind could excavate and explain in terms of the socio-political evolution of European civilization.[29]

By the middle of Louis XIV's reign, the French treasury depended upon a multitude of different taxes. They fell into three main categories: the taille; the tolls and tariffs upon the transit of goods; and the dues, fees, fines, and excises levied upon anything from salt to the inheritance of a title. In addition there were the "free gift" of the clergy, the income from crown lands, and a number of miscellaneous items of income, but most of the yield from these latter sources was allocated to interest on the king's debts. But the mere listing of the taxes does not explain the problem; it was the assessment and administration that proved to be the Achilles' heel of the Bourbon monarchy.

The taille was the backbone of the French treasury, as valuable to the king of France as the mines of the New World were to the king of Spain. Originally it had been a feudal war tax granted by the estates-general and levied exclusively upon the third estate. In actual practice it fell almost exclusively upon the peasants, but with an unequal and unpredictable incidence. In certain provinces, the *pays d'état,* the taille was voted and collected by the provincial estates; there the royal officials had a footing only in the principal towns, since both the amount of the taxes and the methods of collection were beyond their control. Provinces of the *pays d'état* paid a much lighter taille than the *pays d'élection,* where the amount of the tax was decided by the king and the whole machinery of collection was in the hands of treasury officials. But there, too, the taille was unequal and stereotyped. Certain villages and individuals got off lightly by virtue of corruption, favoritism, or tradition, while others staggered under the load. The method of collection was one of the worst administrative abuses: in each village a local collector was designated and, in case of failure to make his neighbors pay, was himself required to make up the difference. The result was that every year the tax collector went bankrupt. Because of the taille the peasants refused to admit to any prosperity: they allowed their houses to fall into ruins and, if they could afford more than a bare minimum of subsistence, they carefully con-

[29] Walter Lotz, *Finanzwissenschaft* (2nd edition, 1931). Cf. first section and bibliography.

cealed the fact from their neighbors. Any sign of wealth merely brought new tax burdens. The taille made many parts of France look like a land that had been devastated by a foreign army.

From ancient times the kings of France had had the right to impose dues, tolls, and tariffs upon the movement of goods on the roads, rivers, and harbors of the kingdom. In earlier ages, when the commodities of trade were light in bulk and of great value, these exactions had not weighed heavily, but by the seventeenth century, when many bulky items were transported, they became onerous. In the second half of Louis XIV's reign they were in part responsible for the decline of commerce and the impoverishment of the land. Only the *traitants* (tax farmers) who collected them became rich.[30]

The king also collected excise and sales taxes upon a long list of commodities necessary to the everyday life. Since the privileged classes escaped the taille entirely, Colbert had increased these taxes fourfold as the only means of making the wealthy bear a share of the tax burden. These excises fell upon candles, soap, leather, and similar necessities, but above all upon wines and liquors. They varied from place to place, but everywhere resulted in higher prices and stifling of trade. A striking example of the effect of the *aides* and *douanes* (excise and tariff) was the fact that Burgundy wine, which sold for one sou a measure in Orléans, cost twenty-four sous in Normandy and Picardy. Historians are generally agreed that these duties wrought economic distress out of all proportion to the income they produced.[31]

The most onerous of the commodity taxes, and the most inequitably levied, was the *gabelle du sel,* the salt tax. This notorious tax varied from province to province; in some it was comparatively light; in others, it drove the price of salt so high as to undermine the health of men and beasts. Furthermore, the hosts of collectors and officials who administered the tax and guarded against smuggling made the *gabelle* one of the big industries of the kingdom, though hardly one that contributed to the prosperity of the people.[32]

The basic weaknesses of the French fiscal structure became painfully apparent as the demands for more money became imperative. The clergy, a wealthy segment of the population, escaped all direct taxation by granting the king a "free gift." The nobility avoided payment of direct taxes on the plea of contributing a "blood tax," which in fact was no

[30] Boisguilbert, *Le détail de la France* (1707), 207.
[31] H. Roberts, *Boisguilbert* (New York, 1935), 119–135.
[32] Beaulieu, *Les gabelles sous Louis XIV* (Paris, 1903).

longer exacted. Privileges of towns, provinces, and corporations involved
further exemptions so that the king had no alternative but to impose
heavier burdens upon the poor and to levy ruinous exactions upon commerce. Louis XIV may have justified the system with the comforting
doctrine preached to him by his confessor, namely, "that all the property
of my subjects belonged to me [Louis], and that that which remained to
them depended upon me, and that they held it from me," [33] but even
such a rationalization could not give him the wealth needed to achieve
his ends on the battlefields of Europe.

It is difficult to draw an accurate picture of the French budget in the
seventeenth century. In 1683, the year of Colbert's death, the income
from taxes was approximately 116 million *livres,* of which 23 million
were spent for collection. The expenditures were 109 million, leaving a
deficit of 16 million. In 1715 the income from taxation was 152 million,
but collection costs and revenues pledged for interest reduced the actual
receipts to 74 million. The expenses of government had meanwhile risen
to 119 million, leaving a deficit of 45 million. Between these years two
great wars had been waged. According to Chamillart, the total expendi-
ture of the war years 1700 to 1706 was 1,100 million, while the income stood
at 350 million. Under Desmaretz, from 1708 to 1715, the outlay mounted
to 1,915 million, while the income was only 461 million. When it is
remembered that these deficits followed almost immediately upon those
incurred during the years 1689–1697 (approximately 1,200 million) it
appears that the total deficit in 1715 was more than three billion *livres.* [34]

In frantic efforts to bring income within hailing distance of expendi-
ture, the successors of Colbert tried many expedients, some of them of
ancient lineage, others daring creations of the hour. For almost two
centuries the sale of offices had been a recognized device of French
kings. "Every time your majesty creates an office," Pontchartrain laugh-
ingly informed the king, "God creates a fool to buy it." [35] There was
usually a ready market for new offices, but when it became difficult to
find purchasers, "gentle pressure" could be applied to wealthy individuals.
In the France of the old regime such offices were regarded both as a sort

[33] H. Roberts, *op. cit.,* 137.

[34] There are two studies of the catastrophe of the French finance system: H. I. Vuitry,
*Le désordre des finances et les excès de la speculation à la fin du règne de Louis XIV et
au commencement du règne de Louis XV* (Paris, 1885), 1–200; A. Vührer, *Histoire de la
dette publique en France,* 2 vols. (1886), 114–140. Cf. also the important article by E.
Esmonin and P. Harsin, "Comment le gouvernement de Louis XIV a-t-il financé la guerre de
succession d'Espagne," *Bulletin de la société d'histoire moderne* (1931–1933).

[35] A. Vührer, *op. cit.,* I, 117.

of annuity and as a source of social prestige. The holder's salary was regulated by the cost of the office, so that the investment usually paid better than state bonds, and, upon payment of an additional tax, the office could be made a hereditary property of the purchaser. The king's treasury in the years 1689–1715 received about 900 million *livres* from such sales. A judicial office brought 500,000 *livres,* a *maître des requêtes,* 190,000. The two posts of directors of finances, created in 1701 to aid Chamillart's financial administration, sold for 800,000 *livres* each! Other, humbler appointments were available at more modest figures.[36]

The sale of patents of nobility paralleled the sale of offices. Louis XIV continued the practice begun by his father of cheapening the title of nobility by multiplying the number of nobles. Saint-Simon's worry over rank and precedence and the relative decay in the worth of even the title "duc" was a repetition of the feeling expressed by the nobility when Louis XIII made Saint-Simon's own ancestor and others great nobles of the land. Louis XIV granted titles as a fiscal measure. It was surprising how many people with money were distinguished enough to warrant the honor.

Another source of income came from tampering with the currency. The *livre* was a token coin, measured in value by gold *louis* or silver *écus.* By changing the value of the *louis* and the *écus* in terms of *livres* the government could reap considerable profit, both in bullion and in the payment of salaries and interest. The profits of the mint in this period have been estimated at 146 million, but they were not made without cost. Good coins simply disappeared, some of them buried in the traditional French fashion, others sent out of the country to Italian and Swiss banking houses.

The issuance of paper money in 1701 seemed to provide a solution for the lack of hard currency. At first the notes of the *caisse des emprunts* circulated freely and took the place of coin. But the government could not resist the temptation to overprint and before long was unable to supply the *caisse des emprunts* with the money to meet claims. The result was depreciation of the paper and extravagant discounting. The prices of commodities were not inflated, for they were quoted in terms of silver and gold; but the paper money lost as much as fifty-four per cent of its value. Attempts to force merchants to accept the paper at par broke down before a barrage of complaints and protests. In the end these

36 A. Vuitry, *op. cit.,* 49 ff.

manipulations, even though they may have brought temporary relief, added greatly to the troubles of the treasury.

Two new taxes made their appearance as war measures: a graduated head tax, the *capitation,* and an income tax, the *dixième.* The *capitation* (1695) involved a division of the people into twenty-two classes or ranks, from the princes of the blood to the meanest of the king's subjects. The first class paid 2,000 *livres,* the second 1,500 *livres,* the following 1,000, 500, 400, 300, 250, 120, 80, 60, and down to the lowest, which paid only one *livre.* The clergy was exempted but required to increase the "free gift" to the king. The taxpayer's problem was, of course, his classification, and each one was naturally seized with the desire to move downward on the royal tax lists. Bribery, favoritism, and arbitrary reclassification reduced the income to the treasury. In place of the 30 million expected, the tax yielded only 22.7 million the first year, and less with each succeeding year. Though suppressed after the Peace of Ryswick, it was re-established during the War of the Spanish Succession.

The second new tax, the *dixième,* was a modification of Vauban's proposed *dîme royale,* created only after the marshal's disgrace. In theory it was a tax of ten per cent upon all income (including the clergy's), but in practice it was unassessable. Within a year after the introduction of the *dixième* (1710) it had become a tax upon the bourgeoisie and the peasantry, the nobility and clergy escaping its incidence. The privileged classes in large part simply refused to pay, and it proved impossible to compel them. The machinery for a workable income tax had not yet been invented.[37]

The French treasury was bankrupt when the War of the Spanish Succession came to an end, and there can be little doubt that this bankruptcy was an important factor in the reverses and defeats which Louis XIV had suffered. Every government in Europe was hard pressed to provide the money needed for the wars, but in France the heavy load resulted in actual financial disaster.

In marked contrast, the splendid position of power and prestige that England held at the end of the period was due largely to the success of the English treasury in raising the money for the ships, iron, powder, and men who won the victories. Perhaps at the very heart of the process which upset the hegemony of France was the political revolution in England which made possible the new fiscal structure of the kingdom. All William's tenacity or Marlborough's genius would have been of little

---

[37] Lavisse, *op. cit.,* VIII, 1, 194–197.

avail had they lacked the wealth to support the armies with which they humbled the marshals of France. After the Revolution of 1688, parliament, co-operating with English treasury officials, assumed the financial reponsibility for government and readily provided the funds necessary for victory. No king, without parliament's aid, could ever have marshalled such funds.

The English kings, like continental rulers, had traditionally depended upon their income from crown lands, dues, fees, and tolls, and upon a direct tax granted by parliament. The ancient tenth and fifteenth and the Tudor subsidies, long since stereotyped at gross undervaluation, had provided for the relatively limited needs of the Tudors. The early Stuarts, unable to make significant changes in this fiscal system even though the expenses of government were growing apace, had no end of trouble with parliament over finance. During the revolutionary era of the mid-century the need for money forced serious reconsideration of the fiscal system. Despite the English conviction that excise taxes provided a basis for tyranny, duties upon beer, soap, cloth, spirits, salt, and meat appeared, on the plea that these were taxes "whereby the said malignants and neutrals may be brought to and compelled to pay their proportional parts. . . ." [38] The customs dues, too, underwent an appreciable change. Theoretically import and export duties had been levied to pay for protection of the merchandise, but in practice they had long since been treated as general revenue. Under the Commonwealth the rise of mercantilist thinking brought abolition of export duties, while import dues assumed a regulatory as well as fiscal character. Cromwell wanted a "favorable balance of trade," as well as the revenue from customs.

Another tax invention of the English revolutionary government was not unlike Louis' *capitation,* a graduated head tax by which a duke paid £100, a squire £10, and others approximately in proportion. This tax easily became stereotyped, but reforms in the years 1641 to 1660 produced the so-called "monthly assessment" which, in effect, was a tax on land rents. Central control over local taxing agencies was too weak, however, to ensure a tax yield anything like what might have been expected.

With the Restoration of 1660 and the return to relative internal tranquillity excise taxes, with the exception of those upon beer and spirits, were abolished. In their place the hearth tax, levied upon family units, was introduced, but attempts to improve the yield from the monthly assessment were unsuccessful.

The Revolution of 1688 and the subsequent war brought about a

[38] Quoted by W. Kennedy, *English Taxation 1640–1799* (London, 1913), 52–3.

thoroughgoing reform of the fiscal structure. The land tax and the excises became the basis of government income. The former had originally been intended as a rate tax, to weigh equally upon all types of income, but the difficulties involved in its assessment and collection at a time when the bureaucracy was still feeble shifted the principal incidence of the tax to land rents. Rent was a form of income that could easily be discovered and, parliament willing, easily collected. During the war years this tax stood at 4 s. on the pound, a tax of twenty per cent. It was levied upon the very people who could best afford to pay: the country squires and the landed nobility. It yielded an income of about £2,000,000 a year. Because good tenants were at a premium, the actual farmers of the land were able to shift the full burden of the tax to the landlords, so it caused no such distress among the agricultural classes as did the taille in France. It was one of the factors that led to the decline in the holdings of the lesser gentry and the increase of the large properties, but it did not impair the efficiency of English agriculture.[39]

The excise taxes and the national debt grew together and became interdependent. In contrast to the continent, England in 1688 had hardly tapped the excise field as a source of revenue. Thus, when the demands for money began to exceed the income and loans became necessary, the excise was available as security for loans. It was not easy to persuade parliament to increase the number of dutiable articles, but in the course of the war taxes on salt, candles, windows, spirits, soap, leather, and a long list of other items came into being. Consciences that were troubled by this violation of the age-old prejudice against taxing the poor were salved by writers like Locke, who said, "everyone who enjoys his share of the protection should pay out of his estate his proportion for the maintenance of it."[40] Others argued that the excise was a fair tax, for everyone, in effect, taxed himself thereby, since the amount paid was conditioned by the amount consumed.

The national debt that resulted from the new loans was popular in the city of London and became one of the mainstays of the Revolution of 1688 and the Protestant succession. It was widely believed that the Pretender, if he gained the throne, would repudiate the debt, so every holder

[39] Habakkuk points out that the rising standard of living in the country, as well as the tax, worked to squeeze out the lesser gentry. They could not "keep up" with their wealthier neighbors and also pay the tax. At the same time, new concentrations of wealth in the hands of generals and statesmen, as well as the assurance of political stability, encouraged the growth of huge estates in the hands of the rich nobility. H. J. Habakkuk, "English Land Ownership, 1640–1740," *Economic History Review*, X (1940), 1–17.

[40] John Locke. *Two Treatises of Civil Government, Book* II.

of government securities became a partisan of the Hanoverian succession. The debt also provided an attractive form of investment at a time when safe investments were hard to find. In the century before 1650, men of money had usually before their death wound up their affairs and bought land so that their families might be sure of their income. But by the end of the century this field of investment was no longer so easily entered, and the amount of loose capital had increased considerably. "Projects" for investment in the latter years of the seventeenth century were multiplying, but few of them paid off as well as a company that raised a Spanish treasure ship with resultant profits of one hundred to one. Indeed, it was as easy to lose the entire investment as it was to gain legitimate profit, and many gentlemen actually put their wealth in coin and bullion and retired to live off their capital. On the continent, annuities and government obligations had long been a field for private investment; the *rentes* of the Hôtel de Ville, for example, were a famous depository for trust funds and estates. But in England royal borrowing from foreign bankers and domestic financiers had been strictly limited by the narrow basis of the king's credit. Parliament suffered from no such limitation; it could create national obligations and provide income to meet the national needs.

Government loans were of various types. Some provided annuities on one life, some on two or three. One had an interesting feature in that, as the subscribers died off, the income to the fortunate survivors increased. Others, like the Hôtel de Ville *rentes,* were perpetual obligations that might never be paid. One very popular form was the lottery loan, which provided large returns for fortunate numbers. Another was the sale at discount of tax tallies which were, of course, unfunded short-term obligations. But to secure a really big loan the government had to grant special privileges. The Bank of England came into being (1694) to float a loan of £1,500,000, and to the surprise of many, it became the mainstay of the treasury.

Banking techniques were already highly developed by the end of the seventeenth century. In Sweden, in the Netherlands, and in several Italian cities, semi-state banks had functioned efficiently, and all over Europe private. banking was common. In England, the goldsmith bankers had served the short-term needs of government and trade, but neither parliament nor the monied classes of London had had enough confidence in the Stuart kings to allow a more powerful institution to be organized. When the cost of King William's War created demands for large sums not quickly repayable, the treasury had to consider extraordinary measures. Charles Montagu, the Whig chancellor of the exchequer, favored a scheme presented by a group of wealthy Londoners for establishing a strong bank to finance the war. The act passed by parliament reveals in its cumbersome title the emergency needs of the government, as well as the failure of its authors to see the full implications of their action:

> An Act for Granting to their Majesties several Rates and Duties upon Tunnage of Ships and Vessels, and upon Beer, Ale, and other Liquors, for securing certain Recompenses and Advantages to such Persons as shall Voluntarily Advance the Sum of Fifteen hundred Thousand Pounds toward Carrying on the War against France.[41]

The new Bank not only loaned the necessary funds, but soon became the most important single economic institution in the kingdom. It accepted deposits from private individuals as well as from the rival banker goldsmiths.[42] It discounted bills, steadied the market for government tax tallies, and issued interest-bearing notes. In a short time it became the treasury's principal ally, but it also had to face several serious crises before its position in the English economy was secure.

A proposed rival bank that would establish credit on the basis of land values was the first threat to the Bank at the Mercers' Hall. The Tory squires, suspicious of the financiers and their "Whiggish Bank," readily gave political support to the project of a land bank that would lend the government £1,200,000. The general principle of the proposed land bank has been successfully used in the twentieth century, but the evidence would indicate that the projectors of this early rival to the Bank of England were financially both naïve and irresponsible. The danger to the Bank passed when, after parliament had authorized the new land bank, it proved impossible to raise the necessary funds. The squires would not risk their money and the city merchants were not interested. The position of the Bank of England, on the other hand, was greatly strengthened when it raised the loan designed for its rival.

The second great crisis arose when the government decided to recoin the silver. The coins in circulation were ancient hammered pieces greatly

---

[41] There are many studies of the Bank of England. Two recent ones provide an excellent introduction: Sir John Clapham, *The Bank of England, A History*, 2 vols. (Cambridge, Eng., 1944); W. M. Acres, *The Bank of England from Within*, 2 vols. (London, 1931). The material in this section is largely drawn from these two books. The quotation is from Acres, I, 9.

[42] Clapham has shown that the reputed hostility between the Bank and the goldsmiths is largely myth. From the very beginning the more stable goldsmiths had good relations with the Bank. Clapham, *op. cit.*, I, 29 ff.

reduced in weight by the practice of clipping the edges and scraping the sides to obtain silver bullion. Six bags of £100 each taken from a goldsmith's strong box actually weighed 230, 222, 198, 190, 182, and 174 ounces. The whole £600 had the weight of £310 in newly minted coins.[43] What made the situation serious was the fact that in spite of the most severe penalties, the practice of clipping was spreading, while newly minted coins immediately disappeared, to be hoarded or melted down for bullion. Business of all kinds was hampered by endless bickering over the coins to be used; even worse, the condition of the coins was resulting in unfavorable exchange in foreign trade. It was suggested that new coins with higher denominations could be issued to compensate for the loss of metal in the old coins, but Locke successfully convinced Montagu that such an expedient would be unjust and at the same time futile. In December, 1695, the government decided upon recoinage as the only solution.

There is reason to believe that this measure caused some injustice. The clever and the informed turned in their light coins before they were outlawed, but many poor, ignorant people, especially those at a distance from London, were left with clipped coins on their hands. Sir Isaac Newton, the director of the mint, organized the recoinage as efficiently as could be expected, and the new coins, when they did appear, were beautifully made and difficult to deface. In the interval, while there was a shortage of money, a run was started on the Bank. To meet the crisis the government issued exchequer bills and the Bank put out interest-bearing notes, England's first large-scale experiment with paper money. A few months later, when coins were again available, the situation cleared, revealing both the strength of the Bank and the stability of the English government. While other governments tampered with the coinage to make profits for the treasury, the English, at great expense, stabilized their coinage on a sound basis. It was a financial maneuver unique in the annals of the period.

In the years of the war over the Spanish succession, the Bank of England became firmly established. It provided money for the government, arranged for payment of troops and allies all over Europe, and stabilized the public credit. At the same time its notes increased the total amount of money in circulation so that the economy could provide the taxes and make the loans necessary to float the war. Paper money and credit turned out to be as effective as gold when they were properly controlled. The

[43] A. Andreades, *History of the Bank of England, 1640–1903* (London ed., 1909), 94.

Bank also acted as a deposit and discount agency and thereby became a mainstay of the ever-growing economic interests of the kingdom.

The other financial institution that helped to build English power was the treasury itself.[44] In the first place the treasury collected revenue without the intermediation of tax farmers, whose "take" on the continent was substantial. Secondly, the treasury developed an *esprit de corps* that transcended party lines. Both Montagu and Godolphin had the "civil service" point of view, and Queen Anne backed up her ministers in preventing the high Tories from irresponsibility removing skilled servants because they had been appointed by the Whigs or held unorthodox views on the Occasional Conformity Bill. The treasury officials, moreover, freely accepted their position of dependence upon the good graces of parliament. The Revolution of 1688–89 forced them to educate the squires in the art of statesmanship and the mysteries of the budget as the price of their successful operation of the royal treasury. "The complicated system of relationship between Treasury experience, Cabinet policy, and Parliamentary control," writes Trevelyan, "was the most original and least advertised invention of English genius under the last Stuart reigns." [45] This was the secret weapon with which England made fluid the resources of the kingdom and mobilized the military forces that assured her a dominant position in eighteenth-century Europe.

The other paymaster of France's enemies was the United Netherlands. In spite of its small population and territory, the republic was a great power in the political and economic life of seventeenth-century Europe. Its wealth derived from the skill and industry of the Dutch merchants, shipbuilders, sailors, and craftsmen who had made their homeland the focal point of international trade. Goods from the north, from the south, and from the Indies were stapled in the Netherlands where some were processed or finished for resale throughout Europe. This trade provided the solid basis for the power that made the Netherlands a crucial factor in the European political system.

The great problem of the Dutch political economy was to maintain a fiscal system that would not weigh so heavily on trade as to destroy the margin of advantage. By the end of the seventeenth century the financial structure of the United Netherlands had fallen into a state of chaos almost impossible to describe in detail. Old taxes were seldom, if ever, repealed; new taxes were added when the need arose without due con-

[44] Doris M. Gill, "The Treasury, 1660–1714," *English Historical Review*, XLVI (1931).
[45] Trevelyan, *England under Queen Anne*, II (London, 1932), 163.

sideration of their place in the total system; and the numerous taxing agencies added divergent interests and views. The admiralty traditionally administered convoy and license taxes upon shipping on the theory that merchandise must pay for its own protection. But since these levies hampered trade there were limits to the amount that could be taken for purposes other than protection. The separate provinces levied taxes upon private property and land, and some of them collected a primitive type of income tax. The excise field was largely, but not entirely, reserved for the general estates. There were excise taxes on almost everything. "He who owned a cow," exclaims Professor Baasch, "had to pay for her a fourfold tax: on the animal, on the pasture, on the butter and cheese, and on the stable." Taxes were imposed upon coffee, tea, wine, beer, salt, soap, coal, candles, wagon wheels, inheritances, rents, interest, and many other items. Commercial and banking capital was almost tax free, but imposts fell heavily upon all the necessities of life. Thus the tax structure was designed to serve the mercantile interests of the state even though it entailed a very high cost of living.[46]

Even this imposing array of taxes was insufficient to meet the costs of war, and the Dutch, like the English and the French, had to borrow money. Provincial public debts had been the rule ever since the wars for independence, and Dutch credit was well established by the end of the seventeenth century. Nonetheless, the mounting costs of war proved too much for the republic. Neither taxes nor credit could be expanded enough to meet the pace set by the War of the Spanish Succession, and by 1707 the English had to take over many of the subsidy obligations that the Dutch had originally assumed.

Much has been written about the causes of the decline of the Netherlands Republic in the eighteenth century.[47] It is undoubtedly true that the rise of multilateral, direct trade connections diminished the importance of the Dutch entrepôt market, that the shifts of commerce resulting from the rise of English and Hamburg merchants, and other commercial factors must be credited with the loss of Dutch prestige in the commercial world, but, as Professor Baasch insists, not the least of the problems of the eighteenth-century Dutch was presented by the tax structure and the debts inherited from the great wars of 1688–1713.[48]

The fiscal systems of the princes in central and Danubian Europe

[46] E. Baasch, *op. cit.*, 182–84.
[47] One of the best discussions is C. Wilson, *Anglo-Dutch Commerce in the Eighteenth Century* (London, 1941).
[48] Baasch, *op. cit.*, 184 ff.

differed in details, but in general followed a common pattern inherited from the German Middle Ages.[49] All these princes, like their ancestors before them, were first of all feudal lords, and their ideas, particularly those of the lesser ones, were but little removed from medieval politico-economic thinking. The more important states like Brandenburg-Prussia, Hanover, Bavaria, and Saxony, however, came to a realization of the modern state idea through the expansion of their military and fiscal institutions. Armies and tax administrations effected the consolidation of the princely units which had attained autonomy in the loose-jointed federal structure of the old Empire. The petty units, too small to build armies, remained feudal baronies without power or vitality, awaiting the day when their stronger neighbors would devour them.

The *Kammer-Verwaltung* (fiscal administration) in the German lands had charge of the prince's crown lands and of the revenues due him as a feudal lord. These *Hofkammer* (treasuries) differed slightly from state to state both in organization and efficiency but they all helped to generate the institutions of eighteenth-century German mercantilism. The princes drew further revenue from direct taxes, usually called "contributions" since they were determined, assessed, and levied by the *Landtage* and the provincial collegial administrations. These parliaments were representative chambers elected by the "orders" in the traditional *Länder*. Any prince who ruled several "lands" would have as many *Landtage* to deal with. The Bohemian crown lands, for example, were under the diets of Bohemia, of Moravia, and of Silesia; the German inheritance of the Hapsburgs included *Landtage* of the three Austrias, of the Tyrol, of Carinthia, etc.; the Hohenzollern domains included *Lantage* for Prussia, for Brandenburg, for Pomerania, for Mark, etc. It could hardly be expected that those who voted the "contributions" would conceive of their prince's problems as an integral whole. Their parsimonious grants of money were made with particularist interests in mind. It is small wonder that the great elector worked to destroy the *Stände's* rights or that Austrian statesmen proposed calling a general *Landtage* from all the Hapsburg domains to force consideration of general problems, for no fiscal reforms could be accomplished through the petty provincial *Landtage*.

The third source of princely revenue was the excise tax. All over central Europe taxes were collected on liquor, beer, wines, soap, meat,

---

[49] Otto Hintze, "Der österreichische und der preussische Beamtenstaat," *Historische Zeitschrift,* LXXXIV (1901), 401–444.

candles, and many other commodities of popular consumption. In Prussia the excise was an urban tax; in the Hapsburg lands it was levied in the rural areas as well as in the towns. The excise taxes were often farmed out to private collectors, but in any case their administration was divorced from the collegial tax-collection agencies. Not until the mid-eighteenth century, under the rule of enlightened despots, were the central European tax agencies consolidated.

The relative poverty of central Europe and the parsimony of the *Stände* combined to impose rather narrow limits on the expansion of tax revenues in times of crisis. It is not surprising, therefore, that German princes had to beg for subsidies from their wealthier allies to meet the costs of keeping their armies in the field.[50]

Although the court at Vienna at times paid subsidies, it was itself often reduced to greatest poverty. The German states contributed either money or soldiers to defend the Empire (the Turkish tax, for example), but these contributions were small compared to the emperor's needs. In the 1680's the subsidies of Pope Innocent XI helped to keep the imperial army in the field. The 500,000 Thl. paid by the prince of Hanover for the electoral dignity, at a moment when only a financial miracle could save the Empire, was only the largest of many sums received in return for honors. The sale of Reichsgraf and Freiherr titles to wealthy bourgeois serves as a reminder that Louis XIV was not the only ruler to cheapen the nobility. The great Jewish banking family, Oppenheimer, was the bulwark of Emperor Leopold's ever-empty treasury, but Dutch and other Jewish bankers also loaned money to the Viennese court in return for mining concessions, tax revenues, and other grants—usually at stiff interest rates. In the midst of the War of the Spanish Succession, the *Wiener Stadtbank* was founded (1706) to prop public credit, and in 1715 the *Universal-Bankalität* came into existence with the combined functions of deposit bank, tax-receiving agency, and public debt administration. It was to be of the utmost importance in Eugene's later wars against the Turks and Maria Theresa's conflicts in the mid-century. Frederick the Great had no comparable credit institution, and had to fight his wars with the aid of subsidies, debasement of the currency, and private credit.[51]

Central European princes were unable to support the financial obliga-

[50] Riedel, A. F., *Der brandenburgisch-preussische Haushalt in den beiden letzen Jahrhunderten* (Berlin, 1866), 34, 47; Riedel provides an interesting discussion of Prussia's problem.

[51] O. Hintze, *op. cit.*, 419–20; A. Sieveking, *Grundzüge der neueren Wirtschaftsgeschichte vom 17ten Jahrhundert bis zur Gegenwart* (Leipsig, 1921), 34.

tions assumed by their contemporaries in the west, but the fiscal structures they created to buttress their military establishments became the very core around which the new states idea developed in Germany. It was the imperious demand for money that called into being the bureaucracies created by men like Ferdinand II and Frederick William earlier in the century, and developed by the statesmen of the late seventeenth and eighteenth centuries into machines for uniting and governing the divergent lands under the prince's authority. These bureaucracies, in turn, became the axis on which the police states of the eighteenth century turned.

It is clear that there were economic limitations to the conduct of war, and reasonably clear that among them fiscal rather than industrial problems were of paramount importance. Governments were apparently able to buy all the war materials they could pay for. Louis XIV himself predicted that the victor would be the prince whose treasury still had in it one piece of gold and, if we substitute credit for gold, his prediction was accurate. By 1713 France was bankrupt, the German princes almost at the end of their resources, and the Dutch forced to curtail expenses. Only England still had credit reserves to be tapped, and England emerged as the victor over allies and enemies alike.

III. COMMERCE AND WAR

There is a "law," wrote Professor Seeley, "which prevails throughout English history in the seventeenth and eighteenth centuries, the law, namely, of the interdependence of trade and war. . . . Trade leads naturally to war, and war fosters trade." [52] Obviously so simple an explanation for so complex a problem is incomplete, but it is undoubtedly true that the mercantilist regulations of trading nations, oriented as much toward the injury of competitors as toward the insurance of benefits for their own merchants, created tensions that led to conflict. Equally important is the fact that, once war was declared, the policies of the contestants were influenced in large measure by commercial considerations. Strategists tried desperately to control the highways of commerce and to shape the course of the war so as to assure their countries a favorable commercial position at the close of hostilities.

Attempts to regulate commerce in time of war immediately raised questions about neutral and belligerent rights. International law was still inchoate and ill-defined; traditional practice, treaty obligations, and political pretensions as expressed in ordinances and proclamations revealed

[52] J. R. Seeley, *The Expansion of England* (Boston, 1909), 110.

great divergences. The Dutch, who had always fought their wars with the slogan "business as usual," supported a liberal position. When war broke out, their prize courts were prepared to apply the formula "free ships, free goods." English practice had generally adhered to the formula of the *Consolat del Mer,* that neutral goods in an enemy ship should be free, but that enemy goods in a neutral ship might be condemned. The French, more severe than either, held that *"la robe d'ennemi confisque celle d'ami"*: a friend's goods in an enemy ship and a friend's ship with enemy goods were both subject to condemnation. Neutrals naturally favored the Dutch position. The Danish and Swedish governments, for instance, as well as the Hanse cities maintained the right of their ships to carry any goods, their own or others', wherever they wished.

As soon as England entered the conflict in 1689 the Whig politicians urged a rigorous prosecution of the trade war. The Whigs resented French trade because it drained bullion and coin from England, and they relished the idea of preventing all nations from enjoying what they wished to deny themselves. The Dutch had not prohibited trade with France even when war broke out; they had merely published a list of goods that could not be imported from or exported to French ports. Whig politicians, convinced that the way to defeat France was to destroy her economic strength, demanded from their ally a much more stringent policy as the price of an Anglo-Dutch alliance.

William III seems to have been singularly uninterested in the commercial aspects of the war; his mind reacted primarily to questions of politics, strategy, and religion, but he was willing to support his aggressive Whig followers. The commission that drew up the alliance treaty of August, 1689, defined Anglo-Dutch naval policy in the most stringent terms. The allied navies undertook to blockade the coast of France and to arrest and condemn all ships and goods going to or from French ports. This treaty "cut the world of commerce into two halves, and it ordered all ships to trade only in the half that belonged to the party of William." [53] Since the French navy maintained its superiority over the allies during the first years of the war, this proclamation proved somewhat unrealistic, but the policy gave free play to Anglo-Dutch cruisers and privateers. French prize practices being equally severe, neutrals were placed in a position where they must either recognize the belligerents' moral right or the *droit de canon.*

[53] G. N. Clark, *The Dutch Alliance and the War against French Trade, 1688–1697* (London and New York, 1923), 33. This little book is an excellent study; it has been freely used in this section.

Swedish merchants, unaccustomed to accept any such restrictions upon their commerce, forced Charles XI to abandon his alliance with the anti-French coalition and to reach an understanding with Denmark on the question of neutral rights.[54] Anglo-Dutch seizures of neutral shipping filled the diplomatic pouches with protests and recriminations. The Danes arrested Dutch ships in reprisal and obstinately enforced the respect of the Danish flag in the Sound. Had the politico-economic machinery been available, William might have appeased Sweden and Denmark by buying up their entire exports, but the seventeenth-century state was utterly unprepared for this type of economic warfare. Scandinavian protests were hazardous to the Anglo-Dutch cause, for the maritime powers were more dependent than was France upon Baltic trade and therefore could not ignore the Danish threat to close the Sound.

The maritime powers were thus placed in an embarrassing position. Their Swedish ally proposed mediation of the war, while the Danes threatened to close the Baltic to allied ships. Furthermore, while the Anglo-Dutch forces gained little by interference with neutral commerce, French privateers really injured English merchants by attacking Swedish ships. "The French," Professor Clark notes, "had been taking Swedish ships with English goods aboard, one recently worth £20,000, whereas . . . no great quantity of French goods had been found on Swedish ships."[55] In the end the British retreated from their policy of strict regulation to the more liberal policy adopted by the Dutch at the opening of hostilities.

The neutrals seem to have been unable to force the French to agree to the formula "free ships, free goods," but French passport policy was so liberal that in practice neutral shipping was fairly free. The Treaty of Ryswick, signed between France and the Netherlands (1697), recognized the principle "free ships, free goods." During the succeeding wars, both in the Baltic and in western European waters, the belligerents acknowledged the right of neutrals to all peaceful trade. Naval policies during the War of the Spanish Succession were more liberal than they were ever to be again.

Though neutral ships were allowed to sail where they wished, their cargoes were carefully searched to prevent contraband from reaching the enemy, and the lists of banned goods grew in length and ingeniousness. At first only metals, guns, explosives, and obvious war equipment were

[54] Rudolf Fåhraeus, *Sveriges Historia till våra Dagar: VIII, Karl XI och Karl XII* (Stockholm, 1923), 282.

[55] G. N. Clark, *op. cit.,* 115.

declared contraband, but with the expansion of the conflict any item that might aid in prolonging enemy resistance came to be classed as contraband. The harvest failures of the early 1690's added grain to the list. In spite of Danish and Swedish protests, the English navy arrested grain fleets and forced them into harbor; the ships were eventually released, but they were forced to sell their grain in England.

War at sea at the turn of the eighteenth century was a nice cross between piracy and modern commerce destroying. The regular navies were not large enough to permit the detachment of many vessels for raiding. Captains were instructed to arrest vessels that came within range, but they were not allowed to hunt for prizes. Special task forces did make spectacular raids, but for the most part patrols, convoy duty, and operational assignments occupied most of the navies' time and attention. After French lost control of the sea, French naval vessels were used for raids, but often enough only after they had been transferred to a privateering syndicate. The capture of the English Smyrna convoy, the interception of the Spanish munitions fleet, and a number of other famous raids were effected by privateers and regular naval vessels combined for a single operation. By and large, however, it was the privateer corsair who made the seas unsafe for commerce and drove insurance rates upward. He was the raider, the sea wolf, ready to pounce upon any likely prize.

These privateers were the descendants of the raiders, filibusters, buccaneers of the sixteenth century. The grant of authority by the government made them a little less like pirates and a little more like regular naval units, but the line between patriotic obedience of the naval ordinances and piracy was often difficult to draw. The privateer was usually backed by a syndicate of owners who supplied the vessel, paid the crew, and expected a share of the booty. The captain carried a letter of marque from the admiralty that legitimized his predatory ventures, regulated his handling of vessels and prisoners, and invited friendly authorities to give him aid and assistance. Before he left port, he had to post a bond to assure his good behavior and his bringing the prize ships into port for condemnation. The admiralty, the crew, and the owners shared in the proceeds. In the two wars of this period, privateering reached its full development; it was to continue to be a characteristic aspect of naval warfare as long as ships were dependent upon sails for motive power.

The cruelty of some captains toward their prisoners, the tricks by which many of them attempted to evade giving full returns, and the riotous and undisciplined behavior of many of their crews, gave the privateers a bad name. On the other hand, some of their exploits, particularly those of the famous French raiders, created around men like Jean Bart and Duguay-Trouin a patriotic mythology that has lasted to our own day. Both these men, as national heroes, were ennobled and given regular naval commissions. One of their English contemporaries earned a reputation and became the subject of a mythology hardly less extensive: Captain Kidd, who, unable to resist the lure of wealth and power, hauled down his king's flag and unfurled the Jolly Roger to make his name synonymous with bloodthirsty piracy. Heroes or villains, the corsairs were an instrument of economic warfare and representatives of an important aspect of the economic life of their era. The ships they captured were either brought into port or paid a fine, so that the privateer became an important factor in the distribution of goods in wartime.[56]

No generalization will do for all privateers. Some of them sailed in big ships mounting 40 or more guns and with crews larger than those of a warship of comparable class. Others used tiny vessels carrying little armament and preyed exclusively on fishermen and small coasters. The larger privateers did not hesitate to give battle to a warship; Duguay-Trouin brought six English and Dutch naval vessels into port to collect the reward of 500 *livres* per gun; the smaller ones had to rely upon stratagems and trickery to bring down an armed merchantman. The numbers operating at one time are difficult to determine. In the Spanish war Dunkirk alone commissioned 800 corsairs, but obviously many of the commissions meant merely a change in captains, many of the ships were captured by the enemy, and not a few of them made only one or two voyages. Malo estimates that there were about 100 at sea from Dunkirk during the most flourishing period of the Spanish succession war. While this harbor was the most important privateering base, it was not the only one; undoubtedly French, English, and Dutch harbors sent forth over 1,000 corsairs. The story of English and Dutch privateering is woefully incomplete, but we know, for example, that Middleburg and Flushing commissioned 47 vessels with 1,004 cannon and 36 mortars in 1702, and three years later, when the general estates increased the rewards, the number approximately doubled. The condemnations of the English prize

56 This section on privateering is largely based upon H. Malo, *Les corsaires dunkerquois et Jean Bart*, 2 vols. (Paris, 1913); *La grande guerre des corsaires, Dunkerque 1702–1715* (Paris, 1925); Monentheiul, *Essai sur la course, son histoire, sa réglementation, son abolition* (Paris, 1898); Leeder, *Die englische Kaperei und die Thätigkeit der Admiralitätsgerichte* (1882), and Johnson's popularly written *Wolves of the Channel 1681–1856* (London, 1931).

courts are clear indications that a sizable fleet of privateers operated from the island.[57]

The sea wolves engaged in work hazardous for themselves as well as for their victims. Countless petty naval actions between privateers, or between a "pack" of privateers and an enemy task force provide thrilling stories of action and bravery. When the English admiralty came under heavy fire in parliament for its "neglect" of English commerce, the defense insisted that the navy had not done badly; between 1702 and 1707 it had taken or destroyed 70 French warships with 1,700 guns, 170 privateers, and 1,346 merchantmen. The admiralty counted its own losses at 35 warships with 800 guns, and 1,146 merchantmen, of which 300 had been retaken.[58] How reliable this figure of losses may have been, it is hard to say. The estimate of 4,000 merchantmen lost in King William's War was probably high; the admiralty estimate for Queen Anne's war may well have been low.

It is as difficult to get a full picture of the depredations as to discover the number of the privateers, for the captains were notorious for evading complete returns even though the business agent of the owners was always on board. Clark estimates an English annual "take" of £60,000 for the years 1689–1697, and £90,000 for 1703–1713. If Malo's estimates are correct, French condemnations were vastly more important. Dunkirk alone had an annual average six and a half times as valuable as the total English figure. An absolute estimate, however, is meaningless unless related to the total shipping figures, but these, too, it is impossible to determine. Insurance rates, however, do reflect the hazard. Posthumus has published the Dutch rates for 1703.[59] They were probably based upon the experience of the preceding war and were undoubtedly too low for the years 1704–1707 when French activity reached its highest point; nonetheless they are instructive. The rate for outgoing ships (from Dutch harbors) to the Levant was 20 per cent, to Italy 16 per cent to 20 per cent, to Portugal 7 per cent to 14 per cent, to the Baltic and North Sea 2 per cent to 8 per cent, to Curaçao and Surinam 10 per cent, to England 2½ per cent with convoy, 5 per cent without. Professor Clark's cautious conclusion is perhaps the best that can be given: ". . . the French took away from the small merchant fleets of their enemies a proportion large enough

[57] G. N. Clark, "Trade War and War Trade, 1701–1713," *Economic History Review*, I (1927–28), 267.

[58] Trevelyan, *England under Queen Anne*, II, 323.

[59] N. W. Posthumus, *op. cit.*, LXIV.

to cause alarm and loss among merchants and financiers, and to threaten and somewhat impair the import and export of goods." [60]

The allied naval and privateering forces worked havoc with French shipping. The fishing fleets suffered severely; the India trade was practically extinguished; trade with the Baltic dwindled to what could be transported in neutral holds; New World commerce continued with great difficulty, for privateers operating out of Boston, Providence, and New York were anxious to capture salt, wine, and furs both before and after they turned to piracy.[61] French Mediterranean trade suffered less severely, but even this was much troubled by the establishment of English bases at Gibraltar, Port Mahon, and Sicily.

Although the belligerent powers believed that their warfare at sea seriously affected the strength of their opponents, it is certain that the war on trade was not decisive. The day had not yet come when economic strangulation could dictate terms. Nevertheless there also can be little doubt that the allied navies influenced the French economy. While the little people in the villages were probably unaware of the war at sea, the commercial and financial classes felt its weight. Louis XIV may not have been forced to surrender by the Anglo-Dutch navies, but his power to impose his will on Europe was undoubtedly weakened after he lost control of the sea.

IV. BUSINESS AS USUAL?

The historian writing in the mid-twentieth century is painfully aware of the impact of war upon economic life, and must, therefore, resist the temptation to read a comparable experience into the past. In the three decades of warfare here under consideration certain areas and cities suffered frightful damage, but, with the possible exception of Hungary, no entire country was ravaged or economically ruined in the twentieth-century manner. Nonetheless, the disorder created by the wars against Louis XIV should not be underestimated. In Belgrade, in Barcelona, in Heidelberg, in Rio de Janeiro, in Deerfield, Massachusetts, and in dozens of other towns the inhabitants could have found little comfort in the knowledge that in a later era Berlin and Hiroshima were to suffer much greater destruction. Compared with the devastation of the religious and

---

[60] G. N. Clark, *The Dutch Alliance*, 128.

[61] The high incidence of change from privateer to pirate along the North American coast can partially be accounted for by the policy of colonial prize courts. Cf. H. M. Chapin, *Privateer Ships and Sailors, The First Century of American Colonial Privateering 1625–1725* (Toulon, 1926), 95 ff. *et passim*.

civil wars of the sixteenth and early seventeenth centuries, however, the conduct of the more disciplined forces of the early eighteenth century was certainly less horrible, except in cases where systematic destruction was undertaken as war policy. On the other hand, earlier wars involved smaller armies and were more restricted in their geographical scope. While recent revaluations have suggested that the destruction of the Thirty Years' War in Germany has been exaggerated, it may well be that, considering the territorial extent of the late seventeenth- and early eighteenth-century wars, the assumed "mildness of limited warfare" was also something of a myth. For each example of generous treatment of the civil population one could adduce a striking case of gross brutality; for each instance of disciplined behavior there was another of license and pillage.

Two studies which deal with the cost of the War of the Spanish Succession to the Duchy of Savoy throw interesting light upon the problem.[62] They reveal not only the tendency toward rising costs of warfare, but indicate also that military operations bore heavily upon populations unfortunate enough to live in theaters of conflict. Piedmont was occupied by both French and Allied troops during the War of the Spanish Succession. Prato's estimates of the damage done by friend and foe illustrate the relationship between military occupation and economic life, and suggest that there may have been a social problem as well.

WAR DAMAGE IN PIEDMONT OCTOBER, 1703, TO 1710
FIGURES QUOTED IN PIEDMONTESE LIBRA

Incendiary damage by foes	£p4,184,608
" " " friends	691,826
Stealing of animals by foes	1,492,032
" " " " friends	325,412
Stealing of other goods (exclusive of hay) by foes	15,039,362
" " " " by friends	3,490,836
Destruction of forests and fruit trees by foes	3,810,882
" " " " " " by friends	2,335,690
Wood, wine, and food commandeered by foes	1,282,871
" " " " " by friends	1,494,801
Indemnities paid to foes	3,177,093
total £p37,325,415	

[62] G. Prato, *Il costo della guerra di seccessione spagnuola e le spese pubbliche in Piemonte del 1700 al 1713* (Turin 1907); L. Einaudi, *La finanza sabauda all'aprisi del secolo XVIII* (Turin, 1908).

These figures assume further significance when it is realized that the average annual budget for courts and justice for these same years was about £p450,000; for the university and schools, £p6,300; for ambassadors, the council of state and the grand chancellery, between £p160,000 and £p210,000. A colonel was paid between £p3,415 and £p7,200, a captain £p1,146 and £p2,360. The expenses of the duke's army of 26,000 men in 1704 (highest) was £p9,877,230, and for the whole period 1703–1709, £p41,000,000.[63] Obviously the predatory behavior of soldiers, their habit of taking souvenirs and any other available goods, and their playful destructiveness were a real burden to provinces in the theaters of war. Piedmont's experience was probably not typical; Hungary, the Baltic provinces, and the Palatinate undoubtedly suffered more severely while other areas suffered less.

Disagreeable as they were, the inroads of soldiers were probably not the most important economic disturbance caused by the wars. During most of the thirty years under consideration, only a relatively small section of Europe was under more or less continuous occupation. For the mass of peasants and townsfolk, the tax collectors, rather than the soldiers, were the constant reminders that the prince had gone to war. Furthermore, the rising taxes, tolls, and excises probably had a more baneful effect upon the economy than the actual depredations of soldiers or privateers. This was certainly true in France, Sweden, and Russia, where taxes became unbearable, and it was probably true also in the United Netherlands, where the tax collector joined the French privateer to blight trade and commerce.

For the Germanies, England, Italy, the three decades of warfare were years of relative prosperity. The German lands had been recovering steadily from the low point of the years 1650–1660, and the wars seem not to have greatly interfered with the process. England, especially in the first decade of the eighteenth century, was extremely prosperous; in spite of French privateers, her sea-borne commerce grew steadily and her internal prosperity was highly gratifying. France, Spain, Russia, Poland, and Sweden were the countries chiefly affected by the economic consequences of the war. Each of these areas suffered a decline in population and a diminution of trade.

The Europe of 1700 was on the threshold of modern economic life, but it was not yet committed to its fullest implications. Certain great seaports were, it is true, tied to an international market, but the inland

[63] The figures are from Prato, *op. cit., passim.*

towns and villages lived within a much narrower economic frame. Villages—and most of the people on the continent still lived in villages— that were at all distant from the large urban centers still operated on a sustenance economy, while the smaller towns depended for their pros- perity more upon the narrow limits of the province than upon the larger markets of Europe. The continent was not closely integrated economi- cally and therefore local weather conditions frequently influenced the welfare of the people more than did war. The drought years of the early 1690's and of 1709–1710 brought a greater distress than the conflicts of the princes.

Even the great marketing centers were less disturbed by the wars than one would expect. Whig statesmen, who regarded trade with France as detrimental to the kingdom even in peacetime, were ready to advocate the complete destruction of all trade with France, but Dutch merchants and statesmen were unwilling to support this policy, especially during the War of the Spanish Succession, when Spain as well as France became an enemy. Textiles, china, leather, shipbuilding, and other industries of the Netherlands depended upon Spain for raw materials, while the Spanish market was extremely important to the mercantile houses of Amsterdam. The Dutch could see no reason for giving up this trade because of war. The states-general published lists of articles that could not be sold to the enemy, but after the failure of the harsh policy at- tempted in 1689, it evaded the English demand for complete cessation of commerce between belligerents. Indeed, the mild penalties almost en- couraged illegal trade. The French government, anxious to get materials and perhaps hoping to drive a wedge between the allies, connived at such trade by issuing generous passports and by according an at least not unfriendly reception to foreign merchants.

The great difficulty for the Netherlands, and for England, too, arose from the fact that prohibition of trade with France did not mean that French goods ceased to flow into the country, or that France would be completely deprived of English and Dutch products. Neutral traders from the Hanse towns, particularly Hamburg, entered the trade and tended to replace the Dutch staple markets. The Dutch markets were threatened with immediate loss and with strong competition when peace finally came. Small wonder, therefore, that the Netherlands government refused to follow English trade policy.[64] Unable to prevent French goods

[64] At the opening of the War of the Spanish Succession the Dutch did sign a treaty with England and the Empire prohibiting trade with France for one year. Exemptions weakened the force of the prohibition, and at the end of the year the Dutch refused to renew the

from entering the international market the English attempted at least to block the flow of gold into France by prohibiting the exchange of bills and bullion between the belligerents. Even this proved difficult, for the overland postal services were not interrupted by the wars,[65] and Dutch financiers continued to enjoy considerable profits from their transactions with France, Italy, and Spain. It is even probable that Louis's war machine was serviced in part by Dutch credit.

The English Whigs could afford to deprecate the value of French trade, for in these very years they were establishing their commercial position in Portugal and the Spanish Empire. The Methuen treaties not only involved allied policy in a hapless attempt to place the Hapsburg prince on the Spanish throne, but also laid the foundation for the Anglo-Portuguese trade of the next two centuries. The exchange of English cloth for port wine became the backbone of a close trade relationship. At the same time, the civil war in Spain allowed English merchants to establish themselves in Spanish America, where they soon succeeded in outdoing both the Dutch and the French, and in building a market for the postwar period. While the Dutch wanted "business as usual" in wartime, the English used the war to develop unusual business that was both profitable and patriotic. With a predatory policy toward their enemy and a ruthless attitude toward their friends, the English made the wars pay dividends even though some losses were involved.

Obviously the wars did interfere with the normal peacetime economy both by their imposts and their destructive exactions by land and sea, but it proved impossible to convert continental buinessmen and statesmen to the Whig view that trade with the enemy must cease and that the business of war must take precedence over all other activity. This fact may well have been crucial in determining the interaction of war and economy at the turn of the eighteenth century. Psychologically and administratively the Europe of Louis XIV was ill-equipped to wage total war. The distinction between public and private life, between the affairs of the prince and those of his subjects, was still too great to permit unlimited warfare, while the administrative machinery necessary to direct public opinion and to organize and control the energy and resources of nations was still in embryo. To be sure, the political revolutions of the

---

agreement. G. N. Clark's excellent article, "War Trade and Trade War, 1701–1703," *Economic History Review*, I, 262–280, gives a penetrating analysis of the problem.

[65] A packet service, free from French jurisdiction, was established between northern Europe and the Iberian peninsula, but it never completely supplanted the overland postal services.

later seventeenth century removed many of the checks that medieval society had imposed upon public power. They made possible the raising and supplying of large military forces at public expense, facilitated the organization and implementation of policy, and cleared the ground for unitary administration. But they did not alter the status of subjects nor did they create the feeling of nationalism necessary to arouse the emotional force of the nation. As long as a man was a subject rather than a citizen, as long as he could distinguish between his private goods and the goods of the nation, it was impossible to check the desire to carry on business as usual, even in wartime. The ancient dualism of king and people had not yet dissolved to the point where identification of both in the welfare of the state became possible.

Chapter Eight

THE FRONTIERS OF KNOWLEDGE

I. THE THIRST FOR KNOWLEDGE

BY THE end of the seventeenth century the breakdown of united Christendom and the transfer of power from religious to secular hierarchies had done much to free the mind of man from the strict controls characteristic of earlier eras. Europe had not yet developed a society so liberal as to disclaim responsibility for the ideas of men, but the political and religious diversity of the continent, as well as the recognition of the fact that intellectual conformity was no longer possible, had created a situation in which any idea, however advanced or fantastic, could somewhere find a forum. The abolition or relaxation of censorship in England, the United Netherlands, and Germany made the Protestant part of Europe appear more liberal than the Catholic, but even in Spain, Italy, and France, where stricter controls prevailed, revolutionary ideas could often find a publisher, and in general the international traffic in books was so imperfectly regulated that ideas could not be excluded from any part of Europe. It is significant that by 1700 it was rare for a book to be burned by the public hangman, and rarer still for an author to suffer such treatment of his own person.

The books that have survived from this era convey the impression that the generation which fought the first world wars and witnessed the rise of the great powers was a most serious-minded one. Men apparently thirsted for knowledge. Booksellers' shelves were loaded with accounts of distant travel, treatises on mathematics, mechanics, physics, and astronomy, catalogues and classifications of plants, insects, animals, fossils, and fishes, books on geography, and works on secular and ecclesiastical history. Where the explorers of the earth, space, matter, and time left off, the philosophers, political theorists, and theologians took up their pens to rationalize man's ways with man, the world, and God in terms of one or another of the fashionable philosophic systems or scientific cosmologies. If we did not know that multivolumed romances, dull and insipid to our age, stories of real and fancied adventure, countless books of devotion,

209

and poetry, essays, and drama supplemented this diet of facts and theorems, we might conclude that never before or since was the literate public so consumed with an avid desire for learning.

The reading public was, of course, only a small segment of the population. Those who were able to grasp the propositions of scientists and philosophers constituted an even smaller group, but their importance transcended their numbers, for they, and not the inarticulate, ignorant, and superstitious masses, shaped the tastes, the forms, and the intellectual outlook of Europe. The gulf between the cosmology and philosophy of the learned and the beliefs of the untutored was abysmal, and no longer marked merely differing degrees of refinement in the comprehension of the same generally accepted ideas. By the end of the seventeenth century the two groups had come to hold mutually exclusive notions about man and the universe. The English judge who freed a convicted witch with the caustic remark that there was no law against riding on a broomstick illustrated the gap that already separated the educated from the ignorant.

The passion for learning among the elite classes created interesting and sometimes amusing situations, for their understanding did not always keep pace with their thirst for knowledge. The first generation of the new scientists and philosophers had worked as individuals or in small companies. Galileo's attempt to popularize his ideas in the *Dialogue on the Two Chief Systems of the World* (1632) had not been so happy as to encourage others to imitate him. In the second half of the century, however, science and learning had become fashionable, and the great minds whose explorations provided so much of the intellectual capital of our own era were joined by an ever-growing number of men anxious to propagate the new truth. Princes in France, England, and Prussia founded, protected, and patronized learned societies more or less modeled upon those already existing in Italy, and all over Europe provincial societies for the study of natural philosophy began to emerge, in imitation of the more illustrious bodies in London and Paris. These learned societies, many of which hardly deserved the adjective, partially satisfied the hunger for knowledge, while popular teachers, some of whom encouraged the belief in the possibility of squaring the circle or making other equally important mathematical discoveries, also helped still the avid, if at times not too enlightened, interest in learning.

One keen observer noted that many of the great and wealthy landlords, whose forebears had expended their energies in war and politics, found in learning a satisfactory substitute for the power that the bureaucratic state was taking from them. The fashionable lady who carried a cadaver in her coach so that she might improve her idle moments by studying anatomy, the young gallants who wooed their ladies with mathematical propositions, and the maidens who refused to accept suitors unless they had made a fundamental discovery in mathematics or mechanics were surely exceptional, but the generation that bought, translated, and read edition after edition of Fontenelle's *A Plurality of Worlds* and John Ray's *Wonders of God,* that made Descartes a household word among the elite, and that patronized the book publishers of London, Amsterdam, Leipzig, and a dozen other cities, was one anxious to know and to understand the world that was being revealed before their eyes.

This generation experienced a great crisis of conscience, a crisis that involved fundamental conceptions honored for centuries. In 1680 most of the educated still thought in terms of Bishop Bossuet: hierarchy, discipline, order, divine right, divine providence, and classic stability. But 1720 Europe was ready to think with Voltaire, ready to discard the old ideals and to accept, indeed to demand, movement and change. Basic to the understanding of this great transformation was the fact that literate Europe was ready to read the books, to accept the findings, and to absorb the ideas of those who were exploring the frontiers of understanding. Old ecclesiastical and secular controls over the minds of men were rapidly dissolving under the impact of facts adduced by those who had explored the globe, had recovered classical learning, had broken the unity of Christendom, had fought civil and religious wars, and were in process of devising new forms of political and economic life.

II. L'ESPRIT GÉOMÉTRIQUE

Copernicus, Vesalius, Kepler, Bacon, and Galileo supplied the brushes with which Descartes, Spinoza, Bayle, Harvey, Huygens, Newton, and Leibniz began to paint a new picture of the universe. To these intellectual giants of the seventeenth century a dozen or more outstanding names could be easily added. These were the philosophers, scientists, and mathematicians who undermined and destroyed age-old preconceptions and oriented the western mind in entirely new directions. The intellectual revolution of the seventeenth century was more than just a new turn in human thought; it was a fundamental remaking of values and an entirely new approach to the problems of the universe. The great seventeenth-century thinkers, with the exception of Leibniz, rejected the teleological explanation of phenomena and the world of harmoniously ascending hierarchies, and posited instead a world in which mathematical relationships and the analysis of data became the key to understanding. They ceased to manipulate a world of gratuitous ideas, and attempted to manipulate the world of things.

No single individual can be credited with this achievement. Kepler's fanatical faith in a Pythagorean world, Galileo's insistence upon observation and experiment, Descartes's intuitive understanding of the need for a new philosophy, and the patient exploration by dozens of researchers of a world theretofore unknown and unconceived—all contributed to the process that was to give man a measure both of understanding and of control over his universe. Two fundamental tools conditioned the process: mathematics and precision instruments. Through logarithms, trigonometric functions, algebra, analytical geometry, and calculus mathematicians devised an accurate language for describing many phenomena; through the barometer, thermometer, telescope, microscope, pendulum clock, air pump, and delicate balances they gradually developed instruments for assembling and measuring significant data. The seventeenth century weighed, measured, and took the temperature of the world; it observed the remote and the minute, and recorded its discoveries in a new synthesis. Pythagoras believed that number ruled the universe, but Kepler performed the heroic task of proving that planetary motion could be reduced to terms of arithmetic. Almost a century later, Newton showed that the whole universe was subject to law describable in mathematical terms.

The achievements of the mathematicians colored the intellectual development of the entire century; this was the era of *l'esprit géométrique* of which Descartes was the shining prophet and Fontenelle the high priest. The latter was merely expressing the conviction of the best minds of his age when he exclaimed: "The geometric spirit is not so attached to geometry that it cannot be disentangled and carried over into other areas of knowledge. A work on morals, on politics, on criticism, perhaps even on eloquence, will be better, all other things being equal, if it is written by the hand of a geometer. The order, the clearness and precision, the exactitude that have characterized good books . . . may well have originated in this geometric spirit." [1] By the end of the century Descartes's disciples had multiplied till their numbers were legion. In the words of one historian: "The universities were cartesian, the marquis, the scientific

[1] *Préface sur l'utilité des mathématiques et de la physique, Oeuvres de Fontenelle,* XVI (Paris, 1790), 67–8.

amateurs, Colbert, the king were cartesian. France conjugated the verb 'to cartesianate' and Europe followed suit enthusiastically." [2] In the same sense Newton, Leibniz, Huygens, Halley, the Royal Society, the Scientific Academy, the *Acta Erudicorum,* and even the gardeners at Versailles were also Cartesian. Descartes had mirrored the spirit of his age and his work became the inspiration of the next several generations.

Descartes was the advocate of skepticism as well as of geometry, and his skepticism served notice that all authorities of the past must brace themselves for the scrutiny of reason. "Descartes proclaimed: 'let us trust reason; it is infallible,' and the chorus of his disciples replied: 'reason alone, it is enough.' 'Common sense is sufficient to judge things,' continued the oracle . . . 'long live common sense and reason,' responded the chorus. 'Pile up experiments and observations.' . . ." [3] Experiment, observation, and reason, these were the sources of knowledge and the keys to the Cartesian world. The authorities of the past, enjoying the prestige of centuries, were subjected to examination in the light of the *Discourse on Method.*

Nonetheless, the seventeenth-century thinkers, for all the rigor of their method, could not escape dependence on postulates of their own. Like their classical and medieval predecessors they assumed an order of things, particularly in nature, that was fundamentally rational. The differences between them were set forth in Galileo's *Dialogues* (1632), which pictured the ancients and the moderns as hopelessly at cross purposes because they asked different questions of the supposedly rational world. Simplicio, the ancient, appealed to reason as much as Sagredo, the modern, but the latter asked *"How* do things happen?" while Simplicio persisted in asking *why* they happened. Professor Whitehead has insisted that Sagredo's appeal to evidence as the final arbiter of truth was actually a revolt against rationalism, ". . . an anti-intellectual movement. It was the return to the contemplation of brute fact; and it was based on a recoil from the inflexible rationality of medieval thought." [4]

This leads to a second assumption of the geometric spirit, namely that it is possible to speak significantly about the world in terms of number or geometric syllogisms. Descartes, by reducing geometry (space) to arithmetic (number), had provided an instrument (analytical geometry) to describe a Pythagorean world. When Newton and Leibniz demonstrated that both the direction and the acceleration of movement on a

[2] P. Rousseau, *Histoire de la science* (Paris, 1945), 249.
[3] *Ibid.*
[4] Alfred N. Whitehead, *Science and the Modern World* (New York, 1935), 12.

curve could also be described by arithmetic (calculus), they reaffirmed the faith of their age in number as a key to understanding. The logic of Aristotle and St. Thomas was thus summarily rejected for the syllogisms of Euclid. The latter seventeenth and the eighteenth centuries were to apply the new method to morals, theology, economics, and politics as well as to physics and astronomy. Here was the basis for a world without human emotions, aspirations, or fears: a world of measured facts.

The belief in a reasonable order of things, subject to the law of number, led Descartes to posit the universe as a machine, and induced Newton to prove that this machine was subject to a law statable in mathematical terms. At this point another postulate introduced limitations upon the development of the system. Like the Platonists, the thinkers of the seventeenth century were seeking unvarying absolutes, universals that would explain all things. They therefore postulated a Creator, a first cause, and then uncritically accepted the notion that His creation was of recent date, perhaps of about 4000 B.C. The historians of the period believed history to be episodical; the naturalists assumed that the earth, its fauna and its flora, had always been the same; and the theologians thought they *knew* within a few years the exact date of creation. It is not surprising, therefore, that the mathematicians and scientists failed to understand that the universe had evolved. Through their "geometry" they were trying to discover the "blueprint" used by the Creator in constructing His time machine. God, they assumed, was a mathematician; all that was needed was to discover His specifications. The question "why" seemed too burdened with superstition and prejudice to merit further consideration.

This inability to see that the world had a history caused less embarrassment to the astronomers and physicists than to the geographers, naturalists, and historians. It was easy enough to accommodate celestial and terrestrial mechanics to a limited conception of time. But the naturalist, confronted with clam shells on mountain tops or deeply embedded in the earth's surface, and faced with fossil plants and animals, some in forms unknown on earth, was forced to resort to curious mental gymnastics. The biblical flood, a whimsical creator, perverse seeds, and other often fantastic explanations had to substitute for history. The historians, in turn, when confronted with the extended chronology of China, India, and Egypt, were perplexed but most reluctant to abandon the biblical story of the earth's novity.

Another problem grew out of the Cartesian concept of the world as an orderly machine describable in terms of mathematics: namely, the question of the relationship between reason and experiment. Descartes was responsible for the idea that man, after discovering a few basic principles by observation and experiment, could reason out the structure of the universe without needing to consult the phenomena at every step. Fontenelle, speaking of the master, explained that Descartes, "taking a bold flight, wished to place himself at the center of all, to make himself master of first principles from which could be derived clear and fundamental conceptions. . . ." [5] Before his death, Descartes himself seems to have lost confidence in this idea, but many of his disciples ignored his doubts, especially when they adapted his method to areas other than mechanics. There is, of course, little difference beween this method of reasoning and Aristotle's. The Cartesians did not start with a nature abhorring a vacuum, but it was not difficult for them, as Goethe said later, to build "little worlds within the greater" by elevating limited ideas to the status of universals. It was this aspect of the geometric spirit that beclouded much of the thought of the Enlightenment and made much of the later Cartesian speculation as arid as Scholasticism.

There was, however, another tenet of *l'esprit géométrique*. Boyle Huygens, and Newton, following in the footsteps of Galileo, insisted upon testing theory by experimentation. In the preface to the second edition of the *Principia Mathematica* (1713) the editor, Roger Cotes, in paraphrasing Newton's famous rules of reasoning in natural philosophy (Book III of *Principia*), explained that natural philosophers, following the Newtonian practice, "derive the causes of all things from the most simple principles possible but, then, they assume nothing as a principle that is not proved by phenomena. They frame no hypotheses, nor receive them into philosophy otherwise than as questions whose truth may be disputed. . . ." Outside the field of science, Newton's own thinking was not based on such rigorous skepticism. His theological writings bristle with postulates and hypotheses accepted unquestioningly. But in his scientific works he did reject all that could not be tested by observation and experiment. It was this side of *l'esprit géométrique* that made possible the great conquests of knowledge and gave Newton's name to the science of the next hundred and fifty years. Obviously it too had limitations, for the Newtonian scientist had to assume that he could actually observe true relationships within a narrow segment of the total phenomena.

[5] *Éloge de Newton*, in *Oeuvres de Fontenelle*, XVII (Paris, 1792), 262 ff.

Cartesian or Newtonian, the learned world and its amateur followers shared the conviction that the world was describable in terms of mathematics and the assumption that human reason aided by observation could unlock its secrets. Generalized, this geometric spirit led to the application of the new science to ethics (Spinoza), to theology (Malebranche), and to politics (Locke). In the eighteenth century it enlarged its empire to include all knowledge. Its impact was felt even in architecture, landscape gardening, war, and daily life. Geometry was to the generation of 1700 what evolution was to be to a later age.

<h3>III. THE TRIUMPHS OF SCIENCE</h3>

As the historian of scientific thought approaches the early eighteenth century, he is confronted with an interesting problem. The first nine decades of the seventeenth century had made great strides in the conquest of scientific knowledge. The great mathematicians had laid the groundwork for modern algebra, trigonometry, analytical geometry, and calculus. The physicists had established the basis for the study of mechanics, statics, and hydrostatics, and had made prodigious gains in the field of optics. The anatomists had discovered the circulation of the blood and had opened the field of microscopic investigation of living tissue. With the thermometer, the barometer, the air pump, others had prepared the way for the study of meteorology and had cleared the ground for the foundations of modern chemistry. In astronomy Newton's *Principia* had crowned a century's labor with the discovery of laws governing all matter. It was an era enormously productive in research that led to fundamental discoveries in "pure" science. But the next thirty-odd years, that is, the three or four decades following the publication of the *Principia,* were almost as barren of important discoveries as the preceding ninety had been rich.[6]

It is difficult if not impossible to explain this strange lapse, for at bottom it touches the problem of rhythm in intellectual development and perhaps even the deeper mystery of the twin problems of learning and genius. In many ways it is interesting that the end of the seventeenth century provokes the question. By 1700 the great scientific academies, charged specifically with the task of expanding human knowledge, were well established in the cultural life of Europe. Subsidized observatories had taken the place of private astrologers in studying the firmament, and

---

[6] Newton and Huygens both published books on optics after 1687, but the research and texts for these books had been completed long before.

in the universities the new scientific learning was slowly but surely establishing itself alongside the traditional disciplines.[7] If institutional assistance and encouragement were the significant factors in the discovery of new truth, the generation of 1700 should have surpassed its immediate predecessors.

Furthermore, by 1700 the diffusion of scientific information was already taking place on an international scale. The publications of the scientific academies of England and France, *The Philosophical Transactions*, the *Mémoires et histoire*, and the *Journal des savants*, as well as the German *Acta Erudicorum*, the two Dutch reviews, *Les nouvelles de la république des lettres* and the *Bibliothèque choisie*, as well as a number of lesser publications in Venice and elsewhere assured an international audience for scientific news and speculation. The voluminous correspondence between scholars all over Europe provided something like a public forum where thinkers could test their ideas before a jury of their peers. We are told by scientists that such international ventilation of opinion and fact contributes to the environment necessary for the healthy development of scientific knowledge, but it obviously does not in itself ensure the progress of knowledge.

At first sight it would seem that the widespread victory of *l'esprit géométrique* should also have created an intellectual climate favorable to the nurture of scientific investigation. By 1700 Cartesianism was definitely the mode. It may be, however, that the disciples clung too closely to the master's words and understood too little of his spirit. The idea that a few fundamental principles, discovered by experiment, would provide the basis for a rational explanation of the world was not conducive to the heartbreaking labor of detailed research. Furthermore, Descartes's personal prestige beclouded his errors. Only his mathematics remained unchallenged by 1700, yet his disciples continued to teach Cartesian cosmology, physics, and zoology, slightly revised, for many decades after they had been superseded. For example, Jacques Ronault's *Traité de physique* (1671), which expounded Descartes's ideas, reached its twelfth French edition in 1708, and its sixteenth English edition in 1739. Long after Cartesian physics was outmoded uncritical readers still accepted it because of the prestige of the master.

Newton, too, had an influence upon his later contemporaries that was

[7] An analysis of the professions of the leading scientists of the period would undoubtedly necessitate a revision of Ornstein's discussion of the universities. Though otherwise excellent, Ornstein's book may be too critical of the universities. Martha Ornstein, *The Role of the Scientific Societies in the Seventeenth Century*, 3rd ed. (Chicago, 1938), 198–212.

not always happy. Knighted by the king, elevated to the presidency of the Royal Society, elected to the house of commons, and named master of the mint, the great scientist dominated the English scene at a time when the intellectual leadership of Europe was passing to his country. There can be no doubt of his deserving the honors and adulations heaped upon him by his fellow countrymen, but the naïve idea that he had fully illuminated the dark corners of the universe may well have discouraged others from prying into them. Furthermore, his supersensitive nature, his curious mixture of diffidence and jealousy about his discoveries, and his theological preoccupations marred his influence. Unwilling to publish his discovery of the calculus, he accused Leibniz of plagiarizing his ideas when the German scholar brought out his own findings. We now know that both men arrived independently at the solution of the problem and that others were on the verge of the same discovery. The scandalous squabble over primacy does Newton no credit and, until long after his death, deprived Englishmen of the use of the superior system of notation developed by Leibniz and Bernoulli.[8] Equally unfortunate was the fact that Newton's prestige enabled his corpuscular theory of light to block the acceptance of Huygens' wave theory, which in any case was more difficult of experimental demonstration, given the laboratory facilities available in the eighteenth century.[9] Newton's reputation as a great scientist was justified as much by his discovery of the nature of color as by his calculus or his principle of gravitation, but his idea that light was made up of infinitely small particles of matter that had "fits" of easy and difficult transmission did not prove fruitful for later research.

The present generation, which has seen war stimulate the development of the atomic bomb, radar, jet engines, and the rocket, might well ask why the great wars that followed the publication of Newton's *Principia* did not provoke similar scientific inventions. The answer to that question may in part supply the explanation of the comparative barrenness of most early eighteenth-century efforts to discover further scientific truths. The weapons of modern warfare do not in themselves constitute fundamental scientific contributions; they are for the most part technological applications of earlier basic discoveries. In that sense, the great wars of 1683–1721 did enhance scientific progress. The fortifications of Vauban and other engineers, the construction of the hundred-gun battleships, the

---

[8] E. T. Bell, *The Development of Mathematics* (New York, 1940), 131.

[9] In the twentieth century the corpuscular theory and the wave theory are both important, but the wave theory is not that advanced by Huygens.

development of mortars and multibarreled cannon and the flintlock musket were all applications of seventeenth-century physics and mathematics to the science of war. Since the generation that fought the first world wars had also to work out the problems in logistics and tactics inherent in the use of large standing armies, it is not surprising that it did not make fuller use of current scientific knowledge.

Leaving aside the so-called basic research of pure science and turning to its technological application, it appears that the technicians of 1700 made many important advances. Denis Papin, Thomas Savery, and Thomas Newcomen, all of them engineers and excellent mathematicians, applied the discoveries of their predecessors to the problem of steam power, and by 1712 Newcomen had developed a serviceable, if inefficient, steam engine. Wren, Pöppelmann, Courtonne, and others applied the new mathematics and physics to the problems of architecture. Others improved pumps for mines, machines for boring cannon, windlasses, treadmills, hoists, and other such mundane instruments so necessary to mining and manufacture. More than a century was to pass before technology had absorbed or exhausted the intellectual capital accumulated by the scientists of the seventeenth century.

The technology of the era was tied to its general cultural pattern; it was not adequate for the production of the precision machinery necessary to utilize fully the systems of mechanics, statics, hydrostatics, and optics discovered by the physicists, nor was it sufficiently advanced to raise questions that would require the answers of chemists and biologists. In one of his most brilliant essays, Carl Becker has suggested that man's conquest of the world rests upon the sword, upon writing, and upon technology. It may be well that man's discovery of so-called "pure scientific knowledge" cannot soar far above the technology of his culture.[10]

IV. THE NEW COSMOS: NEWTON AND FONTENELLE

Scholars of the early seventeenth century were well aware that the cosmology of the ancients was no longer tenable, but the experience of Galileo with the Inquisition naturally discouraged writers whose researches tended to challenge the accepted tradition. In 1686–1687, how-

[10] Carl Becker, *Progress and Power,* 1949 ed. by Leo Gershoy. There are three essays that have tentatively analyzed the problem of science and technology: B. Hessen, "The Social and Economic Roots of Newton's 'Principia,'" *Science at the Crossroads* (London, 1931); R. K. Merton, "Science, Technology, and Society in Seventeenth Century England," *Osiris,* IV (1938), 360–631; and G. N. Clark, *Science and Social Welfare in the Age of Newton* (Oxford, 1937), for an analysis of Hessen's Marxist interpretation.

ever, two books appeared that once and for all broke down the walls of ignorance and forced upon their age the recognition of the need for a new evaluation of man's place in the universe. For centuries philosophers, astrologers, and theologians had assured man that his world was the center of the universe, that the planets and constellations had somehow been set in their places to serve his interests, even that the five planets were connected with his five senses. From a system purposeful in terms of human life, and somehow connected with human destiny, the universe was abruptly transformed into a cold, impersonal system, a time machine obeying its own laws, in which the earth became a minor planet revolving around the sun. This readjustment of values depreciated man in his own eyes, and left him wandering on a small fragment of a great universe that was obviously unconcerned with his existence.

The two books in question were Fontenelle's *Entretiens sur la pluralité des mondes,* which appeared in 1686, and Newton's *Philosophiae Naturalis Principia Mathematica,* published in the following year. These works were to each other something like a pleasure yacht and a 60,000-ton aircraft carrier. Newton's work embodied a series of fundamental discoveries and was perhaps the most important scientific publication of all times; Fontenelle's, on the other hand, was merely a charming popularization of the Cartesian teaching. But for most of the next generation Fontenelle's little treatise was as important as Newton's big one: to read the *Principia,* even after it was translated into the modern languages, required a knowledge of mathematics and a power of concentration far beyond the reach of most of Newton's contemporaries; [11] but to read the *Pluralité des mondes* was and still is a delightful experience, for the author coquettishly combined the beauty of a woman, the charm of a starlit garden, and the wonder of the universe in a meaningful synthesis. Fontenelle's cosmology was out of date a year after its publication, but his popular style and simple explanations made the heliocentric universe understandable to all who could read.

Fontenelle, a nephew of the great Corneille, turned to natural philosophy when he realized that his literary talents would probably not bring him immortal fame. The *Pluralité des mondes* was destined to be only one item in a great shelf of books in which he recorded the scientific achievements of the hundred years of his life. Perhaps more than any

11 This is attested by the fact that although Newton correctly described the effect of the moon on the tides, Herman Moll, when he wrote his *Compleat Geographer, Asia, Africa and America,* still explained the tides in the traditional manner. Cf. edition 1709, Chapter VIII, xli.

other of his generation Fontenelle, as a publicist and as permanent secretary of the French Academy of Sciences, kept abreast of the scientific work of his era. His eulogies on the great figures as they died were masterpieces of style and simplification, as well as evidence of the conscientious labors of this first reporter of the sciences.

The *Pluralité des mondes* expounded a Cartesian universe filled with a subtle celestial fluid that sustained the suns and planets in their places. The sun was the center of a vortex in which the planets revolved. Each planet, in turn, became a vortex with moons or rings spinning about its center. The fixed stars were also each the center of a vortex around which Fontenelle subsumed the revolution of planets not dissimilar to those that circle the sun. The beautiful countess, to whom he presented this world in the course of five evening lectures, was in turn thrilled, alarmed and enchanted by his analysis of the universe, and intrigued by the problems of the beings who might be presumed to inhabit its parts.[12] In the course of his conversations Fontenelle explained to the countess the other cosmologies, European and Asiatic, which the Cartesian universe had superseded, while the countess amusingly and astutely put her finger on a weak spot in the Cartesian theory by admitting a liking for the Indian's elephants that so firmly supported their earth; the celestial fluid seemed to her a very fragile prop for so massive a structure.

Had the countess been entertained by Newton rather than by Fontenelle, and could she have followed the Englishman's mathematical analyses, her questions and fears might have been allayed. For Newton postulated absolute time and absolute space, within which he discovered a rigid mechanism, the universe, held together by absolute mechanical laws. By 1685 the principle of gravitation was literally begging for expression. Much attention had been devoted to the force in planetary motion that acted upon the center: Huygens had shown that a (the force toward the center) in a circle with a radius of r is mv^2/r (m-mass, v-velocity); Kepler's third law of planetary motion, namely that the squares of the periodic times and, therefore, the value of r^2/v^2, vary as r^3, had proved that v^2 varies as $1/r$ and that therefore v^2/r, acceleration, varies as $1/r^2$, which would account for a circle. Halley, considering the movement of a planet, had questioned whether this rule of inverse squares would also support Kepler's first law, namely that the orbit de-

<hr>

[12] The edition of John Glanvill's translation, with a preface by David Garnett (London, 1929), is both a masterpiece of the printer's art and a fine introduction to Fontenelle's thought.

scribed by a planet is an ellipse. He brought the question to Newton, who had already discovered the mathematical solution, but, somehow, had misplaced his notes. The problem involved changes in acceleration on a line; to solve it, Newton had invented the calculus. He was able to recapitulate the formula, and sent it and "much other matter," on to Halley.[13] It was this proof that induced Halley to encourage Newton to write the *Principia*. The next problem was to show mathematically that a sphere of gravitating matter attracts other bodies as if all its mass were concentrated in the center. "No sooner had Newton proved this superb theorem," writes Dr. Glaisher, ". . . than all the mechanism of the universe lay spread before him." [14]

With this formula Newton returned to the question on which he had worked twenty years before, namely, the relationship of the earth and the moon. Recent observations had determined the distance to the moon to be sixty radii of the earth. Picard, in 1670, had established accurately the

[13] The acceleration *a* towards the centre of motion, acting for a short time *t*, will produce a radial velocity *at*. Let us suppose that the velocity in the circular path in Fig. 3, and therefore the velocity at any moment along the tangent to the circle, is *v*. Then, in the small rectangle at the top of the figure, which represents the velocities along the radius and along the tangent, the adjacent sides are in the ratio of at/v, and this ratio is equal to the small angle between the radii drawn to two successive points on the circumference, or vt/r. Therefore

$$\frac{at}{v} = \frac{vt}{r} \quad \text{and} \quad a = \frac{v^2}{r}$$

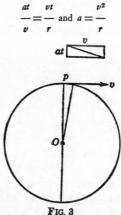

FIG. 3

Since force, as defined by Newton, is measured by the product of mass and acceleration, the centripetal force necessary to maintain a body in circular motion is mv^2/r. (Taken by permission of the publisher from William Dampier, *A History of Science* (New York and Cambridge, Eng., 1932), p. 167.)

[14] William Dampier, *ibid.*, 168.

measurement of a degree of longitude, so that Newton knew that the moon was approximately 60 x 4,000 miles away. Study of the orbit of the moon had shown that that body was falling from a straight line toward the earth at the rate of 0.004 feet a second. If the law of inverse squares were true, a body on the surface of the earth should fall at 60^2 x 0.004 feet (about 16 feet) a second. Since this was in accord with observed facts, Newton could assume that he had discovered that the movement of the planets and the fall of the apple are both due to the same unknown cause.[15]

During his entire life Newton was a secretive man, anxious to avoid criticism and perhaps a little jealous of his methods. He was apparently diffident about his discovery and unwilling to present it without an elaboration of the whole solar system. Halley, anxious to have his friend's work published, financed the printing of the elaborate treatise in which Newton expounded the nature of the universe according to his discovery. In the first and second books of the *Principia* Newton developed the intricate mathematical processes for measuring different velocities and constantly changing directions. He himself had employed the system of fluxions (calculus) which he had evolved in making these calculations, but in the *Principia* he translated them into Euclidian geometry. The third book described the solar system as it appears to the eye. The fourth, after an affirmation of his principles of science, namely the law of parsimony and the assumption that qualities which exist in all bodies without increasing or diminishing shall be postulated as qualities of all bodies, showed how the planets and their satellites obey the law of inverse squares. The moon furnished the final conclusive proof.

It is, of course, impossible to give a satisfactory analysis of the *Principia* in a few pages, and even more difficult to give adequate credit to Newton's predecessors, who made his discovery possible. Newton stood, in his own words, on the shoulders of giants. Between Copernicus and himself had come a host of great men whose discoveries, methods, and measurements supplied the background for the *Principia*. Robert Hooke, professor of geometry and secretary of the Royal Academy, had been on the verge of proclaiming the new theory in 1665. Halley, the discoverer of the orbit of the comet of the 1680's, was near the solution himself, but could not devise the mathematical proof. The great Kepler (1571–1630), who, after a mass of "long hand" calculation that would have deterred anyone but that sun worshiper, had provided the key by describing the orbit of

15 *Ibid.,* 167–8.

the earth and propounding the rule of inverse squares. Galileo's analyses of the force exerted toward the center by the radius, and Boyle's studies on the problems of density all furnished grist to the Newtonian mill. Pope's couplet

> Nature and Nature's laws lay hid in night:
> God said, Let Newton be! and all was light

gives Newton full praise for his genius, but credits God with the discoveries of his predecessors.

It has been asserted that there were not more than three or four people in the Europe of 1687 who were able completely to understand Newton's *Principia*.[16] Certainly Halley, Huygens, and Leibniz could read and understand it and there were undoubtedly others. Of the three, only Halley accepted Newton's findings unreservedly; the Dutchman and the German raised questions that had to wait until the late nineteenth and early twentieth centuries for solutions. Only in England, and to a lesser degree in Holland, did the *Principia* receive immediate and unqualified acceptance; most of the Cartesian thinkers on the continent regarded with much suspicion the mysterious, subtle force of gravity acting through such great distances. Their skepticism was not unlike that of the Pacific islanders who, on being told that flies should be killed because they carried evil germs, courageously informed the medical officers that since they had become Christians, they no longer believed in bad spirits. It was not until almost a half century after 1687 that the Newtonian explanation of the universe supplanted the Cartesian vortex theory. By that time, in the second edition of the *Principia,* the editor, Roger Cotes, was able to dispense entirely with the celestial fluid which even Newton had believed essential. The universe that the young Voltaire learned about on his first trip to England might have made Fontenelle's countess tremble even more than she did and wish for extra elephants to hold up the earth. By 1713 nothing but gravitation held the vast time machine together in a universe of empty space.

The fundamental postulates of both Fontenelle's and Newton's time machines, namely that the sun is the center of the planetary system and that the earth revolves around that sun, were accepted by Europe's elite without serious question. There was a conservative fringe which still insisted on the ancient cosmology, but the evidence was piling up so overwhelmingly in favor of the new that Fontenelle was made secretary of the French Academy of Science and Newton president of the Royal Society. The half century between Galileo's trial and the publication of the *Principia* had worn away effective resistance to the heliocentric universe; by 1700 western man was ready to explore and explain a world that was rapidly becoming meaningless in terms of his own life.[17]

V. THE ADVANCE OF NATURAL HISTORY

Man's interest in the earth and its multitudinous forms of life is probably as old as his self-consciousness, but his ability to understand this ball of mud and water has been limited by the tools for exploration at his disposal, by the postulates he accepted, and by the limitations of his own intelligence. The tools and the postulates at the disposal of seventeenth-century scholars enabled them to make great strides in physics and astronomy, but condemned them to the role of collectors of data and dreamers of tales in the field of natural history. The men who undertook experiments in mechanics and optics, who traced the course of the planets, and who discovered the properties of air could collect almost all their data in Paris, Amsterdam, or London, but students of the earth had either to depend upon the reports of travelers, or themselves laboriously to explore the world. Two hundred years of world trade had taken sailors, soldiers, merchants, and adventurers to many parts of the globe, but in 1700 the lacunae on the cartographers' charts, though no longer filled with fanciful pictures of sea serpents and other strange beasts, gave glaring evidence that men had not yet solved the riddles of the seas, let alone the mysteries of the larger land masses. Without a chemistry to describe matter in precise terms the earth's crust presented an insoluble problem; without a more complete understanding of electricity and meteorology many phenomena of nature could not be unmasked; and above all, without a realization of the enormous age of the earth neither its geological structure nor the biology of its inhabitants could be successfully explained.

Furthermore, although the skepticism inherent in *l'esprit géométrique* pervaded the climate of opinion, it proved to be much more difficult to upset the authority of the ancients in the area of natural history than in the fields of astronomy, physics, and anatomy. Pliny still remained the

[17] Cf. A. E. Burtt, *The Metaphysical Foundations of Modern Science* (New York, 1925), 236; M. H. Nicholson, *Voyages to the Moon* (New York, 1948).

authority on natural phenomena, and Ptolemy, though discredited by astronomers, still had his followers among the mapmakers. The Venetian sailors of the fourteenth century had reasonably accurate charts of the Mediterranean coasts, but the humanists succeeded in imposing Ptolemy's map upon the geographers. The later seventeenth-century cartographers like Sampson, Jaillot, Mallet, and Moll, all continued to show the Ptolemaic elongated Mediterranean. Jaillot's plates for his *Atlas nouveau* (1698) were probably already completed when Cassini drew the planisphere on the floor of the eastern salon of the observatory in Paris, showing the exact location of thirty-nine points on the globe as established by astronomical calculation. Moll in his *Compleat Geographer* (1709) repeated the traditional error, though he knew of Cassini's work and was fully aware that Dampier and his crew had almost lost their lives in the Pacific by relying on a map which, by projecting the error to that region, involved a distortion of over five hundred miles.

The problem of measuring a degree of longitude had been solved thirty years before 1700, but it was not until the middle of the eighteenth century that the mapmakers had digested and incorporated the new astronomical observations in their work. In the *Compleat Geographer,* Moll explained to his readers: "The Gentlemen of the academy [Academy des Sciences] a few years ago made a new Experiment wherein they observed with great Exactness . . . the length of a Degree," but, he went on, "This being premised and the reader informed by what means to correct the common computation, it will not perhaps be amiss to continue the old way. . . ." [18] Moll, like Jaillot and other early eighteenth-century mapmakers, was even more remiss in utilizing available information than this statement would imply. The coastlines of Europe had been accurately charted by astronomers long before they were defined by the cartographers. Moll's Bay of Biscay, for example, reproduced the errors of Mallet and Sampson, even though the "Gentlemen of the French Academy" had correctly measured not only the width but also the coasts of the kingdom. The Scandinavian peninsula and the Baltic, as well as Italy and the Levant, continued to be equally distorted. [19]

The "known world" of 1700 was the world conquered by soldiers or lying within the reach of merchants and missionaries. Very few voyages were made with the primary objective of discovery. It is therefore not

[18] H. Moll, *op. cit.,* xiv.
[19] Late seventeenth- and early eighteenth-century geographies have survived in considerable numbers. It takes but little detective work to trace the errors from one geographer's plates to those of his successors.

surprising that large areas of the earth's surface were either completely unknown or only imperfectly understood. The coastlines of the non-European world, with the exception of South America and a part of the Atlantic seaboard of North America, were often fancifully constructed from fragmentary evidence. From the "island" of Southern California to Japan, the North Pacific was practically a blank. The waters and lands south of the Spice Islands in the direction of both Africa and South America were still waiting for Captain Cook's voyages to unveil their secrets. The interiors of Asia, North America, and Africa were filled with imaginary river and mountain systems. Even the Great Lakes area, which had been visited and described by French missionaries and traders, was very incompletely known. The maps of 1700 certainly gave evidence of two hundred years of travel and exploration, but Moll was unduly optimistic when he assured his prospective purchasers that an investment in his book was a good one since it would not become obsolete.

The problem of understanding the earth's crust was even more difficult than that of accurately describing its contours. The stratifications and fossil remains that were eventually to yield so many secrets had long been noted. Miners had known about faults, seams, and veins of ore, and in the sixteenth century a great student of the earth, Agricola, had laid the foundation for its serious study. By the second half of the seventeenth century several thinkers, among them an Italianized Dane, Bishop Steno, were beginning to fit fossil remains and rock and soil strata into place, but in the closing years of the century a mixture of theology and science was concocted in northern Europe which blighted progress and retarded the scientific study of the earth for another full generation. "Never," Lyell remarks, "did a theoretical fallacy, in any branch of science, interfere more seriously with accurate observation and systematic classification." [20] The great geologist was too specific in his condemnation. It was not just the authority of Moses which shut off the light, for the seventeenth century still thought in terms of absolutes, of static realities and of Platonic ideals; it was not yet ready to think in terms of process and development. Even those who were fast becoming skeptical about the authority of the Bible had no idea of the enormous age of the earth; everywhere the idea of its novity was accepted without question. A short chronology could easily accommodate Newton's cosmology, and the postulates of a Creator, absolute space, and absolute time did not require

[20] Sir Charles Lyell, *Principles of Geology*, 11th and rev. ed. (New York, 1872), II, 37–8.

a history to explain the universe. Fossil remains and stratification, however, were not so easily adaptable to a world created about 4004 B.C.

It is interesting to speculate whether it was the Protestant reliance upon the Bible or the geological structure of England and Germany that most blinded northern scholars, and conversely whether it was the Roman Catholic attitude toward the Bible or the remarkable opportunities for study offered by the geological structure of Italy that allowed the first important steps toward an explanation of the earth to be made in Italy. Whatever it was, the tradition of Steno, followed in the eighteenth century by Lazzaro Moro and his fellow students, carried forward the work started by Agricola, while northern Europe, though strong on the practical level, still indulged in extravagant speculations akin to fairy tales.[21]

It is the proper function of history to describe man's errors as well as his successes. Often wrong guesses supply the fullest explanation of the limiting factors in the process of historical development. The naturalists who wished to understand the earth were profoundly disturbed by fossil remains uncovered in gravel pits, well diggings, and strata outcroppings. These, along with the shells of marine animals discovered on mountain tops, presented baffling problems. In the mid-century Steno had boldly asserted that fossil teeth he had found high above sea level were actually sharks' teeth, but most of his contemporaries regarded such a conclusion as incredible. Edward Lhwyd, a distinguished teacher and collector, rejected the idea that these fossils could have been animals: "For my part," he wrote to a friend, "I am soe farre of the contrary opinion yt I think it all most an absurdity to believe they ever were shells, not doubting but that they are lapides sui generis yt owe their forms to certain salts whose property 'tis to shoot into such figures as these shellstones represent. . . ."[22] Many others argued that the fossils were the acts of a whimsical creator, seeds that grew into the rocks rather than out of the ground, or special "salts" such as Lhwyd posited. The distribution seemed to be too wide to permit any theory of animal or vegetable origin. John Ray, when confronted with clam shells dug up in a well pit one hundred feet below the surface at Amsterdam, put his finger on the difficulty when he remarked " 'Tis a strange thing considering the novity of the world, the age whereof, according to the usual account, is not yet 5600

[21] F. D. Adams, *The Birth and Development of the Geological Sciences* (Baltimore, 1938), 357–372.
[22] R. T. Gunther, *Early Science in Oxford, Life and Letters of Edward Lhwyd,* XIV (Oxford, 1945), 79–80.

years." [23] Ray, however, was too honest an observer to disclaim the animal origin of the shells.

It was at this point that "theological geology" intervened to explain all things. Noah's flood, properly interpreted, could and did permit men to accept the fact that the fossils were true animal and vegetable remains. In 1684–1690, Dr. Thomas Burnet, an English clergyman, produced a two-volume book with the modest title: *The Sacred History of the Earth, containing an account of the Original of the Earth and of all the General Changes which it hath already undergone or is to undergo till the Consummation of all Things.* Burnet did not hesitate to pronounce upon all manner of things; he even solved the problem that bothered many of his generation, namely, whether the Paradise of Adam and Eve was located on this planet or at an indeterminate place between heaven and earth. His assurance led Butler to comment,

> He knew the seat of Paradise,
>   Could tell in what degree it lies,
> And, as he was disposed, would prove it
>   Below the moon, or else above it.

But both Addison and Steele praised the book extravagantly, and the generation of 1700 read it widely. Burnet, like all who tried to fit the observable facts into the scheme of a young and unchanging earth, needed a cataclysm of the first magnitude to explain the data. Noah's flood furnished him with the key to the universe.

Once the way was open, the biblical deluge found its place in many other books. In his *Essay towards a Natural History of the Earth* (1695, revised 1702), John Woodward skillfully combined the Newtonian principle of gravitation and the story of the flood to explain the distribution of fossil remains. William Whiston, with a remarkable display of biblical, mathematical, and astronomical knowledge, produced a book in 1696 that settled the whole question.[24] In the beginning, it seems, the earth did not rotate on its axis; that began with the fall of man and the introduction of sin. Sin continued apace until November 18, 2349 B.C., when a great comet stood above the equator, its tail in contact with the earth. This phenom-

[23] C. E. Raven, *John Ray* (Cambridge, Eng., 1942), 421.

[24] *A new theory of the Earth, from its original to the consummation of all Things, wherein the Creation of the World in six days, the Universal Deluge, and the general conflagration, as laid down in Holy Scripture are shewn to be perfectly agreeable to reason and philosophy* (London, 1696).

enon released the subterranean waters and brought about the deluge, a cataclysm which redistributed matter on the earth's surface. Since so matter-of-fact a person as John Locke congratulated Whiston on having made so many things clear, it is evident that contemporaries of these cosmological mythmakers took their theories quite seriously.[25] Even though Leibniz, in his *Protogaea,* presented the Cartesian idea that primitive matter was fluid because of tremendous heat, and that the spherical form of the earth was the result of the whirling elements or monads, of which it was formed, he finally, if somewhat reluctantly, fitted the whole picture into the framework of Genesis, deluge and all.

The diluvial theory was scarcely strengthened when the great Swiss scholar, Scheuchzer, announced the discovery of the skeleton of one of those "wicked men" whose "sins were responsible for the catastrophe," only to have it shown later that his prediluvial specimen was the remains of a giant salamander. We should, in justice to the Swiss naturalist, call attention to his humorous description of a meeting of the fossil fishes at which they protested against the libels of those who described all fossils as "sports of nature." The explanation provided by the deluge gave the fossils their true character, but denied them their proper place in the earth's history.[26]

There were some men, like John Ray, who, while accepting the fossils as true remains of vegetable and animal life, refused to be satisfied with the facile explanations of Woodward and his followers. But these men had no alternative solution. Ray's own cosmology lacked the precision and insight found in his works on contemporary plants and animals; the postulates of his age were seemingly an insuperable barrier to a solution of the problem.[27] The same Robert Hooke who came so close to the discovery of both oxygen and the law of gravitation, left a posthumous paper in which he not only recognized fossils for what they are, but also suggested that these remains were historical evidence from which a new chronology could be constructed. Instead of attempting this ambitious task, however, Hooke rejected the current diluvial theory only to erect a more complicated one in its place.[28] Not until the next generation was the Venetian priest, Lazzaro Moro, to break through these mythological

[25] H. B. Woodward, *History of Geology* (New York and London, 1911), 13–14; K. A. von Zittel, *History of Geology and Paleontology* (London, 1901), 30–31.

[26] A. Wolf, *A History of Science, Technology and Philosophy in the Eighteenth Century* (New York, 1939), 391–2.

[27] C. E. Raven, *op. cit.,* Chapter XVI.

[28] Sir Charles Lyell, *op. cit.,* I, 43–4; H. B. Woodward, *op. cit.,* 9.

systems and re-establish the study of the earth's crust on the firm basis of the tradition of Agricola and Steno.

The generation of 1700 understood the phenomena of weather a little better than it did the earth's crust, but it is necessary only to refer to Herman Moll's discussion of the subject to realize that, despite substantial advances in meteorology, a host of misconceptions still plagued the human mind. The studies of Perrault, Mariotte, and Halley showed clearly that annual rainfall was sufficient to account for rivers and springs without postulating the existence of subterranean caverns filled with water. Investigations of air pressure, temperature, and the moisture content of the air, as well as more exact weather observations (Hooke and Halley), gave some insight into the nature of storms, while Halley's complex calculation of the angles of the sun's rays at different stages in the earth's orbit clarified some of the seasonal problems. However, the indignation with which Emanuel König attacked the proponents of the "new philosophy" who rejected the idea that the thunder axes (*caraunii*) were the product of lightning is evidence of the tenacity of old ideas. "If nature in the lightning clouds makes stones, resembling various instruments, which fall to earth," he asks, "does it not in the same way make for its pleasure pictures of our domestic things in agate and other gems?"[29] König argued that the thunder axes were really products of the clouds, just as the "figured stones" were products of the earth. Two decades later a prank played upon Johann Beringer by his students at Würzburg answered the argument. The professor had written a book describing the remarkable "figured stones" he had discovered. After the book was published he found a stone with his own name on it! The poor man was financially ruined in his efforts to buy up the whole edition of his book.[30]

Thunder axes, stones with sex, vapors that could turn men and beasts into rock, and a host of similar traditions still haunted the intellectuals. The uneducated, superstitious masses, altogether untouched by the skepticism of *l'esprit géométrique*, still cherished the whole pantheon of European demonology and fairy lore. Oman has suggested that the sixteenth century saw the end of credulity,[31] but while it is true that in the late seventeenth century men no longer expected to find the fountain of youth, the lost continent of Atlantis, or the unicorn, they still

---

[29] Emanuel König, *Regnum Minerale* (1703), 244.
[30] F. D. Adams, *op. cit.*, 259–261.
[31] C. Oman, *The Sixteenth Century* (London, 1936), 43 ff.

explained the universe in terms of the supernatural and the miraculous. They still believed, in spite of Newton's time machine, that man and his activities were the center upon which the universe turned.

The naturalists who attempted to bring order out of the apparent chaos of plant and animal life were more successful than their fellows who explored the earth's crust. The later seventeenth century marked the extensive development of botanical and zoological gardens as well as of observatories and scientific academies. Under the guidance of Joseph Pitton de Tournefort, the famous *Jardin du roi* (now *Jardin des plantes*) in Paris was modeled on the earlier gardens usually connected with medical schools in Bologna, Padua, Leyden and elsewhere. In Dresden, London, and other cities, more or less successful imitations of the Paris botanical garden reflected the current, widespread interest in botany. At the same time the "king's cabinet of curiosities" was expanded to include living animals as well as stuffed skins, eggs, nests, horns, and all sorts of specimens. Wealthy amateurs imitated the princes; they collected and classified items of natural history much as contemporary amateurs collect butterflies, coins, stamps, and pictures. It was for this public that Ray wrote on plants, animals, and reptiles, Woodward on fossils, and Willughby on birds.

The chief concern of these scholars was with classification. The systems of Theophrastus and Pliny were no longer adequate to provide for the plant and animal life brought to light by European activities throughout the world, but the herbalists and naturalists of the sixteenth and seventeenth centuries made little progress towards solving the problem. In the mid-seventeenth century the writings on natural history were almost as chaotic as nature itself appeared to be. Conflicting systems, multitudinous names, and confusing descriptions made the plant and animal world almost incomprehensible. But in the latter seventeenth century two workers did much to reduce the confusion: Rodolf Jakob Camerarius, professor of medicine at Tübingen, produced the first convincing proof of the sexuality of plants, while John Ray, the scholarly English clergyman-naturalist-philosopher, devised classifications which were basic to the later work of Linnaeus and in some respects even more useful than those of that great Swedish naturalist. But none of the naturalists of 1700, nor indeed Linnaeus himself, grasped the principle of development or evolution. They fully believed that God had created plants and animals as they found them, and that any suggestion of change would imply something less than perfection in His work. Ray was several times on the verge of deciding that mutations in species were possible, but, like the geologists, he gave way before the authority of the biblical account of creation and accepted the theory of the earth's novity.[32]

The microscope opened a new world to the naturalists and provided them with a tool for probing into the mechanism of both plants and animals. Malpighi had already shown that this new instrument could be used to demonstrate the circulation of the blood from arteries to veins. Robert Hooke and Nehemiah Grew turned their lenses on vegetable tissue and first described the cell structure of plants. Most famous of all the microscopists was a Dutch cloth merchant, Anton van Leeuwenhoek, who built his own instruments and examined everything from human semen to bacteria. His letters to the Royal Society reported a world theretofore inconceivable. But the scientists of his time failed to apply his findings to medicine or biology; they were as unready for the germ theory of disease as they were for the concept of evolution.

VI. THE IMPACT OF FOREIGN CULTURES

Europe's knowledge of the diverse peoples and civilizations of the earth, like its knowledge of its surfaces, expanded with every generation following the heroic era of discovery. It is impossible to estimate accurately either the number of people who traveled or the effects of the literature produced by travel, but it is certain that the activity itself became more popular and widespread with the passing of each quarter century. By the end of the seventeenth century there was an extensive literature and an interesting collection of guidebooks, catalogues, and similar aids for the prospective voyager. There were guidebooks in many languages for every country and for all the major cities of Europe which gave accounts of the history, customs, and places of interest. The "tourism" that Europeans have since developed into a major industry has, therefore, a long history. Englishmen and Germans, apparently, were the most avid travelers, but Swedes, Dutchmen, Italians, Spaniards, and Frenchmen were also to be found in the growing company of sightseers.

Bibliographies of travel literature indicate that the publication of travel books increased markedly with each generation of the seventeenth century and Jean Le Clerc's testimony, "the title alone of a Voyage is

---

[32] E. Nordenskiöld's *Biologiens Historia,* 3 vols., 1920–1924, translated by L. B. Eyre under the title *The History of Biology* (New York, London, 1928), is the most readable general history of biology. Raven's *John Ray* is indispensable for an understanding of the period and its problems.

enough to arouse interest of readers" indicated an ever-growing market for these books.[33] Since there was little literature available beyond fantastic and often dull romances, the stories of travelers satisfied the need of the reading public for interesting tales as well as for information. The fact that creative writers of this period commonly cast their ideas about men and the world in the form of travel stories is further evidence of the popular interest. Tales of actual and imaginary voyages made up no small part of the intellectual diet of the literate public, and the frequency with which other writers referred to these narratives testifies to their influence in shaping the European mind.

The great wars that filled these decades did not interfere with private travel as much as modern wars do. It was difficult, but far from impossible, to travel in the lands of the king's enemies. Occasionally military operations did make the immediate theater of the war almost inaccessible, but these theaters were usually small and soldiers did not consider it their business to control civilian traffic. Furthermore, passports and letters of safe conduct were relatively easy to obtain. Military courtesy and gallantry, bound to disappear as war later became the business of peoples rather than of kings, allowed soldiers to give passports to their enemies as soon as the winter season set in. Moreover, while the wars may have somewhat reduced civilian mobility, they vastly increased the total number of people on the highways. Soldiers, diplomats, and special agents were constantly traversing the continent, and their reports helped to swell the literature that was teaching Europeans to know one another.

The revocation of the Edict of Nantes (1685) also dispersed a large number of people, many of whom were keen and articulate observers. The accounts of their wanderings as well as their influence in the lands that gave them shelter were important factors in the dissemination of knowledge about Europe and the world. Men like Bayle in Amsterdam or Leguat in the East Indies made contributions to European understanding that can probably be attributed directly to the brutal treatment Louis XIV meted out to his Protestant subjects.

Most travelers undoubtedly confined themselves to Europe, but there was an ever-increasing number who visited distant lands, where customs, manners, and morals were very different from those of the west. The travel books published at the time would seem to indicate that the number of articulate voyagers to non-European lands increased in geometric progression with each quarter century.

[33] For a discussion of travel bibliographies, see P. Hazard, *La crise de la conscience européene, 1680–1715* (Paris, 1934), III, 14–16.

Even more important, perhaps, was the subtle change that took place in the type of travelers. Although monks and friars went along to convert the heathen, the first explorations had been made largely by rough men—soldiers, sailors, and merchants—whose interests were military and commercial and whose understanding and appreciation of foreign societies was usually very limited. By the end of the seventeenth century, however, observers of a different kind had begun to report: men with literary, scientific, and philosophic interests, men of more sensitive understanding, men who for one reason or another had taken the trouble to learn the languages and study the mentality of non-European peoples. A rough fellow like Champlain might appreciate the good qualities of the American Indians, though his training and purposes blinded him to many aspects of their culture. On the other hand Joseph Tournefort's voyages to the Middle East, Paul Lacus' trips to the Levant, Jesuit peregrinations in China and the Americas, or P. Tachard's journeyings in Siam yielded information that a soldier or a merchant would scarcely have found significant. The customs, folklore, religion, and history of non-European peoples as reported by the travelers gave Europeans standards of comparison theretofore unavailable.

Nor was it necessary to read all the travel literature to get an adequate picture of the world at large. In 1683 Alain Manesson-Mallet published a huge work describing the religions, manners, governments, morals, and customs of all the peoples of the earth.[34] The book appeared in German in 1685 and was subsequently translated into several other languages. It was a study of the world's geography, of comparative religions, of military forces, of commerce, and of varieties of dress, manners, and morals. The illustrations were as profuse as they were fanciful, and the book as a whole was so attractive as to inspire many imitators, of whom the most famous was Herman Moll, the Dutch geographer who had settled in England. Moll's text was drawn almost entirely from the accounts of travelers. He professed to save his reader considerable labor by his digest of this material. Voltaire could have written his famous *Essai sur les moeurs* without going beyond these two compendiums of travelers' narratives.

Europeans of the late seventeenth century tended to be sensitive and self-critical. It was therefore inevitable that discussions of other cultures should provoke them to reappraisal of their own. Travelers reported the outrageous behaviour of fellow Europeans abroad who, they declared, had

[34] A. Manesson-Mallet, *Description de l'univers* (Paris, 1683).

made the term "Christian" a symbol for fraud, violence, and dishonor in many parts of the world. In contrast, they gave sympathetic accounts of the civilization and morals of non-Europeans. The Jesuit fathers, who had hoped to find in the emperor at Peking a Chinese Constantine, gave a picture of Chinese morality that left no doubt of its superiority to the European. In Siam, India, Persia, and Egypt other voyagers encountered people whose lives were as moral and as civilized as their own. Even the red men of North America appeared to them virtuous in comparison with Christian Europe. All these reports and interpretations provided philosophers and critics with weapons which they soon turned upon the laws, customs, and religion of Europe.[35]

Man's natural desire to establish types or symbols to reduce the complexity of reality led to the emergence of a mythology that greatly influenced the thinking of the whole eighteenth century. The "noble savage," the "wise Egyptian," the "Mohammedan Arab," the "refined Persian," the "Chinese philosopher," all found their way into the literature of Europe. To be sure, travelers at times recorded less complimentary traits in the foreigner and filled their narratives with stories of the viciousness, treachery and brutality of the savages, the wily cunning of the Orientals, and in general the seamy side of life beyond Europe. But such evidence was of no use for attacking the evils which Europeans were discovering, and was therefore ignored by the myth makers who were intent on demonstrating that Christian civilization had no monopoly of morality and in fact was frequently inferior to the cultures found elsewhere on the globe.

Most travelers who actually visited the East or North America felt bound to report the facts as they observed them. But the writers of imaginary travel accounts suffered no such limitations. Recent studies have shown that such writers based their stories upon the accounts of real travelers, but did not allow themselves to be handicapped by firsthand information that might cramp their style or destroy their thesis.[36] Their narratives followed a standard pattern. The writer pictured himself as by some chance transported to an unknown land where the culture of the people, in comparison with that of Europe, was so superior as to

[35] G. Atkinson, *Les relations de voyage du XVIIe siècle et l'évolution des idées* (Paris, 1924).

[36] G. Atkinson, *The Extraordinary Voyage in French Literature before 1700* (New York, 1920), and *The Extraordinary Voyage in French Literature from 1700 to 1720* (Paris, 1922); N. Van Wijngaarden, *Les odyssées philosophiques en France entre 1616 et 1789* (Harlem, 1932).

show that the Christian religion and the monarchical form of government were barbarous and detestable. One author discovered a society of horses whose morals were superior to man's, and only Gulliver's tiny folk revealed any of the petty feelings and limited viewpoints characteristic of Europe. French writers of such tales seemed possessed with a desire to discredit the traditions, authorities, and institutions of their own land; there was not a single aspect of French civilization that did not come under their attack. It requires but little imagination to picture the readers of these romances in the van of the crowds that pulled down the old regime at the end of the eighteenth century.

VII. THE HISTORY OF MAN

The same generation that invented myths about noble savages, wise Egyptians, and Chinese philosophers began to have doubts about the authority of recorded history. The *esprit géométrique,* when applied to the problems of man's past, was destined eventually to have effects almost as revolutionary as the discovery of the heliocentric universe for, once started, it was impossible to check the mounting doubt of all history, including that found in the Bible and the writings of the church fathers. A few of the men responsible for this questioning of historical authority were intent on chipping at the foundations of revealed religion. Others were concerned to correct the record and to establish an accurate account of the historical past in the naïve belief that such a record would in itself confound their religious or political enemies. Still others were simply overwhelmed by the terrific problem of separating truth from falsehood.

The historians were often guilty of distortions that aroused criticism. The humanistic historians, following classical models, had written of the past for the edification of princes and subjects. To them history was the judge of past rulers of society: kings, popes, and ministers appeared before the bar to account for their actions, while the historian, in a godlike role, passed judgment. But the humanistic historians had regarded themselves as men of letters rather than as scientists, and were more interested in producing literary masterpieces than in giving a solid account of their subject. Their lack of method, their failure to criticize and evaluate their sources, and their unwillingness to make a complete survey of their problems made their histories inaccurate, haphazard, and subject to all sorts of attack. The very fact that no two of them could agree upon the basic outline, that even in details they differed so widely that an event described by one was unrecognizable in the pages of another, led thoughtful men to decide that such history was merely a web of lies or fancies unworthy of serious consideration.

The Reformation and the political problems that flowed from the religious wars produced a new type of historian, the apologist who used documentary evidence to justify his own party's program. Men of this type, who looked upon the *Magdeburg Centuries* and the *Annales* of Baronius as models were attentive to sources because they expected criticism and rebuttal, but they lacked the methodology necessary to evaluate their documents, they were partisan in their attitude, and they were wanting in historical insight. Ponderous tomes were piled up for and against the Lutherans, Catholics, Calvinists, and others, only to make the critically minded suspect that this array of scholarship was merely a screen for falsification.

Since contemporary historians were subject to such criticism, the question naturally arose whether the same charges might not be leveled at the ancients. An age that was becoming skeptical of witchcraft, demons, miracles, and fairy tales, had little trouble in identifying the stories of Romulus and the wolf, of Aeneas and Dido, and indeed the whole fabric of early Roman history, as mythology. "I dislike fame founded on tales or established by the error of false judgment," wrote Saint-Évremond. "There are enough true things to admire in the Romans that it only does them a wrong to endow them with fables." Once Roman historians had come under fire, it was inevitable that the Greeks would be subjected to the same attack, and that finally the Hebrew Bible would have to meet a similar test.[37]

The extent of this historical skepticism may best be judged by the outraged protest of Jacob Perizonius, a distinguished professor of history at the University of Leyden. Before his colleagues, students, and the magistrates of the city, he delivered a lecture on Pyrrhonism (i. e., extreme skepticism), in which he pointed out that the real issue was not whether some history might be false, but whether any history could be true. This spirit of doubt, he continued, was so seducing that, if unchecked, it might lead to a universal skepticism, which he viewed as an unmitigated evil. He therefore affirmed that it was possible to establish historical truth, and exhorted his listeners to check their disbelief.[38]

No one man, however, could successfully contain the skeptics at a time

---

[37] Bayle, for example, wrote that "l'histoire n'est qu'une fable convenue."

[38] Paul Hazard's discussion of this Pyrrhonism is one of the best chapters in a brilliant book, *op. cit.*, I, 38–69.

when authority was crumbling on every side. The rough treatment accorded to Aristotle, Ptolemy, Galen, and other classics made it almost inevitable that the fragile structures of the historians would soon be undermined. Many Cartesians brushed all history aside as more or less useless knowledge of questionable validity, quite unnecessary for an *honnête homme*. Malebranche asserted that Adam, though he possessed perfect science, obviously had no history. The freethinkers, who were asserting their right to reject all authority, insisted that history was simply a compilation of lies designed to justify party, people, or religion. Even the *Acta Eruditorum* asserted that historians were a troupe of charlatans. The simple-minded might wish to read books of martyrs, histories of dead kings, and discussions of church problems, but the men who "knew" were convinced that there was no truth in the yarns the historians were busily creating.

The chronologers added to the confusion. Chronology was an esoteric science, cultivated by a handful of devoted adherents whose aim it was to establish accurately the course of Bible history. These men succeeded in fixing the day and sometimes the hour of many events like Noah's flood, Abraham's mission, the life of Jesus, and even the death of Adam. The credulous hoped that eventually this work would be finished, so that all important events could be recorded in the prayer books for popular edification. But the chronologers could not agree; they argued about the year of creation: was it 4004 B.C. or simply 4000 B.C; did the flood come in 1656 B.C., 1757 B.C. or, as Whiston had it, on November 18, 2349 B.C.? In the second half of the seventeenth century the task was made doubly difficult when the Jesuit fathers in China reported a chronology that purported to stretch back many centuries before the biblical creation, and when John Marshan published collections of Egyptian antiquities (from Greek sources) that made Adam a late comer. How could this be? Men began to scrutinize Babylonian, Greek, and Roman history to find an answer. Herman Moll's cautious remarks about China reflect the general perplexity: "The History of China," he writes, "is very ancient, the Fabulous Legends make it many thousand years before the Creation; but those Histories that may be credited, begin within two or three hundred years after the Flood. . . ." [39]

When the Egyptians and Babylonians were consulted about chronology, however, it became obvious that either the Bible was distorted or the peoples of the Nile and the Euphrates were wrong about their own his-

[39] *Op. cit.*, 139.

tory. Could it be that the Bible was in error about the history of the ancient peoples between Egypt and Mesopotamia? If that were the case, how could one account for the errors of writers inspired by God?

All this study evoked another problem. Could it be possible, as some suggested, that the Jews, including Moses himself, had derived their ideas from the Egyptians, under whose domination they had lived? [40] Marshan's publication of Egyptian antiquities inevitably led to such queries, for the striking similarities between Egyptian and Hebrew beliefs could not be ignored. Bishop Huet suggested that Moses might have inspired the Egyptians as well as the Jews, an idea that Antoine Arnauld considered impious, since it implied that one religion was as good as another. Professor Perizonius tried to stem the tide by suggesting that the Egyptians might be wrong about their own past, but he did not venture to establish dates that would satisfactorily synchronize Egyptian and Hebrew history.

This avalanche of controversy over chronology could not be ignored by other serious students. Even Bishop Bossuet, who had written with such assurance in 1681, revised the third edition of his *Discours sur l'histoire universelle* in 1700 so as to provide the longer period demanded by Egyptian, Chinese, and other histories. Father Pezron had pointed out that there was a difference in the chronology of the Vulgate and Septuagint editions of the Bible that would push the creation back to about 5500 B.C. Bossuet accepted his suggestion, but could not account for the error in the sacred text. Father Pezron, an honest searcher after truth, was himself not satisfied with his own solution. ". . . after all the care that men have taken in our days," he wrote ". . . to know how many centuries have passed between the creation of the world and the coming of the Messiah, not only has one not found the truth, but one is even more distant from it than before. . . ." [41]

By 1700 the assurance with which earlier historians had announced the day and even the hour of the creation had largely vanished. No one was yet prepared for the enormity of time which later generations were to require for the explanation of the history of man and the earth, but the seeds of doubt had been planted, and the outer bastion of the Mosaic fortress had fallen.

On another front the sacred history of the Bible came under fire from

<hr>

[40] John Spencer, *De legibus Hebraeorum ritualibus et earum rationibus Libre tres* (Cambridge, 1685).

[41] Paul Pezron, *L'antiquité des tempes*, quoted by P. Hazard, *op. cit.*, I, 62.

one of the most critical minds of the era. Pierre Bayle, educated by both Jesuits and Calvinists and driven from France to the Netherlands by the persecutions of Louis XIV, was a philosopher and historian as well as a teacher and editor who focused attention on the problems of internal criticism. His seemingly endless observations on comets served notice upon his generation that he was a man willing to apply rational analysis to all sorts of problems, a man to whom superstition and mythology were anathema. Into his *Dictionnaire historique et critique* he poured a lifetime's study and thought, thus providing an arsenal of arguments for the next generation of skeptics and deists. Bayle's method of attack was oblique; to uncover his thought the reader must plow through the long and involved footnotes appended to a comparatively innocuous text, and even then has to struggle with Bayle's difficult style and backhand way of saying things. But those who were willing to accept the limitations of topical treatment and undergo the labor of ferreting out Bayle's ideas found in this *Dictionnaire* one of the taproots of the Enlightenment. Bayle's skepticism extended from Adam to Lazarus: he ridiculed some of the biblical stories and made others completely implausible. David was roughly handled as a "sun of holiness" whose immorality led him to adultery, murder, treachery, and falsehood. Nor did Bayle stop there. He treated the controversies between the sects of Christendom as well as the differences between Christians and non-Christians as all based on false beliefs, equally bad, equally superstitious, equally ridiculous. It is no wonder that his fellow Huguenot exiles looked at him askance.

Bayle used secular as well as ecclesiastical history to draw his moral about the existence of evil. There was hardly an instance of violence brought about by intolerance, superstition, or stupidity that did not find its way into the *Dictionnaire.* Martin, the Manichaean in *Candide,* must have regarded the *Dictionnaire* as a mine of evidence, and Voltaire could have written the story with no other book to guide his thoughts. In Bayle's hands history became a weapon to turn against his enemies; it had no continuity, no philosophy, no spirit. It was brute fact that revealed the ignorance, superstition, and viciousness of man. By throwing doubt upon accepted histories Bayle contributed to the historical Pyrrhonism of his day; by using history as a weapon he paid tribute to the idea that Clio could defend those who were right.[42]

[42] Several histories written in this period had an important effect both upon the men of 1700 and upon their descendants. Bishop Bossuet's *Histoire des variations des églises protestantes* (1688), for example, not only profoundly affected all the later thinking of this greatest of French clerics and orators, but also influenced leaders in Protestant as well

At the very time when historical skepticism was winning converts, another group of writers were endowing history with an intellectual respectability that would eventually satisfy the sternest advocate of *l'esprit géométrique*. Professor Thompson has stated baldly: "Modern historical scholarship had its inception in the Reformation and Counter Reformation." [43] Professor A. C. Krey, however, has pointed out more judiciously that the work of the erudite scholars of the seventeenth century was a continuation of a humanistic tradition as well as an answer to the problems raised by controversial church histories. The discovery, editing, and publishing of texts obviously antedated the Lutheran revolt and the *Magdeburg Centuries,* and many of the intellectual tools that historical scholars pressed into service were forged before 1500. The Reformation undoubedly stimulated historical research, but western man's concern with the problem of editing documents provided a sound foundation for the development of historical methodology.

During the seventeenth century Jesuit priests, who took their name from one of the greatest of their company (John Bolland), undertook the colossal task of editing the *Acta Sanctorum.* Their greatest problem was to sift the authentic from the false, to comb out the mythology that had grown up about the saints, sometimes supported by forged evidence as well as by age-old tradition. By the end of the century, under the leadership of Father Daniel Papebroche, they had developed a documentary criticism that will pass muster even today. Perhaps even more important than the Bollandists were the Benedictine congregation of St. Maur at Saint-Germain-des-Prés. Their leader, Jean Mabillon, was one of the great historical scholars of all times. His book *De Re Diplomatica* (1681) laid the foundation for the science of diplomatics, which, as Bernheim says, proves the honesty or falsity of sources. In the wake of this book came the first volumes of the *Acta Sanctorum O. S. B.* and the *Annales* as well as numerous other great collections. These great editions were the fruit of several centuries of scholarly labor. Textual criticism had developed from

---

as Catholic Europe. Bossuet's thesis was simple but powerful. He showed how individual freedom to interpret religion had led inevitably to a splintering of the Christian community, and, with great foresight, insisted that it must inevitably lead to doubt, deism, and atheism. The pitiless story of reformers of the reformed religions made the Huguenot Pierre Jurieu even more certain that it was a mistake for government to be tolerant of new religious sects; himself a refugee from the religious persecution of Louis XIV, he became an advocate of persecution in Holland. The greatest impact of Bossuet's history came a hundred years later when the Romanticists, frightened by the French Revolution, made it the foundation of their cult of authority. By that time Pyrrhonism had been replaced by a will to believe; the *Histoire des variations* made that belief seem imperative.

[43] J. W. Thompson, *A History of Historical Writing* (New York, 1942), II, 3.

the fourteenth century onward, and by the seventeenth century most of the known works of antiquity had been newly edited. The next task of scholars was to be the critical treatment of medieval materials.[44]

Two other great scholars of this period deserve mention, even in a short discussion of the labors of collectors and editors of historical documents. The first was Louis-Sébastien le Nain de Tillemont, a Jansenist and a friend of Mabillon, who assumed the pious task of collecting and editing the documents relative to the first six centuries of the Christian Church and the Roman emperors. His scholarship was meticulous, his honesty transparent; his translations were made with extreme care and wherever he felt that the sense might be distorted, he printed the original text. Whenever in his notes he allowed himself a personal remark, he showed himself to be a naïve moralist, a role better suited to the priest than the historian, but he did not allow his attitude to interfere with his critical scholarship. What would he have said had he known that his labors were to feed the pen of the Voltairian Gibbon, and would be turned against the church which he hoped to vindicate?

The other great scholar was that universal genius, Gottfried Wilhelm Leibniz. Between diplomatic missions for princes, the writing of essays on ethics and philosophy for princesses, and works on cosmology, logic, and mathematics for scholars, Leibniz found time to begin a great historical collection, the *Annals* of the House of Brunswick. Even so great a scholar as he, however, could not rise above the intellectual outlook of his era. Like the French scholars who were mining the materials for the writing of history, he had no understanding of the sociological, economic, or political process. He was a philosopher dealing with historical materials, but he did not see in them the development that later historians were to discover and explain.

These critical collections of sources for secular and religious history established a firm basis for historical research, and laid the foundation for the development of a historical literature that would satisfy even the most skeptical critic. Skepticism had driven the humanist and partisan historians from the temple; scholarship re-established Clio's respectability. But the new history was destined to be as dangerous to traditional beliefs as the new science had been; it deepened the chasm between the beliefs of the learned and of the ignorant by extending man's time sense and giving him new perspectives on himself and his institutions.

---

[44] Fueter's and Bernheim's books are still the best for balanced accounts. Thompson and Barnes have more evidence, but seem to lack over-all judgment. Cf. E. Bernheim, *Lehrbuch der historischen Methode* (Leipzig, 1889), 97–153; E. Fueter, *Geschichte der neueren Historiographie* (Munich, Berlin, 1911), 246–334.

Chapter Nine

THE CULTURE OF THE ELITE

I. THE BAROQUE STYLE

THE seventeenth century was the age of the baroque. Originally that term was confined to art and architecture, but in our own day it has come to be used increasingly as a period term, like Gothic or Renaissance, to describe the culture of the church and the princely courts from the mid-sixteenth to the eighteenth century.[1] While scientists, scholars, and travelers were lifting man's intellectual horizon, artists, musicians and literary men opened new vistas for expression and new ideals for civilized life. The structure of society was such, however, that only a small section of the population was affected by the new modes. The masses continued to live as they did before, relatively untouched by the splendor of the new culture unfolding in the courts of Europe.

Any attempt to explain the baroque style must inevitably revert to its origins. In both art and architecture the high Renaissance had carried the classic style to a point beyond which there was little possibility of further advance. Artistic genius, however, is rarely thwarted for long by the accomplishments of preceding generations, especially if the society within which it works tolerates new expression. Thus the early baroque was an attempt to meet the needs of artists and society in the changing world of the sixteenth century.[2] More specifically it was, in its beginnings, the artistic counterpart of the Catholic Reformation. Spanish gold and energy, Italian genius, and the lofty idealism of the Roman Catholic Church, purified and rejuvenated by reforming popes, prelates, and princes, produced the first fruits of the baroque style. It was associated with the papacy in Rome, with the Jesuits, with the court at Madrid, with the upsurge of energy that reconquered so much of Europe for the Roman Church. While, in the secular sphere, palaces continued to be built, por-

[1] The bibliography in the *Journal of Aesthetics and Art Criticism,* V (December, 1946), provides striking evidence of the expansion of the term *baroque* since the publication of H. Wölfflin's *Renaissance und Barock* (1888).

[2] Pevsner in his *Barock Malerei in Italien* (Wildpark-Potsdam, 1928) suggests that the early baroque should be called "manerism." The distinction is rather finely drawn.

traits of princes and courtiers to be painted, and music to be composed, the greatest artistic efforts of the later sixteenth century were devoted to the glory of God rather than of man. Churches were built and adorned with loving care to celebrate His glory and His magnificence.

This first period of the baroque centered in Latin Europe, but by the last quarter of the seventeenth century the movement had slowed down in Italy and become dormant in Spain. The wealth and power of Europe had shifted to the north. The great artists of the Spanish baroque were dead, and their unimaginative successors received few important commissions. In Italy the schools were still vital, but the artists, musicians, and architects had to seek employment in Vienna, Munich, Dresden, Paris and other northern capitals. This was the beginning of the great dispersal of Italian genius. By the first half of the eighteenth century colonies of Italian artists, architects, and musicians, scattered from Moscow to Boston, from Stockholm to Budapest, were disseminating the culture of Italy.[3]

In moving northward the baroque style underwent an important change. The Counter Reformation had lost its vitality and the egoism of the emerging monarchical states had become the axis of political and cultural life. This meant secularization; instead of glorifying God, art and architecture were now bent to the glory of princes, and music to their enjoyment. The stately, monumental, heavily ornate style designed by Catholic Europe for the temples of God the King could be admirably adapted to the temples erected for divine-right rulers on earth. In France, England, and Germany new churches were still being erected, but the new temples were intended to commemorate human victories or to expiate the sins of princes. Gone was the simple faith that had constructed the Gothic cathedrals and the defiant belief that raised the great baroque churches of the sixteenth century. Princely pride and secular interests had invaded the temples of God.[4]

Palaces rather than churches now captured the imagination, and particularly one great palace, Versailles, became the focus of interest. Never before had so much magnificence been consecrated to exclusively worldly ends. The Sun King, ruler by divine right, raised to himself a temple that rivaled the greatest monuments of antiquity. The remodeling of

[3] P. H. Lang has an interesting map of the distribution of Italian composers during the height of this dispersal, 1675-1750. If it were enlarged to include architects, artists, sculptors, singers, and instrumentalists, it would be even more striking. P. H. Lang, *Music in Western Civilization* (New York, 1941), 458-9.

[4] In England the great fire of London in 1666 was responsible for the rebuilding of that city. Christopher Wren's St. Paul's Cathedral as well as the many lesser churches which he built in London were part of the reconstruction.

Louis XIII's hunting lodge at Versailles had begun about 1661, but the great period of construction fell in the decade 1675–1685. Only the chapel remained to be built after 1690, and it was not completed until a few years before Louis's death. With its gardens, subsidiary buildings, and reflecting pools, this great palace is even today one of the artistic wonders of the world.[5]

Versailles opened a new phase of the baroque, for the great palace exemplified the new culture that was emerging in Europe. The disciplined, bureaucratic state, centered upon the monarch, was gradually regulating all phases of life. By rigid, ceremonious formalism, by empty conventions and stiff etiquette, the great nobility, no longer able to control politics, were bent to the king's will. Versailles reflected this disciplined order. Lenôtre, the landscape architect, allowed his shrubs and bushes no more self-expression than Louis permitted his courtiers; the clipped hedges, formalized gardens, and disciplined trees all submitted to the royal will. The palace and outbuildings displayed the same order: under the guidance of Mansart, stone, glass, and plaster were brought into a balance of line and form that left no odd edges, no undisciplined sweeps to distract attention from the stately magnificence of the whole.[6] In the decoration of the palace, Le Brun, the apostle of design, imposed upon the painters a pattern of unity. The pictures and bas reliefs may have been pompous and insincere, ludicrous in their glorification of the king's ego, but there could be no question about their unity. Palaces, statues, and decorations all expressed the stately pomp of the French court and the inner discipline of the bureaucratic state.

While Versailles greatly modified the previous baroque style in the direction of French Renaissance architecture, the great churches built in England, France, and Germany adhered more closely to the earlier Italian baroque. This was particularly true of the domes raised in Vienna by Fischer von Erlach and Lukas von Hildebrandt. The Italian influence was stronger in Austria than anywhere else in Europe. The Karlskirche and the Peterskirche in Vienna, the Dom at Passau, and the Klosterkirche St. Florian in upper Austria are magnificent examples of Austrian adaptation of the Italian style. These churches, along with a dozen others built for cloisters and cities, all display the stately grandeur and the

---

[5] A twentieth-century biographer of Louis XIV insists that all the miseries and evils of Louis's regime were outweighed by the creation of this sumptuous monument of French culture. L. Bertrand, *Louis XIV* (New York, London, and Toronto, 1928).

[6] Cf. W. Weisbach, *Die Kunst des Barock in Italien, Frankreich, Deutschland und Spanien* (Berlin, 1924), 56 ff.

rhythmical expression of space characteristic of the earlier baroque.[7] In England, Wren's masterpiece, St. Paul's Cathedral, was completed in the 1690's. The churchmen had desired a Gothic structure, but the need for an imposing monument and the dominant mode of the era dictated the baroque. St. Paul's showed none of the later rococo tendencies, for Sir Christopher Wren was obliged to keep within a "modest" budget and therefore had to let the architectural structure of the building provide its own decoration. The Invalides in Paris was Louis XIV's answer to St. Paul's.[8] It was more characteristic of the Italian baroque than any other of Louis XIV's later buildings. On the other hand, the lighter treatment of the problem of space composition in the chapel at Versailles suggests that the rococo influences, already expressed in the newer interior decoration of the palace, were beginning to affect church architecture.

It is difficult to sum up the many factors that molded the character of the baroque as it moved northward. Obviously the dominant influence even in church architecture was the courtly society of the era.[9] The kings and their courtiers, bureaucrats, and soldiers were all patrons of the art, and their requirements inevitably set the patterns for the artists who served them. Yet both court and artist were also affected to some extent by the broader developments of European society. This was an epoch of expanding horizons and of sensational discoveries, as well as a period of classical humanistic interests. The baroque style reflected both the new and the old conceptions.

Pope, writing in 1711, expressed a credo of his age in the terse remark:

> Those rules of old discovered, not devised,
> Are Nature still, but Nature methodized.
> Nature, like liberty, is but restrained,
> By the same laws which first herself ordained.[10]

This faith in an underlying order of things, basically classic in structure, permeated the society that cultivated *l'esprit géométrique*. Inevitably it

[7] G. G. Dehio, *Geschichte der deutschen Kunst*, Vol. III (Berlin and Leipzig, 1931), 327 ff.

[8] S. F. Kimball, *Creation of the Rococo* (Philadelphia, 1943), 59.

[9] This is not true for Wren's smaller churches in which he combined a Gothic spire with classical decoration. This form, transferred to America, influenced church architecture from Savannah to Portland.

[10] *Essay on Criticism*, lines 88–92.

found expression in literature, music, and architecture. Artists avidly studied classical antiquities as well as the work of the Renaissance; the baroque achieved the symmetry and balance of classic forms as part of the order of things.

Expansion and rhythm, however, were also ideals of the period that was eventually to proclaim the doctrine of progress. According to one critic, "Baroque art emerged out of . . . [a] struggle for freedom from old shackles and inhibitions and spoke with an energetic and highly eloquent rhetoric of progress, expanding the range of human activities, of grandiose achievements, of ceaseless activity and motion." [11] This idea of the baroque can be carried to fascinating lengths. Expansion of a single theme can be discovered in a Corelli composition, in a Le Brun painting, in Mansart's Versailles or Pöppelmann's Zwinger. The baroque style was classical in form, but it also expressed movement, extension, and rhythm. Merely to stand in a baroque cathedral or in the gardens of a baroque palace is to sense the organization of space characteristic of the style. Open alleys that lead the eye on and on with new prospects at every turn, the rhythmic repetition of the central theme of design, these are the most striking characteristics of the baroque. Paintings in this style, unlike those of the Renaissance, could not be considered by sections, for the whole canvas was essential to the understanding of any one part. Was this rhythm and extension of space the artistic expression of an age that conceived a universe regulated by law, an age that arrived at a global conception of humanity with its diverse cultures, of an age that discovered the mathematical structure of the world? Or was it merely the expression of a society of kings, priests, and aristocracy who felt it important to impress the world with their grandeur and magnificence? These are questions the historian probably will never be able to answer, but they open fruitful lines of inquiry into the psychology of the seventeenth century.

The baroque emphasized mass and size; it was often ornate and artificial in its decoration. These characteristics have led to charges of insincerity. Artists, whether they were glorifying God in a church, or a king in his palace, or a nobleman in his chateau, used tinsel and color, extravagant plaster and stone designs, and grandiose patterns and themes to carry out their ideas. In music, too, they ornamented the theme with striking figures, repetitive and elaborate. Lastly, they regimented nature

[11] W. Fleming, "The Element of Motion in Baroque Art and Music," *Journal of Aesthetics and Art Criticism*, V (January, 1946), 121–128.

to conform to their will: in landscape gardening they produced clipped hedges; in music the equal temperament; in opera *castrati* voices. These distortions of the natural and this extensive ornamentation exposed the baroque style to the label "degenerate Renaissance art."

II. ORIGINS OF THE ROCOCO

At the very time when Versailles was adapting the baroque to fit the ceremonial needs of Louis's court, other forces were subtly changing the monumental character of the style to produce the softer, more intimate and elegant forms of the eighteenth century. The Versailles designed and built by Le Vau and Mansart and decorated by Le Brun and his fellows was a proper palace for a great king, but it was too cold and formal for comfortable living. The stiff ceremonial of the court was at first tempered by Louis's love affairs and by gay palace festivals, but during the king's closing years, when disaster stalked his armies, when death invaded his household, and when fear for his soul turned his thoughts to God, the formalism of the life of Versailles became oppressive.

It has been commonly assumed that in the court that saw Madame de Maintenon established as the king's wife men pretended to be pious, and that the gaiety of life was to be found not at Versailles, but in Paris. According to this view Versailles in the early eighteenth century was like a tomb embellished with Le Brun's baroque splendor. Recent research has shown the error of this view. The court, it is true, never recovered the brilliance of the mid-years of Louis's reign, but after the arrival of the young Duchess de Bourgogne in 1697 it could hardly be described as a tomb. Under her influence a new burst of building and decorating activity took place. It was not the regency that first gave Marly, the Trianon, Meudon, and Versailles their rococo decorations, for the "new taste" that became the rococo style can be traced back at least to 1699.[12]

The new style came in being after Mansart had been elevated to the post of *surintendant des bâtiments*. However, neither Mansart nor his brother-in-law De Cotte, who was second in command, could find time to make actual drawings or develop plans. Their most gifted assistant, Pierre Lepautre, was the leading artistic spirit and the true founder of the

[12] S. F. Kimball's *Creation of the Rococo* (Philadelphia, 1943) is a remarkably painstaking and scholarly study that explodes the generally accepted idea that the rococo style originated away from the court. This study is based upon extensive research in the plans and projects for remodeling and redecorating the royal palaces.

new style that led to the rococo.[13] Mansart, the only professional architect to rise to so high an administrative post in the *bâtiments,* encouraged his assistant, but it is improbable that he had much to do with the evolution of the designs.

The rococo first appeared in interior decoration, the field of its greatest triumphs, when Lepautre's work at Marly attracted attention. The living quarters of the royal family rather than the great salons of the palace were the rooms that were first affected by the departure from the stately artistic patterns. The problem was to provide a new treatment for the fireplace and to make the wall mirrors an integral part of the room. "The beauty of these new designs," writes Kimball, "must have been instantly appreciated for ones of similar type, with mirrors 'en toute l'hauteur,' were ordered . . . for the diagonal faces of the salon." Soon every important person at court wanted his or her apartments "done over" in the new mode. It would be impossible in this brief account to show how rapidly the elegance of the new style was adopted by the upper classes. Kimball's study, however, gives clear indication that the interiors of the royal palaces began to be redecorated in the first decade of the eighteenth century. The regency period only accelerated the pace and perhaps increased the flowing elegance of the designs.

The new style "took" in France almost immediately. Its introduction coincided with the early eighteenth-century boom in private construction. In the late seventeenth century the changing conditions of life and taste had outmoded the country and city houses of the rich to such an extent that mere remodeling was no longer sufficient. Order and discipline followed in the wake of the king's soldiers and officials. The uncertainties and disorders of earlier periods gradually disappeared, and those who could afford to live on a grand scale were no longer satisfied with the cold, heavy, fortresslike homes that had been built to meet the more turbulent conditions of the past. Versailles demonstrated that new structures, lighter and more cheerful, with gardens and reflecting pools rather than walls and moats, could be built without fear of consequences. The significance of the new police state can be measured by comparing the chateau built by Sully in the first decades of the seventeenth century with any of the country homes constructed a hundred years later. In the cities the same tendency was manifest. The Place Vendôme, laid out by Mansart

[13] S. F. Kimball, "The Creation of the Style Louis XV," *Art Bulletin,* XXIII (1941), 1–15.

in the latter years of the century, set a new standard for the dwellings of noblemen, financiers, and officials. An era was born, and with it a lighter architecture.

Changes in the pattern of living were reflected in other arts as well as in architecture. The early eighteenth century was marked by gracious manners and witty conversation undreamed of a hundred years before, when Henry IV ruled his court like an ex-guerrilla captain. The salon rather than the stable had become the center of civilized living; conversation, music, and artistic surroundings became essentials for social intercourse. New social trends made demands upon the arts and a new conception of civilized society brought with it new styles of decoration and architecture.

Artistic modes rarely develop abruptly. Like most human achievements, they usually result from trial and error in the effort to meet new requirements. As noted above, the new taste was first developed for the intimate rooms of the royal family at Marly, and later applied to some of the more pretentious salons at Versailles. Not everyone could afford to build on a royal scale, but the new style could be adapted to smaller hotels and country houses. Indeed, the rococo decoration was admirably suited to smaller rooms; with large windows, opposing mirrors, lighter doors, and cool colors, a small room could be planned to give the illusion of spaciousness and still retain the charm of intimacy. The heavy baroque, so appropriate for the glorification of God or king, thus began to give way to this lighter, more elegant decoration which softened the stately magnificence of the earlier baroque style.

The large mirrors and windows took most of the wall space and left no room for historical paintings or mythological tableaux. The artist had nothing but corners and borders on which to paint "the march of the seasons," "the muses," or some other trite subject to provide color. The gracious charm of the oval room in the Hôtel de Soubise, designed by Germain Boffrand and decorated by Charles-Joseph Natoire in 1707, or the interiors of the Parisian home of Sieur Bréthous indicate the change in living and taste in the two decades following Le Brun's death.[14]

The artist had to adjust himself and his work to these new conditions. Such pictures as could be used were expected to either amuse or flatter the owner of the house and his guests. At Versailles it was fitting to por-

[14] Volumes XI and XIII of the *Propyläen-Kuntsgeschichte*, W. Weisbach, *op. cit.*, and M. Osborn, *Die Kunst des Rococo* (Berlin, 1929), are invaluable for understanding this change in style.

252 THE EMERGENCE OF THE GREAT POWERS

tray "Louis crossing the Rhine"; in the *hôtel* of a nobleman or a finan-
cier, a portrait of the owner or his family was appropriate; in the country
chateau landscapes or pictures of rustic activity were thought suitable.
These tastes were reflected clearly in the public showings of pictures at
the Academy. The salons of the 1680's were filled with historical and
allegorical canvases, while in the last salon under Louis XIV (1704) more
than two hundred of the entries were portraits.[15] At the same time, the
leading artists, as we shall see, were moving away from the ponderous
and grandiose school of Le Brun toward the lighter and gayer style that
culminated later in the work of Watteau.

The influence of Versailles upon the imagination of princes, however,
was too strong to permit the easy immediate acceptance of the lighter
style of the rococo-baroque. Versailles was almost as much a challenge to
Europe as Louis's trumpets and soldiers. German rulers, perhaps from a
feeling of inferiority, felt impelled to answer that challenge in stone and
mortar as well as on the field of battle. In Berlin Frederick I (III) began
the *Schloss*. His architect and sculptor, Schlüter, did not have the unlimited funds put at the disposal of Mansart and Le Brun, but between 1698
and 1706 he reared a monument suitable to his master's proud though
newly acquired title of King in Prussia. In England, the queen and
parliament, temporarily grateful to Marlborough, ordered the construction of Blenheim palace, an enormous, impressive monument to the defeat of the French king, but, like Versailles, not a very comfortable
residence. In Vienna, Fischer von Erlach and Lukas von Hildebrandt,
architects to the emperor and to the fabulously rich soldiers and statesmen who conquered Hungary, erected palaces that defied the arrogance
of the French king. The first of these were still of the Versailles-baroque
design but by 1715, when plans for the Belvedere, the Schwarzenberg
palace, and the Bohemian Hofkanzlei were being made, the softer, more
graceful rococo style was beginning to invade Vienna also. In Würzburg,
where Balthasar Neumann and Lukas von Hildebrandt constructed the
Residenz, and in Dresden, where Pöppelmann built the Zwinger, the
baroque of Versailles and the most intimate rococo combined to set the
pattern for eighteenth-century architects and decorators. The difference
between Versailles, completed in the later 1680's, and the Zwinger, begun
in 1711, is an excellent gauge of the change in taste and style from the
heavy magnificence of Louis XIV to the gay elegance of the eighteenth
century.

[15] L. Réau, *Histoire de la peinture française au XVIIIᵉ siècle, I* (Paris and Brussels, 1925–
26), x.

Just as the massive baroque of Versailles was giving way to eighteenth-century patterns, the French palace was outdone in Germany, at least on paper. Paul Decker (1677–1713), a pupil of Schlüter, made his famous architectural drawings, *Der fürstliche Baumeister,* to show what might be done with the monumental baroque if only money were available. His book was only one, though perhaps not the most fantastic, of this era's "better homes and gardens" books for princes. Decker's proposed palace was to be a colossal, architectural monstrosity, surrounded by hundreds of acres of formal gardens, geometric walks and hedges. It was to be the final answer to the Versailles baroque, but by the eighteenth century both the money and the taste for such formal magnificence were lacking.[16] The elegance of the rococo better suited the witty and frivolous society that was emerging. A Decker palace would have been impressive, but a rococo palace was better fitted for the enjoyment of the civilized life of the coming age.

The debate in the French Academy in the 1680's presaged the changing taste in painting. For twenty-odd years Le Brun, the disciple of Raphael and Poussin, had dominated French artistic life. As first painter to the king, head of the Academy, and director of the Gobelin works, he was in a position to dictate style. Even so, revolt broke out against his rule. It was a phase, perhaps, of the conflict between the ancients and the moderns. In art it took the form of the Reubenists against the Poussinists, color against design. Le Brun's death in 1690 left the field to the pro-Flemish party, or rather, to put it more accurately, left French art free to follow its own development without constraint.[17] Le Brun's successor, Mignard, was too old to exercise close control over the Academy and after his death in 1695 no one was to try to dictate to French artists until the rise of David almost a century later.

There were a half-dozen first-rate painters in the period between the death of Le Brun and the rise of Watteau, but many of their finest pieces were destroyed in the turmoil of the French Revolution and of the Commune of 1871, so that only prints remain by which to judge them. Some of these men, like Jouvenet and his nephew Jean Restout, still painted in the style of Le Brun. Jouvenet's *Descent from the Cross* (1697) and his *Mass of Canon La Porte at the Notre Dame* are mag-

---

[16] Cf. illustration,

[17] S. Rocheblave's *French Painting in the XVIII*th *Century,* translated from the French by G. F. Lees (Paris, 1937), contains exceptionally fine illustrations. *The Propyläen Kunstgeschichte* (XI–XIII) is, of course, also an indispensable series for any study of art in this period.

nificent examples of baroque religious painting. Others, like Santerre, were obviously feeling their way toward the forms that Watteau would develop for the eighteenth century. Santerre painted religious as well as secular figures, but he chose religious subjects that allowed him to portray a beautiful nude (*Suzanne*) in a setting as pleasing to the eye as the figure itself.[18] In Noël and Antoine Coypel France had a family of painters who definitely forecast the eighteenth century. Lafosse, Desportes, and Largillière were also artists of a high order. Lafosse's principal works of this period, with the exception of his paintings in the Invalides, have been destroyed, but there is evidence to indicate that they deserved to rank with the great productions of the baroque era.

Outside France, there were few great artists, except portrait painters, to carry on the traditions of Spain, the Lowlands, or Italy. L. Giordano and Tiepolo were painting in Italy, but in spite of the beauty and excellence of their work they marked no great advance over the earlier style. Bega was working in Berlin for Frederick I (III) and Bellacci, another Italian, painted at Vienna; Boonen and Hobraken carried on the traditions of Holland; but none of these men developed a new style. The great period of Dutch, Spanish, and Italian art had come to an end by the last quarter of the seventeenth century and the French painters were still struggling to express the new rococo style that became European in the ensuing century.

With Watteau the spirit of the rococo became fully established in painting. He worked with Claude Audran, a decorator, and Claude Gillot, a scene painter for the opera and the French theater, who also painted humorous pictures from the plays and homely scenes of everyday life. Charles Lafosse and Antoine Coypel also befriended the young Watteau, and probably influenced his development. Lastly, the Rubens gallery in the Luxemburg and the Veronese paintings owned by M. Crozat made a deep impression upon the young painter. In one decade (1709–1721) this youthful artist gave the western world some of its most exquisite masterpieces and established a pattern for a whole generation of painters.[19] With Watteau rococo art emerged as the style of that frivolous and sophisticated society that dominated cultural life of the eighteenth century.

---

[18] Lot and his daughters also provided congenial problems for the painters, a "religious" subject that required two very secular nudes.

[19] L. Réau, *op. cit.*, I, 8–23; L. Gillet, *La peinture de Poussin à David*, 2nd ed. (Paris, 1935), 146–161.

The two most important portrait painters of the period were Hyacinthe Rigaud and Godfrey Kneller. Rigaud's training was French; Kneller's was German and Dutch. Between them they painted practically every important person of the generation 1685–1715. Rigaud in particular was a consummate master of the "grand portrait," in which the individual appears surrounded by the glories of his office and the tools of his profession. His portraits reflect the pomp and circumstance as well as a significant evaluation of the subject. Rigaud was not as cruel to Louis XIV as he was to the electoral prince of Saxony, whose portrait reveals a vacuous young man, heavy with honors and position, but essentially vain and stupid. Sir Godfrey Kneller at his best was as fine a portrait painter as any, but he was often satisfied to show off his technical skill without attempting to penetrate his subject. As a result one critic complains that he made a whole generation of Englishmen look like seventeenth-century Germans.[20] Nonetheless, many of Kneller's portraits show psychological insight as deep as Rigaud's. Anyone who has attempted to paint portraits will be amazed to learn that most of Kneller's pictures were completed in two sittings: he was able to lay a base of silver gray and, while it was still wet, to fix his glazes in the first sitting; in the second, he finished the portrait! Only with great talent and complete technical command can a good portrait be painted so quickly.

There were many other portrait painters of merit whose subjects, not as famous as those of Rigaud and Kneller, paid well and for the most part received first-rate pictures for their money. Neither Rigaud nor Kneller painted women as well as Mignard. In a characteristically Gallic vein, a modern critic has remarked that Mignard alone of his generation painted women so that "one understands why the men committed so many follies."[21] Largillière introduced a light and often humorously friendly motif into his portraits, but one suspects that he flattered his patrons. His work is technically unassailable and even Rigaud could not paint fabrics and furniture more superbly. Jean Jouvenet, better known for his religious paintings, was also a portrait painter of real merit; his picture of the physician Finot is a masterpiece. There were sound portrait painters also in Germany, Italy, the Netherlands, and elsewhere, but most of them did not produce works of high artistic quality. Every city, every court had its complement of painters; by 1700 French-trained artists had begun to supplant the Italians in the Germanies, but in all countries there were native painters to satisfy the demand of the upper

[20] C. H. C. Baker, *Lely and Kneller* (London, 1922), 129.
[21] L. Gillet, *op. cit.*, 114.

classes for portraits much as the photographer does in the twentieth century.

Another form of portraiture, popular in the latter seventeenth century, was the black and white print. Many printmakers were craftsmen, some of them superbly skilled, who merely copied the famous portraits of the great. Kneller, Rigaud, and many other painters were widely known in their own times because of the black and white copies of their canvases. Every inn in Europe wanted a portrait of Charles XII, of Marlborough, of Eugene, of Villars, or one of the vivid battle and siege scenes painted by eminent artists and widely reproduced in black and white.[22] The pictures of philosophers, prelates, and authors also found a market in the ever-increasing demand for prints. Several engravers struck out boldly to compose original plates. Robert Nanteuil and Gérard Edelinck raised engraving above the level of the mechanical arts and secured recognition as artists in their own right. But there was nothing spontaneous about their engravings. Zegrosser remarks, "Every detail is studied and calculated. It is the opposite extreme of the candid camera shot. . . ."[23] Madame de Scudéry wrote:

> *Nanteuil en faisant mon image*
> *A de son art divin signalé le pouvoir,*
> *Je hais mes traits dans mon miroir,*
> *Je les aime dans son ouvrage.*

The sculptors of the period adhered closely to Italian Renaissance and early seventeenth-century baroque patterns. Some of their finest work was for the tombs of great men and wealthy families. In France the tombs of Mazarin and Richelieu, completed in the 1690's by Coysevox and Girardon, were marvelous specimens of baroque art. The tombs of the Pallavicino family, by Mazzuoli, were characteristic of the more exuberant forms of the same style. Aldous Huxley's observation that this marked the high point in the baroque use of the human skeleton, representing death and corruption on mortuary monuments, applies to Italy more than to the rest of Europe.[24] But everywhere the baroque tomb

[22] The sieges of Vienna and Ofen inspired dozens of illustrations. From the surviving prints it seems that the war against the Turks was the most popular theme for this form of pictorial art. The people, Catholic as well as Protestant, were enthralled by this last crusade.

[23] C. Zegrosser, *Six Centuries of Fine Prints* (New York, 1937), 95.

[24] Aldous Huxley, "Death and the Baroque," *Harper's Magazine*, 198 (1949), 80–86.

sculptor rejected the calm classic poses of the Renaissance in favor of those that suggested motion and extension.

In all forms of monumental and portrait sculpture Bernini's influence was decidedly more important than the Renaissance and classical styles. But after 1690 the new generation of French sculptors (Coustou, Dirmont and J. B. Lemoyne) discarded the calm grandeur of the Versailles baroque and began to depict turbulent motion in stone. Their figures were idealized, though obviously taken from nature; they initiated the style that was to reach its zenith in the mid-eighteenth-century French rococo with Falconet's compositions.[25]

Schlüter gave Berlin its first great equestrian monument, the statue of the great elector, and showed that Italian training and German tradition could produce an important sculptor as well as a great architect. His heads of dying warriors on the *Zeughaus* and the allegory Africa in the *Schloss,* as well as the great elector's memorial, place Schlüter among the great artists of his age.[26]

Closely allied to the sculptors were the craftsmen who worked in stone, wood, and plaster. Even a superficial glance at the churches and palaces built at the turn of the eighteenth century will show that this was an age when the artisan's skill made possible the development of architectural styles. The baroque required able craftsmen to execute ornate patterns in stone and plaster, but even more so did the rococo. In the latter style the solid wall masses tend to melt into a flow of rhythm, into constantly moving vibrations of line. To achieve this effect, the architects had to depend upon the anonymous artisan class from which they had liberated themselves by making their profession one of the liberal arts. In no other era have European craftsmen excelled the artistic skill of their fellows of the seventeenth and eighteenth centuries; without them the elegant rococo style would have been impossible to achieve.

The artists, architects, sculptors, and craftsmen of the opening years of the eighteenth century were clearly in harmony with the trends developing in the European society of princes, noblemen, financiers, and merchants. Even before the end of the wars and the death of the Sun King artists were preparing for the elegance of the rococo civilization. While their brethren in science and philosophy were building the temple for the heavenly city of the eighteenth-century philosophers, the men with drafting boards, chisels, and brushes were creating the physical setting in which that city would be most satisfactorily considered.

[25] R. Schneider, *L'art français: XVIIIe siècle (1690–1789)* (Paris, 1926), 67 ff.
[26] Cf. G. G. Dehio, *op. cit.*, 438–440.

III. MUSIC OF THE HIGH BAROQUE

Like other artists, the musicians filled an important role in the society of Europe at the end of the seventeenth century. While the mass of the people continued their traditional religious and secular musical culture, in the courts, as in the society of noblemen and of the patrician bourgeoisie, complex patterns were evolved to satisfy more critical tastes. It has been called the period of the high baroque. The monodic style as it developed in the seventeenth century allowed contrasts of large and light tone masses, and permitted thematic organization through rhythmic patterns and repetitive expressions giving unity to the music. The period's taste for ornamentation and musical color completed the synthesis which musicologists believe warrants the use of the term baroque. Since art historians have no monopoly of the term, there seems to be no valid reason for denying the history of music so useful a concept.[27]

Music probably never had greater opportunity for development than in the later seventeenth century. "Seen in historical perspective," writes Paul Bekker, "the seventeenth century appears as an age of many-sided experiment, of imaginative ingeniousness . . . as a highway . . . between the peaks of the sixteenth and the eighteenth centuries." [28] There were literally hundreds of composers, all of whom could get a hearing. Every court, every important nobleman, every major city maintained or supported musicians, and several dozen opera houses scattered throughout the continent gave further employment. The musicians of the time were both performers and composers. Not all became as rich and famous as Lully, but most of them could count upon a reasonable livelihood.

The composer was not an isolated individual working in a garret far from the "consumers" of his labors; on the contrary, he was closely integrated with his society. His patron or employer expected him to compose music for every "occasion"; his "public" waited anxiously to hear his latest product. If the piece were well received, and often even if it were mediocre, it would be sent abroad to bring prestige to the author and his patron. Scores were published in large number, though publication did not necessarily mean added income to the author. They were distributed

---

[27] Three books are indispensable. M. Bukofzer, *Music in the Baroque Era* (New York, 1947); R. Haas, *Die Musik des Barocks,* Vol. V of *Handbuch der Musikwissenschaft* (Potsdam, 1934); and G. Adler, *Handbuch der Musikgeschichte* (Berlin, 1930), 2 vols. All three of these works have extensive bibliographies. See also William Fleming, *op. cit.,* 121–127.

[28] P. Bekker, *Musikgeschichte als Geschichte der musikalischen Formwandlungen* (Stuttgart, 1926), 80.

through the diplomatic pouches or carried from one end of Europe to the other by traveling artists. Even a cursory glance at the musical activity of the late seventeenth century reveals a flow of energy, a climate favorable to the development of new musical ideas.

Italy held the musical hegemony of Europe long after she had lost her primacy in literature and the fine arts. Venice, Florence, Rome, and particularly Naples sent forth a steady stream of performers, composers, and teachers who carried Italian musical culture as far as Boston and Rio de Janeiro, Moscow and Constantinople.[29] Native schools in France, Germany, and England were not entirely submerged by this Italian flood but, except in France, where an Italian, Lully, composed in the French manner, the Italians were dominant. In England they practically carried the day.[30] In Germany Vienna was the gateway for Italian influence; from there it spread to Munich, Dresden, and even to Hamburg. Agostino Steffani, whose music reconciled the new monodic style with the older contrapuntal tradition, was a primary influence on both Bach and Handel.[31] The compositions of eighteenth-century German masters survived those of most Italians, yet the Italian musicians who flooded all Europe gave the German composers many basic ideas and techniques.

It is difficult to write about musical style, especially when it is impossible to give illustrations. In general, however, it may be pointed out that the monodic style of the seventeenth century was especially suited to spectacle entertainment. The word, or recitative, became the dominant characteristic; genuine musical expression gave way to musically heightened speech. Fortunately this relation of word and music was soon reversed by Monteverdi, who used music to intensify the sense of the words. In another way, too, the monodic style underwent modification; throughout the seventeenth century there was a growing feeling for tonality and with it increased use of chordal relations to circumscribe the key. This technique makes the music of Corelli, Scarlatti, and their contemporaries seem "modern" when compared with the compositions of the first half of the century. These composers laid the foundations for the musical edifice of the next two hundred years.[32]

The evolution of musical instruments was closely connected with the

[29] P. H. Lang, *op. cit.* Cf. map opposite p. 453.

[30] Handel, though a German, was deeply influenced by Steffani and by his own studies in Italy.

[31] D. J. Grout, "German Baroque Opera," *Musical Quarterly,* XXXII (1946), 575 ff.

[32] For an adequate discussion of the technical problem, see M. Bukofzer, *op. cit.,* Chs. III, IV, VII, X, and XI; for a shorter, but skillfully integrated discussion, D. N. Ferguson, *A History of Musical Thought,* 2nd ed. (New York and London, 1948), 240–257.

rise of new musical forms. The seventeenth century saw the viol family reach its fullest development. The rich, soft tones of these instruments were especially suited for chamber music, but the needs of the opera and the concert halls required a stronger, more strident voice. The violin filled this need. Fiddles had long been known in Europe, but they were perfected as concert instruments only when the Amati, the Stradivari, the Guarnieri, and other famous Italian families of craftsmen produced their masterpieces. The violins built at the end of the seventeenth century are still standard and much prized. Later generations raised the bridge and strengthened the neck, but by 1700 the basic form of the violin had been achieved. It is interesting to note, however, that its victory over the older viol was not complete until the mid-eighteenth century.

Keyboard instruments also were improved in the seventeenth century. Technical difficulties in construction were solved, and with the "fixing" of the scale toward the end of the century, the two-keyboard type of instrument tended to disappear. By 1700 the "well-tempered" clavier was becoming a facile and beautiful instrument for chamber music. The types that have survived, either in museums or in pictures, suggest that there was considerable variation in their appearance and construction, but the principle of the clavier had become well established. Horns and woodwinds were also somewhat improved in the latter seventeenth century, but they did not yet offer the possibilities inherent in the violin and the keyboard instruments.[33]

Almost as important as the development of new instruments was the transformation of the role of the composer-conductor into that of the professional director of orchestra and chorus. Lully, Louis XIV's great musician, first perfected conducting. He trained the sections of his orchestra like a modern symphony conductor, and made conducting an exact art. Without such expert leadership the concerto, with its characteristic solo ensemble of two to four violins playing against a whole orchestra, would have been impossible. At Louis's court everything was disciplined and fitted into a pattern: the shrubs, the courtiers, the soldiers, the artists, and the musicians. When the conductor assumed the role of the maestro, of the creative artist who interpreted the score for the whole orchestra, he was filling his part in the court culture of the late seventeenth century.

As in earlier periods, the church was an important patron of music. The glory of God even more than the amusement of princes had always attracted the composer and the performer. The Catholic Church, with the rich symbolism and majestic problems of its services, provided fertile ground for musical experiment, especially at a time when the church had not yet placed liturgical limitations upon the musical score. Some of the larger churches supported not only an organ but also an orchestra, including horns and drums, so that the composer had a free rein in preparing music for the services. The first concertos and sonatas were written for churches, and composers all over Europe, Protestant as well as Catholic, tried their hand at music for the solemn high mass. Some of this music, written by lighthearted and sometimes irresponsible musicians, was nothing more than an adaptation of the dance and operatic styles being developed for secular consumption, yet this highly ornamental music did not seem as incongruous to the churchmen of 1700 as it does today.

In Protestant lands, where the church services required less ceremonial music, the traditions of choral singing were sharpened and refined. The Italian music master may have regarded Protestant hymns as crude, almost barbaric expressions of musical form, but when native musicians had absorbed enough of Italy's teaching, these same Protestant services inspired musical masterpieces. The passions, the oratorios, and the cantatas fitted well within the theological limitations and traditional customs of the north, and by 1700 had taken on the forms and styles which the eighteenth century was to exploit.[34]

In both Catholic and Protestant countries the church organ provided an instrument that challenged the composer. Earlier in the century Frescobaldi (1583–1643), organist at St. Peter's, had initiated a new epoch in organ music. His students spread the new style all over Europe: Rossi and Pasquini were worthy successors in Italy; Froberger, Tunder and others transplanted it to Germany. Buxtehude, the great Lübeck organist whose teaching was so decisive for Bach, as well as hundreds of lesser musicians developed the power of the organ and left an impressive literature of music that even the genius of the great eighteenth-century composers could not completely obliterate.[35]

If the sheer number of musical scores is any indication of importance, however, it would appear that by the opening of the eighteenth century the amusement of men had become more momentous than the glory of God. The operas of the period, for example, had become the most spec-

[34] G. Adler, *op. cit.*, I, 446 ff.
[35] Cf. Lang, *op. cit.*, 362 ff.

tacular and colorful expressions of musical culture. Scarcely a century old, and still very much in the process of development, the opera had already acquired a substantial following. It grew out of several traditions. In England it emerged from the masques; in France from the ballad; in Italy from the pastorale. In Florence, Rome, Vienna, and Paris it was conducted under court auspices and therefore maintained a dignified mien. The English, on the other hand, took it as a form of escape from the Puritan ban on the theater, and consequently opera suffered severely when the Restoration allowed the playhouses to reopen. In Hamburg, Venice, and Naples it was patronized largely by patrician families but it also acquired something of a popular following at an early date. By the opening of the eighteenth century, however, the Italian, particularly the Neapolitan opera had become standard throughout Europe. Lully's operas continued to be played in France; Keiser wrote Italianized German operas in Hamburg; and Purcell and Bow more or less followed the earlier English tradition; but Italian singers and composers were displacing native talent so that opera became almost synonymous with "Italian."

It is quite unlikely that any considerable part of this early operatic music will ever be reproduced, for most of it calls for one or more male sopranos, and there is no reason to suppose that *castrati* will ever again appear in the concert halls. It was for these *castrati* that many of the pieces were written. The more famous of them, apparently, had magnificent voices, and could sing duets with the cornet much as a modern coloratura sings with the flute. Their control of volume, the trick by which they could throw their voices, and the full power and beauty of a male soprano voice had so striking an effect upon the female part of the audience that many people condemned the opera as aphrodisiac. With *castrati* in leading roles, only coloratura and dramatic soprano voices could play the female roles, so that contraltos were forced to take the parts of men. All this made the opera unnatural and unreal; the audience of 1700, however, was willing to accept these conventions without worrying about plausibility.

Professor Grout remarks that "an inherent feature of the opera is its artificiality." [36] This was certainly true of the Italian variety, in which the natural and supernatural elements were freely combined, and no attention at all seems to have been given to the problem of motivation. The audiences did not mind. The opera was a luxurious spectacle; no one cared if the plots were absurd. That was a convention freely accepted by

[36] D. J. Grout, *A Short History of Opera* (New York, 1947), 4.

all who patronized the art. Considering that in the last decades of the seventeenth century over five hundred different operas were produced in Venice alone, and that Scarlatti wrote one hundred and twenty-five of them, it is not surprising that the librettists did not produce great drama. They must have been as hard up for stories as a modern scenario writer.

The audience, then, did not go to the opera to hear a story. The human voice, the prima donna or the great *castrato* was the prime attraction. There probably have never been better trained vocalists than those of the early eighteenth century, and never were singers more warmly acclaimed. Several of them became fabulously rich; many of them were "called" from opera house to opera house, from court to court, and at times these calls were negotiated through diplomatic channels. Composers wrote their operas with this or that singer in mind, and patrons returned night after night to hear their favorite sing the same part. The music and stage settings were designed to give background for the voice; the plot was merely a vehicle to provide occasion for the song.[37]

Opera houses and stage settings had not yet reached the perfection that was to come in the eighteenth century, but in Venice, Paris, Naples, and Vienna the forms that characterized the later operas were already discernible. If the drawings that have come down to us are at all accurate, some of the most typically baroque architecture and decoration were to be seen on the opera stage rather than in palaces or churches. The use of "machines" to achieve the supernatural effects and the elaborate and luxurious costumes and stage props seem all to have become well established by 1700. On the other hand, poor lighting, the ungainly figures of the *castrati,* and the complete absurdity of the plots would make the settings and props incongruous to modern eyes. All opera houses did not reach the high standards set by Venice. The Hamburg Opera, for example, though it could boast of Keiser, Steffani, and Handel, was shabby, with cheap settings, and undisciplined singers. It was to take another half century before the standards of excellence set by the best opera houses became general throughout the continent.[38]

Though the opera was undoubtedly the most spectacular musical entertainment, instrumental music also played a significant part in the court life of Europe and an important role in the cultural pattern of the upper

[37] There are several fine books dealing with the opera. D. J. Grout, *ibid.;* J. Gregor, *Kulturgeschichte der Oper* (Zurich, 1941); and H. Kretzschmar, *Geschichte der Oper* (Leipzig, 1919) are very useful. Both Haas and Bukofzer also have excellent sections on the opera.

[38] D. J. Grout, "German Baroque Opera," *Musical Quarterly,* XXXII (1946), 575 ff.

classes. Every court boasted an orchestra, many noblemen maintained their own little bands of players, and talented amateurs found in music an outlet for creative expression. Compositions ranged from elaborate suites and concertos, calling for masses of viols, violins, wind and percussion instruments, to little pieces for the harpsichord or a small string orchestra. Some of this music is still familiar; most of it has been lost or is buried in libraries and archives. Nonetheless, the period of the high baroque was important because it "fixed" the forms for the music of the next two centuries. The dance suites, with their usual sequence of four dances, of which the *allemande, courante, saraband,* and *gigue* were basic but interchangeable with the *pavan, galliard, minuet, gavotte,* or *bourrée,* emerged as a standard form. Single dances, it was discovered, were not particularly striking, but contrasting dances provided amusement for the dancers and artistic satisfaction for the listeners.[39]

The orchestral concerto, too, became an established form of musical expression about the end of the seventeenth century. The first concertos seem to have been written as sacred music for a combination of voice and instrument, but by 1700 Vivaldi, Albinoni, and Torelli had developed the true orchestral concerto form. The musical differentiation of orchestra and solo was first made by contrasting a trio of violins with the full orchestra. By the first decade of the eighteenth century solo concertos for violin (Torelli and Albinoni) and for cello (Jacchini) had come into being. The solo parts in these works ceased to be merely transitional interludes in the music and assumed equal importance with the orchestra.[40]

Corelli, another Italian, developed the sequence of movements in the sonata. He wrote two types: the *sonata da chiesa* (church) and the *sonata da camera* (chamber). The latter was strongly influenced by the dance suites. Corelli alternated the fast and slow movements, and usually derived one of the fast ones from the old vocal music of the fugal style, yet his compositions were by and large homophonic. Most of his sonatas were apparently written for the violin, while German composers tended to make the clavier and harpsichord the important solo instruments.

The music of many composers of this period was not only popular in their own day, but also significant for the musical thought of the succeeding century. Composers, however, deserve to remain in decent anonymity when it is impossible adequately to describe their life and works. They

[39] C. Gray, *The History of Music* (New York, 1931), 150; McKinney and Anderson, *op. cit.*, 354–355.

[40] M. Bukofzer, *op. cit.*, 59 ff., 64 ff., 224 ff., and *passim;* Haas, *op. cit.*, 215 ff. and *passim.*

labored hard to solve the problems presented by improved instruments, by the conception of tonality, by the obvious advantage of combining the monodic and the polyphonic styles. Their music, played in churches, at the courts, in opera houses, and in the chambers of noblemen and wealthy patricians, was one of the flowers of the period. The characteristic forms of western European civilization were rapidly coming into being, and the artists as well as the soldiers, statesmen, and businessmen contributed their share to the process of development that was to make the latter culture of Europe.

IV. MIRRORS FOR MEN

In the sixteenth and early seventeenth centuries the problem of salvation had overshadowed most other human concerns. In the clamor raised by priests and preachers, theologians and philosophers, soldiers and statesmen, the gentler voices of Erasmus, Montaigne, and others who pleaded for a reasonable approach to humanity were almost completely drowned out. Life on earth, even a Christian life, seemed to pale in significance in the great debate between the forces of Reformation and Counter Reformation. Nonetheless, under the barrages of anathemas and cannon balls of the religious contestants, the determining forces of politics and economics were inexorably shifting the thoughts of western society from theological to secular affairs. To the theologians and preachers it may have seemed that the questions of salvation by faith, election, grace, and good works were still the dominant issues of the day, but the fact remains that attention was being increasingly focused upon the problems of this rather than of the next world.

The expansion of trade brought with it comforts and worldly interests. The growth of new political institutions and the extension of political authority raised questions of power and organization that were exclusively secular. The new learning broke through part of the wall that had obscured the nature of the world, and expounded an apprehensible universe governed by laws. Thus both intellectuals and practical men of affairs found their attention drawn increasingly to the world of the present. By 1700 men might still quarrel about salvation, but they were distracted from their interest in heaven by the problem of man's destiny on earth.

The seventeenth century took a gloomy approach to life. Theological presuppositions had burdened man with original sin and made him a weak creature who without God's assistance could hope to accomplish but little. The evils of life, personified by the devil, were everywhere present to challenge man's courage and devotion. Threatened with eternal damnation, constantly reminded of the crucified Christ whose sufferings had been necessary to expiate their wickedness, and unceasingly prompted to regard their animal nature as evil, men of the seventeenth century could hardly be expected to take an optimistic view of the world. The life they saw about them only confirmed their darkest suspicions, for immorality, public and private, was appalling by any European standards. The stern race of tight-lipped men and unsmiling women who sat for the mid-seventeenth century portrait painters peer pessimistically from their canvases. Only here and there where the softening of manners, the gradual lifting of poverty, and the extension of order and tolerance were making themselves felt, do faces appear that indicate a lighter and happier view of human destiny.

The intellectual life of the mid-century was also under a cloud. The centuries-old idea of an earlier golden age persisted, even though Aristotle was receiving rough treatment at the hands of the new scholars. It was not until the end of the seventeenth century that writers in some numbers could boldly assert that their culture was not a degenerate form of the great Graeco-Roman civilization. The static conceptions inherited from the past almost completely blinded men to the changes going on around them. Even a great creative writer like La Bruyère labored under the impression that all that could be known had already been recorded. The massive backdrop of the ancient world oppressed men with a feeling of futility almost as difficult to overcome as the weight of more primitive superstitions.

Even those who realized the deficiencies of Graeco-Roman science were hardly less pessimistic. The heliocentric cosmos they discovered was an uncomfortable dwelling place for those accustomed to thinking in terms of purpose and to living in a world reasonably finite and man-centered. The new cosmology dwarfed man in his own estimation and robbed him of his traditional place in creation without at the same time providing him with a new conception of his destiny and position. Fontenelle, even when he explained Descartes's universe to the countess and proclaimed the superiority of the moderns over the ancients, looked with incomparable pessimism upon the creature whose wisdom and virtues he extolled. As the world opened before them, thinkers of the seventeenth century found themselves hard pressed to discover the significance of their own existence. Some solved the problem by looking neither left nor right, but continuing to explore the universe in a belief that an answer would present itself. Others attempted to fit old values into the new system, to adapt Christian idealism to the new science. Still others struck out boldly in an effort to find a new meaning for man within the framework of the new learning.

A new vision of man was in the offing, but the first generation of the Enlightenment was to grasp it but imperfectly. The older mirrors for men, for the courtier and the *honnête homme,* were obviously no longer adequate. The accepted courtier was an egocentric person with morals and manners no longer suited to a political world that was outrunning feudalism. The *honnête homme,* who accepted the evils, the trials, and the problems of life with stolid resignation and Christian patience, was equally becoming outmoded. Christian resignation, like Oriental fate, no longer fitted the needs of a society groping toward the idea of progress and of the perfectibility of man. But it was one thing to realize the meaninglessness of the old response and quite another to discover a new and more adequate one. Man had to conceive a new psychology to explain himself, a new morality by which to act, and a new destiny by which to orient his life before he could move confidently forward in the world unfolding before him.

Curiously enough it was a Spanish Jesuit, Baltasar Gracián, who provided one of the mirrors for men that appealed most strongly to the last generation of the seventeenth century. When he wrote in the 1640's and 1650's, he was neglected by Europe and opposed by his own order, yet a half century later his books ran through one edition after another in French, German, Italian, and English. Gracián's man seemed destined to become the pattern accepted by all Europe. The French have a word, *espagnolisme,* almost untranslatable into English; it means the bravado, the conscious self-esteem, the mixture of Don Juan and Don Quixote, of Philip II and Ignatius Loyola that is inherent in human nature. Gracián glorified this *espagnolisme* as an ideal to be striven for. He rejected the bundle of self-effacing, patient, and mediocre virtues required by Christian humility and resignation to fate. Gracián's hero cultivated his greatest talent to the neglect of all others; he strove to be the one, the unique, the exceptional man. He vaguely resembled Nietzsche's superman, but was still clothed in Christian garb. Struggling to achieve, to conquer, to win great fame, he still labored so that he might lay his triumphs at the feet of God.[41]

[41] A. F. G. Bell, *Baltasar Gracián* (Oxford, 1921); E. Mele, "Baltasar Gracián e il Nietzsche," *La Cultura* (April, 1927).

The generation that was searching for a belief that would give man control of his own destiny found Gracián alluring, but his ideal was too Spanish, too flamboyant for the generation that also read Descartes's *Discourse on Method*. His popularity, however, was significant, for it revealed the prevalent desire to escape the inadequate response to traditional forms.

England, which was establishing an intellectual as well as a political and economic hegemony over Europe, rather than decadent Spain, provided the new philosophy needed to give men faith in their own destiny. Among the English even theologians were devising rational systems based upon nature as revealed by the new science, while English society in general, stimulated by the Revolution of 1688 and the subsequent wars, was rapidly taking on the bourgeois character that was to become so well defined in the next century. Commerce, industry, politics, and war joined with science and theology to suggest the need for a new human pattern.

John Locke provided the foundation for the new philosophy. His common-sense arguments, his distrust of metaphysical speculation, and his inevitable appeal to the reasonable made him popular in a society that was becoming skeptical of Aristotle and contemptuous of scholastic learning. His *Essay Concerning Human Understanding* (1690), his *Letters on Toleration* (1689, 1690, 1692), and his book on *Education* (1693) were as important in the field of philosophy and morals as his *Two Treatises on Government* in the field of politics. Locke's empiricism suited admirably the needs and the mood of his era, and his reasonable approach to problems assured him a wide hearing. "He is always sensible," writes Bertrand Russell, "and always willing to sacrifice logic rather than become paradoxical. . . . Whenever strange consequences seem about to appear [as a result of his general principles], Locke blandly refrains from drawing them. To a logician this is irritating; to a practical man, it is proof of sound judgment." [42]

The core of Locke's doctrine was a relatively simple theory of human psychology. "Let us suppose," he writes in an oft-quoted passage, "the mind to be, as we say, white paper, void of characters, without any ideas,—how comes it to be furnished? . . . to this I answer in one word: Experience." The idea that all understanding ultimately comes from experience was not entirely new, but in Locke's pages it was made the very foundation for the study of man. Philosophical conceptions are important because of what men do with them. Locke's proposition pro-

---

[42] B. Russell, *A History of Western Philosophy* (New York, 1945), 606.

voked what amounted to a major intellectual revolution. Swept aside was the impressive volume of metaphysics and theology based upon the proposition that there were innate ideas, placed in men's minds and hearts by God. The new postulates for epistemology were now firmly founded on the earth and man's experience with it, and the new psychology opened vistas for a new conception of man and his place in the universe.

As a corollary to the idea that experience is the sole source of knowledge, Locke insisted that man must restrict his hopes of solving philosophical problems to the concrete and immediate world of experience. The universals and absolutes of earlier philosophers were thus ruled out. Locke's man was like a mariner whose plumb lines will reach bottom on the coasts and in the harbors, but are quite inadequate for sounding the depths of the open sea. He taught that men should probe for certainty wherever possible and that they should accept as probable those things that experience had shown to be acceptable in practice, even though not provable. Everything based upon mere metaphysical speculation was to be regarded as undemonstrated and fruitless to study. Thus Locke was doing for philosophy what Newton was doing for natural science. He scouted questions about the real nature of things so that he might establish a firm basis for explaining the world of reality. "The original value of Locke's philosophy," Hazard observes, ". . . lies in this method of circumscribing and safeguarding an island in an immense sea that dissolves before the eye." [43]

Locke's writings provided a new picture of man as a reasonable creature capable of observing the world and arranging his experience in meaningful patterns. He pointed out that experience involved the grasping of both secondary and primary qualities of the observable world, but in any case allowed man to understand his environment and to live a happy life, secure in the knowledge that he could review all art, science, morality, and nature, and draw from them reasonable conclusions for action. Thus man became the measure of all things, and one more step had been taken on the road leading from the theocentric to the homocentric world. Locke supplied an answer as much to the skepticism of his age as to the scholasticism of the past. By assuring man of his capacity to know certain things as true and others as probable he provided a cure for skepticism that was at the same time a protection against the metaphysical probings that had produced the doubts.

[43] P. Hazard, *La crise de la conscience européene, 1680–1715* (Paris, 1935), II, 16.

Its reasonable practicality as well as its rejection of the concept of innate ideas fitted Locke's philosophy into the movement toward complete secularization of society and development of a new mirror for man. Travelers had reported great differences in morality among the peoples of the earth, and had thereby raised the idea that morality was relative. Locke could explain the variations on the grounds of difference of experience; if there were no innate ideas deriving from God, there could be no universal idea of good and evil, of right and wrong, to which men by nature would subscribe. This argument threw new light upon the destiny of man. It made plausible Bayle's contention, so shocking to good Christians, that a society of atheists could have a morality as pure as the Christian.[44] Furthermore, if morality were actually relative, then a purification of society would lead to higher morality; by eliminating the evils of the world man could hope for moral progress and, as a later generation would add, for perfectibility. The method was at hand. Man was a reasonable being; it should be possible for him to overcome the evils that beset his path. William Temple, Saint-Évremond, La Bruyère, Leibniz and many others were grasping for a new formula, secular in its implications, that would promise man a better future. While all of them did not accept Locke's postulates, their efforts were all akin to those of the *Essay on Human Understanding*.

England was better prepared to elaborate the new ideal than was the continent. The immoral court life of the Restoration was so far out of tune with the vital forces in English society that many Englishmen cried aloud for a transvaluation of values. In this sense the Revolution of 1688 was a moral and social victory as well as a political one. But the years between the Commonwealth and William III had wrought changes in the opponents of the Stuart court also. The rigid, tight-lipped puritanism of the mid-century became more genial as Whig politicos replaced Cromwell's saints. The rapid development of trade and commerce undoubtedly played an important role in the development of the sense of well-being and geniality among the upper classes. The commercial and professional men, the squires and officials who met in the clubs and coffeehouses which were replacing the conventicle as the center of masculine society, lived in a secular atmosphere. The ideas of Locke and Newton as well as the problems of the market place and parliament gave a new turn to the *esprit géométrique*. The ideal of the "gentleman" replaced that of the

---

[44] Actually Bayle, an ardent student of the evils of Christian society, had suggested by inference that it would not be difficult for reasonable, rational atheists to have a purer morality than the Christians had developed.

courtier, and the "gentleman" was thought of as a man whose manners, wealth, and morals, rather than whose blood, established his right to social recognition. The bourgeoisie were coming into their own.

The great essayists of the age of Queen Anne hailed and elaborated this new ideal. Swift and Defoe sometimes struck out with biting irony at the mad remnants of feudalism and intolerant clericalism. Addison and Steele, more genial and understanding, preferred to extol the virtues of the new man who was to inherit social power and prestige. If the essayists were often prudish and occasionally puritanical, it was in reaction to the manners of the Restoration. The fact that both Whig and Tory statesmen, as well as the elite of London society, cheered the performance of Addison's *Cato* and eagerly purchased the *Tatler* and *Spectator* testifies to the widespread acceptance of the new approach. Even Sir Roger de Coverley, a figure at first intended to provoke ridicule of the fox-hunting squires, soon became a fictional character whose foibles were not to be imitated, but whose sterling qualities were accepted as ideal by the English country gentleman of the eighteenth century. The little group of characters associated with Sir Roger de Coverley in the *Spectator,* the quiet pictures of the clubs and coffeehouses of London, the talk, manners, and amusements presented as good form—all contributed to the new pattern. London even more than Amsterdam exemplified the new bourgeois society with its secular interests and reasonable manners and morals.

In France, where Louis XIV and his magnificent court still dominated society, La Bruyère played the role that Addison, Steele, Swift, and Defoe acted out in England. But La Bruyère had no pattern of solid virtues to point to and extol. From his vantage point as a hanger-on of one of the cadet branches of the Bourbon family, he could see only the existing abuses and evils. When he attempted to fashion a model for the future, he had to fall back upon imagination. Nevertheless, La Bruyère's *Characters* (1685–1694) was one of the most important French works of social criticism, well deserving to be ranked with the great books of the eighteenth-century Enlightenment. His portraits of men and manners often involved savage attacks upon the parasitical nobility and upon the vicious immorality and stupidity of his day. More as an enemy of the system than as an observer, he satirized the society in which favoritism and birth rather than merit and ability opened the doors to position and fortune. Without perceiving it himself, La Bruyère bespoke the ideals of the emerging bourgeois classes when he extolled the virtues of the oppressed peasantry and cried aloud for equality of opportunity. The French bourgeoisie had not as yet developed either a class consciousness or a program for the realization of their powers, and so they failed to provide their potential champion with a blueprint of the emerging society. La Bruyère's critical pen was dipped in ink as acid as Swift's when he described and documented the unstable social structure of Louis XIV's court and kingdom; like Addison, he was preparing the way for a new society of which equality, honesty, and good sense were to be the dominant features.

In the general decay of the feudal and renaissance ideal, the soldier lost his glamour and his claim to social precedence. This may seem strange, considering that society depended upon the soldiers for security and order, but it probably reflected the changing pattern of military organization. The new armies drew their rank and file from the lower classes, their officers from the nobility. Society was not yet ready to welcome and honor the democratic citizen-soldier of the ranks, yet the feudal code of the officer no longer fitted the rationalism of bourgeois-minded philosophers and essayists. The whole code of chivalry, with its emphasis upon honor, dueling, and the military virtues had become unsuited to men who would behave reasonably and would eventually conceive of themselves as links in the chain of human progress. Bayle condemned the vices of the army; Addison's retired soldier in the *Spectator's* company had nothing good to say for his profession; Fénelon called the soldier's honor a superstition. These were hard days for men reared in the old traditions.

It must not, of course, be assumed that the old patterns disappeared because moralists and philosophers no longer approved of them. Nor should it be assumed that the changing ideal resulted from the new mirrors created by the critics. The change from the early seventeenth century, when every man with a sword at his side behaved like a sovereign power, to the eighteenth and nineteenth centuries, when the gentleman was a reasonable, law-abiding, genial member of society was the result of the political, economic, and scientific determinants that molded the structure of society. By 1700 men grasped the fact that this change was taking place; they encouraged it, even though they did not invent it.

The problem of morality fascinated the leading intellectuals. Bayle went to great efforts to show that morality and religion were not necessarily united in a single frame of reference. Pitilessly he listed the evils and evil-doings in Christian society, which neither threats of hell nor promises of heaven seemed able to control. By way of contrast, Spinoza, whom men called an atheist, had preached and lived by a moral code so pure and lofty that Bayle could envisage a republic of atheists with a morality superior to the Christian. William Temple, Saint-Évremond, and many other freethinkers pointed to Cicero as the great moralist. His lofty ideas, his saintly life, and his service to the community contrasted favorably with anything the Christian tradition could produce. Steele combatted such pagan ideals by trying, in his *Christian Hero,* to show "that no principles but those of religion are sufficient to make a great man." His own life, however, threw some discredit on his essay. Locke pointed out that there was no ideal imaginable that had not at some time in some society been revered and at other times and places despised. He concluded that the ideals necessary for the conservation of any society are the only ones honored by such a society; all others are violated at will. This was a likely lead to a new morality. If men, through their understanding, could determine the needs of society, they could also discover the required moral code. The eighteenth-century *philosophes* were to carry this notion to fruition.

One book of the time attempted to reverse the whole pattern of morality. In 1705 Mandeville anonymously published *The Fable of the Bees.* This little pamphlet shocked its readers by the terrible paradox it presented and raised a storm of replies. Mandeville pictured a hive that was powerful, prosperous, and creative, but revealed, upon analysis of its organization, vice, luxury, immorality, and individual wickedness. A reform party abolished personal immorality in the hive, but at the cost of the whole bee community. The virtuous hive ceased to be productive; it lost its power, its creative spirit, and its prosperity. Here was the paradox that eighteenth-century moralists had to solve: it was not enough to mouth traditional, pious verbalisms; the rational moralist also had to prove that his system would not upset the social order.

Along with a new pattern for man and hopes for a new morality came the idea that human destiny included happiness on earth. With the lifting of the clouds at the opening of the era of the Enlightenment, the gloom as well as the superstition of earlier ages began to disappear. Freethinkers boldly declared their allegiance to a hedonistic philosophy and denied that the world had to be a vale of tears. By good humor, by art, by science, and by reasonable living man could discover happiness, which became psychologically so important when the earth rather than heaven, man rather than God, became the axis of human thought. One of the most appealing advocates of this ideal of happiness on earth was Anthony Cooper, Earl of

Shaftesbury. Locke had directed his education, he was rich and talented, his father had been a great political figure; at first sight it would seem that he, like most of the freethinkers, would have found it easy to approve of a world so generous in its gifts. But in addition to talents, wealth, and position, Anthony Cooper had a chronic illness that killed him at the age of forty-two. Nonetheless, his writings and his conversations manifested an unfailing faith. It required only the reasonable, the good-natured, the well-intentioned man to make happiness on earth an actuality. Shaftesbury, like his teacher, was one of the writers from whom the utilitarian philosophers of the next century were to draw inspiration for the teachings that so well fitted the emerging, bourgeois society of Europe.

While Englishmen were asking questions about man's understanding of the world and his role in society, Leibniz and his disciple, Christian Wolff, were probing into the problem of the meaning of human life in a mechanistic universe. Less popular than Locke, perhaps because he was more profound, Leibniz was not satisfied with the static conceptions of the Newtonian universe and the Lockian doctrine of man and society. His correction of Locke, unheeded in his day, was fundamental: there is nothing in the mind that does not come from experience *except* the mind itself. Leibniz must have watched a baby and somehow realized that its behavior hardly justified the analogy to a clean sheet of paper. It was the dynamic nature of the world that fascinated him. Like Heraclitus before and Einstein after him, Leibniz saw the universe in terms of motion. His mathematical studies led him to the infinitesimal calculus, a method of describing motion on a line; similarly his observation of society led him to the conclusion that all events were connected in a chain of causation, and that this chain was the important thing to study. But the tools for understanding process in physics, psychology, and history had not yet been discovered, and so Leibniz was forced to fall back upon his postulates to explain the world.

This left him with a mechanistic universe created by a benevolent God. From these assumptions he developed the optimistic doctrine that Voltaire was to satirize in *Candide*. Since God was all-wise and all-good, He must have created the world only after consideration of all possible alternative worlds. Thus the world which He finally did create must have seemed to Him the best of all. In a world governed by law all events must have sufficient cause. Thus the evils that men experience must be necessary for the realization of the good. To anyone convinced by Bayle's Manichaeanism, this optimism seemed intolerable, but Leibniz and his followers in the eighteenth century were persuaded that God was good, and that there-fore His world was right. It was a doctrine that appealed to the German princesses for whom Leibniz wrote many of his books, but it appealed also to men of the world like Eugene of Savoy. European society was ready to say "yea" to the world after so many centuries of negation.

Leibniz' fame as a philosopher would be less had he stopped on this optimistic note. Actually his own generation knew little and understood less of the more profound thinking of this universal genius. His Spinoza-like philosophy, his work on symbolic logic, and some of his more daring excursions into theology were unpublished in his own day; some of his work, in fact, was not honored until the end of the nineteenth century. Nonetheless, Leibniz and Christian Wolff were the founders of the great school of philosophy that gave the German Enlightenment its unique stamp.

While the philosophers pondered God's wisdom in creating the world and attempted to discover a new psychology to explain man to man, an argument dating back to the early years of the seventeenth century dra-matically challenged the basic tradition of the Graeco-Roman civilization as a golden age. Early in the century several Italian thinkers had boldly asserted that the moderns were in many ways at least the equals of the ancients. The scientific and philosophical studies of the century fortified this idea by shaking men's faith in Aristotle and the Roman cosmologists. When Charles Perrault published his poem, "The Age of Louis the Great" (1687), a host of men were ready to assail the citadel of Graeco-Roman prestige. Perrault's poem was a disarming bit of flattery, intended perhaps as much to secure a pension for its author as to expose a great truth, but it resulted in the reopening of the controversy that had broken out when Tassoni attacked Homer earlier in the century. In the two decades follow-ing the publication of Perrault's poem the conflict between the ancients and the moderns raged in France and England. Swift's *Battle of the Books* is perhaps the only item of the controversy still read today, but most of the important literary and philosophical figures of the period joined in the dispute before it died out.

In raising the issue whether or not the moderns of the age of Louis were as great as the ancients of the age of Augustus, the proponents of the moderns attacked a basic assumption, but their arguments failed to undermine the postulate upon which it rested. Both the proponents and opponents of the moderns regarded history as episodical in character; they had no conception of process and development. Perrault, to be sure, came close to developing a theory of the progress of knowledge when he pointed out that the moderns had inherited the wisdom of the ancients and had also added new knowledge of their own discovery. Thus knowledge could advance with time, and the latecomers need not necessarily be inferior to the men of antiquity. He explained the medieval decline in knowledge as a breach in continuity; wars and disorder had obliged men to neglect study in order to meet the imperious demands of the times. But the fact that Perrault, too, failed to see that knowledge was connected with social development deprived him of a powerful argument and blinded him to the idea of progress which the next generation was to proclaim.

While literary men compared Homer and Virgil to their own contemporaries, the proponents of seventeenth-century science explained triumphantly that the work of the Royal Society and of the French Academy of Sciences had overthrown classical learning and was transforming the world of men. Glanvill's optimism (*Plus ultra, or the Progress and Advancement of Knowledge since the days of Aristotle*, 1668) was infectious; even Dryden turned from politics and religion to pay his respects to man's coming mastery of the universe. Fontenelle, when he turned from literature to become the first great popularizer of science, defended the moderns against the ancients and proclaimed the advent of the era *géométrique*.[45] Cartesianism had in it the germ of the idea of progress; its method and its achievements inevitably opened new vistas to man and new conceptions of his destiny on earth.

[45] J. B. Bury, *The Idea of Progress, an Inquiry into its Origin and Growth*, Introduction by C. A. Beard (New York, 1932), 78–126.

Chapter Ten

OF GOD AND MAN

I. THE SPIRITUAL CRISIS

IN THE field of religion and morality the last decades of the seventeenth and the first of the eighteenth century present the historian with a problem formidable in its proportions and fascinating in its ramifications. Within these years a dichotomy developed between the conceptions of God held by the learned and those of the ignorant which threatened a more serious breach in the traditional structure of European religious thought than that of the sixteenth century. Before 1680 isolated thinkers had rejected the traditional story of the Man-God who died on the cross for the salvation of mankind, but it was not until after 1720 that it became fashionable for considerable numbers of the learned to dismiss the tenets of dogmatic Christianity and attempt to justify human life on secular grounds. The implications of this revolution in thought were far-reaching. The structure of politics based upon divine right weakened, sagged, and ultimately came down in ruins. The problem of morality and ethics, the vision of man's relationship to the eternal, the whole question of the significance of human life became involved in a process of reorientation and re-evaluation made necessary by the change in the conception of God.

The roots of the revolution ran deep. The mechanistic cosmos discovered by natural scientists, the enlarged conception of the varieties of culture, manners, and morals both in space and in historical time as set forth by historians and travelers, and the critical methodology that elevated doubt to a primary postulate—all contributed to the new trend of intellectual development. The growth of trade and commerce and the subsequent development of urban society, the rise of the bureaucratic state with its new conception of order and politics, the secular workaday world with its new types of war, social life, and economic exchange provided new patterns. Theologians, philosophers, and moralists could not ignore the secular and scientific interests that were demanding attention.

While the intellectuals were busily creating a conception of God different from the traditional one, movements among the people also tended to alter religious institutions. The state churches that emerged from the Reformation had lost much of their spiritual appeal by the end of the seventeenth century. Formalized ritual and politically minded clergymen had little to offer to satisfy the need for religious experience. The course of the Reformation inevitably continued; in both Protestant and Catholic lands the established churches were put on the defensive by mystical movements and outright heresies as dangerous to the ecclesiastical *status quo* as Luther's reforms had been.

The segmentation of the religious community served further to emphasize the need for secular goals and ideals. As long as society could be held together by a common belief in salvation and a common body of mythology, the state churches were effective as instruments of social control. But with the emergence of heretical sects and the consequent dissolution of the Christian community, society had to grope for other mythologies, other concepts of good and evil, other mystic doctrines that would kindle the imagination of men and keep them united as a social group. The eighteenth century did not find a completely satisfactory solution for this problem; it remained for the nineteenth to establish the ideal of nationalism as a substitute for religious unity.

As was to be expected when the concepts of dogmatic theology and the organization of the state churches were both under attack, ideas about the meaning and destiny of man also underwent considerable change. The generation of 1700 only laid the foundations for the new temple of humanity which the eighteenth century completed. Too much of the old still had to be swept away and too much of the new to be reconciled for one generation to achieve the transition from the traditional Christian conception of human destiny to the secular version demanded by the evolution of European civilization.[1]

II. L'ESPRIT GÉOMÉTRIQUE AND THE IDEA OF GOD

Cartesian skepticism and the new learning proved to be acids that ate deep into traditional beliefs. Descartes himself had stopped short of any conclusions that involved a break with the church, and many of his

---

[1] One of the most interesting early analyses of the work of this first generation of the Enlightenment may be found in a series of articles by Gustav Lanson in the *Revue de mois* for 1910. The most important of these articles was entitled "La transformation des idées morales et la naissance des morales rationnelles de 1680 à 1715." P. Hazard's *La crise de la conscience européenne 1680–1715*, 3 vols. (Paris, 1934), is the most provocative and systematic treatment of the problem. Ernest Troeltsch, Leslie Stephen, and many others have written significantly on the subject. Cf. Bibliographical Essay.

followers tried desperately to do likewise or, even better, to accommodate the new philosophy to the old tradition. Nonetheless, Caraccioli was probably right when, in the mid-eighteenth century, he designated Descartes as a redoubtable enemy of Christianity.[2]

Many of the attacks on traditional ideas seemed innocent enough, yet they released arrows of skepticism that could not be deflected before they had struck the heart of Christianity. Popular superstitions provided an easy target for the rationalists. The comet that was destined to bear Halley's name, for example, made a tremendous impression on the popular imagination of the 1680's. The ignorant both in the streets and in the pulpits took it as an omen, a sign from God, a warning of coming cataclysm; all sorts of events were blamed on this fiery star. Bayle opened the attack against the stupidity of his contemporaries with an essay on comets. Over the next decades he wrote again and again on the same subject, till he might well have become tired of comets. The comet for him was simply an opening wedge for an analysis of human credulity. His arguments were biting and incisive as he exposed the ridiculousness of superstitions and the viciousness of those who used them as a means of social control. Bayle's learning was great, and even though his style was difficult, his books buried one superstition after another under an avalanche of facts.[3]

The next victims of the skeptics were the oracles of antiquity. Their attack was daring since it impinged upon the reasonability of the writings of the church fathers, St. Jerome, St. Augustine, and St. Justin the Martyr, who had not only accepted the Sibylline oracles but had used them to buttress the Christian tradition. The oracles, the accepted argument ran, were obviously inspired either by God or by the devil; their pronouncements could be interpreted to support many facts of the Christian tradition; they ceased to prophesy after the birth of Christ. However, even a cursory study revealed that the oracles did not suspend operations when Christ was born, and only a little detailed research proved conclusively that they were frauds. A dozen or more books were published on oracles, but Fontenelle's *Histoire des oracles* (1686), like his *Pluralité des mondes,* combined sufficient scholarship with elegance of style to make it the most

[2] L. A. Caraccioli, *Dialogue entre le siècle de Louis XIV et le siècle de Louis XV* (Paris, 1751).

[3] *Pensées diverses sur la comète* (Société des textes françaises modernes, Paris, 1911); H. Robinson, *The Great Comet of 1680, a Study in the History of Rationalism* (Northfield, Minn., 1916). Balthasar Bekker and many others joined Bayle in his crusade against the popular beliefs.

telling attack on the impostors. It was a hard conclusion to reach, but clearly the early Christians who tried to use the oracles to bolster their position were either dupes or charlatans, and neither category seemed suitable for St. Augustine.

Sorcerers, witches, werewolves, and wizards were to suffer the same exposure. The first two-thirds of the seventeenth century saw an astonishing outburst of witch-hunting. All over Europe wretched women and men were hauled before courts of law and condemned to death for their alleged association with the forces of evil. By the end of the century Cartesian doubt and the obvious poverty of the evidence against sorcerers reduced the incidence of witch-burning almost to zero. Many lawyers, judges, and publicists fought against the superstition, but it was Balthasar Bekker who struck the mortal blow. His book *De Betoverte Weereld* (1691) was translated into French, German, and English within four years of its first publication. This massive treatment of the "enchanted world" did much to break the spell. Witches were still to be burned in Europe, but they were to be fewer and the day was not far off when skeptical rationalism would put an end to public professions of faith in the occult.[4]

But where would skepticism stop? The miraculous, whether it occurs in the next county or in the tradition of the church, requires faith. The great miracle of the Christian tradition, namely, the life, death, and resurrection of Christ, was grounded firmly in faith rather than reason. Once men assailed the vulgar superstitions of the ignorant, it was impossible to stop them from questioning the sacred tradition of the Christian Church. Theretofore the Bible had been beyond criticism; now it, too, had to submit to the analyses of Cartesian doubters. Spinoza was one of the first to point out that a knowledge of Hebrew was necessary for any serious biblical study, and he proposed to examine the text just as one would analyze any other document. The methods for testing the authenticity of documents could be applied to the Old Testament as well as to the *Iliad*. Spinoza was an impious Jew to whom his own age would not listen, but when Richard Simon, a Roman Catholic priest whose orthodoxy could hardly be questioned, published *A Critical History of the Old Testament* (1679) the problem could no longer be ignored. Simon began with no intention of upsetting traditional beliefs. He merely wanted to set the text straight in order to confuse the bibliolatrous Protestants who depended upon it. His study, however, revealed that the text had been

---

[4] P. Hazard's discussion of comets, oracles, and the occult is excellent. *Op. cit.*, I, 206–239, III, 72–77.

tampered with, that there were curious transpositions, difficulties in chronology, and problems in vocabulary and meaning. The damage was done. By laying clerical hands on the text revealed by God, and then suggesting that, like other texts, it needed careful editing, Simon had raised questions even more penetrating than those of Bayle when he wrote about comets.

The impiety of writing *A Critical History of the Old Testament* shocked Simon's contemporaries; Catholics and Protestants both condemned his book. The king of France forbade its further publication, and ordered all copies burned; the congregation of the Index condemned it in 1683. Nonetheless, a new edition appeared in Amsterdam in 1685 and the worst was yet to come. In rapid succession Simon published *A Critical History of the Text of the New Testament* (1689), *A Critical History of the Versions of the New Testament* (1690), and *A Critical History of the Commentaries on the New Testament* (1693). He excused his impiety by pointing out that he was re-establishing the word of God which centuries of ignorance had corrupted. His argument reduced itself to the proposition that neither theology nor tradition had the key to God's word and that grammar was all that was needed! "Nothing," wrote Arnauld to Bossuet, "could be more favorable to the Socinians." Simon's last volume, *The New Testament of Our Saviour Jesus-Christ, based on the Old Latin Edition with Notes*, appeared in 1702. He explained that he had no other aim than to establish the literal meaning of the text; without this "one often falls into some jargon to which one gives the name spirituality." This volume, like his other ones, was condemned by church and state.

Simon, excluded from the Oratory because of his books, continued to regard himself as a loyal son of the church even though he stubbornly continued his chosen labors. He died peacefully in 1712, after receiving the sacraments, and was buried in holy ground. His words, however, did more than shock theologians by the advice to forsake all studies but grammar. Those already prone to disbelief accepted his argument that the texts of the Holy Bible were corrupted by mistranslations, interpositions, transpositions, omissions, and perhaps deliberate attempts to mislead. They were not interested in his belief that he was only purifying God's words of errors that had crept into the text during centuries of ignorance. These "Critical Histories" thus became batteries trained on the traditional faith. "How is it," asked Baron de Lahontan, "that you wish me to believe in the truth of this Bible written so many centuries ago, translated into several languages by ignorant men who did not understand its true meaning, or by liars who have changed, enlarged, or diminished the words that are found there today . . . ?" Simon's labors, largely confined to grammatical criticism, became the starting point for the long series of analyses of the Holy Writ that were to follow during the next two centuries.[5]

Simon challenged the Bible with a knowledge of Hebrew, Greek, and Latin; Pierre Bayle challenged it with a rational intelligence. In his Encyclopedia he ruthlessly asked questions of the Christian tradition, and answered them by pointing to the Christian Book. One after another of the heroes of Jewish history was subjected to a moral analysis that found them wanting, or to a critical examination that threw doubt upon their credibility.[6] If Simon were the first to apply textual criticism to the Bible, Bayle was the first to apply internal criticism. His studies of the inconsistencies, the contradictions, and the moral improbity of the Old Testament narrative provided the next generation of deists with all the arguments they needed to dismiss the Bible from their thinking. Bayle suffered considerable inconvenience even in tolerant Holland because of his views, but he was not to be deterred. No historian of ideas can pass Bayle by without a profound respect for his scholarship, his originality, and his courage.[7]

While dogmatic theology had to meet Bayle's and Simon's pointed remarks about the sacred text of the Bible, it was assaulted from another side by new theological propositions inspired by Descartes rather than by St. Augustine and St. Thomas. Spinoza's discovery of God in nature should have been a warning of the heretical possibilities in Cartesianism, but Spinoza was a Jew; his "errors" did not deter Malebranche and Fénelon, both Catholic priests, from applying the new learning to theology. Malebranche discovered God in the order of the universe; Fénelon, who at first set out to combat this view, ended by accepting it and displaying a scorn for Augustine greater than Simon had dared express. The God they "discovered" was a perfectly reasonable supreme being who had created the world and its inhabitants and had given to the whole a supreme law. The only difficulty was in making that God fit into the traditional framework of Christianity. Like their English contemporaries, Malebranche and Fénelon overlooked the fact that the religious concepts

---

[5] Albert Monod, *De Pascal à Chateaubriand* (Paris, 1916), Ch. III; Henri Tréville, "Richard Simon et les Protestants," *Revue d'histoire moderne* (1931); P. Hazard, *op. cit.*, I, 240–264, III, 78–79.

[6] Cf. "David," "Saul," "Moses," etc. in *Le Dictionnaire*.

[7] Georges Ascoli, "La critique des croyances: Bayle," *Histoire illustrée de la littérature française* (Paris, 1924), II.

they were creating might not be Christian. In their pages God became a mystic agent in the universe, or maybe the universe itself; His will was supposedly expressed in rational, necessary laws which, in effect, subordinated Him to His own wisdom and love. It was an easy matter for the next generation to strip off the Christian trimmings and reveal a theology suited to the deistic thinking of the eighteenth century.[8]

In England theologians, scholars, and philosophers rallied around the traditional beliefs and attempted to defend them with a powerful array of intellectual weapons. Hobbes, Spinoza, and a corporal's guard of deistic thinkers of the latter seventeenth century alerted the proponents of the Christian faith to the dangers it faced unless the new science could be turned to its account. Robert Boyle, the great chemist, had left funds for lectures in defense of Christianity, and at the turn of the century the Boyle lecturers applied both the Newtonian philosophy and modern criticism to the solution of their problem.[9] Both the pillars of the orthodox Anglican creed and leaders of the dissenters joined hands to make Christianity reasonable in a day when reasonability was becoming the test of faith. As one reads Leslie Stephen's list of the giants who appeared in the Christian vanguard, it seems incomprehensible that their victory should not have been complete,[10] but the English philosophers and theologians, like their French contemporaries, pushed aside dogmatic theology and, having rested their case upon a world of law and reasonableness, then attempted to identify their God with Jehovah. Their arguments, only slightly turned, became the arguments of the eighteenth-century deists.

It was all very well to conceive of God as a first cause, a great mathematician-architect who created the world and gave it a basic constitution. The discovery of God's laws and reverence for this great eternal force might be a satisfactory religious experience for the intellect, but it lacked emotional force and mystery. Furthermore, since God had created the whole world, and since He was assumed to be a reasonable, benevolent being, it was impossible to relegate the millions of men born before Christ and the millions born into cultures other than the European to perdition

[8] It is extremely difficult to compress theological arguments and differences in a short discussion. H. G. Gouhier's two books, *La philosophie de Malebranche et son expérience religieuse* (Paris, 1926), and *Malebranche: (Les moralistes chrétiens; textes et commentaires)* (Paris, 1929), and E. Bréhier's *Histoire de la philosophie* (Paris, 1926–1932), II, part I, 200–227, provide good introductions to the problem.

[9] Anthony Collins remarked that no one doubted the existence of God until the Boyle lectures tried to prove it.

[10] Sir L. Stephen, *History of English Thought in the Eighteenth Century*, I, 2nd ed. (New York and London, 1881), 86–87.

merely to satisfy a theology narrow and exclusive in its understanding. Here was a problem: if one deprived Christianity of its exclusive right to point the road to salvation, did the resultant belief remain Christian? Some of the noblest thinking of the seventeenth century came from the pens of England's rational theologians, but it required little more than rejection of the idea of revelation to give their thinking a turn that was anti-Christian. Like the naturalist John Ray, whose popular *Wisdom of God* aimed to present the animal and plant kingdoms as living evidence of God's love and necessity, the rational theologians created a religious belief that was deistic and Spinozan.[11]

An interesting example of the sort of thinking that unwittingly undermined the traditional belief may be found in a little book written by John Locke, *The Reasonableness of Christianity*. The text is both naïve and tedious. Locke had reread the New Testament and was struck by the fact that Christ had not imposed a creed upon his disciples; the Athanasian Creed, the Thirty-Nine Articles, even the Nicene Creed were absent. All Christ had asked was acknowledgment that he was the Messiah and that there was but one true God. Here Locke discovered a religion far removed from the theological wranglings of the schoolmen, from the imposing confessions of the competing churches. All that was called for was belief in Christ and in His love. Locke thought that by emphasizing this point he was defending his church's beliefs. He was shocked to find that his first disciple was Toland, who immediately expounded his ideas in a book entitled *Christianity not Mysterious*. If Christianity were stripped of mystery, what would be left to make it Christian? Locke repudiated his disciple, but he could not disown in advance the numerous eighteenth-century *philosophes* who read his books and found them a firm basis for their ideas. Happily, Locke died in the conviction that he had defended the Christian religion.

Few writers of Locke's generation, however, broke aggressively with Christianity. Spinoza, of course, had not been Christian, and Hobbes, while showing his contempt for the Christian tradition, had been careful not to separate himself from it. Most of the deists and atheists, if such there were in the seventeenth century, had been reluctant to publish their view, and their existence can only be inferred from the fact that Christian apologists felt impelled to combat their ideas. However, the generation of 1700 did produce deistic books suggesting that the Christian tradition be discarded in favor of a new religion. John Toland, a journalist, Anthony

[11] John Tulloch, *Rational Theology and Christian Philosophy in England in the Seventeenth Century* (Edinburgh, 1872), Vol. 2.

Collins, a country gentleman, and Shaftesbury, a lord, each in turn published works attacking Christianity. In every case their scholarship was inferior to that of the men who answered them, but the boldness of their arguments gave them notoriety beyond the deserts of their intellects and literary skills. One man remarked shortly after the publication of one of Toland's little books that he had to quit church because he heard from the pulpit more about Toland than about God. Toland had to leave England, but Collins, a "respectable" country squire, seems not to have suffered inconvenience. Shaftesbury's attack was oblique rather than direct; he lived most of his life in Italy from choice rather than necessity.

These early deists made but a limited impression upon their age. Their conception of God was naïvely Spinozan, and their idea of a new religion was hardly more than a refurbishing of Christian thinking. While they rejected as mythology the tradition of the Bible and the church fathers, they established the idea of a God of nature who rewarded and punished much like the God of the Christians. Dryden's satirical couplets bespeak their intellectual problem:

> The deist thinks he stands on firmer ground
> Cries Eurêka, the mighty secret's found.
> God is that spring of good supreme and best
> We made to serve, and in that service blest.
> Our Reason prompt us a future state
> The last appeal from fortune and from fate,
> Where God's all-righteous ways will be declared,
> The bad met punishment, the good reward,
> Thus man by his own strength to Heaven would soar,
> And would not be obliged to God for more.

Swift with characteristic irony answered the deists with *An argument to prove that the abolishing of Christianity in England may, as things now stand, be attended with some inconveniences, and perhaps not produce those many good effects proposed thereby* (1708).

The flowering of deism in the eighteenth century owed more to the rationalistic theologians than to the early deists whom the theologians tried to refute. Both the scholarship and the style of the theologians were superior, and their arguments were based on Cartesian philosophy, buttressed by the new science. One had only to reject the idea of revelation, which in a sense was an appendage rather than an integral part of their theology, to derive from them a complete case for a deity of nature.[12]

It goes without saying that these new theological patterns influenced relatively few people. The majority of the population still worshiped in the churches duly established by law and tradition, or newly created by reformers anxious to reform the Reformation. In the churches dogmatic theology of more or less traditional types was still the accepted thing. Toward the end of his life Bishop Bossuet may have felt himself isolated in the rarefied intellectual atmosphere of his time, but had he turned to the masses, he would have found that his strict traditional tenets were still honored and fully accepted. Not only religious belief, but also all manner of superstitious conceptions, had been but slightly touched by the geometric spirit with its concomitant skepticism. Only among the educated elite, who had the wealth, the education, and the leisure necessary for a cultured existence, had the new patterns of thought taken hold at the opening of the eighteenth century.

III. THE STATE CHURCH AND THE CONTINUING REFORMATION

In the century following Luther's revolt from Rome state churches had arisen in both Catholic and Protestant lands as the typical religious institutions of the era. Religious unity was still regarded as the essential basis for political and social solidarity, and therefore both church and university (theology) had been closely integrated with government. Here and there, as a matter of necessity, religious dissenters were tolerated, but Europe as a whole did not accept Bodin's teaching that religious unity was not necessarily the supreme social good. The Reformation had broken Rome's monopoly on religion only to replace it with a series of smaller state monopolies. The individual was not free to worship God as he saw fit. Even in countries where a measure of toleration was granted, there was a strong tendency to revoke such privileges. Thus in Bohemia (1621), in England (1660), in Hungary (1678), in France (1685), dissent had once more become a crime, and dissenters from the state churches were subject to severe penalties.[13]

But the march of events gradually shook the hold of the state churches upon the people. In the first place high positions in the churches were

---

[12] No student should miss Carl Becker's somewhat exaggerated but charmingly provocative *The Heavenly City of the Eighteenth Century Philosophers* (New Haven, 1932).

[13] E. Troeltsch, "Das Wesen des modernen Geisten," and "Leibniz und die Anfänge des Pietismus," *Gesammelte Schriften*, IV, 298–388, 488–531.

commonly awarded for political rather than spiritual reasons, and frequently the incumbents scarcely exemplified the teaching of their confessions. Furthermore, the intimate association between throne and altar tended to make the clergy into timeserving conservatives, and thereby the revolutionary zeal of the Reformation and Counter Reformation degenerated into formalized ritual. Supported by princes, patronized by courts, and dominated by the rich and powerful of the land, the churches adopted the formalized baroque culture of the period. Any expression of religious enthusiasm was frowned upon; any direct appeal to the human heart was regarded with suspicion. Both Catholic and Protestant churches gained in dignity, but lost their hold upon the popular imagination. Worldly clergymen and formalized religion positively invited a renewal of the Reformation designed to free the individual from the monopoly of the state church.[14]

A *sine qua non* for any successful revolt against the state churches was neutrality on the part of government. As long as the prince believed in the necessity for religious unity and protected the religious monopoly by law and force, no reformation that could not be accomplished within the bounds of the state church could possibly succeed. In England after 1688, in the United Netherlands of the later seventeenth century, and in Petrine Russia, where toleration was either open or tacit, sectarianism gradually liberated men from the state churches. But in Catholic Latin Europe and in Lutheran or Calvinistic Teutonic Europe reforms aimed at spiritualizing the state churches were feasible only within the framework of established religious institutions.

The Catholic Church was best fitted by organization and experience to deal with religious innovations. In Catholic lands concordats had accorded the princes a share in the government of the church, but the Pope's right to define heresy was unimpaired and the monarchical constitution of the church assured uniformity in teaching. The Roman church, however, was not immune from the currents of religious reform that continued to flow. Quietism and Jansenism were both typical of reform movements which, at bottom, were hostile to the state church. They called for delicate treatment. The former came so close to the mysticism of many of the saints that it was difficult to specify the heresy. The latter, strongly supported by

---

[14] The life of the state church in Catholic countries was not always serene. Louis XIV, for example, fought a *Kulturkampf* with Rome for almost two decades after the Gallican Articles of 1682. The advantages of maintaining the connection with Rome were so great, however, that the French king finally accepted the anomaly of divided authority within the French church rather than break with Rome and create a Gallican Catholic Church.

some of the most brilliant theological writers of the century, was hard to pin down because the Jansenists would never admit their heretical doctrines when they were condemned by the church.

Quietism appeared as a religious problem in both Rome and Paris and, had it gone unchecked, might well have pervaded the entire Catholic community. In the eyes of the world its two principal exponents, Molinos, a Spanish priest living in Rome, and Madame Guyon, an extremely pious lady of the Versailles court, were God-fearing, saintly people whose lives and teachings might well have led to canonization. Innocent XI himself protected Molinos until the case against him became crystal clear; Fénelon gallantly defended Madame Guyon until he himself was rebuked by the church. Nonetheless Quietism was a direct threat to the established church. The core of the Quietist heresy was the belief that God spoke directly to the human heart, and that man must not reject His promptings. By placing emphasis upon the omnipotence of God and the absolute weakness of man, it was easy to teach the absorption of man's will in a mystic union with God. The Roman Catholic Church quite naturally looked suspiciously upon any doctrine that dispensed with the services of the church as intermediary between God and man, especially when at the same time it discounted personal responsibility and free will. The folly and the danger of such arguments became painfully clear when the Roman Inquisition discovered how much sexual and other immorality could be excused by attributing the impulse to God. Molinos spent his last years in prison; Madame Guyon was silenced and banished from court. The church with its bishops, the Index, the Inquisition, and the good offices of the French court was able to destroy Quietism before its devotees had made many converts.[15]

Jansenism presented Rome with a more stubborn problem, one deeply rooted in ancient theological and political conceptions. In St. Augustine, whose orthodoxy was not open to question, the Jansenists had found a doctrine of predestination that closed the gates of heaven to all save God's elect. The sorry spectacle of widespread personal immorality confirmed the Jansenists in their belief that only an elected few would or should achieve salvation. The Jesuits, who would open the gates wide to admit all sinners desiring salvation, were the natural enemies of the self-righteous proponents of austerity, and for over a half century the Jesuit-Jansenist conflict was averted only by a smoldering truce. The Jansenists

[15] L. Pastor, *The History of the Popes* (St. Louis, 1910), XXXII, 442–9, 609–620; M. Masson, *Fénelon et Madame Guyon* (Paris, 1907).

also incurred the wrath of the French government because of their hostility to statism. Richelieu had put one of their early leaders in prison and Louis XIV hated them with a violence that eventually culminated in the desecration of the graves of their "saints." But to condemn Jansenism was difficult, for the Jansenists cleverly avoided denunciation by insisting that any propositions condemned by the Pope were no part of their doctrine. For fifty years Jansenism hovered between heresy and orthodoxy, at times protected by the Pope, at times on the verge of a sweeping condemnation. At the end of the seventeenth century the Jesuits, joined in uneasy alliance by Bossuet, Fénelon, and a number of others, forced their opponents into the open and obliged them to reveal their heretical ideas about divine grace.

The full story of the Jansenist controversy cannot be told here. The Gallican church, the instability of the new archbishop of Paris, a famous book of devotions by Quesnel, an involved argument before both the Roman court and the theological faculties of the leading French universities, and a series of religio-political intrigues all contributed to produce a complex problem of faith and politics. Rome tried to solve the problem by a half measure, *Vinean Domini* (1705), but in 1713 it finally issued the bull *Unigenitus,* which condemned one hundred and one propositions in Quesnel's *Réflexions morales* and definitely placed Jansenism outside the pale of the Catholic community. Yet even this drastic action did not actually solve the Jansenist problem; for another half century it continued to disturb the peace of the French church.

Although the Jesuits were victorious over their Jansenist enemies, they too came under a cloud at the end of the seventeenth century because of their liberal moral interpretation of sin and their hopes for the conversion of China. The Society of Jesus was composed of fishermen for souls who understood the weakness of man and counted on the mercy of God. They wished to open wide the gates of heaven for all to enter. In moral philosophy this attitude led to the doctrine of probabilism, while in church politics it produced an attempt to write the entire Confucian community of China into the Catholic Church. Probabilism was almost as fraught with moral laxity as Quietism had been. It assumed that if any reputable moral teacher approved an act, a man could follow his teaching even though all the other moral philosophers of the church might have condemned it. With such a generous definition of sin it was indeed difficult to sin! The Jesuits would always find an explanation to satisfy the needs of the sinner and condone his action. The Jansenists had held up this Jesuit probabilism to ridicule and opprobrium. Bossuet, who had allied himself with the Jesuits against the Jansenists, nevertheless induced the assembly of the French clergy to condemn their doctrine. Pope Innocent XI rebuked the order by the appointment of Father Tirso Gonzalez, the only Jesuit who had written against probabilism, as its commander. Gonzalez, however, was unable to extirpate probabilism; the Jesuit order was too strong for him to influence even from the highest post in its ranks. It remained for Alphonsus Liguori to give the doctrine a death blow in the mid-eighteenth century.[16]

In the "Chinese question" the Jesuits were playing for high stakes. They had been the first missionaries in China, and they hoped to find a "Chinese Constantine" in the Emperor Kanghi. The transition from the traditional religion of the Chinese intellectuals to the Roman Catholic Church seemed to the Jesuit missionaries to present no great difficulty. The Chinese believed in one God, their morality was as pure as or purer than that of Europe, and their mythology did not disturb the sensibilities of the fathers. The arrival of missionaries from rival orders and the publication of their own books about China upset their plans. It appeared monstrous to men like Bossuet to suggest that Chinese theism was almost identical with Christianity. The preaching monks who went out to China to teach the doctrine of Christianity to the masses added their objections to the Jesuits' Chinese projects. The monks hated the aristocratic Jesuits, who lived magnificently at the emperor's court rather than in a humble and Christlike way among the people. The result was that the whole project for a Chinese conversion had to be abandoned.

The Roman Church was able to discipline its ranks and stifle heretical doctrines because both church and state co-operated in furthering uniformity. In the Calvinist community there was no comparable authority. The Calvinist churches had no recognized head, and the United Netherlands, the most important Calvinist state, had discovered secular bases for political solidarity and could therefore afford to remain tolerantly neutral in religious controversy. In England the Revolution of 1688 had brought toleration to dissenters. The English government, while not really neutral in religious matters, at least allowed differences within the Protestant community. Like the Netherlands, England was finding other bases for political and social unity. Thus the Anglican and Calvinist churches were left to deal with heretical doctrines as best they could without government intervention.

[16] Ludwig Pastor, *op. cit.*, XXXII, 435–41, 621–33.

The Calvinists were more subject to religious dissension than the Catholics. Even while they were suffering the persecutions of Louis XIV, the French Huguenots continued to wrangle among themselves over questions of theology. Calvin's doctrine of election and predestination encountered much objection in an age that was becoming both liberal and skeptical. The bursting of the bounds of the old cosmos, the realization of the size of the earth and the diversity of its cultures, and the rise of the new science made Calvin sound parochial and smug to many who wished to retain the outer form of the church. In Holland the Huguenot refugees found themselves at the center of a theological debate openly staged and with almost complete freedom of expression. Orthodox Calvinists were confronted by liberals who drew their ideas from Erasmus, from Fausto Sozzini, from Bayle, and from many other thinkers whose views fitted ill with the rigid, self-righteous, self-assured notions that had made the Calvinist communities strong. The sixteenth-century Reformation had given the Bible to men; it had broken with the universal authority of the old church; the seventeenth century had initiated a reform to free men from the tyranny of the Reformation churches.

One of the most interesting groups demanding a hearing were the Socinians. Their influence was effective not so much in the reform of institutions as in the liberalization of religious thinking during the next century. Their founder, Sozzini, was born in Poland in the sixteenth century. Like the Quietists, he wished to dispense with the church as a barrier between God and man by giving the individual complete freedom to interpret the word and the will of God. This was a serious threat to the authority of the preachers and elders who, sure of their knowledge of God's will, had erected thousands of petty papal stools all over the Calvinist countries. Socinianism could not easily be institutionalized, but it did yeoman's service in the liberalization of religious thought.[17]

In England the Revolution of 1688, by freeing dissenters from many of their legal disabilities, opened wide the floodgates of religious enthusiasm. The Church of England had become cold and formal. The close association between the university-trained parsons and the fox-hunting squires tended to make it almost the exclusive preserve of the wealthy Tories, while its dignified tone and its rejection of religious emotion as in bad taste further alienated it from much of the population. Furthermore, its almost complete disregard for the spiritual and intellectual welfare of the lower classes cut it off from many city dwellers and weakened its

[17] C. Vanslee, *De Geschiedenis van het Socianisme in Nederland* (Haarlem, 1914).

position among the rural workers. The sons of the Roundheads, the moneyed classes of the cities, and many intellectuals were hostile to the church on religious or political grounds; they provided both the brains and the funds to make the dissenting conventicles effective in the lives of the people. Dissent took many forms. Most types had emotional overtones that presaged John Wesley's Methodism in the next generation. Anabaptists, Quakers, Ranters, and many such groups had mushroomed into existence in the seventeenth century. When toleration gave them legal status they quickly proceeded to build churches and schools and to expand their congregations. Their emotional fervor seemed almost strong enough to overwhelm the old church in the urban areas. In Queen Anne's reign this danger became so apparent that the established church took measures to create new urban parishes and even attempted to close the dissenting schools.

English dissenters had one thing in common: they all urged separation of church and state. Within this frame, however, there were several divergent trends. The Levellers, Fifth Monarchy men, and Diggers, to mention only a few, sought to reorganize civil life for the sake of a free state and a free church. In their hands the New Testament became an inspiration for active resistance as well as for mystic experience. Other groups, Brownists, Familists, Quakers, and the like, were less visionary, less willing to adopt extreme measures. They advocated nonresistance as a Christian virtue, self-government within the church, a lay ministry rather than a theologically trained priesthood, and a democratic, voluntary membership. The Baptists and Congregationalists in England and America derived from this school of thought, which was actually little more than a home-rule Presbyterianism reinforced with a revivalist type of service. When the Methodists appeared in the next generation they made conquests from among these earlier sectarians as well as from the ranks of the established church.

In Lutheran countries the association between church and princely authority and the splintering of sovereignty among hundreds of petty states destroyed what little revolutionary spirit had been left in Luther's church after the first era of rebellion. The transfer of authority from Rome to the prince made the Lutheran clergy into a band of complacent conservatives and seriously weakened the spiritual force of the church. The Thirty Years' War, with its destruction of life and culture, accentuated the process until Germany too became ripe for further reform. Pietism, the dominant reform movement, was confined largely to the bourgeoisie and part of the nobility; in the countryside the dull routine of poverty and ignorance seems to have left no scope for religious emotion.

Pietism was mystical, "practical" Christianity. Prayer, meditation, Bible reading, and Christian ethics formed the core of its teaching. It was both anti-intellectual and puritanical in origin, and encouraged its devotees to experience Christian love of God as an act of intuition. The movement seemed to have in it an element of Spinoza's acceptance of the universal being, but it was also deeply grounded in the traditional Christianity of the Bible. Philipp Jakob Spener, a Lutheran pastor at Frankfurt, was its most articulate leader. His career in Dresden, Berlin, and finally in the newly established University of Halle is evidence of the fact that in Germany, as in other parts of Europe, there were many who sought in religion a spiritual satisfaction no longer supplied by the formalized state church. Pietism was to have a deep influence both in Germany and abroad in the eighteenth century. Its converts gave a new tone to German society; even though pietistic morality was puritanical and narrow, the movement flowered in literature as well as in theological discussion. Its most important non-German influence was upon John Wesley and the rise of English Methodism.

Not all who were anxious to continue the process of reformation were willing to remain within the traditional framework of Christianity. Unitarians, for instance, refused to accept the trinitarian conception of God.[18] Deists and freethinkers went even further and rejected the whole structure of Christianity in favor of a natural religion with postulates drawn from the Graeco-Roman philosophers and from natural science. At the opening of the eighteenth century, under the leadership of John Toland, a group of English deists held regular meetings with prayers and ritual appropriate to a society of freethinkers. Only a few years later (1717) the Masonic order was founded in London with similar religious implication. Perhaps only time was needed to transform deists into atheists; in any case contemporaries often confused the two. Whether or not there were considerable numbers of genuine atheists is difficult to say. Probably not, for seventeenth-century postulates were unsuited to atheism. But there were certainly a few and those few were the target for much hostile comment.

While the state churches of western Europe were forced on the defensive by sectarian and heretical movements, the Russian Orthodox Church was suffering from a schism that resulted from the reforms introduced in

---

[18] Sir Isaac Newton was preoccupied with Unitarian theology.

the mid-seventeenth century. The Russian texts of the Holy Books had been badly translated, but when the Patriarch Nikon joined hands with reformers who knew Greek as well as Russian to purify the texts, a substantial part of the clergy and people clung tenaciously to the old forms. These "Old Believers" became the progenitors of a series of sectarian movements. Freed from control of the patriarch, they developed their own church organization. One of their problems was to secure a proper clergy; since the bishops stayed with the reformers, no new priests adhering to the old tradition could be regularly ordained. The first split in the dissenting faction came between the priestless and the priestists. The former dispensed with a regular clergy, the latter lured away regularly ordained priests from the state church. By 1700 numerous other variations were beginning to appear. A millenarian idea permeated most of them, but some were devoted to a mystical spiritual brotherhood unlike anything to be found outside Russia.

The coming of the Petrine reforms further agitated the religious scene. Peter did not behave like an anointed ruler. His drunken debauches were more famous than his piety, and he obviously had no respect for the religious taboos of Russian society. The belief that the world would soon come to an end had brought men in 1669 to lie in coffins and spend nights in hollow trees, but the world had not come to an end. There had clearly been some error in the calculations. By 1702 Peter's butchery of the *streltsy*, his new calendar that "stole eight years from the Lord," his reforms of dress and manners, and his outrageous behavior in general had convinced the "old ritualists" that he was actually the anti-Christ. By omitting the M from "Emperor," the new title behind which he was hiding, the remaining letters were found to correspond in Slavonic figures with numerals that would total 666. This meant the apocalyptic beast. Again, as in 1669, people awaited the end of the world; but again there was some mistake, for there was no cataclysm in 1702.

Government persecution of the dissenting groups was surprisingly mild. Perhaps the fact that the "priestless" largely migrated to northeast Russia, where neither feudal landlords nor established tradition interfered with their beliefs, and where, in the course of time, many of them found freedom and wealth, accounts for their relative immunity from official pressure. The suppression of the patriarchate in the early years of the eighteenth century also helped to spare them persecution. After Peter became involved in his wars he was too preoccupied with immediate problems of politics to inquire too closely into religious developments on the sparsely populated frontier.

The sectarian movements took various forms. Women and maidens shared the "priesthood" with men, were called "Prophets," "Apostles," "Christs," "Mothers of God," and taught a mysticism congenial only to a people with a pagan folklore like Russia's.[19] Some of the sects enjoined celibacy, forbade wine, beer, and liquor, and prescribed long midnight vigils of prayer. "The white shirts and burning candles of the vigilants," writes Miliukov, "recalls the schismatic expectations of the end of the world, while the older songs . . . approach the folklore and serve as a guide to the popular views on the Day of Judgment, Paradise, etc. The holding of two fingers in making the sign of the cross also reminds one of the schismatic origin of the sect."[20] The Dukhobors, who some years later won fame in the New World, grew out of these earlier sects.

Meanwhile, the state church of Russia was brought under the complete control of the government. From the proud position occupied under the patriarch in the first half of the seventeenth century, the church sank to the status of a mere organ of the state. Its tendency to emphasize ritual and formal, rather than spiritual, ideals became ever more marked. Its clergy remained, for the most part, essentially ignorant. Priests were elected, but neither theological knowledge nor spiritual ardor seems to have played a part in the selection. The parishioners chose men who would perform the rituals at the lowest possible salary, with the result that in many villages the priesthood became hereditary. One dynasty, Miliukov tells us, ruled over the same parish for two hundred years.[21] Those who wished either a spiritual or an emotional Christianity had no choice but to join the schism.

Thus by the end of the seventeenth century the religious structure of Europe had produced something like the confusion of tongues after the destruction of the tower of Babel. From one end of Europe to the other men were deriving new religious forms from the old books; the unity of Christendom was a thing of the past. Sensitive souls whose background and training were deeply rooted in the Christian ideal deplored this disorder. There seemed to be no answer to the thesis of Bishop Bossuet's famous book on the *Variations of the Protestant Churches,* namely that

[19] For a penetrating analysis of this problem see G. P. Fedotov, *The Russian Religious Mind* (Cambridge, Mass., 1946), Chs. I and II.

[20] P. Miliukov, *Outlines of Russian Culture,* I, *Religion and the Church* (Philadelphia, 1942), 91.

[21] *Ibid.,* 123.

the breakdown of authority would eventually end in religious skepticism and atheism. But the problem of reuniting Christendom was appallingly difficult. The papacy had been working for centuries without appreciable success to bring the Orthodox churches of the east into the Roman fold. Yet even the victories of Christian arms on the Danube and in the Morea failed to convince the Greeks that their destiny lay with Rome. The splintering of the western church by the Reformation, and the violent hostilities created by a century and a half of religious warfare and intrigue made the problem of reuniting the western church equally insuperable. The division was rooted in the hearts of men as well as in theological faculties and in governments.

Nonetheless, from the end of the Thirty Years' War onward, one proposal after another was broached for the reunion of western Christianity. The effort at the end of the seventeenth century was to be no more successful than earlier ones, but the fact that both Leibniz and Bossuet were involved in the negotiations make the attempt significant in the religious history of Europe. If anyone could have achieved the unity of the churches, Leibniz should have been the man. Known and respected throughout Catholic and Protestant Europe, this great philosopher, who already had invented the calculus, had proposed a universal language for symbolic reasoning, had championed the new science, and had written significantly in practically every field, was an ideal champion for a universal church. His lofty idealism as well as his ability as a diplomat fitted him for the task. Leibniz approached Bishop Bossuet, the subtle, learned, dogmatic defender of authority and true representative of the religion he so eloquently preached, in the hope that a compromise could be found. Bossuet's conviction that disunity and disbelief were synonymous, and his dislike of the skepticism of the age, made Leibniz see in him the man who would most surely welcome a chance to heal the fissures in the Christian community. Bishop Bossuet, however, was temperamentally unsuited to support any move that might jeopardize the one authority that he believed was alone capable of checking the lapse into atheism.

The discussions between the two men extended over almost the entire last decade of the century. Bossuet's attitude, however, foredoomed them to failure. It almost seems that the good bishop was fishing for Leibniz' soul rather than seeking a compromise. Leibniz, willing to accept much of the Catholic position, attempted to put aside the decisions of the Council of Trent and to have a new council called to solve the problems of the Reformation. Since the Gallicans spoke of conciliar superiority, since France had not published the Tridentine decrees, and since there was the historical precedent of the Council of Basel in connection with the Bohemian heresy, he hoped for success. But in the end Bishop Bossuet stood intransigently by the infallibility of the church. He feared that any breach in the wall of authority would open the way for a flood of new heresy. With more realism than Leibniz, he saw that the historical process could not be reversed.[22]

For all his insight Leibniz failed to understand the full implications of the Reformation. To a friend he wrote: "If five or six men wished it, Louis XIV, the Pope, the Emperor, a couple of Protestant princes, it could be done. . . ."[23] He still thought of religion as an affair of princes and prelates, at the very time when the princely era of the Reformation was drawing to a close. Leibniz did not see that, for all their childishness and apparent simplicity, the sectarian movements that were further segmenting Christianity and demanding freedom from the state churches, were a significant part of the process that was liberating western man. The heroic age of the Reformation had broken the power of Rome; the sectarian age of the Reformation now challenged the power of the state church. In so doing the religious extremists were acting to free man's conscience. Who can say that their work was not as significant as that of the brilliant minds of the Cartesian revolution? Perhaps they, as much as the Newtons and Fontenelles, expressed the crisis in the conscience of Europe that set men free from ancient theological controls.

III. THE SECULARIZATION OF POLITICAL THOUGHT

The seventeenth century was an age of princes patterned on Machiavelli's prototype and anointed with the Christian oil of divine right. From one extreme of Europe to another, philosophers, statesmen, and prelates, at times naïvely, at times with great show of scholarship, joined in extolling the wisdom of God as expressed in the divine structure of the *status quo*. In this great chorus celebrating the princely prerogatives, the voice of Bishop Bossuet was the clearest and most eloquent. He summed up the case for kingship as a divine office, borrowing the ideas of his predecessors to support his argument. Bodin, Hobbes, and Grotius as well as James I, the Oxford divines and the other great traditional

[22] F. X. Kuf, *Der Friedensplan des Leibniz zur Vereinigung der getrennten Kirchen* (Paderborn, 1913); P. Hazard, *op. cit.*, I, 289–317; G. J. Jordan, *The Reunion of the Churches, A Study of G. W. Leibniz and His Great Attempt* (London, 1927).

[23] H. J. T. Hettner, *Geschichte der deutschen Literatur im achtzehnten Jahrhundert* (Leipzig, 1929), 46.

defenders of the divine origin of royal power, were fitted into his thesis at the very moment when the historical development was beginning to make the divine-right king an anachronism.

For the eloquent bishop the case was relatively simple. Man must obey God, the king was God's representative on earth, hence man must obey the king. One God, one king, one law, that was his credo. But Bossuet was so completely impregnated with Aristotelian logic, derived directly or indirectly through St. Thomas, that he felt constrained to erect a powerful, reasonable argument to establish his point. The contemporary belief in the miraculous nature of the king, the attempts to heal the sick by the king's touch, the quasi-idolatrous reverence given his person, all reveal the emotional force behind the belief in divine right.[24] Bossuet as priest and subject shared the popular belief in the royal powers, but in his argument he stressed the idea that history was the work of God, and that therefore every established authority, no matter what form it might take, was God's handiwork, against which rebellion would be sacrilegious. Bossuet was a champion of authority, holding that without authority society would distintegrate into anarchy, and religion into disbelief. He had little faith in man's natural goodness; man was a creature who had to be saved from himself, and God had provided the power and authority to accomplish this end. It is not surprising that Bossuet discovered that the absolutism manifest in the government of Louis XIV was the highest expression of God's will, or that he concluded that those suffering from bad or tyrannical government had no redress save tears and prayers.[25]

Even though kings were to heal the sick by miraculous touch for another century, the pace of European development was rapidly secularizing their position. Seventeenth-century theorists were slow to realize that the prince by divine right was being transformed into the king who was the first servant of the state. Bossuet had hardly proclaimed that

[24] M. Bloch, *Les rois thaumaturges, étude sur le caractère surnaturel attribué à la puissance royale* (Strasbourg, London, New York, 1924), 344 ff. The rite of the royal touch was practiced both in England and in France. William III dropped it as superstitious, but Anne revived it after 1702. The Hanoverian kings did not attempt royal miracles, but the Stuart pretenders continued the practice in exile.

[25] H. Sée's *Les idées politiques en France au XVIIe siècle* (Paris, 1923), 145–181, is the best short account of Bossuet's political philosophy. Joseph Hitier's *La doctrine de l'absolutisme* (Paris, 1903) is still useful. Sée's discussion of the inversion of thinking by which the theorists of absolutism, Bossuet in particular, absorbed the state in the person of the prince is excellent, in that it shows the development of the idea as a historical phenomenon. A recent article, written by a man in search of authority in the modern world, is an interesting discussion of Bossuet's ideas: L. de Lichtervelde, "Bossuet et le problème du gouvernement," *Revue générale belge*, XXXII (June, 1948), 208–221.

Louis XIV with his pomp, his splendor, and his power was the ultimate of the divine wisdom when the onrush of war forced that king into a role subservient to the state and called forth critics who did not hesitate to question either his wisdom or his right to rule. When the needs of the state and the rights of its subjects rather than the will of the monarch and the wisdom of God became the axis of political speculation, the theorists began to catch up with political practice, and to reflect the forces of European development.

The French Huguenots were among the first to raise their voices in criticism of Louis XIV. After Richelieu had destroyed their dream of a republic within the kingdom, the Huguenots had been profoundly royalist, but when the dragonnades and the revocation of the Edict of Nantes made life miserable for the psalm-singing congregations, they recalled their ancestors' arguments against tyrannical kings. Because their interests were concentrated upon the preservation of their religious community rather than upon the formulation of a complete theory of politics, the Huguenot writers contributed but little toward the secularization of political thought. They, like Bossuet, believed that the end of the state was the glory of God.

Of all the Huguenot intellectuals who entered the debate, Jurieu stands out as the most vigorous; he was almost a Huguenot pope, at least a Huguenot Bossuet.[26] His criticism of Louis's policies had begun before the revocation of the Edict of Nantes; after he had settled in Holland his pastoral letters to his dispersed flock continued his campaign against Bossuet and Arnault. But Jurieu became a tragic figure. He dreamed of a universal church almost as much as did Bossuet himself. By temperament and conscience a conservative, his radical and revolutionary words were forced upon him when his beloved religion came under attack. Furthermore, he had hardly opened fire on his French enemies when he was obliged to defend his church from another side. Men more liberal than himself, men infected with Cartesian skepticism and with un-Calvinistic notions about salvation were undermining John Calvin's church in Holland. Poor Jurieu was soon in the uncomfortable position of a man who demanded toleration for his own beliefs and at the same time advocated the suppression of the views of others. Perhaps Bossuet's taunting pages in the *History of the Variations of the Protestant Churches* aroused his conservatism as much as Louvois's dragoons had enraged his sense of justice.

[26] G. H. Dodge, *Political Theory of the Huguenots of the Dispersion* (New York, 1947), gives an excellent full-length portrait of the ideas of Jurieu and his companions.

The English Revolution of 1688 sharpened Jurieu's thinking, for he naturally assumed the role of defender of the act that placed the Calvinist William III on the throne vacated by the Catholic James II. But Jurieu's deep-seated distrust of the masses, the monster with a thousand heads, prevented him from drawing the conclusions that were to make Locke the high priest of eighteenth-century political philosophers. Like the author of the earlier *Vindiciae contra Tyrannos,* Jurieu refused to accord the individual the right of rebellion. The natural orders and hierarchies of society, the magistrates, the army, the estates, the great nobles, were to him all endowed, like the king, with divine right. They could therefore legitimately resist the encroachments of tyrannical kings, even rebel against them. For all his talk about natural rights, Jurieu had too much medieval theological bias to stand out forcefully on purely secular principles.

The dramatic march of events was rapidly outmoding thinkers like Jurieu and Bossuet. By 1700 the religious cloak of European political society had worn threadbare in a secular world of business, politics, and war. Men would still hark back to the old ideas, but new conceptions of the meaning and end of the state were beginning to be heard. Locke, the oracle of the Whig party, Vauban, Boisguilbert, the cameralist thinkers in Germany, Fénelon, a bishop in the Catholic church, and Saint-Simon, a courtier in Louis's court were all helping to shift the emphasis in political thinking from the authority of the king to the rights of his subjects and the needs of the state. Some still thought in theological terms, but their arguments no longer implied absolute submission to the whims of a ruler, no matter how carefully anointed. The new political thinkers did not ignore God but, like the natural philosophers and some of the theologians who placed God on a new plane with reference to the affairs of the earth, they adapted their concepts to the situation that was developing before their eyes.

More than any of the others, John Locke broke completely with the idea of divine right. His task was to justify the revolution that had deposed a ruler by divine right and to buttress the throne of William III. The Whig politicians would hear nothing of divine right; they had to find secular justifications for authority. Like many theorists before him, Locke used the medieval concept of a contract as the basis for society, but he avoided the theological implications of the *Vindiciae contra Tyrannos* as well as the cynical materialism of Hobbes' *Leviathan.* Man, he assumed, was good, and in his natural state enjoyed certain rights such as those to life, liberty, and property. He did not give up those rights by agreeing to the original contract that brought society into existence, nor could they legitimately be taken from him. Each individual, therefore, retained his natural rights. This is the basic argument of Locke's doctrine. The original contract endowed the rulers with power, but it reserved the right (authority) to the people. In Bossuet's thinking both power and authority were gifts of God; Locke, on the other hand, separated power and authority (the ability and the right to rule) so as to leave the subject redress against a tyrant.

Locke developed no concept of a general will, but he did define the limits of power. As long as a ruler conducted his government in the interests of the governed and within the framework of law, he was to be left undisturbed. But if he used his power unjustly, tyrannically, or beyond the law, then his subjects could "appeal to heaven," namely revolt, and expel him from his throne. The people thus retained the right, the authority, to set up a new ruler if the present one became a tyrant. The God of the divine-right theorists vanished entirely from this doctrine, which made government a purely secular affair.

Perhaps without fully intending to do so, Locke struck a violent blow at the old conception of an organic society by his emphasis upon individual rights. By centering his argument on political man, endowed with rights, he substituted a homocentric for the old theocentric idea of society. By giving man an inalienable right to life, liberty, and especially property, Locke prepared the way for the eighteenth-century liberals and early nineteenth-century radicals who were to picture man as sovereign and fully cognizant of his interests. Once the break was made with the idea of society as the will of God, it was easy to develop the conception of an atomistic social structure in which men served the greatest good of the greatest number by simply seeking their own best interests.

In his discussion of the organization of government, Locke followed the pattern of the Revolution of 1688. He divided power between the executive and the legislative branches, but insisted that in any conflict the latter must be supreme. His theoretical analysis of the revolution, in other words, vindicated William's succession but also presaged the development of the cabinet government that was to arise in England. Curiously enough, although the rise of an independent judiciary was one of the finest fruits of the Revolution of 1688, Locke remained silent about its function as the third factor in political life. It remained for Montesquieu to "discover" the judiciary as a separate force in the balance of powers within the state.

Europe as a whole was more interested in Locke's philosophy than in his politics. Not until the second quarter of the eighteenth century did his political ideas begin to influence continental thinking. In England, however, his prestige and position as the foremost Whig theorist brought him fame even in his own lifetime. His secular spirit, his frank recognition of political realities, and his interest in the practical problems of politics were entirely consonant with the actual trend of English development. But his failure to see the significance of the rise of standing armies and civil bureaucracies, so typical of the continental states, made his doctrines less useful to those who were intent on discovering means for making government more efficient and on removing the abuses inherent in either ineffective bureaucratic machinery or arbitrary personal power. Locke hailed the rise of mixed government; continental thinkers were preparing the way for enlightened despotism.

In France frustration and misery of defeat brought the evils of Louis's arbitrary power into sharp focus. Louis was evolving a modern state, but he ruled it in the spirit of a Renaissance prince. His dynastic interests, his love of splendor, his personal whims often overrode the reason of state and the interests of his subjects. When disaster overtook his policy, a clamor of protest rose against him, not from wild-eyed radicals or revolutionaries anxious to overthrow the government, but from clergymen, soldiers, courtiers, and bureaucrats who fully recognized the king's right to rule but desired to reorient his regime and provide his government with institutions capable of more effective administration and sounder policy.

Fénelon, Saint-Simon, and Boulainvilliers, all of them courtiers at Versailles, hoped to secure relief from the arbitrary rule of the Sun King by influencing his heir, but Louis XIV ruined their plans by surviving both his son and his grandson. All three of these critics wanted to adapt the ancient federal constitution of France to the political reality of their own day. Saint-Simon had a childlike faith in the peers of the realm, of whom he was one; Fénelon wished to give responsibility to the entire nobility, great and small, and thereby create organic institutions that could share with the king the government of the land. None of these men advanced practical suggestions of significance for the further development of France or Europe, but their criticisms of Louis's policy, their insistence that the interests of the state transcended those of the ruler.

and their conception of power all foreshadowed the ideas of enlightened despotism.

More courageous than others, and more clever in his political thinking, Fénelon did not hesitate to submit his scathing criticism to the king himself. His *Examination of Conscience on the Duties of Royalty* was so bold a censure of Louis XIV that its authenticity was doubted until an autographed copy was discovered.[27] Like the Huguenot author of the anonymous *Sighs of Enslaved France,* Fénelon denounced the personal policies of the king that ran counter to the paramount interests of his subjects. The people and their well-being, he argued, rather than the king and his personal interests should be the chief concern of government and have the first claim on the attention of the ruler. Coupled with this, Fénelon expounded an idea of law by which he hoped to tie the king's hands. The king, he wrote in his *Dialogue des mortes* "ought to be obedient to the law; his person, detached from the law, is nothing; it is only consecrated in so far as it is itself the living law for the good of men." Even more important for later political thinking was Fénelon's conception of history. For him history was a science for discovering the truth about the past, but the most important historical truth yielded by his own studies was the fact of historical change. "Without going further back than the reign of Henry IV," he exclaimed, "the changes in customs are almost unbelievable."[28] If society is not static, as assumed by so many earlier philosophers, then it should be possible to consider it in terms of growth, development, and progress. The political philosopher might, in fact, forecast the future development of society. "Thus," writes Henri Sée, "Fénelon undoubtedly opened the way for the thinkers who believed in the possibility of creating a new society, and by his humanitarian conceptions, his optimistic tendencies, and his instinctive belief in evolution and progress, he is a precursor of the *philosophes* of the eighteenth century."[29]

An entirely different line of thought, but also provoked by the disastrous disorder of Louis XIV's later years, produced the protests and proposals of Vauban and Boisguilbert. The soldier-engineer, whose career took him from one end of France to the other, and the civil servant, who personally witnessed the financial disorders of his own district, both approached the problem of government from the practical, workaday

---

[27] P. Smith, *History of Modern Culture,* II (New York, 1934), 205.

[28] *Lettre sur les occupations de l'académie française* (1714).

[29] H. Sée, *op. cit.,* 233. Chérel's study, *Fénelon au XVIIIᵉ siècle en France, 1715–1820* (Paris, 1917), amply justifies this conclusion.

side. Vauban, like Colbert before him, regarded the well-being of the kingdom and the growth of a prosperous, happy population as the principal end of government. When the king's wars and financial extortions impoverished the kingdom and caused a flight of population, Vauban became aroused. He was convinced that both the unwise politics of the court and the inefficiency and venality of the bureaucracy were responsible for the existing evils. His suggestions for a new system of taxation would have appealed to Colbert, but they were far too daring for a country which still accepted privilege and inequality as part of the divine order of things. The tough, honest old marshal, unable to get a hearing from his king, appealed to the literate public by publishing his views, even though he knew his action might lead to considerable personal inconvenience. Vauban was important not only because of his ideas, many of which furnished later writers with ammunition, but also because of his willingness to risk royal displeasure by insisting that policy was a subject suitable for public discussion. His prestige as the builder and taker of fortifications gave weight to his ideas as a political economist, and by his appeal to public opinion he made policy a subject for debate in the market place as well as in the king's chamber.

Boisguilbert's interest in reform was also rooted in the misery of the kingdom, and like Vauban he was unable to get a hearing from Louis's government. His thinking, however, was more purely economic, and indeed suggested the later theory of the *laissez-faire* school. If Adam Smith was not influenced by his *Dissertation on the Nature of Wealth,* the similarity of views was truly remarkable.[30] In contrast to Vauban, whose thinking was essentially Colbertian, Boisguilbert pointed the way to the economic doctrines of the eighteenth century.

While French political and economic thinkers sought reforms to relieve the misery resulting from defeat and personal absolutism, and while English theorists vindicated the revolution that ended the divine-right monarchy of the Stuarts, the political writers of central Europe concerned themselves with the problems of the bureaucratic state which was revolutionizing the political life of Germany and the Danubian lands. Politics in Germany were simpler, more elementary, than in the western states. The issue was joined between two forces: the feudal, decentralizing tendency inherent in the political ideas of the great landed nobility, and the centralizing tendency of the bureaucratic princely governments.

[30] H. van D. Roberts, *Boisguilbert, Economist of the Reign of Louis XIV* (New York, 1935), 273-330.

Leopold I of Austria, Frederick William of Prussia, Maximilian of Bavaria and a half-dozen lesser princes, who were setting up centralized institutions for all of their domains, were the ones who were forcing the changes. Their interests were practical: finance, justice, and police problems rather than speculation about the nature of the Holy Roman Empire or the idea of sovereignty permeated the thinking of their advisers and officials. Later generations have tended to regard the theorists who articulated the ideas of German cameralism as economic thinkers, and have rightly identified them as German counterparts of Colbert. But it would be a mistake to separate their political from their economic ideas. Seventeenth-century Germany knew nothing of pure economics; it understood only political economy. The abstract economic man had not yet been born.

The most important cameralist thinkers of the period were, as might be expected, servants of Leopold I. The political development of the Hapsburg domains was as much an object lesson as was the Revolution of 1688 in England, and just as Locke explained and justified the new English constitutional system, so Becher, Hörnighk, and Schröder theorized about the Leopoldian revolution. They drew inspiration and arguments from Bodin, Hobbes, Pufendorf, and, above all, Seckendorff, the first great cameralist. Consequently, while they never questioned the prince's divine right to rule, they looked to reason rather than to divine law or biblical tradition. As Srbik puts it, with the rise of the bureaucratic police state, national economy broke loose from theology and imperial law and "won for itself a separate existence." [31] The reason is not hard to find, for the rapid march of events that produced the idea of the Danubian Monarchy brought in its train problems of police, finance, and military organization that required revolutionary action. The older forms had to give way to new ones, and the men who were creating the bureaucratic police state were naturally intent on justifying their work. German cameralist thinking reflected the process begun in Germany in the late sixteenth century; its development in the seventeenth and eighteenth centuries was to give central Europe the ideal of the paternalistic bureaucratic state. [32]

[31] H. Ritter von Srbik, "Wilhelm von Schröder, Ein Beitrag zur Geschichte der Staatswissenschaften," *Sitzungsberichte der Philosophisch-Historischen Klasse der Kaiserlichen Akademie der Wissenschaften*, CLXIV (1910), I, 90.

[32] In 1909 A. W. Small published a study analyzing this tradition with the view of discovering which, if any, of its conceptions could be acclimated to American democratic institutions. Although his study was primarily concerned with economic ideas, it is still

Like Vauban, the early cameralists started with the idea that the essential basis for a powerful state is a healthy, prosperous people. Their preoccupation with finance, the life blood of political and military power, led them to place great emphasis upon ways and means of strengthening the economy. From England and France they learned to think in what later came to be called mercantilistic terms; from their own experience they knew the importance of efficient administration and bureaucratic organization. Their basic belief that the prosperity of his subjects determined the wealth of the prince forced upon them the idea that the state must act paternalistically to further the welfare of the people. Johann Joachim Becher, chemist and natural philosopher, was the real founder of the Vienna cameralist group. He died in 1682, but his son-in-law, Hörnighk, and his friend, Schröder, developed his conception of the service or welfare state as the basis for political and military power. Hörnighk's *Österreich über alles—wann es nur will* (1684) laid the theoretical foundation for the Leopoldian state. Schröder's books of the late 1680's elaborated the methods to be followed. All these men tended to propound rules and administrative procedures rather than to attempt any philosophical analysis. The little verse on the title page of Schröder's *Fürstliche Schatz-und Rentkammer* (1686) is characteristic: [33]

> *Wenn eines klugen Fürsten Herden*
> *Auf diesem Fuss genützet werden*
> *So können sie recht glücklich leben*
> *Und den Regenten Wolle geben,*
> *Doch wer sogleich das Fell abzieht*
> *Bringt sich um künftigen Profit."*

In Protestant Germany the cameralist ideas were originally advanced by Veit Ludwig von Seckendorff, whose *Der Teutsche Fürsten Staat* (1655) was almost a bible for the princes of the latter seventeenth century. Seckendorff, an official at the court of Gotha, lived the life of a scholar and administrator-statesman; at the end of his life he became the first chancellor of the University of Halle. His later book, *Der Christen Staat* (1685), emphasized the cameralist teachings of his earlier volume, and added the idea that a Christian prince rules his lands in the interests of his subjects. For a century and a half German princes were to talk about

---

the best book in English on the cameralists. *The Cameralists, the Pioneers of German Social Policy* (Chicago and London, 1909).

[33] Quoted by A. Oncken, *Geschichte der Nationalökonomie* (Leipzig, 1902), part I, 231.

the extension of German Christian culture. One of the chief ingredients of this culture was efficient government by a bureaucratic police state oriented to serve the popular welfare. This was the item of export that German princely culture sent down the Danube, and into the border lands between Germany and Russia. It was Christian in that it assumed the Christian religion, but its interests were worldly and its methods were practical. In this new teaching the secular interests transcended the spiritual.

Thus cameralism fitted into the process of European development during the next two centuries. The theological presuppositions that had dominated so many areas of human action in the past were being rapidly discarded as worldly, secular values became more significant to human life. The new cosmology and the Cartesian philosophy, the new patterns for culture and the extended economic horizons, the new political structure that hinged on the state and on international relations all tended to draw attention to worldly problems. After a thousand years during which heaven was man's goal and theology queen of the sciences, man was giving up the attempt to manipulate the world with religious and philosophical ideas, and turning to mundane explanations of his physical environment and his social problems.

THE bibliographical essay of a book like this is necessarily a compromise, for it is apt to be too extensive for the casual reader, too limited for the scholar. There is no real solution for this problem, for it is obviously impossible to list thousands of titles and it is extremely difficult to make a selection that will assuredly include all the significant works, for the word "significant" is itself subject to interpretation. I have, therefore, attempted to call attention to the books that will be of general interest, and to suggest works—a limited number—of primary interest to those who wish to make a more intensive study. As much because of my own linguistic limitations as because of those of most prospective readers, I have omitted books in Magyar, Turkish, Finnish, and the Slavic languages. Those conversant with such languages will have little difficulty in finding the bibliographical assistance they need. Cf. E. M. Coulter and M. Gerstenfeld, *Historical Bibliographies* (Berkeley, 1935).

I have tried not to duplicate unnecessarily the excellent bibliographical essays found in the other volumes of this series. P. Roberts, *The Quest for Security, 1715-1740* (New York, 1947), W. L. Dorn, *Competition for Empire, 1740-1763* (New York, 1940) and Leo Gershoy, *From Despotism to Revolution, 1763-1789* (New York, 1944). Nor have I attempted to include all the works cited in the text of the present volume.

GENERAL HISTORIES

The *Propyläen Weltgeschichte* and the *Peuples et civilisations, histoire générale* are attempts by European scholars to present a synthesis of European history. A. Saint-Léger and P. Sagnac, *La prépondérance français, Louis XIV, 1661-1715* (Paris, 1935) in the series *Peuples et civilisations, histoire générale,* has been republished in an enlarged and corrected edition with the title, *Louis XIV, 1661-1715* (Paris, 1949), but the work is marred by Saint-Léger's attempt to justify the French conquest of the Rhineland and his curiously ambivalent feelings about Louis XIV. It fails also as a general history, since the whole volume is narrowly focused on France. Nonetheless, it is a very useful book. *Propyläen Weltgeschichte,* Vol. VI, *Das Zeitalter des Absolutismus, 1661-1789,* by W. Goetz, W. Platzhoff, F. Schnabel, O. Walzel, H. Wätjen, H. Plischke, and F. Saloman (Berlin, 1931) is intended for the general reader. Despite the fact that Platzhoff himself suggested a European approach to the high politics of the era of Louis XIV ("Ludwig XIV, das Kaisertum und die europäische Krisis von 1683," *Historische Zeitschrift* [1919], 121, 377-412) this volume is largely oriented toward Germany. It is beautifully illustrated and the material presented is well written and scholarly. The most interesting general history yet to be published is Roland Mousnier's *Les XVIᵉ et XVIIᵉ Siècles, Les progrès de la civilisation Européenne et le déclin de l'Orient (1492-1715)* in the new *Histoire Générale des Civilisations,* Paris, 1953.

The *Cambridge Modern History,* Vol. V, *The Age of Louis XIV* (New York, 1908), is much less valuable to the general reader, but still useful for several of the excellent chapters. E. Lavisse et A. Rambaud, *Histoire générale du IVᵉ siècle à nos jours,* Vol. VI, *Louis XIV, 1643-1715* (Paris, 1895; 2nd ed. Paris, 1912) is still useful as much because of the straightforward style as for a summary of the best French historical scholarship at the end of the nineteenth century. J. A. G. Pflugk-Harttung, and others, ed. *Weltgeschichte; die Entwicklung der Menschheit in Staat und Gesellschaft, in Kultur und Geistesleben,* 7 vols. (Berlin, 1908-1925), Vol. V, *Neuzeit, 1650-1815* is more useful than either the *Cambridge Modern History* or the old *Histoire générale.*

Max Immich, *Geschichte des europäischen Staatensystems von 1660 bis 1789* (Munich and Berlin, 1905) is still the most valuable short handbook. The bibliographies up to the time of its publication are complete; the text is most useful. A new edition of this work would be highly desirable. E. Préclin and V. L. Tapié, *Le XVIIᵉ siècle (Monarchies centralisées, 1610-1715),* Vol. VII of *Clio: introduction aux études historiques* (Paris, 1943), while extremely useful, does not actually supplant Immich's work. All students, however, are indebted to Préclin and his colleagues, both for the bibliographical aids and for the suggestions of fruitful lines of inquiry.

G. N. Clark, *The Seventeenth Century* (Oxford, 1929; Galaxy paperback also) is one of the most stimulating books on the period, essential reading for every student. David Ogg, *Europe in the Seventeenth Century,* 4th ed. (London, 1943) is good for the earlier part of the century, but weak for the latter. M. Philippson, *Das Zeitalter Ludwigs des Vierzehnten* (Berlin, 1897), Vol. V, Section III of *Allgemeine Geschichte in Einzeldarstellungen,* ed. by W. Oncken is good for the earlier years of Louis's reign. H. A. L. Fisher, *A History of Europe,* 3 vols., new rev. ed. (London, 1939) is suggestive but untrustworthy. A. H. Johnson, *The Age of Enlightened Despots, 1660-1789,* 11th ed. (London, 1925) is a well-known text, now outmoded. O. Hintze, *Staatsverfassung und Heeresverfassung* (Dresden, 1906) and "Staatsverfassung und Staatsentwicklung," *Historische und politische Aufsätze* (Berlin, n. d.), Vol. IV are penetrating and brilliant essays worthy of any student's attention.

NATIONAL HISTORIES

The best history of France for this period is E. Lavisse, ed. *Histoire de France depuis les origines jusqu'à la révolution,* 9 vols. in 18 (Paris, 1900-1911), Vol. VIII, Part I, E. Lavisse and others, *Louis XIV, la fin du règne 1685-1715.* It is a little pedantic in tone, but nonetheless the most complete single secondary work on the last thirty years of Louis's reign. L. Madelin, *Histoire politique, de 1515 à 1804* (Paris, 1924), which is Vol. IV of G. Hanotaux, *Histoire de la nation française,* is a readable popular account, clear, concise and to the point. Another series, *The National History of France,* edited by Funck-Brentano, has two volumes dealing with the seventeenth and eighteenth centuries: J. R. Boulenger, *The Seventeenth Century* (London, 1920) and C. Stryienski, *The Eighteenth Century* (New York, 1916). They are competent but thin.

P. Sagnac, *Formation de la société française moderne* (Paris, 1945-1946) 2 vols. is indispensable for social history. August Bailly, *Le règne de Louis XIV* (Paris, 1946) and G. Pagès, *La monarchie d'ancien régime en France (de Henri IV à Louis XIV)* (Paris, 1946) are shorter, less valuable attempts to educate Frenchmen about their past. The little book by G. Pagès is interesting for its attempt to devalue Louis XIV.

Louis XIV has not yet found a biographer, and probably will have to wait long before anyone undertakes a full scale study to supplant the one made by Lavisse (cf. above). Louis Bertrand's volume is the best known life of the king, but it is almost worthless as history. There are five short biographies written in a popular style: David Ogg (1934), M. Ashley (1948), Hubert Méthivier (1950), de Saint-Aulaire (1950), W. H. Lewis (1959), and a two volume essay by Jacques Roujon. This latter study pretends to be a full-length portrait, but it is marred by the author's *Action Française* views and his inability to grapple with foreign policy. An interesting study is Ph. de Vries, *Het Beeld van Lodewijk XIV in de Franse Geschiedschrijving* (1947), which analyses the development of the image of Louis XIV from the eighteenth century to our own. Louis XIV still presents many problems for the historian.

The number of special studies of the period is enormous. The student who wishes to probe deeply should consult Émile Bourgeois and Louis André, *Les sources de l'histoire de France: le XVII*ᵉ *siècle, 1610-1715,* 8 vols. (Paris, 1913-1935), as well as the other standard bibliographies.

Any bibliography of English history for this period must start with Macaulay. In spite of its age and its Whig bias, his book remains a monument to historical scholarship and literary skill. Sir Charles H. Firth, *A Commentary on Macaulay's History of England* (London, 1938) is a useful corrective, and his edition is probably the best of the many that have been published: T. B. M. Macaulay, *History of England from the Accession of James II,* 6 vols. (London, 1913-1915). G. M. Trevelyan, *England under Queen Anne* (London, 1930-1934), 3 vols., is a continuation of Macaulay's study into the next reign. It is one of the most brilliant single historical works of our times. With the tools of modern scholarship, the monographic collection of a hundred years of the research, and an unsurpassed historical style, Trevelyan has written the sequel to Macaulay as his great forebear would have written his own work had he had the materials available. Two other books by Trevelyan on this period also deserve high praise. *England under the Stuarts* (London, 1904; 12th ed. rev. London, 1925), Vol. V of C. Oman's *History of England,* is an excellent example of his skill as an historian; *The English Revolution, 1688-1689* (London, 1938) is a remarkable study that should prove a model for future historians dealing with complex problems like the Revolution of 1688.

The most colorful historical work on the England of this period is W. S. Churchill, *Marlborough, His Life and Times* (New York, 1933-1938), 6 vols. It has a slightly apologetic tone, but by and large both the scholarship and the interpretation are unassailable. Even if he had the assistance of trained historians, Churchill's reputation as an historian is as secure as his fame as a statesman. Despite its title, O. Klopp, *Der Fall des Hauses Stuart und die Succession des Hauses Hannover in Gross-Britannien und Irland im Zusammenhange der europäischen Angelegenheiten von 1660-1714* (Vienna, 1875-1888), 14 vols. is not merely an English history but a history of Europe, 1660-1714. It includes masses of materials unavailable elsewhere, but its tone is narrow, its vision limited, and the distribution of its ample space unbalanced.

This period of English history has rightfully attracted many fine scholars. G. N. Clark, *The Later Stuarts, 1660-1714* (Oxford, 1934) *(Oxford History of England)* is a good book, but not up to the other works of this careful and thoughtful scholar. Sir R. Lodge, *The History of England from the Restoration to the Death of William III, 1660-1702* (London, New York, etc., 1910) and I. S. Leadam, *The History of England from the Accession of Anne to the Death of George II, 1702-1760* (London, New York, etc., 1909), Vols. VIII and IX of the *Political History of England* (London and New York, 1905-1910) are part of the 12-volume series of political histories edited by Wm. Hunt and R. L. Pool. Maurice Ashley's *England in the Seventeenth Century (1603-1714)*, (London, 1952), is an interesting "conservative interpretation of English history."

It is difficult to pick and choose among the many monographic studies. William T. Morgan, *English Political Parties and Leaders in the Reign of Queen Anne, 1702-1710* (New Haven, etc., 1920) is a careful, detailed study with an excellent bibliography. K. Feiling, *A History of the Tory Party, 1640-1710* (Oxford, 1924), despite its style and organization, is one of the most useful books on the period. M. A. Thomson, *A Constitutional History of England, 1642-1801*, ed. by R. F. Treharne (London, 1938) is a good handbook, interestingly presented, but too thin for close study. There are a number of interesting biographies of the Stuart kings. The student might begin with Sir A. C. Petrie, *The Stuarts* (London, 1937) and *The Stuart Pretenders: A History of the Jacobite Movement, 1688-1807* (Boston and New York, 1933) for a review of the problems of the house. H. Belloc, *James the Second* (London and Philadelphia, 1928), while not profound, is a charmingly written book; N. M. Waterson, *Mary II, Queen of England, 1689-1694* (Durham, 1928) is the best available for Mary. N. Connell, *Anne, the Last Stuart Monarch* (London, 1937) and M. R. Hopkinson, *Anne of England, the Biography of a Great Queen* (London and New York, 1934) are satisfactory for Anne. The latter is an apology.

H. F. H. Elliott, *The Life of Sidney, Earl of Godolphin, K. G., Lord High Treasurer of England, 1702-1710* (London and New York, 1888) and Sir C. A. Petrie, *Bolingbroke* (London, 1937) give some insight into the politics of Anne's reign. S. J. Reid, *John and Sarah, Duke and Duchess of Marlborough, 1660-1744, based on unpublished letters and documents at Blenheim Palace* (London, 1914) should be read after Churchill's work if only to get another view of the Marlboroughs.

The above list touches only a few of the available works. For more complete bibliographical assistance see Godfrey Davies, *Bibliography of British History, Stuart Period, 1603-1714* (Oxford, 1928), issued by the Royal Historical Society and the American Historical Society; W. T. Morgan, *A Bibliography of British History, 1700-1715, with special reference to the Reign of Queen Anne* (Bloomington, Ind., 1934), 2 vols.; and C. L. Grose, *A Select Bibliography of British History, 1660-1760* (Chicago, 1939).

V. O. Kliuchevskii (V. O. Kluchevsky), *A History of Russia*, trans. by C. J. Hogarth, 5 vols. (London, 1911-1931) is the standard non-Marxian large-scale history by a Russian scholar. It is available also in French, German, and Italian; the English translation is awkward. P. N. Milioukov, C. Seignobos, and L. Eisenmann, *Histoire de Russie*, 3 vols. (Paris, 1932-33), Vol. I, *Des origines à la mort de Pierre le Grand* is an excellent co-operative work, systematic, detailed, and scholarly. A. Brückner, *Geschichte Russlands, bis zum Ende des 18-ten Jahrhunderts*, 2 vols. (Gotha, 1896-1913), considering its dates of publication is a remarkable study, still, perhaps, the best analysis of institutions and society. K. Stählin, *Geschichte Russlands von den Anfängen bis zur Gegenwart*, 4 vols. (Stuttgart, 1923-1939) is the standard work produced by a non-Russian scholar; it is thorough, critical, and full. A. Leroy-Beaulieu, *The Empire of the Tsars and the Russians*, 3 vols. (London and New York, 1893-1896), trans. by Z. A. Ragozin, is a classic, outmoded today, but still readable. E. Hanisch, *Geschichte Russlands*, Vol. I, *Von den Anfängen bis zum Ausgang des 18. Jahrhunderts* (Frieburg in Breisgau, 1943) is a recent German work by a thoroughly competent historian; it is better for the later eighteenth century. M. N. Pokrovsky, *History of Russia from Earliest Times to the Rise of Commercial Capitalism,* trans. from the Russian by J. D. Clarkson and M. R. M. Griffiths (New York, 1931), is the work of a communist historian whose strict adherence to the party line of Lenin led to disapproval when Stalin decided that personalities were important in the historical process.

Peter the Great has attracted many biographers. A. Brückner, *Peter der Grosse* (Berlin, 1879) an old book, is still good. V. O. Kluchevsky's *Peter the Great* is now available in a Vintage paperback edition (New York, 1961). K. Waliszewski, *Peter the Great,* trans. from the French by Lady Mary Loyd (New York, 1897) is a classic; its lively tone excuses occasional exaggeration and errors. E. Schuyler, *Peter the Great,* 2 vols. (New York, 1884), is accurate, judicious and occasionally dull, but still a useful and important study. S. Tereshchenko (D. Novik, pseud.) and V. Llona, *Pierre le Grand* (Paris, 1931), 2 vols., is a recent detailed life of Peter worthy of serious consideration. Georges Oudard, *Peter the Great,* trans. by F. M. Atkinson (New York, 1930), is a popular, often flippant account.

R. J. Kerner, *Slavic Europe, a selected bibliography in the western European languages, comprising history, languages, and literatures* (Cambridge, Mass., 1918) is an excellent bibliography for materials published before 1918. It should be brought up to date to preserve its reputation and usefulness.

The best general work on the Hapsburg state is Alfons Huber, *Geschichte Österreichs,* Vols. I-V, to 1648 (Gotha, 1885-1896); Vol. VI, 1648 to 1705 under the subtitle, *Österreichs Grossmachtbildungin der Zeit Kaiser Leopolds I* (Gotha, 1921) was finished by O. Redlich. O. Redlich, *Das Werden einer Grossmacht: Österreich von 1700 bis 1740* (Leipzig, 1938) is the continuation of this monumental work into the eighteenth century. All these volumes are narrowly political and military, but they are indispensable for the study of the period. H. Kretschmayr, *Geschichte von Österreich* (Vienna und Leipzig, 1936) and H. Hantsch, *Die Entwicklung Österreich-Ungarns zur Grossmacht* (Freiburg im Breisgau, 1933) are modern histories. The latter is an excellent study, competently written, though popular in tone. F. M. Mayer, R. Kaindl, H. Pirchegger, *Geschichte und Kulturleben Deutschösterreichs* (Wein and Leipzig, 1929-1937) 3 vols.; Vol. II, *Von 1526 bis 1792,* is a co-operative work, thin for any given period.

The constitutional problems of the Danube Monarchy have attracted many competent scholars. J. Redlich, *Das österreichische Staats-und Reichsproblem* (Leipzig, 1920), Vol. I, *Der dynastische Reichsgedanke und die Entfaltung des Problems bis zur Verkündigung der Reichsverfassung von 1861* is a standard work. The first section is very useful for the eighteenth century. R. Zehntbauer, *Gesamtstaat, Dualismus und pragmatische Sanktion* (Freiburg, Switzerland, 1914), G. Turba, *Geschichte des Thronfolgerechtes in allen habsburgischen Ländern bis zur pragmatischen Sanktion Karls VI, 1156 bis 1732* (Vienna and Leipzig, 1903), G. Turba, *Die pragmatische Sanktion, authentische Texte samt Erläuterungen und Übersetzungen; im Auftrage des k. k. Minister-Präsidenten Carl Grafen Stürgkh* (Vienna, 1913) and G. Turba, *Die Grundlagen der pragmatischen Sanktion* (Leipzig and Vienna, 1917) provide an introduction to the idea of the *Gesamtstaat* and the Pragmatic Sanction. J. Nadler and H. Ritter von Srbik, *Österreichs Erbe und Sendung im deutschen Raum* (Salzburg and Leipzig, 1936) and H. Ritter von Srbik, *Deutsche Einheit* (München, 1935) Vol. I, *Das tausendjährige Reich, Die leere Lebensform* are both brilliantly conceived, though the orientation may have been inspired by contemporary politics. There are several histories of Hungary but few are good. F. Eckhart, *A Short History of Hungary* (London, 1934) and D. G. Kosáry, *A History of Hungary* (Cleveland, 1941) are reasonably objective. A. Domanovsky, *Die Geschichte Ungarns* (Munich and Leipzig, 1923) is also acceptable. Theodore Mayer, *Verwaltungsreform in Ungarn nach der Türkenzeit* (Vienna, 1911) is the best study of the reforms of 1688-1710; B. Bretholz, *Geschichte Böhmens und Mährens,* 4 vols. (Reichenberg, 1921-1924), Vol. III, *Dreissigjähriger Krieg und Wiederaufbau, bis 1792,* is a pro-German history of Bohemia, while E. Denis, *La Bohéme depuis la Montagne-Blanche,* 2 vols. (Paris, 1903) is pro-Czech. There seems to be no objective treatment.

Curiously enough there is no good, indeed practically no biography of Leopold I; V. Baumstark, *Kaiser Leopold I* (Berlin, 1873) is old, G. Guillot, "Léopold Ier et sa cour," *Revue des questions historiques,* April 1, 1907, no more than suggestive. Like Louis XIV, Leopold I awaits his biographer.

The most useful single volume for the study of the Hapsburg state is K. and M. Uhlirz, *Handbuch der Geschichte Österreichs und seiner Nachbarländer Böhmen und Ungarn,* 3 vols. (Graz, Leipzig, Vienna, 1927-1939); it is indispensable as a bibliography and useful as a handbook.

For Germany, Bernhard Erdmannsdörffer, *Deutsche Geschichte vom Westfälischen Frieden bis zum Regierungsantritt Friedrichs des Grossen, 1648-1740,* 2 vols. (Berlin, 1892-1893), is still the best general history. Its primary emphasis on politics can be corrected by K. G. Lamprecht, *Deutsche Geschichte,* 12 vols. in 16 parts: Vol. VII, I, ii, *Neuere Zeit, Zeitalter des individuellen Seelenlebens* (Berlin, 1909-1911); in which there is adequate discussion of social and intellectual problems. F. C. Dahlmann and G. Waitz, *Quellenkunde der deutschen Geschichte,* 9th ed. (Leipzig, 1931), is the famous, indispensable bibliography, the starting point for any study of German history.

For Prussia, J. G. Droysen, *Geschichte der preussischen Politik* (Leipzig, 1868-1886), 5 vols. in 14, despite many criticisms, is still one of the most valuable histories. Hans Prutz, *Preussische Geschichte,* 4 vols. (Stuttgart, 1900-1902), Vol. II, *Die Gründung des preussischen Staates (1655-1740),* is in many ways the best general history of Prussia, a corrective to Droysen's partiality; its emphasis upon the east gives it better balance than most German histories. Albert Waddington, *Histoire de Prusse,* 2 vols. (Paris, 1911-1922), Vol. I, *Des origines à la mort du Grand Électeur (1688),* Vol. II, *Les deux premiers rois (1688-1740),* is a famous book, the classic on Prussia written by a non-German. O. Hintze, *Die Hohenzollern und ihr Werk: Fünfhundert Jahre vaterländischer Geschichte* (Berlin, 1915), even though it was a "command volume" is an important study, which reflects Professor Hintze's wisdom as well as his scholarship. L. Tümpel, *Entstehung des brandenburgisch-preussichen Einheitsstaates in Zeitalter des Absolutismus, 1609-1806* (Berlin, 1915), is a constitutional study by a legal scholar, fundamental for the period.

P. Geyl, *History of the Netherlandish Race (Geschiedenis van de Nederlandsche Stam),* 3 vols. (Amsterdam, 1930-45), and B. H. M. Vlekke, *Evolution of the Dutch Nation* (New York, 1945), are the best short histories, and P. J. Blok, *History of the People of the Netherlands,* 5 vols. (New York and London, 1898-1912), is still the best extended treatment of the United Netherlands available in English. G.

Edmundson, *History of Holland* (Cambridge, England, 1922), is a good general account, but uninspired; H. Brugmans, *Geschiedenis van Nederland,* 8 vols. (Amsterdam, 1935-1936) is the latest detailed history. The latter is beautifully illustrated, but the text seems to contribute little that is new to the period of the present volume. H. Pirenne, *Histoire de Belgique,* 6 vols. (Bruxelles, 1900-1926): Vol. V, *1648-1790* (Bruxelles, 1921) is a fine work, absolutely indispensable.

Like his great contemporaries Louis XIV and Leopold I, William III of Orange still awaits a good biographer. G. J. Renier, *William of Orange* (New York, 1933) and A. A. van Schelven, *Willem van Oranje, een boek ter gedachtenis van idealen en teleurstellingen* (Haarlem, 1933) do not fill this gap.

There are two large-scale political histories of Sweden. The fact that one scholar played a leading role in the planning of both probably accounts for the similarity of their organization. E. Hildebrand and others, *Sveriges Historia intill tjugonde Seklet,* 11 vols. in 6 (Stockholm, 1903-1910) is the older series, now superseded by E. Hildebrand and L. Stavenow, eds., *Sveriges Historia till våra Dagar* (Stockholm, 1919-1926), 13 vols. which is, in effect, a radically revised edition of the former. R. Fåhraeus, *Sveriges Historia till våra Dagar,* Vol. VIII, *Karl XI och Karl XII* (Stockholm, 1923) is the volume dealing with the Caroline period. It is judicious, balanced and fair. O. Sjögren, *Sveriges Historia,* Vol. III, *Storhetstiden Vasaskedet, Pfalziska Skidet* (Stockholm, 1925) is the third volume of a beautifully illustrated and scholarly written series on social and cultural history.

There are many one-volume histories of Sweden. The best available in English are R. Svanström and C. F. Palmstierna, *A Short History of Sweden* (Oxford, 1934) and C. J. H. Hallendorff and A. Schück, *A History of Sweden* (Stockholm, 1929).

There seems to be no good life of Charles XI; O. Sjögren, *Karl den Elfte och Svenska Folket på Hans Tid ett 200-Art-Minne* (Stockholm, 1897) is popular and patriotic. The most authoritative work on Charles XII is F. Bengtsson, *Karl XII's Levnad till uttåget ur Sachsen* (Stockholm, 1935) and *Karl XII's Levnad från Altranstädt till Fredrikshall* (Stockholm, 1936), a truly admirable, brilliant biography. E. Carlson, *Sveriges Historia under Karl den Tolftes Regering* (Stockholm, 1910), 3 vols. is an older study, but still useful. E. Godley, *Charles XII of Sweden, a Study in Kingship* (London, 1928) is popular.

Polish histories for this period are disappointing. There are several brief accounts available in English, but Polish historians rarely write with objectivity. O. Halecki, *A History of Poland* (New York, 1943) is very brief; W. F. Reddaway and others, eds., *The Cambridge History of Poland from Augustus II to Pilsudski, 1697-1935* (Cambridge, England, 1941) and G. E. Slocombe, *A History of Poland* (rev. and enl. ed., London and New York, 1939) are the best. E. Hanisch, *Die Geschichte Polens* (Bonn and Leipzig, 1923) is a good German treatment. There are two reasonably good lives of Sobieski: O. Laskowski, *Jan III Sobieski* (Lwow, 1933) and J. B. Morton, *Sobieski, King of Poland* (London, 1932). Augustus the Strong has attracted more attention. C. Gurlitt, *August der Starke,* 2 vols. (Dresden, 1924) and the two volumes by P. Haake, *August der Starke im Urteil seiner Zeit und der Nachwelt* (Dresden, 1922) and *König August der Starke, eine Charakterstudie* (Munich, 1902) are the best. W. Schlegel, *August der Starke, Kurfürst von Sachsen, König von Polen* (Berlin, 1938) is marred by German nationalism. L. Konopczyński, *Liberum veto* (French trans., Paris, 1930) is a brilliant monograph that throws much light on the whole constitutional problem of Poland.

For Turkey Freiherr von Hammer-Purgstall, *Geschichte des osmanischen Reiches,* 2nd rev. ed., 4 vols. (Pesth, 1834-1836), French trans. by J. J. Hellert, *Histoire de l'empire ottoman, depuis son origine jusqu'a nos jours,* 18 vols. and atlas (Paris, 1835-1843) is still extremely useful. It is almost unreadable as history, but is a mine of information otherwise unavailable to most Western scholars. J. W. Zinkeisen, *Geschichte des osmanischen Reiches in Europa,* 7 vols. (Hamburg, 1840-1863): Vol. V, *Fortschreitendes Sinken des Reiches vorzüglich unter dem Einfluss der wachsenden Macht Russlands, vom Ausgange des Krieges mit Venedig im Jahr 1699 bis zum Frieden zu Kutschuk-Kainardsche im Jahre 1774* (1857) is perhaps more valuable than Hammer's work because the author is more critical of his sources. N. Jorga, *Geschichte des osmanischen Reiches,* 5 vols. (Gotha, 1908-1913) is the only extensive modern study. It is poorly organized, badly written and quite undigested, but is one of the few sources for the history of the subject peoples of the Balkans. K. Ritter von Sax, *Geschichte des Machtverfalls der Türkei bis Ende des 19. Jahrhunderts und die Phasen der "orientalischen Frage" bis auf die Gegenwart* (Vienna, 1908) is an excellent little work; it relies on the older studies, but makes them quite intelligible. A. La Jonquière, *Histoire de l'empire ottoman depuis les origines jusqu'au traité de Berlin,* 1 vol. (1881) (rev. ed., entitled *Histoire de l'empire ottoman depuis les origines jusqu'à nos jours;* 2 vols. [Paris, 1914]) is the most easily read and best-proportioned general history of the empire. It relies heavily upon Hammer and Zinkeisen for material.

W. L. Wright, Jr., *Ottoman Statecraft, The Book of Counsel for Vezirs and Governors of Sari Mehmed Pasha, the Defterdâr* (London and Princeton, 1935) (*Princeton Oriental Texts,* Vol. II) is a remarkable book. The introduction is the most careful analysis of the machinery of government of the empire available in any language. The text is admirably edited and provides fascinating insight into the Turkish mind.

Spanish historians approach the last Hapsburg kings in a penitent mood; their works on the period emphasize cultural rather than political history. A. Ballesteros y Beretta, *Historia de España y su influencia en la historia universal,* 9 vols. in 10 (Barcelona, 1918-1941) is the most recent modern large-scale general history. R. Altamira y Crevea, *Historia de España y de la civilización española* (Barcelona, 1900-1930) 5 vols. in 6 is the most famous treatment, a classic that deals with society, institutions, and cultural development. R. Altamira y Crevea, *A History of Spanish Civilization,* trans. from Spanish by P. Volkov (London, 1936) is an American translation of another work by Altamira, and not merely an abstract of the larger book. C. E. Chapman, *A History of Spain, founded on the Historia de España y de la civilización española de R. Altamira* (last ed., New York, 1937) is a good condensation of Altamira's big book. A number of one-volume general histories of Spain have appeared in the last two decades. R. Konetzke, *Geschichte des spanischen und portugiesischen Volkes* (Leipzig, 1939), Vol. VIII of *Die grosse Weltgeschichte* is the best short account for this period, perhaps for the whole story of Spain. A. Ballesteros y Beretta, *Geschichte Spaniens* (Munich and Berlin, 1943) is a translation of a nationalistic history. J. B. Trend, *The Civilization of Spain* (London, New York, 1944) is somewhat dull, but reasonably sound.

Prince Adalbert von Bayern, *Das Ende der Habsburger in Spanien* (Munich,

1929), 2 vols. is the most complete study of the reign of Charles II, excellent for an understanding of the European implications of the problems presented by Spain as well as for its clearly drawn portrait of the personalities of the court. Ludwig Pfandl, *Karl der Zweite* (Munich, 1940) relies largely upon von Bayern's study, but is more popular in tone. J. Juderías y Loyot, *España en tiempo de Carlos II el hechizado* (Madrid, 1912-1918), 2 vols. is the best Spanish history on the topic.

Italy was more interesting as a cultural and artistic force than as a political factor in the late seventeenth century. E. Rota, *Il problema italiano dal 1700 al 1815 (l'idea unitaria)* (Milan, 1938) is a usable book, but not very full for the early eighteenth century. E. Callegari, *Preponderanze staniere, 1530-1789* (Milan, 1895), from the series *Storia politica d'Italia*, ed. by Vallardi, is not altogether trustworthy when it goes beyond Italy. G. Cantù, *Storia degli Italiani;* Vol. XII (Torino, 1877) is valuable for extensive quotations from documents.

K. D. Vernon, *The Story of Italy from the End of the Roman Empire to the Beginning of the Italian Kingdom* (London, 1939) and L. Salvatorelli, *A Concise History of Italy* (New York, 1940) are one-volume general histories. The latter is an excellent short text. For the cultural and artistic history of Italy, cf. other sections of this bibliography.

INTERNATIONAL RELATIONS AND WARFARE

In addition to the general and national histories of Europe there is an enormous literature, largely pre-1914, dealing with politics and war. Any selection will omit important books, but that is inevitable. C. G. Picavet, *La diplomatie française au temps de Louis XIV, 1661-1715* (Paris, 1930) is one of the finest studies of its kind, a careful analysis of the process and institutions of French diplomacy. It also contains an extensive bibliography. O. Krauske, *Die Entwicklung der ständigen Diplomatie vom fünfzehnten Jahrhundert bis zu den Beschlüssen vom 1815 und 1818* (Leipzig, 1885) gives a longer sweep, but without the richness of detail. Max Immich, *Geschichte des europäischen Staatensystems von 1660 bis 1789* (Munich and Berlin, 1905) is the best manual; Émile Bourgeois, *Manuel historique de politique étrangère,* 4 vols. (Paris, 1900-1926) is a classic. Two recent books treat the international relations of this period with considerable insight: Louis André's *Louis XIV et l'Europe* (Paris, 1950), and Gaston Zeller's *Les Temps Modernes, II: De Louis XIV à 1789* (Paris, 1955). This latter is volume III of Pierre Renouvin (Ed.), *Histoire des Relations Internationales* (seven volumes).

G. N. Clark, *The Dutch Alliance and the War against French Trade, 1688-1697* (Manchester, London, New York, etc., 1923) is an excellent little monograph, but distorts the entire picture of the war by too great emphasis upon the west. M. R. R. Marquis de Courcy, *La coalition de 1701 contre la France* (Paris, 1886), 2 vols. is a classic—well written, straightforward, and detailed. It needs surprisingly little correction. Even more interesting is a fragment by L. von Ranke, *Die grossen Mächte, Sämmtliche Werke,* XXIV, 1-40. Roberts' *The Military Revolution, 1560-1660,* s.a. (1956), and Sir George Clark's *War and Society in the 17th Century* (Cambridge, 1958), underline the basic thesis of my study.

For a study of Louis's policy Ezéchiel Spanheim, *Relation de la cour de France en 1690* (Paris, 1882) gives a close-up view, by a somewhat hostile but well-informed ambassador to the French court. Pierre Rain, *La diplomatie française d'Henri IV à*

Vergennes (Paris, 1945) and René Pinon, *Histoire diplomatique, 1515-1928* (Paris, 1929), Vol. IX of G. Hanotaux, *Histoire de la nation française,* provide brief studies of the period in a longer time sequence. W. Platzhoff, "Ludwig XIV, das Kaisertum und die europäische Krisis von 1683," *Historische Zeitschrift,* 121 (1920), 377-412 is a very stimulating essay attempting a synthesis. F. A. M. A. Mignet, *Négociations relatives à la succession d'Espagne, sous Louis XIV; ou, correspondances, mémoires et actes diplomatiques concernant les prétentions . . . de la maison de Bourbon au trône d'Espagne* (Paris, 1835-1842), 4 vols. and A. Legrelle, *La diplomatie française et la succession d'Espagne* (Gand, 1888-1892), 4 vols., 2nd ed. (Braine-le-Comte, 1895-1899) 6 vols. are famous collections that have had tremendous influence upon all latter historiography.

B. Auerbach, *La France et le Saint Empire romain germanique depuis la paix de Westphalie jusqu' à la révolution française* (Paris, 1912) is an indispensable book for the study of Louis's German policy, while his *La diplomatie française et la cour de Saxe, 1648-1680* (Paris, 1888) and *La France et le Saxe, 1648-1789* (Paris, 1912) give considerable insight into the actual mechanics of French diplomacy. Vast, "Les tentatives de Louis XIV pour arriver à l'empire," *Revue historique,* 65 (1897), 1-45 is an important essay whether one agrees with its conclusions or not. Charles Gérin, "Le Pape Innocent XI et l'élection de Cologne en 1688," *Revue des questions historiques,* Vol. 33 (1883) is one of a number of excellent monographs by Gérin on Louis and Innocent XI. I. Hudità, *Histoire des relations diplomatiques entre la France et la Transylvanie au XVIIe siècle, 1635-1683* (Paris, 1927) and Kurt Köhler, *Die orientalische Politik Ludwigs XIV, ihr Verhältnis zu dem Türkenkrieg von 1683* (Leipzig, 1907) are the best books on Louis's Balkan policies.

Fester, *Die Augsburger Allianz von 1686* (Munich, 1893) is the standard work on the League of Augsburg, but the criticism in R. Fåhraeus, "Sverge och forbundet i Augsburg ar 1686," *Historisk Tidskrift,* XVI (1896) provides an interesting footnote on the policy of Charles XI toward that League. M. Immich, *Zur Vorgeschichte des orleanischen Krieges: 1685-1688* (Heidelberg, 1898) is an attempt to orient the war around the Palatinate.

H. Reynald, *Succession d'Espagne, Louis XIV et Guillaume III, histoire des deux traités de partage et du testament de Charles II* (Paris, 1883), 2 vols., G. F. Preuss, "Oesterreich, Frankreich, und Bayern in der spanischen Erbfolgefrage, 1685-1689," *Historische Vierteljahrschrift,* IV (1901), 309-333, 481-503, and G. F. Preuss, *Wilhelm III von England und das Haus Wittelsbach im Zeitalter der spanischen Erbfolgefrage* (Breslau, 1904) are indispensable for the complex development of the Spanish succession after 1690. A. Gaedeke, *Die Politik Österreichs in der spanischen Erbfolgefrage,* 2 vols. (Leipzig, 1877) now an old book, is still valuable for Hapsburg policy.

H. Uebersberger, *Oesterreich und Russland seit dem Ende des 15. Jahrhunderts* (Vienna and Leipzig, 1906) and *Russlands Orientpolitik in den letzten zwei Jahrhunderten* (Stuttgart, 1913) are both essential for the eastern question.

There are a great number of Swedish studies of the Great War of the North. A. P. Tuxen, *Bidrag til den Store Nordiske Krigs Histoire, 1709-1720* (Stockholm, 1899-1922), 7 vols., is a miscellaneous collection. H. Brulin, *Sverge och Frankrike under Nordiska Kriget och Spanska Succéssionkrisen Aren 1700-1701. Till Belysning af Sveriges Utrikespolitik under Karl XII* (Uppsala, 1905) shows the inner workings of Charles' policy at the opening of the war. N. Herlitz, *Från Thorn till Altranstädt.*

Studier över Karl XII:s Politik, 1703-1706 (Stockholm, 1916) covers the war in Poland. The bibliographical guides in Fåhraeus, *Karl XI och Karl XII* are of considerable value. See also bibliography under Sweden.

A. Legrelle, *Notes et documents sur la paix de Ryswick* (Lille, 1894) is valuable for Ryswick; R. M. Popovič, *Der Friede von Carlowitz* (Leipzig, 1893) for Carlowitz. On the Congress at Utrecht, James W. Gerard, *Peace of Utrecht: A Historical Review of the Great Treaty of 1713-1714, and of the principal events of the War of the Spanish Succession* (New York, 1885) is semipopular; it covers the war as well as the treaty. Ottocar Weber, *Der Friede von Utrecht, Verhandlungen zwischen England, Frankreich, dem Kaiser und den Generalstaaten, 1710-1713* (Gotha, 1891) is more complete in its analysis and contains important primary materials. G. M. Trevelyan, *Bolingbroke's Defence of the Treaty of Utrecht* (Cambridge, 1932) is an interesting monograph by a great historian.

As might be expected, there is a voluminous literature on the wars and warriors of this period. The general histories are often as good as some of the specialized monographs for a coverage of military events. H. Delbrück, *Geschichte der Kriegskunst im Rahmen der politischen Geschichte* (Berlin, 1920), 4 vols.: Vol. IV, *Neuzeit* is still the best general history of the art of war and has become a classic. O. L. Spaulding, Jr., H. Nickerson, and J. W. Wright, *Warfare: a study of military methods from the earliest times* (New York, 1925) is a concise, ably executed textbook. L. Montross, *War through the Ages* (New York, rev. ed., 1946) is a more recent book, popularly written, and, as far as it goes, competently done.

No complete analysis of the French army has yet been made. Col. Réboul, *Histoire militaire et navale*, in Hanotaux, *Histoire de la nation française* (Paris, 1925), Vol. VII is competently done. G. A. M. Girard, *Le service militaire en France à la fin du règne de Louis XIV (Racolage et milice, 1701-1714)* (Paris, 1922) is an admirable little book of great value. Général É Hardy de Périni, *Batailles françaises*, Vol. V, *Louis XIV, 1672-1700* (Paris, 1906), Vol. VI, *Les armées sous l'ancien régime, 1700-1789* (Paris, 1906) is an extensive study, useful to the military historian. Gaston Zeller, *L'organization défensive des frontières du nord et de l'est au XVII° siècle* (Paris, 1928) is an excellent monograph that reverses the role usually assigned to Louis and Vauban. K. von Clausewitz, *Die Feldzüge Luxemburgs in Flandern, 1690-1694*, in *Gesammelte Werke*, Vol. IX (Berlin, 1862) and M. Sautai, *La bataille de Malplaquet, d'après le correspondance du duc de Maine à l'armée de Flandre* (Paris, 1904) are examples of numerous studies on particular battles; the former is interesting because of its author as well as for the material presented.

C. E. Walton, *History of the British Standing Army: A.D. 1660 to 1700* (London, 1894) is excellent for the organization of the English army; John W. Fortescue, *A History of the British Army*, 13 vols. in 14 (London, 1899-1930) is the standard work for English military history. The author's prejudice occasionally mars its value.

M. Jähns, *Geschichte der Kriegswissenschaften, vornehmlich in Deutschland* (Berlin, 1889-1891), 3 vols., Vol. II, *XVII und XVIII Jahrhundert bis zum Auftreten Freidrichs des Grossen, 1740*, is an admirable study for military problems in Germany. Gen. C. Jany, *Geschichte der königlichen preussischen Armee bis zum Jahr 1807*, 4 vols. (1928-1933): Vol. I, *Von den Anfängen bis 1740* is a model study of military history, a truly remarkable book. H. Helfritz, *Geschichte der preussischen Heeresverwaltung* (Berlin, 1938) is an interesting, able monograph on a limited area. A. Wrede, *Geschichte der kaiserlichen und königlichen Wehrmacht*, 5 vols. (Vienna, 1898-1905) does the same task for Austria that Jany does for Prussia, but not as effectively.

The great captains of the era have attracted more and better historical studies than the kings and politicians. Eugene and Marlborough vie with one another in bibliographies. The former has attracted the larger number of biographers, but Winston Churchill has righted the balance for his illustrious ancestor. *Feldzüge des Prinzen Eugen von Savoyen*, 21 vols., 2nd ser. (Vienna, 1876-1892), was edited by the historical section of the War Archives in Vienna; it is complete and detailed. Albert DuCasse, *Mémoires et correspondance politique et militaire du prince Eugène*, 10 vols. (Paris, 1858-1860) is an indispensable source. A. Arneth, *Prinz Eugen von Savoyen*, 3 vols. (Vienna, 1858; new ed., Vienna, 1864), is still a standard work. In the last thirty years at least nine shorter lives of Eugene have appeared in English, German, and Italian. They all follow Arneth rather closely for the facts, but advance various interpretations. W. Schüssler, "Prinz Eugen von Savoy" in *Meister der Politik*, ed. by E. Marcks and K. A. von Muller, 2 vols. (Stuttgart and Berlin, 1922) is sound; O. Redlich, *Prinz Eugen* in *Menschen die Geschichte machten* (1922) is also good; Paul Frischauer, *Prince Eugene; a Man and a Hundred Years of History* (London, 1934) is popular and superficial; V. Bibl, *Prinz Eugen, ein Heldenleben* (Vienna, 1941) is good. I. Jori, *Eugenio di Savoia* (Turin, 1934), G. MacMunn, *Prince Eugene, twin marshal with Marlborough* (London, 1934), W. Molo, *Eugenio von Savoy* (Berlin, 1936), G. Assum, *Eugenio di Savoia* (1933) are passable; R. Lorenz, *Prinz Eugen von Savoyen, Die grossen Deutschen, Neue Deutsche Biographie*, Vol. II (1935), is the best short account. M. Braubach, "Prinz Eugen von Savoyen" in *Historische Zeitschrift*, I (1936) is a suggestive essay. *Memoirs of Prince Eugene of Savoy written by himself*, trans. from French by W. Mudford (New York, 1841), is interesting, but unfortunately too brief; Eugene fought better than he wrote. B. Böhn, *Bibliographie zur Geschichte des Prinz Eugen von Savoyen und seiner Zeit* (Vienna, 1943) is a new bibliography on Eugene.

Marlborough's reputation has suffered somewhat from Tory propaganda and from his own unscrupulous love of money and prestige; however, Winston Churchill's monumental work (cf. under England) has at last given us a full, if at times apologetic, picture. Actually, as Trevelyan has pointed out, Marlborough needs no apology. William Coxe, *Memoirs of the Duke of Marlborough, with his original correspondence*, 3 vols. (London, 1847-1848), and Sir George Murray, ed., *Letters and Dispatches of J. Churchill, first Duke of Marlborough, from 1702-1712*, 5 vols. (London, 1845), are still indispensable, if incomplete. Sir J. C. Fortescue, *Marlborough* (London and New York, 1932), is sound but completely superseded by the six-volume life by Churchill and the three-volume history by Trevelyan (cf. under England). C. T. Atkinson, *Marlborough and the Rise of the British Army* (New York and London, 1921) is a complete work, but unimaginative. Frank Taylor, *The Wars of Marlborough, 1702-1709*, 2 vols. (Oxford, 1921), is a brilliantly written military history, favorable to Marlborough. There are three relatively recent lives of Vauban: D. Halévy, *Vauban* (Paris, 1923), *Vauban, Builder of Fortresses*, trans. by C. J. C. Street (London, 1924), which is popular; P. E. Lazard, *Vauban, 1633-1707* (Paris, 1934), and Sir R. T. Blomfield, *Sebastien le Prestre de Vauban, 1633-1707* (London, 1938), which are more extensive.

C. F. M. Rousset, *Histoire de Louvois et son administration politique et militaire*, 3rd ed., 4 vols. (Paris, 1863-1864), and L. André, *Michel Le Tellier et l'organisation de l'armée monarchique* (Paris, 1906) are indispensable not only for military affairs but also for the political picture of the French court. E. de Broglie, *Catinat l'homme et la vie, 1637-1712* (Paris, 1902), H. Carré, *Le maréchal de Villars, homme de guerre et diplomate* (Paris, 1936), and P. de Ségur, *Le maréchal de Luxembourg* (Paris, 1904), are studies that have exploded the idea that Louis had no good generals after Turenne and Condé.

Alfred T. Mahan, *The Influence of Sea Power upon History, 1660-1783* (Boston, 1890, 32nd ed., Boston, 1928) is still the most famous book on naval history. It is thin and ill informed for this period, but cannot be entirely ignored. W. O. Stevens and A. F. Westcott, *A History of Sea Power* (New York, 1920, 1942) is a recent textbook, brief but accurate. Recently a number of important books on naval history have appeared in France. C. G. M. B. de La Roncière, *Histoire de la marine française*, Vols. 1-6 (Paris, 1899-1934) is one of the best; scholarly, broad, and interestingly written. The books of René Memain, *Le matériel de la marine de guerre sous Louis XIV* (Paris, 1936), *La marine de guerre sous Louis XIV—Le matériel* (Paris, 1937), *Matelots et soldats des vaisseaux du roi—Livrées d'hommes du departement de Rochefort, 1661-1690* (Paris, 1937) are excellent examples of the best in historical scholarship. R. Jouan, *Histoire de la marine française* (Paris, 1932) is also a fine piece of work and J. M. M. H. Tramond, *Manuel d'histoire maritime de la France des origines à 1815* (new ed. Paris, 1947) in its revised form is a sound handbook. Georges Lacour-Gayet, *La marine militaire de la France sous les règnes de Louis XIII et Louis XIV* (Paris, 1911) is an older book, but still useful.

Of the books on French privateers H. Malo's works are the most complete. H. Malo, *Les corsaires dunkerquois et Jean Bart*, 2 vols. (Paris, 1913), and *La grande guerre des corsaires, Dunkerque, 1702-1715* (Paris, 1925). L. Lemaire, *Jean-Bart, 1650-1702* (Dunkerque, 1928) is also good. W. B. Johnson, *Wolves of the Channel, 1681-1856* (London, 1931) is a popular, but essentially sound account.

The best recent book on the English navy for this period is J. H. Owen, *War at Sea under Queen Anne* (Cambridge, England, 1938). Michael Lewis, *The Navy of Britain, a Historical Portrait* (1948) is an excellent general text. Sir William L. Clowes, ed. *The Royal Navy, a History from the Earliest Times to the Present*, 7 vols. (London and Boston, 1897-1903) is still a standard work, filled with general as well as specific information. G. A. R. Callender, *The Naval Side of British History* (London, 1924) is useful in that it treats the question of the influence of naval power on English history. Sir J. S. Corbett, *Fighting Instructions, 1530-1816* (London, 1905) and *England in the Mediterranean, a Study of the Rise and Influence of British Power within the Straits, 1603-1713*, 2 vols. (London and New York, 1904) are two of Corbett's best books. Robert G. Albion, *Forests and Sea Power: The Timber Problem of the Royal Navy, 1652-1862* (Cambridge, Mass., 1926) is an indispensable study, thorough and scholarly. Paul W. Bamford's *Forests and French Sea Power, 1660-1789* (Toronto, 1956), is an excellent companion volume.

ECONOMIC HISTORY

The war of 1914-18 may have been responsible for the fact that the economic historians have given relatively less attention to the seventeenth- and eighteenth-century wars than the publication of G. Prato's *Il costo della guerra* (Turin, 1907) and W. Sombart's *Krieg und Kapitalismus* (Leipzig, 1913) seemed to promise. As far as I know, no other theater of war of this period has been as carefully studied as the kingdom of Savoy during the War of the Spanish Succession. Prato's carefully detailed study and L. Einaudi's *La finanza sabauda all'aprirsi del secolo XVII e durante la guerra di successione spagnuola* (Torino, 1908) were models that have found no imitators. Sombart's brilliant, if superficial, analysis has been somewhat corrected by several later studies. G. N. Clark's *The Dutch Alliance and the War against French Trade, 1688-1697* (London and New York, 1923), and his "War Trade and Trade War, 1701-1713," *Economic History Review*, Vol. I (1928) are excellent. J. U. Nef's articles, "War and Industrial Civilization, 1640-1740," *Review of Politics*, VI (1944), 275-314, "Wars and the Rise of Industrial Civilization, 1640-1740," *Canadian Journal of Economics and Politics*, Vol. X (1944), and "The Enlightenment and the Progress of War," *Measure*, I (1949) 17-25 are brilliant attempts to relate war, economics, and morality, but some of their tentative conclusions will require further buttressing and perhaps correction.

As an introduction to the general problems of economic development H. J. Sieveking, *Grundzüge der neueren Wirtschaftsgeschichte vom 17. Jahrhundert bis zur Gegenwart*, 4th rev. ed. (Leipzig, 1923) provides a valuable summary and broad generalizations, while W. Sombart, *Der moderne Kapitalismus: historischsystematische Darstellung des gesamteuropäischen Wirtschaftslebens von seinen Anfängen bis zur Gegenwart*, 3 vols. in 6 parts, rev. ed. (Munich, 1928), is a mine of information for any study of economic history.

The series of handbooks of economic history edited by Brodnitz is very useful: E. Baasch, *Holländische Wirtschaftsgeschichte* (Jena, 1927), A. E. H. Nielsen and others, *Dänische Wirtschaftsgeschichte* (Jena, 1933), J. Kulischer, *Russische Wirtschaftsgeschichte*, Vol. I (Jena, 1925), and H. Sée, *Französische Wirtschaftsgeschichte* (Jena, 1930), the last available also in French translation. E. Lipson's *The Economic History of England*, 3 vols., 7th ed. rev. and enl. (London, 1937) is the best survey in English, but is rather wooden and often uninteresting. G. Martin's *Histoire économique et financière*, Vol. X of G. Hanotaux, *Histoire de la nation française* (Paris, 1927) is both scholarly and popular. H. Sée's *Esquisse d'une histoire économique et sociale de la France depuis les origines jusqu'à la guerre mondiale* (Paris, 1929) and his *La France économique et sociale au XVIIIe siècle*, 2nd ed. (Paris, 1933), along with his volume in the Brodnitz series, are the best general studies of French economy. For the Netherlands an old study still deserves to be read: O. Pringsheim, *Beiträge zur wirtschaftlichen Entwickelungsgeschichte der Vereinigten Niederlande im 17. und 18. Jahrhundert* (Leipzig, 1890).

Perhaps the most important recent research in economic history has been in the publication of the International Scientific Committee on Price History under the direction of Sir William Beveridge. These studies are indispensable to anyone wishing to do research in this field: W. Beveridge, *Prices and Wages in England from the Twelfth to the Nineteenth Century*, Vol. I, *The Mercantile Era* (London, New York, Toronto, 1939); M. J. Elsas, *Umriss einer Geschichte der Preise und Löhne in Deutschland*, Vol. I (Leiden, 1936): H. Hauser, *Recherches et documents sur l'histoire des prix en France de 1500 à 1800* (Paris, 1936): A. F. Pribram, *Materialien zur Geschichte der Preise und Löhne in Österreich* (Vienna, 1938); E. J. Hamilton,

War and Prices in Spain, 1651-1800 (Cambridge, Mass., 1947), and N. W. Post-humous, *Inquiry into the History of Prices in Holland* (London, 1946). A book with merit and importance equal to the price studies is Pierre Goubert's *Beauvais et le Beauvaisis de 1600 à 1730* (Paris, 1960). It is a superb anthropological study of a limited area that will open many avenues for future research. Warren C. Scoville's *The Persecution of the Huguenots and the French Economic Development, 1680-1720* (Berkeley and Los Angeles, 1960) is an excellent work that will require revision of the traditional thesis about the Huguenots in France.

The two older studies of the French public debt and Louis XIV's financial prob-lems, A. Vührer, *Histoire de la dette publique en France* (Paris, 1886), 2 vols. and A. Vuitry, *Le désordre des finances et les excès de la spéculation à la fin du règne de Louis XIV et au commencement du règne de Louis XV* (Paris, 1885) are still useful, although E. Esmonin and P. Harsin, "Comment le gouvernement de Louis XIV a-t-il financé la guerre de succession d'Espagne," *Bulletin de la société d'histoire moderne* (1931-1933) somewhat corrects the latter study. Lavisse, *Histoire de France,* Vol. VIII, contains the most concise account of French finance. For England, W. Kennedy, *English Taxation, 1640-1790, an essay on policy and opinion* (London, 1913) is the most useful study of taxation and E. L. Hargreaves, *The National Debt* (London, 1930) the best study on that subject. P. Milioukov, *Les finances publiques de la Russie pendant le premier quart du XVIII⁰ siècle et la réforme de Pierre le Grand* (Paris, 1905) is a pioneer study used by all subsequent writers. It throws considerable light on Peter's financial problems, and should be consulted along with the standard works on Russia (cf. above).

The rise of the Bank of England was probably the most important single financial fact of this period. A. Andréadès, *History of the Bank of England, 1640-1903* (3rd ed., London, 1935) is an older standard work, first published in 1904; it is still useful, but Sir J. H. Clapham, *The Bank of England, a History,* 2 vols. (Cambridge, 1944) and W. M. Acres, *The Bank of England from Within, 1694-1900,* 2 vols. (London, 1931) have superseded it by combining both scholarship and literary skill. They have become indispensable for any study of English finance.

Many monographs have appeared on industrial and commercial problems of the seventeenth and eighteenth century. Most of them, however, ignore the fact that there were wars that might have had considerable influence on the economic process. G. Martin, *La grande industrie sous le règne de Louis XIV, plus particulièrement de 1660 à 1715* (Paris, 1898), P. Sagnac, "L'industrie en France, de 1683 à 1715," *Revue d'histoire moderne et contemporaine* (1902-03), Vol. IV, 5 and 89, and J. Kulischer, "La grande industrie aux XVII⁰ et XVIII⁰ siècles" in *Annales historiques, économiques et sociales* (1931), p. 11-46, are useful additions to Sée's books on French economy; M. I. Tugan-Baranovskii, *Geschichte der russischen Fabrik* (Berlin, 1900) is valuable for Russian industry even though its emphasis is on social history. L. Beck, *Die Geschichte des Eisens in technischer und kulturgeschichtlicher Bezie-hung,* Vol. II, *Das XVI und XVII Jahrhundert* (Braunschweig, 1893-1895) is an indispensable book even though its organization is trying to the searcher for specific developmental processes.

William Cunningham, *Growth of English Industry and Commerce* (1882) (rev. ed., 3 vols., Cambridge, England, 1922-1929) is still valuable both for commerce and industry. Its vision was broader than Lipson's even though the later book has more facts. Henri Sée, *L'évolution commerciale et industrielle de la France sous l'ancien régime* (Paris, 1925) is excellent. C. H. Wilson, *Anglo-Dutch Commerce and Finance in the Eighteenth Century* (Cambridge, England, 1941) and C. H. Wilson, "The Economic Decline of the Netherlands," *Economic History Review*, IX (1939), 111-127, more important for the period after Utrecht, are generally suggestive as well as informative.

HISTORIES OF SCIENCE, ART AND RELIGION

Paul Hazard's *La crise de la conscience européenne, 1680-1715*, 3 vols. (Paris, 1934) is undoubtedly the most stimulating single work on the cultural history of this period. The style is sparkling, the organization intelligently planned, and the scope extensive. At times, however, one must guard against Hazard's generalizations and at all times one should bear in mind his postulate that travel, scholarship, and heterodoxy rather than science were the roots of the enlightenment. P. Smith, *History of Modern Culture*, 2 vols., Vol. I, *The Great Renewal, 1543-1687* (New York, 1930), Vol. II, *The Enlightenment, 1687-1776* (New York, 1934) is a much more pedestrian type of study, but in a stubborn way more convincing in its general thesis, namely, that the expansion of man's factual knowledge was the key to intellectual change. Both Hazard and Smith provide extensive bibliographies. E. Friedell, *A Cultural History of the Modern Age*, 3 vols. (New York, 1930-32), Vol. III, Book 2, *Baroque and Rococo: From the Thirty Years' War to the Seven Years' War*, trans. by C. F. Atkinson, is a more extended and ambitious work than either of the above and perhaps for that very reason less valuable for the restricted period of this book. J. H. Randall, *The Making of the Modern Mind*, rev. ed. (Cambridge, Mass., 1940) is intended primarily as a textbook for college classes, but is at the same time a penetrating and thoughtful account that should not be overlooked by the serious student. G. N. Clark, *Science and Social Welfare in the Age of Newton* (Oxford, 1937) is another highly instructive study. Professor Clark, however, spends more time than necessary refuting communist notions as developed in *Science at the Crossroads*, a collection of papers presented by the Soviet delegates to the International Congress of the History of Science and Technology held in London from June 20 to July 3, 1931 (London, 1931). Of these Marxist essays, B. Hessen, "The Social and Economic Roots of Newton's 'Principia'" is especially interesting. The communist collection and Professor Clark's excellent work may be supplemented by R. K. Merton's interesting article, "Science, Technology, and Society in Seventeenth Century England," *Osiris*, IV (1938), 360-632. Equally suggestive on another line of general investigation are M. Bloch, *La société féodale; les classes et le gouvernement des hommes* (Paris, 1940) and A. Sorel, *L'Europe et la Révolution Française—Les moeurs politiques et les traditions* (Paris, 1885). The latter is a famous book, the former only one of a number of Bloch's important studies on the nobility and the social conceptions that came down from feudal Europe.

Those interested in social history for this period should consult the next volume in this series, P. Roberts, *The Quest for Security, 1715-1740* (New York, 1947).

The histories of science are for the most part disappointing. The bibliography is enormous, but most of the books can hardly be classed as histories despite their promising titles. A. N. Whitehead's *Science and the Modern World* (1935; NAL paperback available) and Burtt's *Metaphysical Foundations of Modern Physical*

Science (1925; Anchor paperback available) are indispensable to anyone interested in more than brute fact. P. Rousseau, *Histoire de la science* (Paris, 1945), Sir William Cecil Dampier, *A Shorter History of Science* (New York and Cambridge, England, 1944; Meridian paperback available), W. T. Sedgwick and H. W. Taylor, *A Short History of Science* (rev. ed., New York, 1939), and G. Sarton, *The Study of the History of Science* (Cambridge, Mass., 1936; Dover paperback available) and H. Butterfield, *The Origins of Modern Science* (London, 1939) are the most successful short histories of science. The *Histoire Générale des Sciences,* edited by René Taton is surprisingly well conceived and executed, considering the large number of contributors. Volume II, *La Science Moderne de 1450 à 1800* (Paris, 1958), is particularly worth reading. H. T. Pledge's *Science since 1500* (New York, 1947; Harper Torchbook edition, 1959) is written by a distinguished and learned scholar, but falls short of being a history. The two big books by A. Wolf, *The History of Science, Technology, and Philosophy in the Sixteenth and Seventeenth Centuries* (London, 1935; Harper Torchbook edition, 1959), and *A History of Science, Technology, and Philosophy in the Eighteenth Century* (New York, 1939; Harper Torchbook edition, 1961) are excellent encyclopedias but fail as syntheses. J. B. Conant, *On Understanding Science; An Historical Approach* (New Haven and London, 1947) is a stimulating little book that may eventually have important consequences for the study of the history of science. D. Stimpson, *Scientists and Amateurs: A History of the Royal Society, 1660-1940* (New York, 1848), and M. Daumas, *Histoire de Science* (Paris, 1957) provide a good picture of the problems of the scientist.

Although difficult for a layman to read, M. B. Cantor, *Vorlesungen über Geschichte der mathematik* (Leipzig, 1894-1908), Vol. III, *Von 1668-1758* (Leipzig, 1901) is still recognized as a fundamental study in the history of mathematics. J. E. Hofmann, *Geschichte der Mathematik,* 3 vols. (Berlin, 1953-1957), is the latest full-length history. D. E. Smith, *History of Mathematics,* 2 vols. (Boston and New York, 1923-1925) is an extensive account, but G. Sarton, *The Study of the History of Mathematics* (Cambridge, Mass., 1936), and the two books by E. T. Bell, *The Development of Mathematics* (New York, 1940) and *Men of Mathematics* (New York, 1937) are more suitable for the general reader.

In many ways Fontenelle's *Choix d'éloges* (Paris, 1888) (there is an eighteenth-century edition of his complete works), a little volume edited by Paul Janet, is one of the best introductions to the astronomy, mathematics, and physics of the period. Fontenelle was an amazing person; his *Éloges* are still worth attention and the "Preface sur l'utilité des mathematiques et de la physique" is one of the best introductions to Cartesian thought.

D. Stimson, *Gradual Acceptance of the Copernican Theory of the Universe* (Hanover, N. H., and New York, 1917) shows how the heliocentric world finally won general recognition. There are five recent biographies of Newton, none of them definitive: J. W. N. Sullivan, *Isaac Newton, 1642-1727* (London and New York, 1938), L. T. More, *Isaac Newton, A Biography* (New York and London, 1934), G. S. Brett, *Sir Isaac Newton* (1928), D. Brewster, *The Life of Sir Isaac Newton* (London and New York, 1931) and Lieut.-Col. R. De Villamil, *Newton the Man* (London, 1931). Two recent books by I. Bernard Cohen are most helpful: *Franklin and Newton* (Philadelphia, 1956) and *Isaac Newton's Papers and Letters On Natural Philosophy* (Cambridge, 1958).

S. A. Arrhenius, *Lehrbuch der kosmischen Physik* (Leipzig, 1903), although almost fifty years old, is still worth consideration. F. Cajori, *A History of Physics in its elementary branches, including the evolution of physical laboratories*, rev. ed. (New York, 1938) seems to be the most useful history of physics. P. Mouy, *Le développement de la physique cartésienne, 1646-1712* (Paris, 1934) is an interesting study.

The historical chapters in Sir Charles Lyell, *Principles of Geology*, 11th and rev. ed. (New York, 1872) 2 vols., are still noteworthy both because of the distinction of the author and the insight of his presentation. F. D. Adams, *The Birth and Development of the Geological Sciences* (Baltimore, 1938) is a first-rate modern work that should serve as a model for histories of other sciences. K. A. Ritter von Zittel, *History of Geology and Paleontology to the End of the Nineteenth Century*, trans. by Marie Ogilvie-Gordon (London, 1901), Sir Archibald Geikie, *Founders of Geology*, 2nd ed. (London and New York, 1905) are useful.

E. Nordenskiöld, *The History of Biology; a survey*, trans. by Leonard B. Eyre (New York, London, 1928) is the standard text for the history of biology and deserves its fine reputation. A most interesting and useful book is the collection of Leeuwenhoek's papers by Clifford Dobell, *Anthoy van Leeuwenhoek and his "Little Animals"* (New York, 1958).

There are many bibliographies of travel literature. The list given by Hazard (*La crise de la conscience européenne*, III, 14 ff.) seems to be complete. J. N. L. Baker, *A History of Geographical Discovery and Exploration*, ed. rev. (London, 1937) is the best general history of exploration, while E. Heawood, *A History of Geographical Discovery in the Seventeenth and Eighteenth Centuries* (Cambridge, Eng., 1912) is particularly strong on the Pacific and the interiors of the continents. C. Madrolle, *Les premiers voyages français à la Chine—La compagnie de la Chine, 1698-1719* (Paris, 1901), Mlle H. Belevitch-Stankevitch, *Le goût chinois en France au temps de Louis XIV* (Paris, 1910), Ting Tchao-Ts'ing, *Les descriptions de la Chine par les Français, 1650-1750* (Paris, 1928), V. Pinot, *La Chine et la formation de l'esprit philosophique en France 1640-1740* (Paris, 1932), and V. Pinot, ed., *Documents inédits relatifs à la connaissance de la Chine en France de 1685 à 1740* (Paris, 1932) reflect the impression made by China on Europe. C. Wilkinson, *Dampier; explorer and buccaneer* (New York, 1929) and W. H. Bonner, *Captain William Dampier, Buccaneer-Author; some accounts of a modest buccaneer and of English travel literature in the early eighteenth century* (Stanford University and London, 1934) are two recent studies based on the life and works of an adventurer who made a deep impression on his contemporaries.

Two men have done important work on the relationship between travel, real and imaginary, and literature and philosophy. Gilbert Chinard's *L'Amérique et le rêve exotique dans la littérature française au dix-septième et au dix-huitième siècles* (Paris, 1913) and *L'éxotisme américan dans la littérature française au dix-seizième siècle* (Paris, 1911) deal primarily with French exotic notions about America; G. Atkinson's *The Extraordinary Voyage in French Literature before 1700* (New York, 1920), *The Extraordinary Voyage in French Literature from 1700 to 1720* (Paris, 1922) and *Les relations de voyages du XVIIe siècle et l'évolution des idées; contributions à l'étude de la formation de l'esprit de XVIIIe siècle* (Paris, 1924) include both real and imaginary voyages. The thesis developed in these books, namely, that the French revolutionary movement had deep roots in travel literature often depends upon the interpretation given to segments of the literature.

Some of the most interesting interpretive writing on the history of religion in this period is to be found in E. Troeltsch, *Aufsätze zur Geistesgeschichte und Religions-Sociologie*, Vol. I, *Die Soziallehren der christlichen Kirchen und Gruppen*, Vol. II, *Zur religösen Lage, Religionsphilosophie und Ethik*, Vol. III, *Der Historismus und seine Probleme*, Book I: *Das logische Problem der Geschichts-Philosophie (Gesammelte Schriften* [Tübingen, 1912-1925]). *Protestantismus und Kirche in der Neuzeit* (Berlin, 1922), "Religionswissenschaft und Theologie im 18. Jahrhundert," *Preussische Jahrbücher*, Vol. 114 (1903) and *Die Bedeutung des Protestantismus für die Entstehung der modernen Welt* (5th ed., Munich and Berlin, 1928).

J. Tulloch, *Rational Theology and Christian Philosophy in England in the Seventeenth Century* (Edinburgh, 1872), 2 vols. is an old book, but still valuable. F. J. Powicke, *The Cambridge Platonists* (Cambridge, 1927) is a more readable discussion of that famous school. A. C. McGiffert, *Protestant Thought before Kant* (New York, 1911) is a good survey. Henri Gouhier's *La philosophie de Malebranche et son expérience religieuse* (Paris, 1926) and *Malebranche et les moralistes chrétiens; textes et commentaires* (Paris, 1929) and E. Bréhier's *Histoire de la philosophie* (Paris, 1932) Vol. II, 223 ff. provide the best recent expositions of Malebranche's theology.

Completely indispensable for any study of religious history is L. von Pastor's *Geschichte der Päpste seit dem Ausgang des Mittelalters* (Freiburg im Breisgau, 1899-1919), trans. from the German and ed. by Dom Graf, *The History of the Popes, from the Close of the Middle Ages* (London, 1891-1940; St. Louis, 1942), 32 vols. The bibliographies in the Pastor volumes are excellent. The greatest of the Catholic churchmen, Bishop Bossuet, has attracted many historians. G. Lanson, *Bossuet* (Paris, 1891) is the most stimulating of the older studies. Three recent studies have considerable merit. Victor Giraud, *Bossuet* (Paris, 1930), Philippe Bertault, *Bossuet intime* (Paris, 1927), and Gonzague True, *Bossuet et le classicisme religieux* (Paris, 1934). Gabriel Brunet's *Évocations littéraires* (Paris, 1930) proposes an interesting psychological interpretation of the bishop. E. K. Sanders, *Jacques Bénigne Bossuet; a study* (New York and London, 1921) is the only reasonably good work in English.

To supplement the treatment of religion in the standard works on Russian history cited above, P. Miliukov, *Outlines of Russian Culture*, Vol. I, *Religion and the Church* (Philadelphia, 1942) ed. by M. Karpovich, trans. by V. Ughet and E. Davis, 3 vols. is indispensable.

In addition to the studies on theology, a great number of works deal with both philosophical and theological problems. B. Russell, *A History of Western Philosophy and its Connection with Political and Social Circumstances from the Earliest Times to the Present Day* (New York, 1945, London, 1946) and H. G. Gouhier, *La philosophie et son histoire* (Paris, 1944) are two short general surveys. The former may irritate those devoted to the platonic tradition, or anxious for fair play, but others will like its sparks of brilliance. The latter is more pedestrian and less controversial. René Lote, *Histoire de la philosophie*, in Gabriel Hanotaux, *Histoire de la nation française*, Vol. XV (Paris, 1924) is good for a short history of French thought. Sir L. Stephen, *History of English Thought in the Eighteenth Century*, 2 vols. (3rd ed., New York, 1902) remains a classic. F. Ueberweg, *Grundriss der Geschichte der*

Philosophie, Part III by M. Frischeisen-Köhler and W. Moog, *Die Philosophie der Neuzeit biz zum Ende des XVIII Jahrhunderts* (Berlin, 1924) is not more than a handbook, but useful as an introduction to the questions of philosophy. Émile Bréhier, *Histoire de la philosophie,* 2 vols. (Paris, 1926-1932), and *La philosophie et son passé* (Paris, 1940) are excellent for Cartesianism. E. Cassirer's *Die Philosophie der Aufklärung* (Tübingen, 1932) is already a classic and his *Die platonische Renaissance in England und die Schule von Cambridge* (Leipzig, 1932) is a useful addition to the works cited above on the Cambridge School.

One of the best general histories of music is P. H. Lang, *Music in Western Civilization* (New York, 1941). It may be supplemented by H. D. McKinney and W. R. Anderson, *Music in History, The Evolution of an Art* (New York, 1940), a conventional but useful textbook. D. N. Ferguson, *A History of Musical Thought,* 2nd ed. (New York and London, 1948), is a scholarly and penetrating analysis of the problems of musical expression. P. Bekker, *The Story of Music; an historical sketch of the changes in musical form* (New York, 1927), translated by M. D. Herter Norton and A. Kortschak, is a very useful manual.

Of the larger studies dealing with music of the baroque period M. F. Bukofzer, *Music in the Baroque Era* (New York, 1947) and R. Haas, *Die Musik des Barocks,* Vol. V of E. Bücken, ed., *Handbuch der Musikwissenschaft* are outstanding. Professor Bukofzer's bibliography is most complete. G. Adler, *Handbuch der Musikgeschichte* (Berlin, 1930) 2 vols., J. Combarieu, *Histoire de la musique des origines à la mort de Beethoven,* 3 vols. (Paris, 1913-1919), and *The Oxford History of Music,* W. H. Hadow, ed. Vol. III by C. H. H. Parry, *The Music of the Seventeenth Century,* 2nd ed. (London, 1938) are very useful. These books are basic for the study of seventeenth-century music.

Three important studies on the opera should not be overlooked: D. J. Grout, *A Short History of Opera,* 2 vols. (New York, 1947), is a distinguished book by an American musicologist; H. Kretzschmar, *Geschichte der Oper* (Leipzig, 1919) has long been a standard work but is in part at least supplanted by Grout's book; and P. Bekker, *The Changing Opera,* translated by A. Mendel (New York, 1935, London, 1936) is an interesting though rather popular story.

H. Wölfflin, *Renaissance und Barock; eine Untersuchung über Wesen und Entstehung des Barockstiles in Italien,* 4th ed. (Munich, 1925-26), is the fundamental book reinterpreting the era of the baroque. The extensive bibliography in *The Journal of Aesthetics and Art Criticism,* Vol. V (December, 1946) and the section, "Histoire de l'art," *Clio: Introduction aux études historiques,* Vol. VII indicate the lines of inquiry followed by art historians since Wölfflin's publication.

H. Cysarz, *Hoch und Spätbarock* (Leipzig, 1937) serves well as an introduction to baroque art, but the serious student must consult the great multivolume studies produced by German scholars and printers in the last two generations. A. H. Springer, ed., *Handbuch der Kunstgeschichte,* 4 vols. (Leipzig, edition of 1901-1902), is the oldest, but is still valuable. The *Handbuch der Kunstwissenschaft* (1913-1939), 17 vols. in 30 books and the *Propyläen Kunstgeschichte,* 16 vols. (Berlin, 1923-29) are as fine examples of the printer's art and the scholar's care as can be found. A. Michel, ed., *Histoire de l'art depuis les premiers temps chrétiens jusqu'à nos jours* (Paris, 1905-1929), 8 vols., is a French series comparable to the *Handbuch der Kunstwissenschaft,* but not as pretentious. L. Gillet, *La peinture en Europe au XVII siècle*, 2nd ed. (Paris, 1934) is an excellent little volume that should be read with the more heavily illustrated editions close at hand.

Since French painters assumed European leadership at the opening of the eighteenth century it is not surprising that they have attracted more attention than others. L. Gillet, *La peinture de Poussin à David*, 2nd ed. (Paris, 1935) is a most beautiful example of reproduction. R. Schneider, *L'art français: XVII*e *siècle, 1610-1690* (Paris, 1925), and *L'art français: XVIII*e *siècle, 1690-1789* (Paris, 1926) are indispensable for a general view of the development of French painting. L. Réau, *Histoire de la peinture française au XVIII*e *siècle*, 2 vols. (Paris and Brussels, 1925-26), is charmingly written and carefully illustrated. P. Marcel, *La peinture française de la mort LeBrun à la mort de Watteau, 1690-1721* (Paris, 1906) and L. Hourticq, *De Poussin à Watteau; ou, des origines de l'école parisienne de peinture* (Paris, 1921) are interesting studies showing the rise of the rococo style in France: both are important for an understanding of the conflict in the academy. G. G. Dehio, *Geschichte der deutschen Kunst*, 2nd ed., 4 vols. (Berlin, 1930-1934) is the best general study on German painting, architecture and sculpture for this period.

Sir E. W. Gosse, *British Portrait Painters and Engravers of the Eighteenth Century, Kneller to Reynolds* (Paris, London, New York, etc., 1906) and C. H. C. Baker, *Lely and Kneller* (London, 1922) are useful for their discussions of Kneller, an artist whose career was both fantastic and fascinating.

The student interested in the teaching of art may well start with the excellent volume of N. Pevsner, *Academies of Art, past and present* (Cambridge, England, 1940), a scholarly survey rich in suggestions and bibliographical material.

S. F. Kimball and G. H. Edgell, *A History of Architecture* (New York and London, 1918) is an admirable general account written by distinguished scholars. Kimball's *Creation of the Rococo* (Philadelphia, 1943) is perhaps the most significant single volume on the architectiure of the period. Sir R. T. Blomfield, *A History of French Architecture from the Death of Mazarin till the Death of Louis XV, 1661-1774* (London, 1921) is a standard work, but for Versailles one should consult the numerous works of Pierre de Nolhac, among them *La création de Versailles d'après les sources inédites; études sur les origines et les premières transformations du château et des jardins* (Versailles, 1901), *Versailles et la cour de France: Versailles, residence de Louis XIV* (Paris, 1925), *Versailles et la cour de France: L'art de Versailles* (Paris, 1930). H. Schmitz, *Preussische Königsschlösser* (Munich, 1926) is good for the palaces of Frederick I. T. F. Reddaway, *The Rebuilding of London after the Great Fire* (London, 1940) discusses the reconstruction of London in the latter seventeenth century.

INDEX

Achmed III, 93
Act of Settlement of 1701, 113, 119
Acta Eruditorum, 213, 217, 239
Acta Sanctorum, 242
Acta Sanctorum O.S.B., 242
Addison, 229; *Cato*, 271
Administrative monarchy, rise of, 3–4
Administrative organization, A u s t r i a n, 135 ff.; English, 114 ff., 193; French, 98–101; Ottoman, 167–168; Prussian, 138 ff.; Swedish, 143
Agricola, 228, 231
Albinoni, 264
Alexis, Tsar, 30
Alliance, Grand, 1688–97, 36 ff., 42–43, Ch. II *passim*
Alliance, Grand, 1701–13, 63–64, 67, Ch. III *passim*
Altranstädt, Treaty of, 77
Amati, 260
American Colonies and Revolution of 1688, 116
Anabaptists, 292
Analytical geometry, 213
Anglo-French negotiations, 1711–14, 89
Anglo-Portuguese trade, 207
Anglo-Swedish Alliance, 57
Anne, Queen, 2, 86, 114–120, 182, 193
Antonio de Vera y Cuniga, *El Ambaxador*, 6
Apprentices Act and English army, 104
Apraksin, Grand Admiral, 161
Arbuthnot, *History of John Bull*, 63
Architecture, baroque, 245 ff.; rococo, 249 ff.
Arco, d', 71
Armies, graft and corruption in, 10; methods of recruiting, 9; rise of, 8–12; weapons, 11–12
Arms manufacturers, 178
Arms manufacturing, ownership of, 178
Army organization, 8–11; Austrian, 135 f.; English, 103, 104, 107, 113; French, 99–100; Prussian, 9; Russian, 156; Swedish, 143–144
Arnauld, Antoine, 240, 281
Asia, War in, 1688–97, 47
Asiento, 91
Aspremont, Count, 45
Astrakhan, revolt in, 160
Athens, fall of, 1687, 33
Audran, Claude, 254
August of Saxony, Poland, 10, 50, 53, 76–78, 165

Austrian central government, 135 ff. *See also* Danubian monarchy
Austro-Russian rivalry, in Near East, 167
Aviano, Father, Marco d', 26, 27, 33
Azov, campaigns, 150–152

Bach, 261
Bank of England, 190–192
Banking techniques, 190–191
Baptists, 292
Baronius, 238
Baroque style, 244–249
Bart, Jean, 201
Battle of the Books, 275–276
Bayle, Pierre, 234, 272, 273, 291; *Dictionnaire*, 241; on comets, 279
Beachy Head, 44, 45
Becher, 305, 306
Bekker, *De Betoverte Weereld*, 280
Belgrade, 28, 31; capture of, 1688, 33; siege of, 39; Turkish capture of, 45
Belvedere, 252
Bender, 93–94
Beringer, Johann, 231
Berlin *Schloss*, 252, 257
Bernini, 257
Berwick, Marshal, 73, 80
Biblical criticism, Bayle, 282; Simon, 280–282
Biblical flood, 214 ff.
Bibliothèque choisie, 217
Blenheim, campaign, 70–72; palace, 252
Blockade, 198 ff.
"Blue Guards," 63
Bodin, 297, 305
Boffrand, Germain, 251
Bohemian Hofkanzlei, 252
Boisguilbert, 300, 303, 304
Bolingbroke, Viscount, 88–90, 120
Bolland, John, 242
Bonrepaus, 38
Booksellers, 209
Boonen, 254
Bossuet, Bishop, 23, 211, 240, 281, 286, 289, 290, 296, 297; *Variations of the Protestant Churches*, 295, 299
Boston, 47
Botany, 232 ff.
Boufflers, Marshal, 68, 85
Boulainvilliers, 302
Bourgeoisie, English, 268 ff.; French, 100–101; Ottoman, 167; Russian, 147
Bourgogne, Duchess de, 249

329

Revised June, 1967

harper torchbooks

HUMANITIES AND SOCIAL SCIENCES

American Studies: General

THOMAS C. COCHRAN: The Inner Revolution. *Essays on the Social Sciences in History* TB/1140

HENRY STEELE COMMAGER, Ed.: The Struggle for Racial Equality TB/1300

EDWARD S. CORWIN: American Constitutional History. *Essays edited by Alpheus T. Mason and Gerald Garvey* △ TB/1136

CARL N. DEGLER, Ed.: Pivotal Interpretations of American History TB/1240, TB/1241

A. HUNTER DUPREE: Science in the Federal Government: *A History of Policies and Activities to 1940* TB/573

A. S. EISENSTADT, Ed.: The Craft of American History: *Recent Essays in American Historical Writing*
Vol. I TB/1255; Vol. II TB/1256

CHARLOTTE P. GILMAN: Women and Economics: *A Study of the Economic Relation between Men and Women as a Factor in Social Evolution.* ‡ *Ed. with an Introduction by Carl N. Degler* TB/3073

OSCAR HANDLIN, Ed.: This Was America: *As Recorded by European Travelers in the Eighteenth, Nineteenth and Twentieth Centuries. Illus.* TB/1119

MARCUS LEE HANSEN: The Atlantic Migration: 1607-1860. *Edited by Arthur M. Schlesinger* TB/1052

MARCUS LEE HANSEN: The Immigrant in American History. TB/1120

JOHN HIGHAM, Ed.: The Reconstruction of American History △ TB/1068

ROBERT H. JACKSON: The Supreme Court in the American System of Government TB/1106

JOHN F. KENNEDY: A Nation of Immigrants. △ *Illus.* TB/1118

LEONARD W. LEVY, Ed.: American Constitutional Law: *Historical Essays* TB/1285

LEONARD W. LEVY, Ed.: Judicial Review and the Supreme Court TB/1296

LEONARD W. LEVY: The Law of the Commonwealth and Chief Justice Shaw TB/1309

RALPH BARTON PERRY: Puritanism and Democracy TB/1138

ARNOLD ROSE: The Negro in America TB/3048

MAURICE R. STEIN: The Eclipse of Community. *An Interpretation of American Studies* TB/1128

W. LLOYD WARNER and Associates: Democracy in Jonesville: *A Study in Quality and Inequality* ¶ TB/1129

W. LLOYD WARNER: Social Class in America: *The Evaluation of Status* TB/1013

American Studies: Colonial

BERNARD BAILYN, Ed.: Apologia of Robert Keayne: *Self-Portrait of a Puritan Merchant* TB/1201

BERNARD BAILYN: The New England Merchants in the Seventeenth Century TB/1149

JOSEPH CHARLES: The Origins of the American Party System TB/1049

CHARLES GIBSON: Spain in America † TB/3077

LAWRENCE HENRY GIPSON: The Coming of the Revolution: 1763-1775. † *Illus.* TB/3007

LEONARD W. LEVY: Freedom of Speech and Press in Early American History: *Legacy of Suppression* TB/1109

PERRY MILLER: Errand Into the Wilderness TB/1139

PERRY MILLER & T. H. JOHNSON, Eds.: The Puritans: *A Sourcebook of Their Writings*
Vol. I TB/1093; Vol. II TB/1094

EDMUND S. MORGAN, Ed.: The Diary of Michael Wigglesworth, 1653-1657: *The Conscience of a Puritan* TB/1228

EDMUND S. MORGAN: The Puritan Family: *Religion and Domestic Relations in Seventeenth-Century New England* TB/1227

RICHARD B. MORRIS: Government and Labor in Early America TB/1244

KENNETH B. MURDOCK: Literature and Theology in Colonial New England TB/99

WALLACE NOTESTEIN: The English People on the Eve of Colonization: 1603-1630. † *Illus.* TB/3006

JOHN P. ROCHE: Origins of American Political Thought: *Selected Readings* TB/1301

JOHN SMITH: Captain John Smith's America: *Selections from His Writings. Ed. with Intro. by John Lankford* TB/3078

LOUIS B. WRIGHT: The Cultural Life of the American Colonies: 1607-1763. † *Illus.* TB/3005

American Studies: From the Revolution to 1860

JOHN R. ALDEN: The American Revolution: 1775-1783. † *Illus.* TB/3011

MAX BELOFF, Ed.: The Debate on the American Revolution, 1761-1783: *A Sourcebook* △ TB/1225

RAY A. BILLINGTON: The Far Western Frontier: 1830-1860. † *Illus.* TB/3012

EDMUND BURKE: On the American Revolution: *Selected Speeches and Letters.* ‡ *Edited by Elliott Robert Barkan* TB/3068

WHITNEY R. CROSS: The Burned-Over District: *The Social and Intellectual History of Enthusiastic Religion in Western New York, 1800-1850* △ TB/1242

GEORGE DANGERFIELD: The Awakening of American Nationalism: 1815-1828. † *Illus.* TB/3061

CLEMENT EATON: The Freedom-of-Thought Struggle in the Old South. *Revised and Enlarged. Illus.* TB/1150

CLEMENT EATON: The Growth of Southern Civilization: 1790-1860. † *Illus.* TB/3040

---

† The New American Nation Series, edited by Henry Steele Commager and Richard B. Morris.

‡ American Perspectives series, edited by Bernard Wishy and William E. Leuchtenburg.

* The Rise of Modern Europe series, edited by William L. Langer.

** History of Europe series, edited by J. H. Plumb.

¶ Researches in the Social, Cultural and Behavioral Sciences, edited by Benjamin Nelson.

§ The Library of Religion and Culture, edited by Benjamin Nelson.

Σ Harper Modern Science Series, edited by James R. Newman.

º Not for sale in Canada.

△ Not for sale in the U. K.

LOUIS FILLER: The Crusade Against Slavery: 1830-1860. †
Illus.   TB/3029
DIXON RYAN FOX: The Decline of Aristocracy in the
Politics of New York: 1801-1840. ‡ *Edited by Robert
V. Remini*   TB/3064
WILLIAM W. FREEHLING, Ed.: The Nullification Era: *A
Documentary Record* ‡   TB/3079
FELIX GILBERT: The Beginnings of American Foreign
Policy: *To the Farewell Address*   TB/1200
FRANCIS GRIERSON: The Valley of Shadows: *The Coming
of the Civil War in Lincoln's Midwest: A Contem-
porary Account*   TB/1246
FRANCIS J. GRUND: Aristocracy in America: *Social Class
in the Formative Years of the New Nation*   TB/1001
ALEXANDER HAMILTON: The Reports of Alexander Ham-
ilton. ‡ *Edited by Jacob E. Cooke*   TB/3060
THOMAS JEFFERSON: Notes on the State of Virginia. ‡
Edited by Thomas P. Abernethy   TB/3052
JAMES MADISON: The Forging of American Federalism:
*Selected Writings of James Madison. Edited by Saul
K. Padover*   TB/1226
BERNARD MAYO: Myths and Men: *Patrick Henry, George
Washington, Thomas Jefferson*   TB/1108
JOHN C. MILLER: Alexander Hamilton and the Growth of
the New Nation   TB/3057
RICHARD B. MORRIS, Ed.: The Era of the American Revo-
lution   TB/1180
R. B. NYE: The Cultural Life of the New Nation: 1776-
1801. † *Illus.*   TB/3026
FRANCIS S. PHILBRICK: The Rise of the West, 1754-1830. †
Illus.   TB/3067
TIMOTHY L. SMITH: Revivalism and Social Reform:
American Protestantism on the Eve of the Civil War
                                               TB/1229
FRANK THISTLETHWAITE: America and the Atlantic Com-
munity: *Anglo-American Aspects, 1790-1850* TB/1107
ALBION W. TOURGÉE: A Fool's Errand. ‡ *Ed. by George
Fredrickson*   TB/3074
A. F. TYLER: Freedom's Ferment: *Phases of American
Social History from the Revolution to the Outbreak
of the Civil War. 31 illus.*   TB/1074
GLYNDON G. VAN DEUSEN: The Jacksonian Era: 1828-
1848. † *Illus.*   TB/3028
LOUIS B. WRIGHT: Culture on the Moving Frontier
                                               TB/1053

American Studies: The Civil War to 1900

W. R. BROCK: An American Crisis: Congress and Reconstruction, 1865-67 ° △   TB/1283
THOMAS C. COCHRAN & WILLIAM MILLER: The Age of Enter-
prise: *A Social History of Industrial America* TB/1054
W. A. DUNNING: Essays on the Civil War and Reconstruc-
tion. *Introduction by David Donald*   TB/1181
W. A. DUNNING: Reconstruction, Political and Economic:
1865-1877   TB/1073
HAROLD U. FAULKNER: Politics, Reform and Expansion:
1890-1900. † *Illus.*   TB/3020
HELEN HUNT JACKSON: A Century of Dishonor: *The Early
Crusade for Indian Reform. ‡ Edited by Andrew F.
Rolle*   TB/3063
ALBERT D. KIRWAN: Revolt of the Rednecks: *Mississippi
Politics, 1876-1925*   TB/1199
ROBERT GREEN MC CLOSKEY: American Conservatism in
the Age of Enterprise: 1865-1910   TB/1137
ARTHUR MANN: Yankee Reformers in the Urban Age:
Social Reform in Boston, 1880-1900   TB/1247
WHITELAW REID: After the War: *A Tour of the Southern
States, 1865-1866. ‡ Edited by C. Vann Woodward*
                                               TB/3066
CHARLES H. SHINN: Mining Camps: *A Study in American
Frontier Government. ‡ Edited by Rodman W. Paul*
                                               TB/3062
VERNON LANE WHARTON: The Negro in Mississippi:
1865-1890   TB/1178

American Studies: 1900 to the Present

RAY STANNARD BAKER: Following the Color Line: *Ameri-
can Negro Citizenship in Progressive Era. ‡ Illus.
Edited by Dewey W. Grantham, Jr.*   TB/3053
RANDOLPH S. BOURNE: War and the Intellectuals: *Col-
lected Essays, 1915-1919. ‡ Edited by Carl Resek*
                                               TB/3043
A. RUSSELL BUCHANAN: The United States and World War
II. † *Illus.*   Vol. I TB/3044; Vol. II TB/3045
ABRAHAM CAHAN: The Rise of David Levinsky: *a docu-
mentary novel of social mobility in early twentieth
century America. Intro. by John Higham*   TB/1028
THOMAS C. COCHRAN: The American Business System:
A Historical Perspective, 1900-1955   TB/1080
FOSTER RHEA DULLES: America's Rise to World Power:
1898-1954. † *Illus.*   TB/3021
JOHN D. HICKS: Republican Ascendancy: 1921-1933. †
Illus.   TB/3041
SIDNEY HOOK: Reason, Social Myths, and Democracy
                                               TB/1237
ROBERT HUNTER: Poverty: *Social Conscience in the Pro-
gressive Era. ‡ Edited by Peter d'A. Jones*   TB/3065
WILLIAM L. LANGER & S. EVERETT GLEASON: The Challenge
to Isolation: *The World Crisis of 1937-1940 and
American Foreign Policy*
                      Vol. I TB/3054; Vol. II TB/3055
WILLIAM E. LEUCHTENBURG: Franklin D. Roosevelt and
the New Deal: 1932-1940. † *Illus.*   TB/3025
ARTHUR S. LINK: Woodrow Wilson and the Progressive
Era: 1910-1917. † *Illus.*   TB/3023
GEORGE E. MOWRY: The Era of Theodore Roosevelt and
the Birth of Modern America: 1900-1912. † *Illus.*
                                               TB/3022
RUSSEL B. NYE: Midwestern Progressive Politics: *A His-
torical Study of Its Origins and Development, 1870-
1958*   TB/1202
WILLIAM PRESTON, JR.: Aliens and Dissenters: *Federal
Suppression of Radicals, 1903-1933*   TB/1287
WALTER RAUSCHENBUSCH: Christianity and the Social
Crisis. ‡ *Edited by Robert D. Cross*   TB/3059
JACOB RIIS: The Making of an American. ‡ *Edited by
Roy Lubove*   TB/3070
PHILIP SELZNICK: TVA and the Grass Roots: *A Study in
the Sociology of Formal Organization*   TB/1230
IDA M. TARBELL: The History of the Standard Oil Com-
pany: *Briefer Version. ‡ Edited by David M. Chalmers*
                                               TB/3071
GEORGE B. TINDALL, Ed.: A Populist Reader ‡   TB/3069
TWELVE SOUTHERNERS: I'll Take My Stand: *The South
and the Agrarian Tradition. Intro. by Louis D. Rubin,
Jr., Biographical Essays by Virginia Rock*   TB/1072
WALTER E. WEYL: The New Democracy: *An Essay on Certain Political Tendencies in the United States. ‡ Edited
by Charles B. Forcey*   TB/3042

Anthropology

JACQUES BARZUN: Race: *A Study in Superstition. Re-
vised Edition*   TB/1172
JOSEPH B. CASAGRANDE, Ed.: In the Company of Man:
*Twenty Portraits of Anthropological Informants.
Illus.*   TB/3047
W. E. LE GROS CLARK: The Antecedents of Man: *Intro.
to Evolution of the Primates. ° △ Illus.*   TB/559
CORA DU BOIS: The People of Alor. *New Preface by the
author. Illus.*   Vol. I TB/1042; Vol. II TB/1043
RAYMOND FIRTH, Ed.: Man and Culture: *An Evaluation
of the Work of Bronislaw Malinowski* ¶ ° △   TB/1133
DAVID LANDY: Tropical Childhood: *Cultural Transmis-
sion and Learning in a Puerto Rican Village* ¶
                                               TB/1235
L. S. B. LEAKEY: Adam's Ancestors: *The Evolution of
Man and His Culture. △ Illus.*   TB/1019
ROBERT H. LOWIE: Primitive Society. *Introduction by
Fred Eggan*   TB/1056

2

EDWARD BURNETT TYLOR: The Origins of Culture. *Part I of "Primitive Culture."* § *Intro. by Paul Radin*   TB/33
EDWARD BURNETT TYLOR: Religion in Primitive Culture. *Part II of "Primitive Culture."* § *Intro. by Paul Radin*   TB/34
W. LLOYD WARNER: A Black Civilization: *A Study of an Australian Tribe.* ¶ *Illus.*   TB/3056

Art and Art History

WALTER LOWRIE: Art in the Early Church. *Revised Edition. 452 illus.*   TB/124
EMILE MÂLE: The Gothic Image: *Religious Art in France of the Thirteenth Century.* § △ *190 illus.*   TB/44
MILLARD MEISS: Painting in Florence and Siena after the Black Death: *The Arts, Religion and Society in the Mid-Fourteenth Century. 169 illus.*   TB/1148
ERICH NEUMANN: The Archetypal World of Henry Moore. △ *107 illus.*   TB/2020
DORA & ERWIN PANOFSKY : Pandora's Box: *The Changing Aspects of a Mythical Symbol. Revised Edition. Illus.*   TB/2021
ERWIN PANOFSKY: Studies in Iconology: *Humanistic Themes in the Art of the Renaissance.* △ *180 illustrations*   TB/1077
ALEXANDRE PIANKOFF: The Shrines of Tut-Ankh-Amon. *Edited by N. Rambova. 117 illus.*   TB/2011
JEAN SEZNEC: The Survival of the Pagan Gods: *The Mythological Tradition and Its Place in Renaissance Humanism and Art. 108 illustrations*   TB/2004
OTTO VON SIMSON: The Gothic Cathedral: *Origins of Gothic Architecture and the Medieval Concept of Order.* △ *58 illus.*   TB/2018
HEINRICH ZIMMER: Myth and Symbols in Indian Art and Civilization. *70 illustrations*   TB/2005

Business, Economics & Economic History

REINHARD BENDIX: Work and Authority in Industry: *Ideologies of Management in the Course of Industrialization*   TB/3035
GILBERT BURCK & EDITORS OF FORTUNE: The Computer Age: *And Its Potential for Management*   TB/1179
THOMAS C. COCHRAN: The American Business System: *A Historical Perspective, 1900-1955*   TB/1080
THOMAS C. COCHRAN: The Inner Revolution: *Essays on the Social Sciences in History* △   TB/1140
THOMAS C. COCHRAN & WILLIAM MILLER: The Age of Enterprise: *A Social History of Industrial America*   TB/1054
ROBERT DAHL & CHARLES E. LINDBLOM: Politics, Economics, and Welfare: *Planning and Politico-Economic Systems Resolved into Basic Social Processes*   TB/3037
PETER F. DRUCKER: The New Society: *The Anatomy of Industrial Order* △   TB/1082
EDITORS OF FORTUNE: America in the Sixties: *The Economy and the Society*   TB/1015
ROBERT L. HEILBRONER: The Great Ascent: *The Struggle for Economic Development in Our Time*   TB/3030
ROBERT L. HEILBRONER: The Limits of American Capitalism   TB/1305
FRANK H. KNIGHT: The Economic Organization   TB/1214
FRANK H. KNIGHT: Risk, Uncertainty and Profit   TB/1215
ABBA P. LERNER: Everybody's Business: *Current Assumptions in Economics and Public Policy*   TB/3051
ROBERT GREEN MC CLOSKEY: American Conservatism in the Age of Enterprise, 1865-1910 △   TB/1137
PAUL MANTOUX: The Industrial Revolution in the Eighteenth Century: *The Beginnings of the Modern Factory System in England* ○ △   TB/1079
WILLIAM MILLER, Ed.: Men in Business: *Essays on the Historical Role of the Entrepreneur*   TB/1081
RICHARD B. MORRIS: Government and Labor in Early America △   TB/1244
HERBERT SIMON: The Shape of Automation: *For Men and Management*   TB/1245

PERRIN STRYKER: The Character of the Executive: *Eleven Studies in Managerial Qualities*   TB/1041
PIERRE URI: Partnership for Progress: *A Program for Transatlantic Action*   TB/3036

Education

JACQUES BARZUN: The House of Intellect △   TB/1051
RICHARD M. JONES, Ed.: Contemporary Educational Psychology: *Selected Readings*   TB/1292
CLARK KERR: The Uses of the University   TB/1264
JOHN U. NEF: Cultural Foundations of Industrial Civilization △   TB/1024
NATHAN M. PUSEY: The Age of the Scholar: *Observations on Education in a Troubled Decade*   TB/1157
PAUL VALÉRY: The Outlook for Intelligence △   TB/2016

Historiography & Philosophy of History

JACOB BURCKHARDT: On History and Historians. △ *Introduction by H. R. Trevor-Roper*   TB/1216
WILHELM DILTHEY: Pattern and Meaning in History: *Thoughts on History and Society.* ○ △ *Edited with an Introduction by H. P. Rickman*   TB/1075
J. H. HEXTER: Reappraisals in History: *New Views on History & Society in Early Modern Europe* △   TB/1100
H. STUART HUGHES: History as Art and as Science: *Twin Vistas on the Past*   TB/1207
RAYMOND KLIBANSKY & H. J. PATON, Eds.: Philosophy and History: *The Ernst Cassirer Festschrift. Illus.*   TB/1115
ARNALDO MOMIGLIANO: Studies in Historiography ○ △   TB/1288
GEORGE H. NADEL, Ed.: Studies in the Philosophy of History: *Selected Essays from History and Theory*   TB/1208
JOSE ORTEGA Y GASSET: The Modern Theme. *Introduction by Jose Ferrater Mora*   TB/1038
KARL R. POPPER: The Open Society and Its Enemies △
  Vol. I: *The Spell of Plato*   TB/1101
  Vol. II: *The High Tide of Prophecy: Hegel, Marx and the Aftermath*   TB/1102
KARL R. POPPER: The Poverty of Historicism ○ △   TB/1126
G. J. RENIER: History: *Its Purpose and Method* △   TB/1209
W. H. WALSH: Philosophy of History: *An Introduction* △   TB/1020

History: General

L. CARRINGTON GOODRICH: A Short History of the Chinese People. △ *Illus.*   TB/3015
DAN N. JACOBS & HANS H. BAERWALD: Chinese Communism: *Selected Documents*   TB/3031
BERNARD LEWIS: The Arabs in History △   TB/1029
BERNARD LEWIS: The Middle East and the West ○ △   TB/1274

History: Ancient

A. ANDREWES: The Greek Tyrants △   TB/1103
ADOLF ERMAN, Ed. The Ancient Egyptians: *A Sourcebook of Their Writings. New material and Introduction by William Kelly Simpson*   TB/1233
MICHAEL GRANT: Ancient History ○ △   TB/1190
SAMUEL NOAH KRAMER: Sumerian Mythology   TB/1055
NAPHTALI LEWIS & MEYER REINHOLD, Eds.: Roman Civilization. *Sourcebook I: The Republic*   TB/1231
NAPHTALI LEWIS & MEYER REINHOLD, Eds.: Roman Civilization. *Sourcebook II: The Empire*   TB/1232

History: Medieval

P. BOISSONNADE: Life and Work in Medieval Europe: *The Evolution of the Medieval Economy, the 5th to the 15th Century.* ○ △ *Preface by Lynn White, Jr.*   TB/1141
HELEN CAM: England before Elizabeth △   TB/1026
NORMAN COHN: The Pursuit of the Millennium: *Revolutionary Messianism in Medieval and Reformation Europe* △   TB/1037

3

G. G. COULTON: Medieval Village, Manor, and Monastery
TB/1022

CHRISTOPHER DAWSON, Ed.: Mission to Asia: Narratives and Letters of the Franciscan Missionaries in Mongolia and China in the 13th and 14 Centuries △
TB/315

HEINRICH FICHTENAU: The Carolingian Empire: The Age of Charlemagne △
TB/1142

GALBERT OF BRUGES: The Murder of Charles the Good. Trans. with Intro. by James Bruce Ross   TB/1311

F. L. GANSHOF: Feudalism △
TB/1058

DENO GEANAKOPLOS: Byzantine East and Latin West: Two Worlds of Christendom in the Middle Ages and Renaissance
TB/1265

EDWARD GIBBON: The Triumph of Christendom in the Roman Empire (Chaps. XV-XX of "Decline and Fall," J. B. Bury edition). § △ Illus.
TB/46

W. O. HASSALL, Ed.: Medieval England: As Viewed by Contemporaries △
TB/1205

DENYS HAY: Europe: The Emergence of an Idea   TB/1275

DENYS HAY: The Medieval Centuries o △   TB/1192

J. M. HUSSEY: The Byzantine World △   TB/1057

ROBERT LATOUCHE: The Birth of Western Economy: Economic Aspects of the Dark Ages. o △ Intro. by Philip Grierson
TB/1290

FERDINAND LOT: The End of the Ancient World and the Beginnings of the Middle Ages. Introduction by Glanville Downey
TB/1044

MARSILIUS OF PADUA: The Defender of the Peace. Trans. with Intro. by Alan Gewirth
TB/1310

G. MOLLAT: The Popes at Avignon: 1305-1378 △ TB/308

CHARLES PETIT-DUTAILLIS: The Feudal Monarchy in France and England: From the Tenth to the Thirteenth Century o △
TB/1165

HENRI PIRENNE: Early Democracies in the Low Countries: Urban Society and Political Conflict in the Middle Ages and the Renaissance. Introduction by John H. Mundy
TB/1110

STEVEN RUNCIMAN: A History of the Crusades. △
Volume I: The First Crusade and the Foundation of the Kingdom of Jerusalem. Illus.   TB/1143
Volume II: The Kingdom of Jerusalem and the Frankish East, 1100-1187. Illus.   TB/1243
Volume III: The Kingdom of Acre and the Later Crusades
TB/1298

FERDINAND SCHEVILL: Siena: The History of a Medieval Commune. Intro. by William M. Bowsky   TB/1164

SULPICIUS SEVERUS et al.: The Western Fathers: Being the Lives of Martin of Tours, Ambrose, Augustine of Hippo, Honoratus of Arles and Germanus of Auxerre. △ Edited and trans. by F. O. Hoare   TB/309

HENRY OSBORN TAYLOR: The Classical Heritage of the Middle Ages. Foreword and Biblio. by Kenneth M. Setton
TB/1117

F. VAN DER MEER: Augustine The Bishop: Church and Society at the Dawn of the Middle Ages △   TB/304

J. M. WALLACE-HADRILL: The Barbarian West: The Early Middle Ages, A.D. 400-1000 △   TB/1061

History: Renaissance & Reformation

JACOB BURCKHARDT: The Civilization of the Renaissance in Italy. △ Intro. by Benjamin Nelson & Charles Trinkaus. Illus.   Vol. I TB/40; Vol. II TB/41

JOHN CALVIN & JACOPO SADOLETO: A Reformation Debate. Edited by John C. Olin
TB/1239

ERNST CASSIRER: The Individual and the Cosmos in Renaissance Philosophy. △ Translated with an Introduction by Mario Domandi
TB/1097

FEDERICO CHABOD: Machiavelli and the Renaissance △
TB/1193

EDWARD P. CHEYNEY: The Dawn of a New Era, 1250-1453. * Illus.
TB/3002

G. CONSTANT: The Reformation in England: The English Schism, Henry VIII, 1509-1547 △   TB/314

R. TREVOR DAVIES: The Golden Century of Spain, 1501-1621 o △
TB/1194

G. R. ELTON: Reformation Europe, 1517-1559 ** o △
TB/1270

DESIDERIUS ERASMUS: Christian Humanism and the Reformation: Selected Writings. Edited and translated by John C. Olin
TB/1166

WALLACE K. FERGUSON et al.: Facets of the Renaissance
TB/1098

WALLACE K. FERGUSON et al.: The Renaissance: Six Essays. Illus.
TB/1084

JOHN NEVILLE FIGGIS: The Divine Right of Kings. Introduction by G. R. Elton
TB/1191

JOHN NEVILLE FIGGIS: Political Thought from Gerson to Grotius: 1414-1625: Seven Studies. Introduction by Garrett Mattingly
TB/1032

MYRON P. GILMORE: The World of Humanism, 1453-1517. * Illus.
TB/3003

FRANCESCO GUICCIARDINI: Maxims and Reflections of a Renaissance Statesman (Ricordi). Trans. by Mario Domandi. Intro. by Nicolai Rubinstein   TB/1160

J. H. HEXTER: More's Utopia: The Biography of an Idea. New Epilogue by the Author   TB/1195

HAJO HOLBORN: Ulrich von Hutten and the German Reformation
TB/1238

JOHAN HUIZINGA: Erasmus and the Age of Reformation. △ Illus.
TB/19

JOEL HURSTFIELD, Ed.: The Reformation Crisis △   TB/1267

ULRICH VON HUTTEN et al.: On the Eve of the Reformation: "Letters of Obscure Men." Introduction by Hajo Holborn
TB/1124

PAUL O. KRISTELLER: Renaissance Thought: The Classic, Scholastic, and Humanist Strains   TB/1048

PAUL O. KRISTELLER: Renaissance Thought II: Papers on Humanism and the Arts   TB/1163

NICCOLÒ MACHIAVELLI: History of Florence and of the Affairs of Italy: from the earliest times to the death of Lorenzo the Magnificent. △ Introduction by Felix Gilbert
TB/1027

ALFRED VON MARTIN: Sociology of the Renaissance. Introduction by Wallace K. Ferguson   TB/1099

GARRETT MATTINGLY et al.: Renaissance Profiles. △ Edited by J. H. Plumb
TB/1162

MILLARD MEISS: Painting in Florence and Siena after the Black Death: The Arts, Religion and Society in the Mid-Fourteenth Century. △ 169 illus.   TB/1148

J. E. NEALE: The Age of Catherine de Medici o △ TB/1085

ERWIN PANOFSKY: Studies in Iconology: Humanistic Themes in the Art of the Renaissance. △ 180 illustrations
TB/1077

J. H. PARRY: The Establishment of the European Hegemony: 1415-1715: Trade and Exploration in the Age of the Renaissance △
TB/1045

J. H. PLUMB: The Italian Renaissance: A Concise Survey of Its History and Culture △
TB/1161

A. F. POLLARD: Henry VIII. o △ Introduction by A. G. Dickens
TB/1249

A. F. POLLARD: Wolsey. o △ Introduction by A. G. Dickens
TB/1248

CECIL ROTH: The Jews in the Renaissance. Illus.   TB/834

A. L. ROWSE: The Expansion of Elizabethan England. o △ Illus.
TB/1220

GORDON RUPP: Luther's Progress to the Diet of Worms o △
TB/120

FERDINAND SCHEVILL: The Medici. Illus.   TB/1010

FERDINAND SCHEVILL: Medieval and Renaissance Florence. Illus.   Volume I: Medieval Florence   TB/1090
Volume II: The Coming of Humanism and the Age of the Medici
TB/1091

G. M. TREVELYAN: England in the Age of Wycliffe, 1368-1520 △
TB/1112

VESPASIANO: Renaissance Princes, Popes, and Prelates: The Vespasiano Memoirs: Lives of Illustrious Men of the XVth Century. Intro. by Myron P. Gilmore
TB/1111

Intellectual History & History of Ideas

Psychology

Sociology

RELIGION

Ancient & Classical

Biblical Thought & Literature

The Judaic Tradition

Christianity: General

Christianity: Origins & Early Development

Christianity: The Middle Ages and The Reformation

H. G. FORDER: Geometry: *An Introduction* △   TB/548

S. KÖRNER: The Philosophy of Mathematics: *An Intro-duction* △   TB/547

D. E. LITTLEWOOD: Skeleton Key of Mathematics: *A Simple Account of Complex Algebraic Problems* △   TB/525

GEORGE E. OWEN: Fundamentals of Scientific Mathematics   TB/569

WILLARD VAN ORMAN QUINE: Mathematical Logic   TB/558

O. G. SUTTON: Mathematics in Action. ○ △ *Foreword by James R. Newman. Illus.*   TB/518

FREDERICK WAISMANN: Introduction to Mathematical Thinking. *Foreword by Karl Menger*   TB/511

Philosophy of Science

R. B. BRAITHWAITE: Scientific Explanation   TB/515

J. BRONOWSKI: Science and Human Values. △ *Revised and Enlarged Edition*   TB/505

ALBERT EINSTEIN et al.: Albert Einstein: Philosopher-Scientist. *Edited by Paul A. Schilpp*   Vol. I   TB/502
Vol. II   TB/503

WERNER HEISENBERG: Physics and Philosophy: *The Revolution in Modern Science* △   TB/549

JOHN MAYNARD KEYNES: A Treatise on Probability. ○ △ *Introduction by N. R. Hanson*   TB/557

KARL R. POPPER: Logic of Scientific Discovery △   TB/576

STEPHEN TOULMIN: Foresight and Understanding: *An Enquiry into the Aims of Science.* △ *Foreword by Jacques Barzun*   TB/564

STEPHEN TOULMIN: The Philosophy of Science: *An Introduction* △   TB/513

G. J. WHITROW: The Natural Philosophy of Time ○ △   TB/563

Physics and Cosmology

JOHN E. ALLEN: Aerodynamics: *A Space Age Survey* △   TB/582

STEPHEN TOULMIN & JUNE GOODFIELD: The Fabric of the Heavens: *The Development of Astronomy and Dynamics.* △ *Illus.*   TB/579

DAVID BOHM: Causality and Chance in Modern Physics. △ *Foreword by Louis de Broglie*   TB/536

P. W. BRIDGMAN: Nature of Thermodynamics   TB/537

P. W. BRIDGMAN: A Sophisticate's Primer of Relativity △   TB/575

A. C. CROMBIE, Ed.: Turning Point in Physics   TB/535

C. V. DURELL: Readable Relativity. △ *Foreword by Freeman J. Dyson*   TB/530

ARTHUR EDDINGTON: Space, Time and Gravitation: *An Outline of the General Relativity Theory*   TB/510

GEORGE GAMOW: Biography of Physics Σ △   TB/567

MAX JAMMER: Concepts of Force: *A Study in the Foundation of Dynamics*   TB/550

MAX JAMMER: Concepts of Mass *in Classical and Modern Physics*   TB/571

MAX JAMMER: Concepts of Space: *The History of Theories of Space in Physics. Foreword by Albert Einstein*   TB/533

G. J. WHITROW: The Structure and Evolution of the Universe: *An Introduction to Cosmology.* △ *Illus.*   TB/504

Code to Torchbook Libraries:

TB/1+   : The Cloister Library
TB/301+   : The Cathedral Library
TB/501+   : The Science Library
TB/801+   : The Temple Library
TB/1001+   : The Academy Library
TB/2001+   : The Bollingen Library
TB/3001+   : The University Library
JP/1+   : Jewish Publication Society Series